THE CAMBRIDGE COMP
GAY AND LESBIAN WI

In the last two decades, lesbian and gay studies ha .... studies
and developed into a vital and influential area for students and scholars. This
Companion introduces readers to the range of debates that inform studies of
works by lesbian and gay writers and of literary representations of same-sex
desire and queer identities. Each chapter introduces key concepts in the field in
an accessible way and uses several important literary texts to illustrate how these
concepts can illuminate our readings of them. Authors discussed range from
Henry James, E. M. Forster and Gertrude Stein to Sarah Waters and Carol Ann
Duffy. The contributors showcase the wide variety of approaches and theoretical
frameworks that characterize this field, drawing on related themes of gender and
sexuality. With a chronology and guide to further reading, this volume offers a
stimulating introduction to the diversity of approaches to lesbian and gay writing.

HUGH STEVENS is Senior Lecturer in English at University College London. His
publications include *Henry James and Sexuality* (Cambridge, 1998) and
Modernist Sexualities (co-edited with Caroline Howlett, 2000).

A complete list of books in the series is at the back of this book.

THE CAMBRIDGE
COMPANION TO
GAY AND LESBIAN
WRITING

EDITED BY
HUGH STEVENS
University College London

CAMBRIDGE
UNIVERSITY PRESS

CAMBRIDGE UNIVERSITY PRESS

Cambridge, New York, Melbourne, Madrid, Cape Town, Singapore,
São Paulo, Delhi, Dubai, Tokyo, Mexico City

Cambridge University Press
The Edinburgh Building, Cambridge CB2 8RU, UK

Published in the United States of America by Cambridge University Press, New York

www.cambridge.org
Information on this title: www.cambridge.org/9780521716574

First published 2011

Printed in the United Kingdom at the University Press, Cambridge

A catalogue record for this publication is available from the British Library

Library of Congress Cataloguing in Publication data
The Cambridge companion to gay and lesbian writing / edited by Hugh Stevens.
p. cm.
ISBN 978-0-521-88844-8 (hardback)
1. Gays' writings – History and criticism. 2. Literature – History and
criticism. 3. Homosexuality and literature. 4. Homosexuality in literature.
5. Gays – Intellectual life. 6. Gays in literature. I. Stevens, Hugh. II. Title.
PN56.H57C36 2011
809'.8920664–dc22
2010019536

ISBN 978-0-521-88844-8 hardback
ISBN 978-0-521-71657-4 paperback

CONTENTS

NOTES ON CONTRIBUTORS

DAVID BERGMAN is the author of *Gaiety Transfigured: Gay Self-Representation in American Literature* (1991) and *The Violet Hour: The Violet Quill and the Making of Gay Culture* (2004), among other books. He teaches English at Towson University in Maryland.

JOSEPH BRISTOW is Professor of English at the University of California, Los Angeles. His books include *The Fin-de-Siècle Poem: English Literary Culture and the 1890s* (2005) and *Oscar Wilde: The Making of a Legend* (2008). In 2009–10 he directed the year-long Mellon Sawyer Seminar, 'Homosexualities, from Antiquity to the Present', at UCLA. He is researching a history of British writing of the 1875–1914 period.

RICHARD R. BOZORTH is Associate Professor of English at Southern Methodist University in Dallas, Texas, and the author of *Auden's Games of Knowledge: Poetry and the Meanings of Homosexuality* (2001).

RICHARD CANNING has published *Gay Fiction Speaks: Conversations with Gay Novelists* (2001) and *Hear Us Out: Conversations with Gay Novelists* (2004), which won the 2005 Editors Choice Lambda Literary Award. He is also editor of *Between Men* (2007) and *Between Men 2* (2009), two collections of gay male fiction, and of *Vital Signs* (2007), an anthology of American AIDS fiction. His other publications include *Brief Lives: Oscar Wilde* (2008), and a critical biography of the English novelist Ronald Firbank is forthcoming. He lives in Lincoln and London, and heads English studies at Bishop Grosseteste University College Lincoln.

TIM DEAN is Director of the Humanities Institute at the University at Buffalo (SUNY), where he is also a professor of English and Comparative Literature. He is the author of *Beyond Sexuality* (2000) and *Unlimited Intimacy: Reflections on the Subculture of Barebacking* (2009), as well as a co-editor of *Homosexuality and Psychoanalysis* (2001) and *A Time for the Humanities* (2008).

JANE GARRITY is an Associate Professor of English at the University of Colorado, Boulder. She is the author of *Step-Daughters of England: British Women Modernists and the National Imaginary* (2003); the co-editor, with Laura Doan, of *Sapphic Modernities: Sexuality, Women, and National Culture* (2006); and the editor of a Special Issue of *ELN: English Language Notes*, on Queer Space, Spring 2007. She is currently at work on a book on modernism and fashion.

TIRZA TRUE LATIMER is Associate Professor and Chair of Visual and Critical Studies at California College of the Arts, San Francisco. Her research and publications explore intersections of social subjectivity and visual culture. She is co-editor, with Whitney Chadwick, of the anthology *The Modern Woman Revisited: Paris Between the Wars* (2003) and author of *Women Together / Women Apart: Portraits of Lesbian Paris* (2005). Latimer is also an independent curator, and is currently collaborating on a major exhibition about the life and afterlife of Gertrude Stein, organized by the Contemporary Jewish Museum, San Francisco.

HEATHER LOVE teaches gender studies, twentieth-century literature and film, and critical theory at the University of Pennsylvania. She is the author of *Feeling Backward: Loss and the Politics of Queer History* (2007) and is currently at work on a project on social stigma.

JODIE MEDD is Associate Professor of English at Carleton University in Ottawa, Canada. Her work on lesbian history, modernist literature and contemporary literature has appeared in *GLQ*, *Modernism/Modernity* and collections on law and society, lesbian literature and lesbian history. She is finishing a book on lesbian sexual scandal in the early twentieth century and at work on a new project on modernist patronage.

HUGH STEVENS is a Senior Lecturer in the Department of English Language and Literature of University College London, where he teaches American and British literature and lesbian and gay writing. He is the author of *Henry James and Sexuality* (1998) and co-editor of *Modernist Sexualities* (2000).

KATHRYN BOND STOCKTON is Professor of English and Director of Gender Studies at the University of Utah. Her book *Beautiful Bottom, Beautiful Shame: Where 'Black' Meets 'Queer'* (2006), was a national finalist for the Lambda Literary Award. She has also authored *God between Their Lips: Desire between Women in Irigaray, Brontë, and Eliot* (1994) and *The Queer Child, or Growing Sideways in the Twentieth Century* (2009).

RUTH VANITA is Professor of Liberal Studies and Women's Studies at the University of Montana, and was formerly a Reader in English at Delhi University. She was the founding co-editor of *Manushi*, India's first feminist journal, which she edited from 1978 to 1990, and is the author or editor of several books, including *Sappho and the*

Virgin Mary: Same-Sex Love and the English Literary Imagination; *Same-Sex Love in India* (with Saleem Kidwai); *Love's Rite: Same-Sex Marriage in India and the West*; *Gandhi's Tiger and Sita's Smile: Essays on Gender, Sexuality and Culture* and *A Play of Light: Selected Poems*. She has translated many works from Hindi to English and published widely on Shakespeare, most recently in *Shakespeare Survey*.

ANDREW WEBBER is Reader in Modern German and Comparative Culture at the University of Cambridge and a Fellow of Churchill College. He has published widely on the relationships between gender, sexuality and psychoanalysis. His books include *The European Avant-garde: 1900–1940* (2004) and *Berlin in the Twentieth Century: A Cultural Topography* (Cambridge University Press, 2008).

JOANNE WINNING is Senior Lecturer in Literary and Cultural Studies in the School of English and Humanities, Birkbeck College, University of London. She has published widely in the fields of modernist critical studies and lesbian and gay studies. She is currently completing the book *Lesbian Modernism: A Cultural Study*, which explores the art, literature, photography, architecture and cultural production of the Anglo-American lesbian modernists.

ACKNOWLEDGEMENTS

Many thanks, first of all, to the contributors to this volume, who were always good-humoured and prompt in replying to editorial queries. I have greatly enjoyed the intellectual engagement of working with them.

I should like to thank the Department of English Language and Literature, University College London, for a period of research leave which I largely spent working on this volume.

Santanu Das has always been patient and smart when I have discussed this *Companion* with him. The staff at Cambridge University Press, particularly Maartje Scheltens, have been very helpful during all the stages of preparation for this volume. I am also very grateful to Ray Ryan of Cambridge University Press, who first suggested that I work on this *Companion* and has always been encouraging and supportive. Caroline Howlett's copy-editing was wonderfully careful, thorough and intelligent. It has been a tremendous pleasure to work with her again.

CHRONOLOGY

This chronology should not be read as attempting to delineate an objective record of gay and lesbian writing. It gives some events important to gay and lesbian history, and lists some representative and influential texts.

Unknown	Zeus, king of the gods, abducts Ganymede, a Trojan prince, from Mount Ida. Greek mythology has many instances of youths desired and pursued by male deities.
Unknown	Orpheus, unsuccessful in his attempt to retrieve Eurydice from the underworld, teaches the men of Thrace the art of loving boys.
Unknown	David loves his friend Jonathan, as recorded in the first book of Samuel. When Jonathan dies, David laments, 'your love to me was wonderful, passing the love of women'.
c. 625–570 BCE	Life of Sappho, the lyric poet of Lesbos, whose nine books of lyric poetry, of which approximately 200 fragments remain, include many love poems addressed to women.
c. 427–327 BCE	Life of Plato, whose dialogues *Symposium* and *Phaedrus* are influential for the views they advance on male–male love.
54 CE	Nero becomes Emperor of Rome. According to Suetonius, in *Lives of the Twelve Caesars*, Nero married two men in legal ceremonies, Sporus (whom he first castrated) and Doryphorus.
98	Trajan, 'devoted to boys and to wine' (Cassius Dio, *Roman History*), becomes Emperor.
130	Antinous, beloved of Emperor Hadrian, drowns in the Nile. Hadrian deifies Antinous and founds the city Antinopolis in his memory.

218–22	Reign of Roman Emperor Elagabalus. Cassius Dio writes that Elagabalus 'carried his lewdness to such a point that he asked the physicians to contrive a woman's vagina in his body by means of an incision, promising them large sums for doing so'.
342	Constantius II and Constans, joint Emperors, issue a decree prohibiting men 'marrying a man as a woman'.
390	Emperors Valentian II, Theodosius and Arcadius issue a law against sexual acts between men. Passive partners in same-sex acts were to be punished by being burned alive in public.
527–65	Justinian's reign as Byzantine emperor. The Code of Justinian criminalizes both active and passive same-sex partners, and applies the death penalty.
c. 1050	Saint Peter Damian's *Book of Gomorrah* condemns sodomy as 'the vice . . . never to be compared with other vices because it surpasses the enormity of all vices'.
1265–74	Saint Thomas Aquinas, *Summa Theologiae*, condemns 'unnatural' sexual acts, including same-sex behaviour, masturbation and bestiality.
1534	Under King Henry VIII, the 'Buggery Act' (25 Henry VIII, c. 6) is introduced, with hanging the punishment for buggery.
1592 or 1593	Christopher Marlowe, *Edward II*, gives a bold portrayal of Edward's relationship with his 'sweet friend' Gaveston.
1594	Richard Barnfield, *The Affectionate Shepherd*, a collection of homoerotic pastoral poems, followed in 1595 by *Cynthia, with Certaine Sonnets*, which contains more homoerotic sonnets describing Daphnis's yearning for Ganymede.
1598	William Shakespeare, *The Merchant of Venice*. Queer criticism has been absorbed by the question of how to interpret Antonio's love for Bassanio.
1598	Marlowe, *Hero and Leander*, in which Leander is abducted by Neptune, who confuses him with Ganymede.
1603	Shakespeare, *Troilus and Cressida*. Its portrayal of Achilles and Patroclus is the most homoerotic representation of loving friendship in Shakespeare's oeuvre.

1609	Shakespeare, *Sonnets*, the first 126 of which consist of love poems addressed to a young man.
c. 1640–89	Life of Aphra Behn, novelist, poet and playwright. Many of her poems celebrate gay male and lesbian relationships.
1664 and 1667	Posthumous publication of poems by Katherine Philips, containing many passionate erotic celebrations of female friends.
c. 1672	In *The Farce of Sodom, or the Quintessence of Debauchery*, thought to be by John Wilmot, Second Earl of Rochester, King Bolloxinion proclaims 'that buggery may be used / O'er all the land', and he and his subjects find creative ways of obeying the proclamation.
1709	Ned Ward, *History of the London Clubs*, describes London's subculture of sodomites, or 'mollies'.
1748	Tobias Smollett, *The Adventures of Roderick Random*, includes portraits of an effeminate sodomite, naval captain Whiffle, and his 'crowd of attendants, all of whom, in their different degrees, seemed to be of their patron's disposition'.
1782	While imprisoned in the Bastille, the Marquis de Sade writes *The 120 Days of Sodom*, which describes libertines systematically enjoying every imaginable sexual activity. The novel was first published in 1904.
1791	In Revolutionary France, the Penal Code of 1791 decriminalizes sodomy. This principle stands in the Napoleonic Penal Code of 1810. France is the first Western European country to decriminalize sexual acts between men.
1791–1840	Life of Anne Lister, a Yorkshire Landowner whose partially encrypted diary records her many seductions of women.
c. 1784	Jeremy Bentham, *Offences Against One's Self*, an unpublished essay arguing against the sodomy laws.
1795	Matthew Lewis, *The Monk*, Gothic novel about a pious and handsome monk in love with a young male novice, who turns out to be a woman.
1796	Anna Seward, *Llangollen Vale*, a long poem celebrating the romantic friendship of 'the Ladies of Llangollen', Eleanor Butler and Sarah Ponsonby.

1810	The Vere Street affair, in which several men are arrested at a London gay tavern and later savagely pilloried.
1806–36	In England in this period there are on average two hangings a year for male–male sodomy.
c. 1833	*Don Leon*, anonymous poem (falsely attributed to Lord Byron) which advocates the decriminalization of sodomy.
1850	Lord Alfred Tennyson, *In Memoriam*, a long elegy for his friend Arthur Henry Hallam.
1860	Third edition of Walt Whitman, *Leaves of Grass*, with the 'Calamus' poems celebrating 'adhesiveness' or 'the manly love of comrades'.
1861	In England the Offences Against the Person Act removes the death sentence for buggery. The penalty is changed to imprisonment for between ten years and life.
1864–5	Karl Heinrich Ulrichs, the German sexologist, publishes five books under the title *Researches on the Riddle of Male–Male Love*.
1869	The Austro-Hungarian writer Károly Mária Kertbeny publishes two pamphlets criticizing anti-homosexual laws. These pamphlets contain the first written examples of the word 'homosexuality' (German *Homosexualität*).
1884	*Callirrhoë*, and *Fair Rosamond*, verse dramas, the first publication of Michael Field, the pseudonym of Katherine Bradley and her niece Edith Cooper, a lesbian couple who went on to publish many more plays and books of poetry.
1885	The Labouchere Amendment to the Criminal Law Amendment Act makes 'any act of gross indecency' committed by a man with another man, 'in public or in private', punishable by imprisonment for up to two years.
1886	Henry James, *The Bostonians*, in which the feminist Olive Chancellor falls in love with Verena Tarrant, the beautiful daughter of a mesmerist.

1891	Death of Herman Melville. His posthumously published *Billy Budd* (1924) describes the Master-at-arms John Claggart's tortured desires for a handsome young sailor. Oscar Wilde, *The Picture of Dorian Gray*, often read as a novel about homosexuality.
1895	The 'Wilde Trials'. Wilde is found guilty of 'gross indecency' under the Criminal Law Amendment Act of 1885 and sentenced to two years' imprisonment.
1896	Willa Cather, 'Tommy the Unsentimental', a short story showing a tomboy's strategies of dealing with small-town disapproval.
1897	Wilde, *De Profundis*, a long letter to Lord Alfred Douglas in which Wilde refers to the 'perverse pleasures' of his life as a 'fact about me'.
1912	Thomas Mann, *Death in Venice*, describing the elderly Gustav von Aschenbach's obsession with Tadzio, a beautiful Polish adolescent boy.
1913	E. M. Forster, *Maurice* (published 1971), tells of a gentleman who falls in love with his friend's gamekeeper.
1915	Gertrude Stein, *Lifting Belly*, one of Stein's many innovative texts which can be read as celebrating lesbian sexuality. D. H. Lawrence, *The Rainbow*, prosecuted for its sexual explicitness, describes a love affair between Ursula Brangwen and her teacher Winifred Inger.
1919	Magnus Hirschfeld founds the *Institut für Sexualwissenschaft* (Institute for Sexual Science or Institute for Sexology) in Berlin. The Institute was closed by the Nazis in 1933.
1922	Death of Marcel Proust. His *À la recherche du temps perdu*, a *roman fleuve*, continues to fascinate readers with its daring explorations of male homosexuality, lesbianism, jealousy, cruising and perversion.
1923	Ronald Firbank, *The Flower Beneath the Foot*, one of his many camp novels, in which Laura de Nazianzi joins the lesbian Convent of the Flaming Hood. D. H. Lawrence, *The Fox*, portrays a female couple running a farm.

1924   André Gide, *Corydon*, a collection of essays about homosexuality and culture.

1928   Radclyffe Hall, *The Well of Loneliness*, novel about Stephen Gordon, a female 'sexual invert'.
Djuna Barnes, *Ladies Almanack*, a humorous *roman à clef* about lesbian life in Paris.
Virginia Woolf, *Orlando*, about a young man who becomes a woman, inspired by Woolf's love for Vita Sackville-West.

1929   Nella Larsen, *Passing*, portrays the complicated friendship between two light-skinned African-American women, and suggests parallels between concealing sexual and racial identities.

1933   In Germany, the Nazis begin a policy of banning homosexual groups, shutting down gay and lesbian locales and sending homosexuals to concentration camps.

1936   Djuna Barnes, *Nightwood*, describes the love of Robin Vote for Nora Flood, and the nocturnal adventures of the inverted Dr Matthew O'Connor.

1937   W. H. Auden, 'Lullaby', one of his many great gay love poems.
The pink triangle begins to be used to identify gay men in Nazi concentration camps. It later becomes a symbol of gay liberation.

1939   Christopher Isherwood, *Goodbye to Berlin*, describes homosexual life in the German capital just before the Nazis come to power.

1939–45   During the Second World War, awareness of homosexuality increases, in particular because of the United States Armed Forces' policy of discharging gay men and lesbians as unfit for service.

1943   Jane Bowles, *Two Serious Ladies*, about two female friends, Christina Goering and Mrs Copperfield, who leaves her husband when she falls in love with Pacifica, a young prostitute.

1945   Evelyn Waugh, *Brideshead Revisited*, explores tensions between homosexuality, Catholicism and class.

1948	Gore Vidal, *The City and the Pillar*, portrays the 'coming out' of protagonist Jim Willard and the gay life of New York.
	Alfred Kinsey, *Sexual Behavior in the Human Male* (followed by *Sexual Behavior in the Human Female* in 1953), raises awareness of homosexuality by suggesting it was much more prevalent than had been believed.
1949	Patricia Highsmith, *Strangers on a Train*, one of her many suspense novels exploring homosexual themes; later filmed by Alfred Hitchcock (1951).
1950	The Mattachine Society is founded in Los Angeles, and begins campaigning for greater tolerance and the repeal of sodomy laws. Several other 'homophile organizations' are formed shortly afterwards.
1952	In Angus Wilson, *Hemlock and After*, Bernard Sands, a homosexual, confronts various problems: a paranoid wife, a young lover with an overly possessive mother, and Mrs Curry, a procuress for paedophiles who wants to blackmail him.
	Patricia Highsmith publishes a novel about a lesbian love affair, *The Price of Salt* (later entitled *Carol*), under the pseudonym Claire Morgan.
1953	James Baldwin, *Go Tell It on the Mountain*, describes the growing sexual awareness of a fourteen-year-old African-American, John Grimes.
1954	In Britain, Peter Wildeblood, Michael Pitt-Rivers and Lord Edward Montagu of Beaulieu are found guilty of homosexual offences and imprisoned. The Wolfenden Committee is formed to examine the legal treatment of homosexuality.
1955	Daughters of Bilitis, a lesbian rights organization, is founded in San Francisco.
1956	James Baldwin, *Giovanni's Room*, a novel describing how young American David falls in love with the Italian Giovanni in Paris.
	Alan Ginsberg, *Howl and Other Poems*, the title poem of which contains frank descriptions of homosexual acts.

1957	The Wolfenden Committee publishes its report recommending that 'homosexual behaviour between consenting adults in private should no longer be a criminal offence'.
1958	In Britain, the Homosexual Law Reform Society is founded.
1962	Illinois repeals its sodomy law, becoming the first US state to do so.
1964	Jane Rule, *Desert of the Heart*, an optimistic lesbian love story.
1966	Death of Frank O'Hara. His *Collected Poems* (1972) contain many bold celebrations of gay life in New York.
1967	In Britain, the Sexual Offences Act decriminalizes homosexual acts in private between two adult men; the age of consent is set at twenty-one.
1969	The Stonewall riots occur in New York after police raid the Stonewall Inn, a gay bar in Greenwich Village, Manhattan. The riots are typically seen as the beginning of 'gay liberation'. After the riots, gay activist groups such as the Gay Liberation Front and the Gay Activists Alliance are formed in New York.
1970	On 28 June, the first anniversary of the Stonewall riots, the first gay pride parade is held in New York.
1972	On 27 June, *Gay News*, Britain's first gay magazine, begins publication.
1973	The American Psychiatric Association removes homosexuality from its *Diagnostic and Statistical Manual of Mental Disorders*.
1977	Rita Mae Brown, *Rubyfruit Jungle*, an unusually explicit lesbian novel which becomes enormously popular.
1978	Adrienne Rich, *The Dream of a Common Language*, contains her celebrated sequence, 'Twenty-One Love Poems'. Larry Kramer, *Faggots*, and Andrew Holleran, *Dancer from the Dance*, both describe the exuberant contemporary gay scene of Manhattan.

1979	Death of Elizabeth Bishop. Her *Complete Poems, 1927–1979* (1983) contains many lesbian love poems, although homosexual themes are dealt with only obliquely or discreetly.
1980	The first AIDS-related deaths are observed in the United States. By the end of 1981 there have been 121 deaths, but the cause of these deaths is unknown.
1982	Audre Lorde, *Zami: A New Spelling of My Name*, a 'bio-mythography' merging history, biography and mythology, tells the life of a black lesbian poet. Alice Walker, *The Color Purple*, describes the love of young Celie for the singer Shug Avery. James Merrill, *The Changing Light at Sandover*, poetic trilogy in which Merrill and his lover David Jackson communicate with spirits, including dead friends such as W. H. Auden, using a ouija board. Edmund White, *A Boy's Own Story*, an influential 'coming out' novel. The term AIDS – acquired immune deficiency syndrome – is introduced.
1983	A team of scientists led by Luc Montagnier identify the HIV virus, which causes AIDS, at the Pasteur Institute in Paris.
1985	Jeanette Winterson, *Oranges Are Not the Only Fruit*, a *Bildungsroman* about a lesbian girl growing up in an evangelist working-class family.
1986	Vikram Seth, *The Golden Gate*, a novel in verse exploring gay and bisexual themes in San Francisco. In the *Bowers* v. *Hardwick* case, the Supreme Court rules that there is no constitutionally protected right to engage in homosexual sex. This decision allows individual states to retain laws against 'sodomy'.
1991	Tony Kushner, *Millennium Approaches*, the first part of his two-part drama about AIDS, *Angels in America*. The second part, *Perestroika*, opens in 1992. Denmark becomes the first country in the world to introduce same-sex civil unions.

1992	Thom Gunn, *The Man with Night Sweats*, a collection of poems containing many moving elegies and poems about friends with AIDS.
1995	Mark Doty, *My Alexandria*, acclaimed collection of poems responding to the AIDS epidemic.
1995	Highly active antiretroviral therapy (HAART) slows development of HIV infection to AIDS, and helps lower AIDS-related death rates.
1998	Michael Cunningham, *The Hours*, gay novel which wins the 1999 PEN/Faulkner Award for Fiction. Sarah Waters, *Tipping the Velvet*, acclaimed for its fictional recreation of Victorian sexual subcultures.
2000	Vermont becomes the first US state to introduce same-sex civil unions.
2001	Jamie O'Neill, *At Swim, Two Boys*, gay novel set in Dublin during the 1916 Easter Rising. Holland becomes the world's first country to legalize same-sex marriage.
2003	In *Lawrence* v. *Texas*, the Supreme Court finds that state sodomy laws violate the individual's right to privacy under the fourteenth amendment.
2004	Alan Hollinghurst, *The Line of Beauty*, a novel set in 1980s Britain, wins the Booker Prize. Colm Tóibín, *The Master*, a novel based on Henry James's life in the late 1890s, is shortlisted for the Booker and wins a number of other prizes.
2005	Carol Ann Duffy, *Rapture*, a series of poems about a love affair, wins the T. S. Eliot Prize for Poetry.
2006	Elizabeth Bishop, *Edgar Allan Poe & The Juke-Box: Uncollected Poems, Drafts, and Fragments*, reignites debate about lesbianism in Bishop's poetry.

HUGH STEVENS

Homosexuality and literature: an introduction

'I wish we were labelled,' said Rickie. He wished that all the confidence
and mutual knowledge that is born in such a place as Cambridge could be
organized. People went down into the world saying, 'We know and like
each other; we shan't forget.' But they did forget, for man is so made that
he cannot remember long without a symbol; he wished there was a
society, a kind of friendship office, where the marriage of true minds
could be registered.

E. M. Forster, *The Longest Journey* (1907)[1]

In many parts of Europe – though not in most states of America – the wish
that Forster's Rickie made just over a century ago has been granted. Since the
Second World War, we have gradually entered an era of greater tolerance.
Homosexuality has been decriminalized in most of the world's democracies,
and since the 1990s same-sex marriages and partnerships have begun to be
recognized in an ever-growing number of countries.[2] This greater tolerance
has led to changes in the ways that same-sex relationships and same-sex desire
are recognized, given 'symbols'. Rickie thinks mournfully that 'a few verses of
poetry is all that survives of David and Jonathan'.[3] Today, however, Davids
and Jonathans, Ruths and Naomis, are marrying their true minds in various
kinds of friendship offices. Followers of gay and lesbian trends are wondering
how same-sex marriages, or 'civil unions', will be represented on celluloid and
between book covers. And how will same-sex couples negotiate the challenges of divorce?

Girl meets boy, they fall in love, marry, have children. In this story, so
central to our culture, identities are formed, identities of wife, husband,
mother and father, daughter and son. Children, it is assumed, will repeat
the story, move from outcome of one story to cause of another, and this
story's repetition constitutes not only the continuation of cultural values but
also the continuation of culture itself. In a private, romantic sense, marriage is
viewed as a fulfilment of desire. In a social sense, marriage creates kinship,
merges families, and defines legally binding relationships. It links individuals,
but also creates wider networks of relations.

Yet what if boy loves boy, or girl loves girl? Should they ignore or forget their love for each other? Are the girl-loving girl, and the boy-loving boy, defined by a culture which appears not to accept their very possibility? Or do they exist outside that culture? Will their love always be a story which goes against the grain of another, dominant story, or is it something that can exist alongside the other story, in a relationship of benign equality?

Literature has always been concerned with questions of kinship, love, marriage, desire, family relationships. The central and privileged stories have tended to assume that desire will be desire between girl and boy. Obstacles are thrown in the way of desire. In Shakespeare's *Romeo and Juliet* (1597), the heroine and hero cannot marry because their families, the Montagues and the Capulets, are feuding. The obstacles that stand in the way of same-sex romantic entanglements have been much more encompassing. Before the twentieth century, they have, for the most part, been represented as an impossibility rather than a desirable outcome thwarted by circumstance.

'Gay and lesbian writing' constitutes a problematic category, in large part because the meanings of 'gay', 'lesbian' and other related concepts such as 'queer' and 'homosexual' have been so intensely contested. Defining gay and lesbian writing is by no means a straightforward, or even a desirable, task. Are we dealing with writing by lesbians and gay men? Much of the literature that has been discussed in connection with homosexuality has not been written by writers who would identify themselves as gay. Are we dealing with literary representations of same-sex desire? This might seem to be a more promising way of approaching the subject, but it, too, has its pitfalls. Are representations of desire between male friends, or female friends, 'gay and lesbian'? Are Antonio and Bassanio, the two friends in Shakespeare's *The Merchant of Venice* (1598), gay?[4] Is Henry James's Olive Chancellor, in his novel *The Bostonians* (1886), with her desire to have 'a friend of her own sex with whom she might have a union of soul', a lesbian?[5] Different critical answers can be given to these questions, but the answers remain tentative, in part because Antonio never declares his homosexuality, and James never tells us, in so many words, that Miss Olive is a lesbian. The identification of Antonio and Olive as gay or lesbian is dependent on another question: the question of the extent to which it is possible to assert or understand homosexual identities in cultural and historical contexts in which the concept of homosexual identity has scarcely developed.

In 1976 Michel Foucault made his much-quoted claim, in *The History of Sexuality: An Introduction*, that not until 1870 was the 'psychological, psychiatric, medical category of homosexuality ... constituted ... less by a type of sexual relations than by a certain quality of inverting the masculine and the feminine in oneself ... The sodomite had been a temporary aberration; the homosexual was now a species.'[6] Since then, much has been written on the history of homosexuality which might modify and refine Foucault's claim, but not categorically refute it. However, there is still no consensus on vital questions surrounding homosexual identities and history. Disagreement exists over the question of when homosexual identities become visible, and also over theoretical questions important in the writing of queer history. According to essentialist approaches, there are always within human culture beings whose sexual desires are directed exclusively or predominantly towards members of their own sex, and who might be thought of as homosexual, even if expressions of homosexual identity and desire are so clandestine in much of the historical archive as to make scholarly documentation of them impossible. On the other hand, constructionist approaches hold that it only makes sense to talk of homosexual identities when there is a cultural understanding of what it means to be homosexual.[7] These approaches shape historical inquiry as well as discussions about homosexuality in different parts of the world today.

Tensions between different approaches are evident in historical accounts of homosexuality in Western culture. Randolph Trumbach has influentially argued that although '[t]he terms *heterosexual* and *homosexual* were nineteenth-century inventions … the behavioral patterns they described came into existence in the first generation of the eighteenth century'.[8] In England, France and northwestern Europe, a 'new world of sexual relations' began to emerge, characterized by 'a division of the world into a homosexual minority and a heterosexual majority'.[9] Trumbach connects this emergence with the larger 'vast transformation that is sometimes called modernization', and names 'religious skepticism and the enlightenment' and 'romantic marriage' as factors that can be associated with this new identification of individuals and groups according to sexual identity. (He is not alone in connecting homosexual identities to modernization.[10]) In this 'new world', sexual contact between men 'was now tied to a deviant gender role'.[11] In English literature, glimpses of this new subculture, and of the 'molly houses' and 'sodomites' walks' where these men would meet, are provided in works such as Ned Ward's *History of the London Clubs* (1709), and in several press reports of trials of 'sodomites'.[12] The Societies for the Reformation of Manners, which worked to repress homosexual activity by sending their agents to arrest men engaged in or looking for sex, and brought a number of victims of their vigilance to trial, helped raise awareness of the subculture they were aiming to suppress. There is some disagreement, however, as to whether a homosexual subculture is being formed in the early part of the eighteenth century, or whether an existing subculture is being publicized by legal proceedings and the press. Another historian of sexuality, Rictor

Norton, has commented: 'What is spoken of as "birth" by the historian Randolph Trumbach and others should really be recognized as merely "public knowledge". Or, to put it another way, the birth of the subculture is nothing more than (a) the birth of efficient policing and surveillance, and (b) the birth of the popular press.'[13]

In any case, the growth of awareness of gay and lesbian identities was tentative and slow. From 1774, the British utilitarian philosopher Jeremy Bentham began to write in favour of reforming the sodomy laws, and in defence of same-sex relations. In the 1780s Bentham claimed that 'paederasty ... produces no pain in anyone. On the contrary it produces pleasure, and that a pleasure which, by their perverted taste, is by this supposition preferred to that pleasure which is in general reputed the greatest.'[14] But Bentham's views on homosexuality had no influence, as they remained unpublished.[15]

Notwithstanding the presence of urban gay subcultures in Europe's major cities from the early eighteenth century, it was only in the late nineteenth century that a substantial literature appeared which described recognizably contemporary notions of homosexual identities. Modern homosexuality, it might be said, was an Anglo-Austro-German invention. While it is commonly regarded as a construct arising from the new late nineteenth-century discipline of 'sexology', the original writings on modern same-sex identity were produced by Karl Heinrich Ulrichs, a journalist who had studied law in Göttingen and Berlin, and who had worked for the civil service as a legal official in Hannover until 1854. Ulrichs's writing aimed to demonstrate that same-sex love was associated with a particular character type, a 'third sex', and argued that this 'sex' should not be criminalized for desires that were intrinsic to its nature. In 1864 and 1865 he published a series of five booklets with the title *Forschungen über das Räthsel der mannmännlichen Liebe* (*Researches on the Riddle of Male–Male Love*). Ulrichs used the term Uranism to characterize male–male love, and 'urnings' who felt this love were said to possess *anima muliebris virili corpora inclusa* (a female soul enclosed in a male body).[16]

Ulrichs's ideas were taken up and disseminated by sexologists with medical and neurological trainings. Particularly important was Carl Friedrich Otto Westphal, whose article 'Die conträre Sexualempfindung' ('Contrary Sexual Feeling'), published in 1869, Foucault identified as a founding document of modern homosexuality.[17] Westphal cited Ulrichs extensively, and was influenced by him in associating same-sex attraction with gender deviance. Ulrichs and Westphal in turn influenced Richard von Krafft-Ebing, whose *Psychopathia Sexualis* (1886), the period's most influential sexological text, contained several case studies of male and female homosexuality.[18] This burgeoning sexological literature made its way into English culture in translation, and also through the works of the sexologist Havelock Ellis and the poet and literary critic John Addington Symonds (see Joseph Bristow, 'Homosexual Writing on Trial', Chapter 1 in this volume, 17–33). Early psychoanalytic writing on sexuality, in particular Freud's *Three Essays on the Theory of Sexuality*,[19] cited sexological literature extensively, and gave further authority to concepts of 'sexual inversion'. The trials of Oscar Wilde in 1895 have been recognized as the nineteenth century's greatest promotion of homosexuality.[20] But what they publicized had been formed through the shared influence of early homophile activism and scientific writing.

As Eve Kosofsky Sedgwick argued in *Epistemology of the Closet*, late nineteenth-century gay writing often figured modern homosexual identities as a secret which could not be divulged. In the early twentieth century, Wildean and sexological notions of homosexuality begin to appear more openly in literary texts. The novels of Ronald Firbank and a short story by Willa Cather, 'Paul's Case' (1905), are some of the notable texts to paint homosexuality in the flamboyant colours of the Wildean aesthete.[21] Another story by Cather, 'Tommy the Unsentimental' (1896), describes the efforts of a mannish lesbian, Theodosia Shirley, the 'Tommy' of the title, to marry off her effeminate, carnation-wearing friend Jay Harper with Miss Jessica, 'a dainty, white languid bit of a thing' whom 'Tommy took to being sweet and gentle to'.[22] Tommy is acting in part to ward off the disapproval she and Jay face in the small town in which they live, but the date of the story's appearance gives a more international context to unsentimental Tommy's urgent efforts to see her fey friend married. The story registers both sexological concepts of sexual inversion and the publicity attached to Wilde's trials and imprisonment.

This *Companion* does not attempt to cover the literary history of representations of same-sex desire and love in English literature from the medieval period onwards. Rather it discusses a range of themes relevant to lesbian and gay culture, and shows how these themes are treated in literary texts. The chapters reflect the plurality of voices and approaches within lesbian and gay studies as well as the diversity of queer life today, and show how questions of homosexuality frequently intersect with other aspects of politics and culture.

A specifically lesbian and gay criticism might trace its roots to the late nineteenth century, to texts like J. A. Symonds's *A Problem in Greek Ethics* (1884; see Bristow, 25) and Oscar Wilde's 'The Portrait of Mr. W. H.' (1889).[23] Gay and lesbian criticism became identifiable as a major part of literary studies in the 1980s. Before this period, there were some important studies of homosexuality in literature, including Roger Austin's *Playing the Game: The Homosexual Novel in America* and Jeannette Foster's outstanding *Sex Variant Women in Literature*.[24] Only rarely, however, did English departments teach lesbian and gay writing as a distinct literary topic, and few critical books on homosexuality were published by university presses. Now there are many lesbian and gay writing courses in English departments throughout the world, and questions of homosexuality are routinely discussed in period courses.

Studies from the early 1990s typically regarded lesbian and gay identities as dissident, subversive, transgressive, and as having been subject to repression. In addition, the very discussion of lesbian and gay writing was assumed to be oppositional.[25] This oppositional stance was necessary in Britain under Conservative Prime Ministers Margaret Thatcher and John Major, and in the United States under Republican presidents Ronald Reagan and George Bush Part One. Egregiously poor government responses to the AIDS epidemic in both the UK and the US fuelled scholarly activism in a time when gay and lesbian criticism became 'queer' criticism. The equation of lesbian and gay studies with 'queer' studies received some backlash within lesbian and gay communities – particularly in the United States, where Bruce Bawer's *A Place at the Table* (1993) and Andrew Sullivan's *Virtually Normal* (1995) struck a populist vein of sentiment with their polemics urging that gay and lesbian politics should be reconceived as a non-radical advocacy of tolerance towards homosexuality as a 'normal' identity. Nevertheless queer theory, criticism and history remain highly visible and voluminous, whether in specialist journals such as *GLQ*, *Differences* and *Genders*, or in academic monographs, many of which have appeared in specialist series such as Duke University Press's 'Series Q' or Columbia University Press's 'Between Men – Between Women: Lesbian and Gay Studies'.

In the process, 'queer' has inevitably lost some of its radical charge, become neutralized. This is not only because of the growing familiarity of the term itself, but also because of the increasing legitimation of gay and lesbian identities in our culture. Gay and lesbian studies are indeed 'kinda subversive, kinda hegemonic', in the memorable words of the late Eve Kosofsky Sedgwick.[26] The chapters in this *Companion* reflect that ambiguous status. The study of gay and lesbian writing, they show, can also reflect differences within lesbian and gay culture, and demonstrate the multiplicity of forms gay and lesbian identities take.

In the first section of this *Companion*, 'Repression and Legitimation', contributors discuss lesbian and gay writing in relation to various institutions: the law, psychoanalysis and the press. Joseph Bristow's chapter demonstrates the extent to which homosexual writing has been censored as obscene or blasphemous under British law. Intellectual and literary writing about homosexuality – by figures as diverse as Havelock Ellis, Edward Carpenter, J. A. Symonds, Radclyffe Hall and James Hanley – was often subject to legal intervention, with many major works being seized and destroyed. Lesbian and gay writers faced stark choices under these conditions: there were limits on how openly they could write if they wanted their works to circulate freely. Bristow concludes his examination of 350 years of censorship with the affirmation that homosexual writings in Britain are no longer on trial.

The scientific writing on homosexuality that began to appear in the late nineteenth century was aimed at a specialist audience, and was not subject to legal control to the same extent as more popular forms of writing. In his discussion of homosexuality in the writing of Sigmund Freud and in German modernist literature, Andrew Webber notes that 'psychoanalysis has achieved rather ambivalent forms of recognition for gay and lesbian sexualities' (34). Psychoanalysis provided an articulation of homosexuality which departed from the biological reductionism of sexological writing, and refused to regard homosexuality as a pathology, yet it also associated homosexuality with 'particular forms of mental illness, from hysteria and melancholia to paranoia' (35). Webber shows how many of Freud's case studies construct sexual identity using peculiarly literary tropes. Homosexuality in Freud's writing can recall the Romantic figure of the *Doppelgänger*, embodying a 'narcissistically inflected and sexually charged relationship between men' (37). The sexual curiosity of children in Freud's case studies leads them, like children in fairy tales, to encounters with beasts in enclosed spaces. Webber explores correspondences between Freud's case studies and a wide range of German modernist writing, reading formative scenes 'located in a variety of closet spaces, between private and public exhibition, with more or less explicit indications of homoerotic attachment' (43).

Closet spaces are a focus in Joanne Winning's chapter. The closet, Winning writes, has been conceived of as 'the private, hiding space' (50) in which dissident sexual identities are kept secret. Winning follows Eve Kosofsky Sedgwick in emphasizing how the closet is a shaping presence in understandings of homosexuality, but also suggests ways in which the closet is losing its force as contemporary lesbian and gay life is led more openly. Winning shows how lesbian modernists – in particular H. D. and Bryher – challenge 'the dialectics of outside and inside that pervades our own formulations of sexual identity' (55). For these women writers, the text is not a place of secrets, but an artefact enabling 'the progress towards both self-inscription and sexual self-knowledge' (58).

Power and resistance are central to Tim Dean's chapter on 'The Erotics of Transgression'. The growing acceptance of homosexuality has shifted the meaning of transgression: lesbian and gay sexualities, Dean notes, 'have no essential or privileged relation to transgression' (68). Transgression concerns not the law but the limit, the violation of taboos, of thresholds constructed through shame, disgust and moral sanction. Dean identifies two traditions of transgressive writing in late twentieth-century American fiction. In the first, represented by John Rechy, homosexuality is identified with the figure of the sexual outlaw, and repressive laws augment the lust of a 'dance of mediated desire' (74). In another, represented by Samuel R. Delany, writing explores disturbing fantasies which violate taboos rather than laws or conventions.

My own chapter, 'Normality and Queerness in Gay Fiction', further upsets the equation of gay writing with transgression by showing how contemporary gay fiction negotiates with family structures in ways which refuse to figure the (heterosexual) family as that hegemonic monstrosity against which gay identities define themselves. In the fiction I discuss, homosexual identities negotiate with familial structures, and nuanced accounts are given of the ways in which homosexuality is neither wholly queer nor fully accepted. This fiction challenges concepts of queerness which figure homosexuality as resistant to power. I place a conversation between queer theory and gay fiction in a historical context of tensions between assimilation and radicalism within homophile activism, gay liberation and queer theory.

The second section of the *Companion* explores affiliations between homosexual writing and other forms of identity: cultural, national and racial identities, transgender identities and urban identities. In her chapter 'The Homoerotics of Travel: People, Ideas, Genres', Ruth Vanita suggests ways in which homophobia and notions of homosexual identity are internationally disseminated, and discusses tales of protagonists moving 'in search of more congenial climes and of the hidden self' (99). Vanita shows how a wide range of writers work within national traditions but also cross between nations, religious communities and linguistic groups. European and American writers discussed by Vanita – including Thomas Mann, Radclyffe Hall and Edmund White – travel widely in search of 'places where they feel freer precisely because they are foreigners there' (104). Vanita also discusses how twentieth-century Indian writers Pandey Bechan Sharma ('Ugra') and Suniti Namjoshi draw not only on Indian but also on European literary traditions. Local lesbian and gay traditions negotiate with imported and exported homosexual identities, and queerness remakes itself in this contact between cultures.

Kathryn Bond Stockton, in her chapter on 'The Queerness of Race and Same-Sex Desire', examines the rich complications arising from 'the place where race and queerness cross'. Noting that the 'linguistic binds and conceptual fields' of 'queerness' and 'race' can be markedly distinct, Stockton discusses a range of films and plays which provocatively dramatize the challenges racial and sexual identities pose to liberal sensibilities. She then offers readings of Richard Bruce Nugent and Langston Hughes which address the mélange of queer overtones and undertones in the Harlem Renaissance. In addition, her chapter explores 'switchpoints' between race and queerness as they are played out in Chicano/a writing (the works of John Rechy and Cherríe Moraga), and, in readings of David Henry Hwang's play *M. Butterfly* (1988) and Deepa Mehta's film *Fire* (1996), shows how conflict over meanings of queer sexualities takes place within imperial contexts.

AIDS, we are often told, is not a 'gay disease', but we are still taking stock of its continuing impact on gay communities. Richard Canning's chapter on 'The Literature of AIDS' begins by discussing 'the contemporary dearth of representations of AIDS in culture' (132). Despite the 'huge quantity of novels, memoirs, films, dramas and collections of verse' (133–134) responding to the epidemic, there is now what Canning calls 'an unnatural calm, even silence' around AIDS. Canning links this silence to the introduction of anti-retroviral therapies in 1997, and notes how recent works on AIDS – notably Alan Hollinghurst's *The Line of Beauty* – 'return to the days of uncertainty with the hindsight of a post-treatment consciousness' (135). His chapter explores the astonishing variety of AIDS literature produced in the 1980s and 1990s, including fiction, poetry, memoirs, short stories and plays. Although the majority of this literature was written 'by and about Caucasian gay men' (137), Canning also discusses fiction and memoirs by non-white writers.

In the 1990s 'transgender' emerged as a term to describe a range of forms of gender variance, and to provide a space for resistance against the process of compulsory gendering. Questions about the convergence and disparity of transgender and homosexual identities have led to a re-thinking of the history of gender difference. Heather Love begins her chapter on transgender identities, literature and politics by noting how certain key lesbian modernist texts – Djuna Barnes's *Nightwood*, Virginia Woolf's *Orlando* and Radclyffe Hall's *The Well of Loneliness* – and accounts of sexual inversion from sexological writing, based on testimonies of 'individuals who felt that they were born in the "wrong" body' (149), might persuasively be read not as lesbian but as transgender. Love goes on to discuss a wide range of late twentieth-century self-conscious transgender and transsexual memoirs and novels, and comments on relationships between lesbian and gay politics and transgender issues. Love concludes her chapter by urging that the 'mainstreaming' of lesbian and gay identities should not take place at the cost of newly stigmatizing gender deviance.

The chapters in the final section of the *Companion* show how gay and lesbian literary creation takes place through reference to other queer writing, or writing re-imagined as queer. Jodie Medd uses Stuart Hall's remark that 'Identities are the names we give to the different ways we are positioned by, and position ourselves within, the narratives of the past' (168) as a departure for an examination of contemporary gay and lesbian literature's engagement with the Victorian and modernist past. Alan Hollinghurst's *The Swimming-Pool Library* and Jamie O'Neill's *At Swim, Two Boys* explore the homosexual past within national and imperial contexts, and Michael Cunningham's *The Hours* juxtaposes a queer present in contemporary New York with the re-imagining of an iconic moment in British modernism, Virginia Woolf composing *Mrs. Dalloway* in 1923. Noting that 'the historiography of same-sex desire is diacritically marked by gender' (174), Medd shows how contemporary lesbian writers like Sarah Waters and Jeanette Winterson take 'strategic historical liberties' (177) with the archive of lesbian experience. In creative responses to the faint or 'apparitional' presence of lesbianism in the historical record, they re-imagine lesbian pasts while also reflecting on the processes by which we create historical narratives.

Lesbian and gay literature is produced by individuals, but it has also depended on the writer's contact with networks which stimulated, supported and sustained queer cultural production. Jane Garrity and Tirza True Latimer challenge separatist stereotypes of lesbian and gay culture by emphasizing collaborations between lesbians and gay men. The circle of gay men that formed around Gertrude Stein after the First World War were involved in every form of artistic life: not only writing but also dance and choreography, photography and painting. Collaborations took various forms, and Latimer and Garrity discuss the shared creative enterprise that fed into *Dix Portraits*, a book merging visual and literary portraits, and the opera *Four Saints in Three Acts*. They then focus on the sexual nonconformity of the Bloomsbury group, and connect the erotic and artistic entanglements of the group's married men and women, sapphists and buggers, with their modernist innovations in various fields, including painting, literature and interior design.

Richard Bozorth's chapter discusses 'some of the most influential and representative love poetry written and read by gay men and lesbians since the time of Shakespeare' – figures including Christina Rossetti, Walt Whitman, Emily Dickinson, Hart Crane, Gertrude Stein, W. H. Auden, Adrienne Rich and Mark Doty. Bozorth describes how lesbian and gay love poetry speaks 'the love that dare not speak its name', and exploits unspeakability 'to speak sexuality and the body as subtext' (204). Bozorth uncovers complex networks of poetic influence, and describes a range of poetic strategies, including modernist experimentation, lyric introspection, poignant addresses to an ungendered 'you', erotic celebration in free verse or finely crafted lyric verse which deals with themes of death and loss.

If gay and lesbian communities are imagined communities, then nowhere have they been so powerfully imagined and developed as in New York. The inspiration New York has provided for gay and lesbian literature is the focus of David Bergman's chapter, which traces the development of gay cultural networks in Manhattan from the 1920s. New York's queer literary scene, Bergman shows, is one of great cultural diversity, shaped by the city's 'openness to the strange, foreign or merely different' (219). Much of the writing Bergman describes takes its energies from the street – from what dance critic Edwin Denby called 'the many kinds of walking you can see in this city' (225) – and from the city's night life. The difficulty of writing about New York is precisely the difficulty of capturing the city's infinite variety. Gay and lesbian literature, like New York's streets, shows 'many kinds of walking', and we are still finding out where our long journeys are heading.

NOTES

1. E. M. Forster, *The Longest Journey*, ed. Elizabeth Heine (London: Edward Arnold, 1984), 64.
2. Some of the best scholarship on same-sex partnership and marriage can be found in Yuval Merin, *Equality for Same-Sex Couples: The Legal Recognition of Gay Partnerships in Europe and the United States* (Chicago: University of Chicago Press, 2002), William N. Eskridge, Jr, and Darren R. Spedale, *Gay Marriage: For Better or For Worse?: What We've Learned From the Evidence* (New York: Oxford University Press, 2006) and Katharina Boele-Woelki and Angelika Fuchs, eds., *Legal Recognition of Same-Sex Couples in Europe* (Antwerp: Intersentia, 2003).
3. Forster, *The Longest Journey*, 64.
4. For debates about the meanings of same-sex desire in *The Merchant of Venice*, and the Renaissance more generally, see Alan Bray, *Homosexuality in Renaissance England*, updated edn (New York: Columbia University Press, 1995) and Bruce R. Smith, *Homosexual Desire in Shakespeare's England: A Cultural Poetics* (Chicago: University of Chicago Press, 1991).
5. There are many discussions of lesbianism in *The Bostonians*: see for example Terry Castle, 'Haunted by Olive Chancellor', *The Apparitional Lesbian: Female Homosexuality and Modern Culture* (New York: Columbia University Press, 1993), 150–85, and Annamarie Jagose, 'Unmarriageable: The Housing of Sexual Cultures in *The Bostonians*', *Inconsequence: Lesbian Representation and the Logic of Sexual Sequence* (Ithaca, NY: Cornell University Press, 1992), 57–76.
6. Michel Foucault, *The History of Sexuality: An Introduction*, trans. Robert Hurley (London: Allen Lane, 1979), 44.
7. For a provocative discussion of debates between essentialism and constructionism, see Diana Fuss, *Essentially Speaking: Feminism, Nature and Difference* (New York: Routledge, 1989).
8. Randolph Trumbach, *Sex and the Gender Revolution: Heterosexuality and the Third Gender in Enlightenment London* (Chicago: University of Chicago Press, 1998), 4.
9. Randolph Trumbach, 'Modern Sodomy: The Origins of Homosexuality, 1700–1800', in Matt Cook, H. G. Cocks, Robert Mills and Randolph Trumbach,

eds., *A Gay History of Britain: Love and Sex Between Men Since the Middle Ages* (Oxford: Greenwood World Publishing, 2007), 78.

10. Other scholars making similar claims include John D'Emilio, in 'Capitalism and Gay Identity', *Making Trouble: Essays on Gay History, Politics, and the University* (New York: Routledge, 1992), 3–16. See also Jeffrey Weeks, *Sex, Politics and Society: The Regulation of Sexuality since 1800*, second edn (London: Longman, 1989).

11. Trumbach, 'Modern Sodomy', 80.

12. [Edward Ward], *The Second Part, Of the London Clubs* (London: J. Dutton, 1709). For an account of early eighteenth-century gay subculture in England, see Rictor Norton, *Molly Clap's Molly House: Gay Subculture in England, 1700–1830* (London: Gay Men's Press, 1992). A collection of eighteenth-century documents is available online at Rictor Norton, 'The Gay Subculture in Early Eighteenth-Century London', *Homosexuality in Eighteenth-Century England: A Sourcebook*, updated 15 June 2008, www.rictornorton.co.uk/eighteen/molly2.htm.

13. Rictor Norton, 'The Gay Subculture in Early Eighteenth-Century London'.

14. Jeremy Bentham, 'Offences Against One's Self', written about 1784, www.columbia.edu/cu/lweb/eresources/exhibitions/sw25/bentham/index.html#50, accessed 20 May 2009. This essay was first edited by Louis Crompton and published in *Journal of Homosexuality*, 4 (1978), 91–107.

15. Louis Crompton, *Homosexuality and Civilization* (Cambridge, MA: Harvard University Press, 2003), 530.

16. Hubert Kennedy, 'Karl Heinrich Ulrichs, First Theorist of Homosexuality', in V. A. Rosario, ed., *Science and Homosexualities* (New York: Routledge, 1997), 26–45.

17. Foucault's date of 1870 is one year out. See Foucault, *The History of Sexuality: An Introduction*, 43. 'Die conträre Sexualempfindung' was published in *Archiv für Psychiatrie und Nervenkrankheiten* 2:1 (Berlin, 1869), 73–108. An online transcription of the article (in German) is available at www.schwulencity.de/WestphalContraere1869.html.

18. Richard von Krafft-Ebing, *Psychopathia Sexualis. Eine klinisch-forensische Studie* (Stuttgart: Ferdinand Enke, 1886).

19. Sigmund Freud, *Three Essays on the Theory of Sexuality* (1905), in James Strachey, ed., *Standard Edition of the Complete Psychological Works of Sigmund Freud*, 24 vols. (London: Hogarth Press, 1953–74), vol. VII: 135–243.

20. See in particular Alan Sinfield, *The Wilde Century: Effeminacy, Oscar Wilde, and the Queer Moment* (London: Cassell, 1994).

21. *The Complete Ronald Firbank* (London: Duckworth, 1961); Willa Cather, 'Paul's Case', in Virginia Faulkner, ed., *Collected Short Fiction, 1882–1912* (Lincoln: University of Nebraska Press, 1970), 243–61.

22. Willa Cather, 'Tommy the Unsentimental', in *Collected Short Fiction, 1882–1912*, 476.

23. Oscar Wilde, 'The Portrait of Mr W. H.' (1889), in Ian Small, ed., *Complete Short Fiction* (London: Penguin, 1994), 47–79.

24. Roger Austen, *Playing the Game: The Homosexual Novel in America* (Indianapolis: Bobbs-Merrill, 1977); Jeannette Foster, *Sex Variant Women in*

Literature: A Historical and Quantitative Survey (1956; Tallahassee, FL: Naiad, 1985).

25. For examples of politically engaged critical writing on homosexuality from the late 1980s and 1990s, see Douglas Crimp, ed., *AIDS: Cultural Activism, Cultural Analysis* (Cambridge, MA: MIT Press, 1988); Judith Butler, *Gender Trouble: Feminism and the Subversion of Identity* (New York: Routledge, 1990); Diana Fuss, ed., *Inside/Out: Lesbian Theories, Gay Theories* (New York: Routledge, 1991); Jonathan Dollimore, *Sexual Dissidence: Augustine to Wilde, Freud to Foucault* (Oxford: Clarendon Press, 1991); Terry Castle, *The Apparitional Lesbian: Female Homosexuality and Modern Culture* (New York: Columbia University Press, 1993); Leo Bersani, *Homos* (Cambridge, MA: Harvard University Press, 1995). All of these works are in the guide to further reading.

26. Eve Kosofsky Sedgwick, 'Queer Performativity: Henry James's *The Art of the Novel*', *GLQ*, 1 (1993), 15.

PART I
Repression and legitimation

I

JOSEPH BRISTOW

Homosexual writing on trial: from *Fanny Hill* to *Gay News*

Shortly after the English capital suffered two rare earthquakes in February and March 1750, the Bishop of London, Thomas Sherlock, rushed into print with a controversial pamphlet declaring that the seismic ructions expressed nothing less than a 'strong summons, from God, to repentance'.[1] Sherlock asserts this 'particular mark of divine vengeance' was a stern reminder of the 'destruction of Sodom by fire from heaven' recorded in many parts of the Bible (7). More to the point, he blames these cautionary events on the 'unnatural lewdness, of which we have heard so much of late' (7). Here he implicitly refers to the 'vile book' that he had, a year earlier, done his utmost to 'stop' in its 'progress'.[2] In March 1749, Sherlock had already expressed his dismay to the Secretary of State that the 'prosecution against the printer and publisher of the *Memoirs of a Lady of Pleasure*' (commonly known as *Fanny Hill*, first published in two instalments in November 1748 and February 1749) had resulted in an expurgated edition that 'le[ft] out some things, which were thought most liable to the law and to expose the author and publisher to punishment' (56–7). The very idea that even a heavily edited version of this erotic narrative should remain in circulation, after some sixty copies of the first edition had been sold, contributed greatly to his belief that the time had come for Londoners to suffer God's wrath (56). The *Memoirs*, which had subjected its author, John Cleland, to a fine of £100 and a short spell in jail, remained for Sherlock a 'reproach to the honour of the government, and the law of the country' (57).

Ever since the Secretary of State issued a warrant for the arrest of Cleland (together with his printer and bookseller) for publishing the *Memoirs*, this lively novel has stood as the first original work in the history of English literature to be explicitly banned on the grounds of giving offence – as its author observed – to 'Public Manners'.[3] Since there was no legislation that specifically prohibited obscene publications at the time, it might appear that the seizing of Cleland's book simply amounted (in Walter Kendrick's words) to a 'small fuss'.[4] But, given that the *Memoirs* subsequently became a centrepiece in legal disputes over literary obscenity, the controversy surrounding its initial publication makes one point clear. By the middle of the eighteenth century, the state (abetted by churchmen such as Sherlock) had begun to exercise censorship in a recognizably modern way, insofar as it adopted the role of moral guardianship on behalf of the nation. Events relating to the suppression of Cleland's *Memoirs* show that the state, in meting out punishments against obscene works, held in greatest contempt depictions of male homosexuality.

Although no records remain of Cleland's trial in November 1749, the textual history of the *Memoirs* – a novel that remained illicit in the English-speaking world until the 1960s – has been well documented. Especially interesting to students of homosexual writing is the fact that the most offensive aspect of Cleland's narrative appears to have been the scene where the first-person narrator, the former prostitute Fanny Hill, recalls the time she spied on the sexual antics of two young men in an adjacent room. No sooner had the older of the two teenagers begun 'to embrace, to press, to kiss the younger, to put his hands in his bosom, and give such manifest signs of an amorous attention' than the young Fanny Hill witnessed him 'moistening well with spittle his instrument' so that it 'seem'd to move, and go pretty currently on, as in a carpet-road [i.e. rod], without much rub, or resistance' inside his lover's anus.[5]

This vivid episode, which lasts for scarcely more than two pages, occurs towards the end of an exuberant story where the middle-aged Fanny recounts the sometimes lurid ways in which she acquired increasing expertise in sexual pleasures and practices after she arrived at London, an ingenuous country-girl, at the age of fifteen. Her colourful career begins with the initiation into the 'satiety of enjoyments' that she receives from an experienced sex worker, Phoebe (12). Fanny's adventures, if avoiding the vulgarity of French precursors such as *l'École des filles* (1655), shift briskly from tribadism to more and more sensational experiences. Yet even though Fanny must steel herself when she services several repulsive clients, nothing disgusts her more than 'so criminal a scene' as that of the young sodomites' joyful love-making (159). As Rictor Norton reveals, Fanny's wording is literally true, in so far as this kind of homosexual sex, if discovered, was subject to severe punishments, either in the pillory or by hanging, under the terms of the Buggery Act of 1533.[6] Little wonder that Fanny, even though she maintains a livelihood that itself exists under constant legal threat, recoils so violently from the older man's 'continuing to harass' his partner's 'rear' that she burns with 'rage, and indignation' (159). Unfortunately, once she struggles to 'raise the house upon' these sexual criminals, her 'unlucky impetuosity' results in a moment of absurd comedy when she trips up on a loose floorboard and crashes 'senseless on the ground' (159).

If, however, this risible description dramatizes the 'senseless' nature of Fanny's fury, it also prefaces a conversation in which another character vents her spleen against such 'worthless and despicable' men (159). After she returns home to the brothel, Fanny divulges what she has witnessed to her employer, Mrs Cole, who informs her that 'there was no doubt of due vengeance one time or other overtaking these miscreants' (159). In tones that sound barely different from those of Thomas Sherlock, Mrs Cole remarks that the 'air and climate' of England has a 'peculiar blessing' over that of other nations because it leaves 'a plague-spot visibly imprinted on all that are tainted with' such 'infamous passion' (159). Such men, she says, are 'stript of all the manly virtues of their own sex' because of their 'monstrous inconsistency' in 'loathing and contemning women' (159–60). This modern mark of Cain is most visible in their effeminacy, their 'apeing' women's 'manners, airs, lips' (160). Mrs Cole, however, has another reason – one connected with economic necessity – for denouncing male homosexuality. She resents these men-loving men because they undermine her business; in her view, they 'take something more precious than bread' (i.e. the penis) 'out of the mouths' (i.e. the sexual organs) of women (159). Clearly, Mrs Cole's circumlocutions impugn a 'criminal scene' that Cleland's novel has depicted, just as it depicts all of Fanny's erotic encounters and espials, in such graphic – arguably titillating – detail.

Cleland's evident delight in generating such moral instability is most evident at the conclusion where Fanny reveals that she has for many years lived the life of a happily married woman who has learned to 'pity ... those who, immers'd in a gross sensuality, are insensible to the so delicate charms of VIRTUE' (187). Yet long before we read what she smugly calls her 'tail-piece of morality' (189), it becomes plain that she likes to present herself as a woman who respectfully fulfilled her part of each sexual contract. Fanny's sense of duty to her clients is particularly noteworthy when she abides by the 'necessary previous instructions on how to act and conduct' herself as she gives pleasure to one Mr Barvile, who bears more than a passing resemblance to a disciplinarian Methodist. Cleland's *Memoirs* indulge our humour when they depict a sex worker behaving with almost religious obedience to a follower of John Wesley, whose prudish advocacy of sexual segregation in church made him the butt of much mid-century satire.

Since Fanny's spirited narrative both exults in and repudiates the sexual history it recounts, it has remained difficult for readers to assess the degree to which the novel stands for or against sexual liberation. For this reason, as Peter Sabor has shown, the numerous scholarly essays that address this novel from standpoints informed by feminist critique, lesbian and gay studies and queer theory have reached little consensus about the reactionary or progressive nature of the tireless precision with which Cleland articulates many different types of sexual behaviour.[7] But, as Hal Gladfelder implies, the very idea that Cleland's *Memoirs* should be evaluated along such lines is probably beside the point when we consider the prohibitive legal circumstances in which this work emerged.[8] Gladfelder contends that by 1728, when the Attorney General prosecuted the bookseller Edward Curll after he published translations of two works of French erotica, English law for the first time deemed that obscene libel existed when a printed work could be said – in the words of the prosecution – to 'corrupt the morals of the king's subjects, and ... [to be] against the peace of the king'.[9]

As Gladfelder sees it, authors such as Cleland laboured under an obligation to 'write freely about the wickedest acts' in a 'posture of moral correction' (135). In other words, Cleland's novel proceeds to uncover the eighteenth-century sexual underworld through a narrative where Fanny, no matter how much she delights in her debaucheries, at times expresses strategic propriety. Gladfelder assumes that Fanny's moments of moralizing are shaped by the writer's sense of duty to self-regulate explicit sexual representations in order to deflect objections from the authorities. While there might be more than an element of truth in this claim, it seems possible that Cleland was just as intolerant as everyone else – including Fanny, the Bishop of London and the Secretary of State – when it came to sodomy: a complicated term, as Mark D. Jordan reminds us, whose purpose for Christian theologians in 'categorizing – for uniting and reifying, for judging and punishing – genital acts between members of the same sex' can be traced back to the work of the eleventh-century theologian Peter Damian.[10] In his letter to the Secretary of State's office, where he expresses some regret for publishing the *Memoirs*, Cleland also pointedly remarks that while it took several months before 'the pious indignation of my Lords the Bishops' objected to his novel, it was the case that a much more offensive work – 'a Pamphlet in defence of *Sodomy*' – was suppressed in the very instant it had been 'advertised in all the papers'.[11]

The work in question is *Ancient and Modern Pederasty Investigated and Exemplify'd* (1749), which the *Gentleman's Magazine* publicized in its 'Register of Books'. Until recently, not much was known about this prohibited publication, apart from the fact that in January 1750 the Attorney General requested the prosecution of the author, Thomas Cannon, and the printer, John Purser.[12] In a remarkable piece of sleuthing, Gladfelder discovered that one of the reasons why Cleland languished in Fleet Prison, where he completed drafting the *Memoirs*, was that he owed a considerable debt of £800 to his onetime friend Cannon.[13] On his release, Cleland affixed to

Cannon's chambers in New Inn an offensive note that denounced 'Molly Cannon' as 'that execrable, white-faced catamite', who was also a murderer (25). (The term 'molly' was common street slang for a homosexual man.) Foolishly, it seems, Cannon responded by lodging a complaint against Cleland. The Attorney General's action, which demanded recognizances (i.e. pledges to keep the peace) of £400 each for the release of Cannon and Purser, prompted Cleland's enemy to escape abroad before the trial was scheduled to take place. After a deferred trial in 1751, Purser was sent down for a month in the Marshalsea. Even though all copies of Cannon's pamphlet have disappeared, large portions of it are preserved in the indictment against Purser. What is left of the offending work comprises for Gladfelder 'the most extensive and varied treatment of male same-sex desire in all of eighteenth-century literature' – 'matched only', he claims, by the 'sodomitical interlude' in Cleland's *Memoirs* (34–5). The indictment reveals Cannon to have been a highly informed sexual historian who unapologetically declared that among 'high-flown Philosophers' it was 'Socrates, their great founder' who was 'a most devoted Pederast', as we can see, he reminds us, in Plato's *Symposium*.[14] Cannon's views were certainly in advance of their time. In the next century, such a statement about the *Symposium* would sound notes of alarm among teachers of the Classics, particularly in places such as Victorian Oxford where there were pressing debates about including this sexually contentious dialogue on the university syllabus.[15]

The state's suppression of Cannon's pamphlet should not lead to the conclusion that during the mid eighteenth century most writings on homosexual themes either went underground or never made it into print. Even if the period does not contain many works that represent sexual intimacy between men as explicitly as Cleland's *Memoirs* does, it nonetheless abounds in literature that features cross-dressing lesbians, such as Charlotte Charke, and men-loving men, including Samuel Foote.[16] Henry Fielding's *The Female Husband* (1746) is a case in point. This ostensibly high-minded work elaborates a sensational picaresque derived from the recent trial of Mary Hamilton, who was convicted for living as the spouse of a young woman in Wells, Somerset. At the outset, Fielding condemns his lesbian protagonist because her susceptibility to sexual advances from women – the first of whom happens to be a convert to much-maligned Methodism – shows that 'once our carnal appetites are let loose … there is no excess and disorder which they are not liable to commit'.[17] But that hardly stops him from revelling in the details of Hamilton's disproportionate eroticism. In many ways, *The Female Husband* anticipates the contradictory tactics of Cleland's *Memoirs* by reprehending Mary Hamilton's 'monstrous and unnatural desires' while encouraging readers to imagine her sexual use of a euphemistic '*wherewithal*' – namely, the dildo that she needs not only to satisfy her spouses but also to mask the fact that she is a woman (23).

Yet it is noticeable that while Fielding could write on such topics with impunity, even pirated editions of Cleland's sexually explicit version of the *Memoirs* omitted the passage featuring the two men's love-making. Noticeably, in the edition that G. P. Putnam's issued in 1963, which stood at the centre of a series of obscenity trials that eventually reached the Supreme Court of the United States, the episode was omitted.[18] Had this episode remained in the text, Putnam's might have found it harder to defend the literary value of the *Memoirs* against the charge that the work (to use a key legal phrase) would 'deprave and corrupt' its readers. This point becomes clear when we examine the ways in which nineteenth-century legislation impacted not only depictions of same-sex intimacy but also, more urgently, the representation of homosexual identity.

Over a hundred years later, in 1857, Lord Campbell witnessed his Obscene Publications Bill pass through parliament. This particular law built on the provisions of the Customs Consolidation Act (1853), which sought to ban the importation of pornography from the Continent. According to Campbell, his legislation had been spurred by his recent discovery that in London there had been 'a sale of poison more deadly than prussic acid, strichnine, or arsenic – the sale of obscene publications and indecent books'.[19] Under Campbell's act, such works could be seized and destroyed. Some of his parliamentary colleagues had doubts about his initiative to transform obscenity from a misdemeanour under common law into a statutory offence. Lord Lyndhurst wondered what was 'the interpretation which [was] to be put on the word "obscene"'; he grasped immediately that countless works could be prohibited through the broad scope of this epithet.[20] In particular, he expressed concern that works from the English canon – including John Dryden's translations of Ovid's *Art of Love*, the Earl of Rochester's satires and the bawdier Restoration comedies – might run afoul of a law whose application could extend well beyond those publications that were (in Campbell's words) 'written for the single purpose of corrupting the morals of youth and of a nature calculated to shock the common feelings in a well regulated mind'.[21] Campbell's legislation made no provision for protecting many writings of literary prestige from the broad charge that they were obscene.

Yet while it is true that respected literary productions were not immediately affected by the 1857 law, eleven years later a ruling ensured that the reach of Campbell's legislation embraced works very different from the kinds of pornography whose sale it purportedly aimed to prohibit. In 1868, this law was refined after a militant Protestant was taken to court for an anti-Catholic tirade called *The Confessional Unmasked*; the pamphlet accused Catholic priests of engaging in sexual assaults against women parishioners in the confessional box. In his assessment of an appeal against a regional magistrate's decision to destroy copies of this volume, Chief Justice Cockburn upheld the work as obscene. His conclusion, he said, depended on the following principle, whose wording would become the main point of reference for all subsequent obscenity trials, both in England and Wales and in America: 'The test of obscenity is whether the tendency of the matter charged as obscenity is to deprave and corrupt those whose minds are open to such immoral influences and into whose hands a publication of this sort might fall.'[22] As legal historians have always pointed out, the precise meaning of the two striking verbs is open to wide interpretation. In *Regina* v. *Hicklin*, where Cockburn made this problematic pronouncement, he contended that this test would be proven if the offending works were deemed to arouse 'most impure and libidinous thoughts'. Such a line of argument assumes that courts could exercise an almost telepathic understanding of the ways in which printed matter might succeed in inducing an erotic response in its suggestible consumers. But what was more disquieting about the Hicklin test (as it became known) was that it opened a door for judges to apply the insidious verbs 'deprave' and 'corrupt' to any printed work that touched on sexual subject-matter, regardless of whether it had pornographic content. It was in this legal context that works on homosexual topics that could scarcely be labelled pornographic proved especially vulnerable to prosecution. As I explain here, it became increasingly difficult to circulate publicly several important volumes (both fiction and non-fiction) that represented emergent understandings of male and female homosexual identity. In the meantime, works of homosexual pornography could escape the grasp of the law through clandestine publication with small presses that sold their titles to exclusive lists of private subscribers.[23]

Part of the reason why serious studies of homosexuality became targets for the Hicklin test relates to the 1877 notorious prosecution of an American medical work, dating from the 1830s, that advocated birth control. After a Bristol bookseller had been bound over after admitting his guilt for selling this volume, two fearless freethinkers, Annie Besant and Charles Bradlaugh, challenged the law by publishing their own edition of Charles Knowlton's *Fruits of Philosophy* (1832) – the book that the courts had deemed obscene. As reports of the proceedings show, the jury reached a baffling conclusion when faced with Besant's and Bradlaugh's respective arguments in defence of their case. Since Chief Justice Cockburn presided over the trial, he could see that the Hicklin test was itself under scrutiny. The jury's confused reply exposed an inner contradiction in obscenity law: 'We find that the book is calculated to corrupt public morals, but we entirely exonerate the defendants from any corrupt motives in publishing it.'[24] Although Cockburn instantly assumed that this response amounted to a guilty verdict, the defendants contested the judgment by stating they would continue to sell the book. Cockburn, offended by their affront, sentenced Besant and Bradlaugh to two months in jail, with a hefty fine of £200 each. But just at the point when the defendants were about to be bound over, Cockburn relented over a technicality, since he acknowledged that the prosecution had been based on indicting only the title of Knowlton's book and not its complete text. As a result, the destruction order was removed, and the antiquated volume became an overnight bestseller.

Subsequent freethinkers, such as Havelock Ellis, would not always have such good fortune when they produced works that sought to advance historical and theoretical knowledge of human sexuality, especially with regard to same-sex desire. Even when he focused in his early career on literary editing, Ellis (who trained as a medical practitioner in London) ran into serious trouble with his maverick publisher, the well-established Henry Vizetelly, who had already experienced censorship when the popular circulating libraries operated by W. H. Smith and Mudie's refused to stock one of his titles: the naturalist novel *A Mummer's Wife* (1884), by the Irish writer, George Moore. The fact that Moore's woman protagonist is a sexually promiscuous alcoholic insulted the libraries' sense of propriety, and once they banned the novel Vizetelly promptly issued Moore's protest, *Literature at Nurse, or Circulating Morals* (1885). Vizetelly had good reason for defending Moore, since at the time he was in the midst of publishing some seventeen translations of Zola's sexually provocative novels. By 1888, when he issued a translation of Zola's *La terre*, Vizetelly was fined £100 for publishing a work that embodied (in the words of the Solicitor-General, Sir Edward Clarke) 'so much bestial obscenity'.[25] When the elderly Vizetelly, with the help of his son, issued slightly expurgated translations of Zola's fiction in response to this case, he was imprisoned for three months.

At the time this controversy exploded, Vizetelly decided to discontinue another of his publishing ventures: the series of unexpurgated works by Elizabethan dramatists that Ellis took over editing in 1884. As editor of Vizetelly's 'Mermaid' series, Ellis did his utmost to ensure that he not only used reliable texts but also drew on established writers to furnish authoritative critical introductions. Ellis's own edition of Christopher Marlowe's works featured an opening essay by John Addington Symonds, a respected (though not entirely uncontroversial) authority on early modern culture. By the time Ellis was preparing his edition of Marlowe's works, Symonds had made a great impression with his mammoth seven-volume *Renaissance in Italy* (1875–86), a work that itemized the extraordinary sexual excesses of the

Borgias and the Medici, among others. Symonds, though, was also known for his inquiries into Classical literature, in which he discreetly addressed the sensitive topic of love between men in Ancient Greece. His widely noted *Studies of the Greek Poets* (1873, 1876) had already prompted one reviewer to observe that this work touched 'upon the very delicate subject which Mr. Symonds by an [*sic*] euphemism which is not too misleading designates Greek chivalry'.[26] Ellis, however, troubled Symonds's sense of tact when he brought for the first time before the public the charges of blasphemy that the Elizabethan dramatist Richard Brome had levelled against Marlowe. Not only did Ellis's decision offend Symonds, it also disturbed Vizetelly so much that he withdrew the work. (Subsequent editions omitted Brome's note on Marlowe's 'damnable opinions'.[27]) It is a sign of Vizetelly's desire to protect the sanctity of English literature that he denounced Ellis for making such 'monstrous abominations ... public'.[28] The very idea that Marlowe could be thought a blasphemous writer might be viewed as a legal taunt. The unapologetic secularist G. W. Foote, after all, had been sent to jail in 1883 for his defiant atheism.[29] Perhaps, too, Vizetelly was upset by Ellis's assertion that Marlowe was an advanced thinker in more ways than just defying religious orthodoxy. In Ellis's words, Marlowe also anticipated a modern mindset that could see 'the connection between Jesus and John and those relationships that were common among the noblest of the Greeks' (431).

Ellis's passing statement on passion between men, however, is likely to have struck a chord with Symonds, since by 1890 he sent Ellis an appreciative letter in which he states that there is 'a deep critical sympathy between us'.[30] Symonds's remark arises in his admiring comments on Ellis's recent book of essays about sexual and social liberation, *The New Spirit* (1890). In particular, Symonds observes that he wishes that Ellis had discussed in more detail a noteworthy aspect of Walt Whitman's 'Calamus' poems, where the American poet celebrates male comradeship, which were added to his epic *Leaves of Grass* in 1860. To Symonds it appears that Whitman 'is hinting at Greek feeling' (*Letters*, vol. III: 458). 'I should much like to hear your views upon the matter', Symonds adds (*Letters*, vol. III: 459). By approaching Ellis in this exploratory manner, Symonds was venturing onto ground where he recognized there were palpable risks, not only because of the ample pressures of obscenity legislation but also given the increased legal prohibitions on sexual relations between men laid down in the Criminal Law Amendment Act (1885). Since Symonds knew that public discussion of 'Greek feeling' could cause offence to his fellow Classicists, he published his inquiry on this topic, *A Problem in Greek Ethics* (1884), in a private edition of ten copies. By 1891, when he had read widely in European writing belonging to the emergent science of sexology, Symonds issued another work, *A Problem in Modern*

Ethics: Being an Inquiry into the Phenomenon of Sexual Inversion; this, too, appeared in a strictly limited edition, and on this occasion (as we read on the title page) it was 'Addressed Especially to Medical Psychologists and Jurists'.[31] In no respect was this study of such writings as Richard von Krafft-Ebing's *Psychopathia Sexualis* (1886) intended for public consumption. Nor did Symonds's volume treat uncritically all of the medical sources in his discussion of 'sexual inversion': a model of homosexuality drawn from the work of the Hanoverian jurist Karl Heinrich Ulrichs, who proposed that men-loving men inhabit bodies that have been 'differentiated as masculine, but whose sexual instinct has not progressed beyond the feminine stage' in the 'evolution of the embryo'.[32] If Ulrichs's comments sound crude in their biological determinism, it is worth bearing in mind that he advanced these ideas in the name of liberating German homosexuals from the prohibitions of the Prussian government's Paragraph 175 (1871).[33]

A year after his *Problem in Modern Ethics* appeared, Symonds grew bolder in his ambition to make the debate about 'sexual inversion' public, and he approached Ellis to see if he 'would take a book ... on "Sexual inversion" for his Science Series' published by Walter Scott (*Letters*, vol. III: 691). Symonds's intention was to fuse his 1883 and 1891 *Problem* volumes, in the firm belief that 'the historical study of Greece is absolutely essential to the psychological treatments of the subject now' (*Letters*, vol. III: 691). 'It is', Symonds continues, 'being fearfully mishandled by pathologists and psychiatrical professors, who know nothing whatsoever about its real nature' (*Letters*, vol. III: 691). Symonds, as he informed the homophile campaigner Edward Carpenter, wanted to show that European sexologists 'from [Paul] Moreau & [Johann Ludwig] Casper to [Albert] Moll' were 'totally ignorant of Greek customs' (*Letters*, vol. III: 798). Yet Symonds soon learned from Ellis there was 'too much at stake to involve the [Science] Series in any really risky pioneering investment'.[34]

In the event, Symonds discovered that it would be best to collaborate with Ellis on the volume, with a view to finding a different outlet for their different researches, which would contain a number of Ellis's case studies of sexual inverts. Since Symonds died in 1893, Ellis was left with an incomplete manuscript on his hands, and it took until 1896 before a German translation of the work – one that pushed Symonds's historical contributions to the margins – appeared in Leipzig. Later, Ellis placed it with Wilson and Macmillan. But, as Phyllis Grosskurth observes, Symonds's biographer, Horatio Brown, 'attempted to buy up the entire edition'[35]; the title page upset Symonds's family because it bore his name. Thereafter, since Ellis wanted to see the book in print, the only company that would accept it was the obscure Watford University Press, an outfit run by the questionable Roland de Villiers (also known as G. Astor Singer). This press also published the freethinking Legitimation League's journal, the *Adult*; the League, which advocated free love, attracted the police's attention because anarchists attended its meetings. George Bedborough, who headed this radical organization, agreed to sell copies of *Sexual Inversion* from his home. When a police officer acquired one, he promptly applied for a warrant to arrest the vendor. In 1898 Bedborough was indicted for selling 'a certain lewd wicked bawdy scandalous and obscene libel in the form of a book'.[36] Although Ellis did not have to defend his work before the jury, it was clear that his research was regarded as degraded when the Recorder of London pronounced that *Sexual Inversion* was in no respect a 'scientific work' but 'a pretence and a sham' – nothing more than an 'obscene publication'.[37] (In response to this verdict, the medical press observed that while Ellis's subject-matter 'is to most persons extremely disagreeable', there was nothing in the volume that could 'pander to the prurient mind'.[38]) The upshot of these clumsy proceedings was that Bedborough (through some underhand dealings with the prosecution) was released on recognizances amounting to £100. And when Ellis eventually learned that the man posing as both de Villiers and Singer was a German fraudster, he transferred publication of what became his multi-volume *Studies in the Psychology of Sex* (1901–28) from Britain to the medical publisher F. A. Davis in Philadelphia.

The court's hostility to *Sexual Inversion* did not derive solely from the police's wish to stem anarchism. Its antipathy arose from the legacy of the trials that Oscar Wilde endured three years earlier. Wilde, who at the time enjoyed success with two society comedies in London, never anticipated what could happen when he took out a libel case against an enemy. His suit against his male lover's father, the petulant Marquess of Queensberry, occurred because the volatile aristocrat had left at Wilde's club, the Albermarle, an offensive visiting-card – one featuring an infamous misspelling – that denigrated Wilde as a 'somdomite'. Queensberry objected to Wilde's intimacy with his son, Alfred Douglas. But rather than humiliate a member of his own family, Queensberry chose to use spies whose investigations would prove that Wilde had indulged in sexual liaisons with several dubious (mostly working-class) young men. Although Douglas never testified in court, some of his writings, along with those of Wilde, were subject to rigorous cross-examination. The eminent barrister Edward Carson persuaded the jury that their poetry and prose on homoerotic themes proved that Queensberry was justified in making his allegation. 'I believe you have written an article', Carson remarked of Wilde's novella 'The Portrait of Mr W. H.' (1889), 'pointing out that Shakespeare's sonnets were practically sodomitical.'[39] Earlier, Carson had asked Wilde to define what Douglas meant in his poem 'Two Loves' (1894), by 'the Love that dare not speak its name' (68). But

Carson reserved his harshest comments for the first edition of Wilde's only novel, *The Picture of Dorian Gray* (1890), which had provoked a handful of reviewers to complain so loudly about its 'medico-legal' interest and its appeal to 'perverted telegraph boys' that newspaper vendors removed it from their shelves.[40] Carson, once he had quoted this offensive review, contended 'that some people upon reading the book ... might reasonably think that it deals with sodomy' (78). Noticeably, Carson's phrasing does not make any appeal to obscenity, since Wilde's novel could hardly be called explicit in its numerous suggestions that Dorian Gray engages in sexual relations with other men. For the most part, Wilde's narrator hints that part of Dorian Gray's intimate (and highly troubled) world is homosexual by exploiting allusions to the Classics and the Renaissance, ones that Wilde frequently (though by no means exclusively) gleaned from Symonds's research.

Wilde lost his suit, and with it he relinquished his worldly possessions, since he went bankrupt when forced to defray considerable costs after his counsel (embarrassed by the disclosures about his client) conceded that Queensberry was not guilty. Unexpectedly, once Wilde stepped out of the Old Bailey the Crown issued a warrant for his arrest. For reasons that may have had to do with a governmental wish to cover up other potential homosexual scandals, the Home Secretary, H. H. Asquith, supported the prosecution of the writer, who had (in the words of Queensberry's defence) long been tolerated in London for 'bringing boys into the Savoy Hotel' (277). Such information, together with the parade of young men with whom Wilde had been intimate, was rehearsed in the subsequent two trials that disgraced his name so much that on his release, in the spring of 1897, he deserted England for ever, living on the Continent under an incognito.

The exposure of Wilde's involvement in London's homosexual underworld created a scandal like no other before, and his sentence encouraged the publisher T. Fisher Unwin to cancel its contract to publish Carpenter's *Homogenic Love*. Although Wilde had some supporters who protested against his punishment, the demeaning press reports of his appearance in court – often accompanied by unflattering caricatures – did everything they could to make this otherwise dapper aesthete look as grotesque as possible. In many ways, the journalists ensured that Wilde appeared to bear the physical marks of racial degeneration that Max Nordau popularized in his widely discussed work *Entartung*, whose English translation, *Degeneration*, became available in the months leading up to the trials.[41] From this point on, as a number of historians have observed, the repellent image of the degenerate Wilde came to embody the figure through a modern word that Symonds reluctantly used. The word of course is *homosexual*: an awkward etymological hybrid of Greek and Latin that in the twentieth century shifted from adjective to noun in order to define the 'necessarily morbid' features that Symonds scorned in medical accounts of people attracted to their own sex (*Letters*, vol. III: 694). By the turn of the twentieth century, the public had grown aware that the homosexual – like its coeval, the sexual invert – categorized a specific kind of sexual being, whose presumed pathology should not evoke sympathy in the nation. As a consequence, when E. M. Forster completed the draft of his homophile novel, *Maurice*, in 1913, he felt disinclined for the rest of his life to make public his defence of a male protagonist who overcomes his anguish after divulging to a doctor that he is 'an unspeakable of the Oscar Wilde sort'.[42]

Yet the one writer who boldly wished to defend the sexual invert was Radclyffe Hall, whose fourth novel, *The Well of Loneliness* (1928), became by far the most controversial of several narratives – including Rosamond Lehmann's *Dusty Answer* (1927) – that sought to give greater visibility to lesbian identity in the 1920s: a decade when parliament contemplated outlawing sexual relations between women. In his preface to the first edition, Ellis declared that Hall's novel presented 'in a completely faithful and uncompromising form, one particular aspect of sexual life as it exists among us today'.[43] Nowhere does Ellis even specify the 'certain people' whom Hall's novel represents (36). But when Hall's story of female inversion fell into James Douglas's hands at the conservative *Sunday Express*, the journalist protested that Hall's traditionally structured novel (a work that contains only two passing allusions to intimacy between women) was 'an intolerable outrage – the first outrage of the kind in the annals of English fiction' (*Palatable Poison*, 36). In many respects, the controversy that this rather muted work managed to generate was certainly the first of its kind. *The Well of Loneliness*, as Elisabeth Ladenson observes, 'differs from most of the other books famously suppressed on grounds of obscenity ... in that what made it dangerous was not any particular scene ... but the subject itself'.[44] The very suggestion that Hall's mannish female protagonist might enjoy affairs with other women struck Douglas as 'moral poison that kills the soul' – something far worse, as Lord Campbell had stated more than seventy years before, than the 'prussic acid' that he would prefer to 'give a healthy boy or a healthy' girl than subject them to pornography (*Palatable Poison*, 38). Removing Hall's *Well* from circulation was imperative, Douglas insisted, because literature had 'not yet recovered from the harm done to it by the Oscar Wilde scandal' (38).

In judging that Hall's *Well* committed an obscene libel, Sir Chartres Biron took particular offence at the work not because it rendered any sexual details intolerably graphic (in the manner, for example, that led to the ban on D. H. Lawrence's *Lady Chatterley's Lover* (1928)). Instead, this magistrate rested his objections, in relation to the Hicklin test, on the grounds that Hall's novel would 'deprave and corrupt' anyone open to 'immoral influences' for the very reason the work was well written (*Palatable Poison*, 41). Just as Lord Lyndhurst had anticipated in 1857, in this trial literary quality could not be defended when faced by charges of obscenity. In court, as Hall discovered, it was the very fact that there were no 'gross and filthy words' in what Biron admitted was a polished narrative that made the *Well* so culpable: 'The more palatable the poison', he said of Hall's writing, 'the more insidious' its effect on an impressionable readership (41).

For over twenty years, Hall's *Well* was not republished in Britain, and in the intervening period a number of works that had homosexual content were seized and destroyed, including James Hanley's fine novel, *Boy* (1931). But by the 1960s, when a series of court cases on both sides of the Atlantic ensured that publishers could issue editions of *Lady Chatterley's Lover* and *Fanny Hill* with impunity, the very idea of taking lesbian and gay writing through obscenity trials looked less and less viable. By 1976 the moral campaigner Mary Whitehouse successfully turned to blasphemy law in order to prosecute *Gay News* and its editor, Denis Lemon, for publishing a sacrilegious poem, 'The Love that Dares to Speak Its Name' (an echo of Alfred Douglas's famous line) by James Kirkup. This monologue, which gay activists illegally reprinted and recited in protest against the banning of it, describes the Saviour having sex with a centurion after his crucifixion. Even though several Victorian radicals such as Foote had been found guilty of blasphemy, the charge was so uncommon in the twentieth century that no one before Whitehouse had invoked it since 1922. In 1979 the Law Lords dismissed an appeal by *Gay News* and Lemon against the earlier guilty verdict, since they concluded that the defendants had – in words that to some degree echo those of Thomas Sherlock – committed 'a blasphemous libel concerning the Christian religion'.[45] But, even if this case made it look as if Kirkup's 'Love' would never be legally reprinted, the removal of the blasphemy laws in 2008 finally liberated his poem, thus bringing a symbolic end to more than 350 years of homosexual writings on trial.

NOTES

1. [Thomas Sherlock,] *A Letter from the Lord Bishop of London to the Clergy and People of London and Westminster; on the Occasion of the Late Earthquakes* (London: Vertue and Goadby, Stationers at the Royal Exchange, 1750), 4. Spelling and presentation of quotations from this work have been modernized; further page references appear in parentheses.

2. Thomas Sherlock, 'To Thomas Pelham-Holles, Duke of Newcastle', 15 March 1749, in David Foxon, *Libertine Literature in England, 1660–1745* (London: Book Collector, 1964), 57. Spelling and presentation of quotations from this work have been modernized; further page references appear in parentheses.

3. This phrase appears in Cleland, 'To Lovel Stanhope, Law Clerk to the Secretary of State', 13 November 1749, in Foxon, *Libertine Literature*, 54. The pornographic *Sodom* (c. 1684) (sometimes attributed to John Wilmot, Earl of Rochester) is also a candidate for the earliest work to be censored by the state for obscenity, especially its advocacy of same-sex sexual practices. This work, which is probably by diverse hands, is a violent political satire on the court of Charles II.

4. Walter Kendrick, *The Secret Museum: Pornography in Modern Culture* (New York: Viking, 1987), 98.

5. John Cleland, *Memoirs of a Woman of Pleasure*, Unexpurgated Text, ed. Peter Sabor (Oxford: Oxford University Press, 1999), 157, 158; further page references appear in parentheses.

6. Rictor Norton, *Mother Clap's Molly House: The Gay Subculture in England, 1700–1830*, second edn (Stroud: Chalford Press, 2006), 170–225.

7. Peter Sabor, 'From Sexual Liberation to Gender Trouble: Reading *Memoirs of a Woman of Pleasure* from the 1960s to the 1990s', *Eighteenth-Century Life*, 33:4 (2000), 561–78.

8. Hal Gladfelder, 'Obscenity, Censorship, and the Eighteenth-Century Novel: The Case of John Cleland', *Wordsworth Circle*, 35:3 (2004), 134–41; further page references appear in parentheses.

9. These remarks, which were made by the judges in the case against Curll, are quoted by Foxon, *Libertine Literature*, 15.

10. Mark D. Jordan, *The Invention of Sodomy in Christian Theology* (Chicago: University of Chicago Press, 1997), 9, 29.

11. Cleland, 'To Lovel Stanhope', in Foxon, *Libertine Literature*, 54.

12. Foxon brings this information to light in *Libertine Literature*, 54–5.

13. Hal Gladfelder, 'In Search of Lost Texts: Thomas Cannon's *Ancient and Modern Pederasty Investigated and Exemplify'd*', *Eighteenth-Century Life*, 31:1 (2007), 25; further page references appear in parentheses.

14. Hal Gladfelder, ed., 'The Indictment of John Purser: Containing Thomas Cannon's *Ancient and Modern Pederasty Investigated and Exemplify'd*', *Eighteenth-Century Life*, 31:1 (2007), 51–2.

15. See Linda Dowling, *Hellenism and Homosexuality in Victorian Oxford* (Ithaca, NY: Cornell University Press, 1994), 67–103.

16. Charlotte Charke (1713–60) was the youngest child of poet laureate Colley Cibber (1671–1757) and the actress Katherine Shore (d. 1734). Her unconventional life in the theatre, together with the fact that she cross-dressed to pass as the husband of her female companion, 'Mrs. Brown', is recorded in *A Narrative of the Life of Charlotte Charke* (1755). Samuel Foote (1720–77) was an actor, playwright and theatre manager. A year before his death, the journalist William Jackson and Foote's former servant, John Sangster, publicly stated that Foote was homosexual.

17. [Henry Fielding,] *The Female Husband: Or the Surprising History of Mrs Mary, alias Mr George Hamilton* (London: M. Cooper, 1746), 1; a further page

reference appears in parentheses. Spelling and presentation of quotations from this work have been modernized.

18. See John Cleland, *Memoirs of a Woman of Pleasure* (New York: G.P. Putnam, 1963), 256.

19. *Hansard's Parliamentary Debates*, third series, 145 (1857), 102.

20. *Ibid.*, 331.

21. *Ibid.*, 327.

22. *Law Reports* 3 *Queen's Bench*, 60; further quotation appears on this page.

23. The two best-known works of male homosexual pornography to be published through small presses are the anonymous *Sins of the Cities of the Plain: Or the Recollections of a Mary-Ann, with Short Essays on Sodomy and Tribadism* (London: Lazenby, 1881) and *Teleny, or the Reserve of the Medal: A Physiological Romance of To-Day* (London: Cosmopoli, 1893). For details of these publications, together with Victorian reprints of such erotic works as *Memoirs of a Woman of Pleasure*, see Peter Mendes, *Clandestine Erotic Fiction in English, 1800–1930: A Bibliographical Study* (Aldershot: Scolar Press, 1993), 181–7, 214–17 and 252–5.

24. 'Law Report: The Queen v. Bradlaugh and Another', *Times* (22 June 1877), 11.

25. 'Central Criminal Court', *Times* (1 November 1888), 13.

26. G.A. Simcox, Review of J.A. Symonds, *Studies of the Greek Poets* (1873), *Academy* (15 July 1873), 262.

27. *Christopher Marlowe*, ed. Havelock Ellis, Mermaid Series, Unexpurgated Edition (London: Vizetelly, 1887), 428; a further page reference appears in parentheses.

28. Havelock Ellis, *My Life: Autobiography* (Boston: Houghton Mifflin, 1939), 167, quoted in Phyllis Grosskurth, *Havelock Ellis: A Biography* (New York: Knopf, 1980), 113.

29. See Arthur Calder-Marshall, *Lewd, Blasphemous and Obscene* (London: Hutchinson, 1972), 169–92.

30. John Addington Symonds, 'To Havelock Ellis', 6 May 1890, in Herbert M. Schueller and Robert L. Peters, eds., *The Letters of John Addington Symonds*, 3 vols. (Detroit, MI: Wayne State University Press, 1867–9), vol. III: 458; further volume and page references appear in parentheses.

31. My own copy of this work is a limited, privately published edition issued in 1896; this reprint of the 1893 edition was also limited to 100 copies.

32. John Addington Symonds, *A Problem in Modern Ethics: Being an Inquiry into the Phenomenon of Sexual Inversion* (London: Privately Published, 1896), 90, 89.

33. See Hubert Kennedy, *Ulrichs: The Life and Works of Karl Heinrich Ulrichs, Pioneer of the Modern Gay Movement* (Boston, MA: Alyson, 1988).

34. Ellis, quoted in Grosskurth, *Havelock Ellis*, 175.

35. Phyllis Grosskurth, *The Woeful Victorian: A Biography of John Addington Symonds* (New York: Holt, Rinehart and Winston, 1964), 291. I discuss the controversies surrounding the publication of *Sexual Inversion* in 'Symonds's History, Ellis's Heredity: *Sexual Inversion*', in Lucy Bland and Laura Doan, eds., *Sexology in Culture: Labelling Bodies and Desires* (Cambridge: Polity Press, 1998), 79–99.

36. The indictment is quoted in Grosskurth, *Havelock Ellis*, 194.

37. Quoted in Grosskurth, *Havelock Ellis*, 201.

38. [Anon.,] 'Medico-Legal', *British Medical Journal* (5 November 1898), 1466.

39. Merlin Holland, ed., *Irish Peacock and Scarlet Marquess: The Real Trial of Oscar Wilde* (London: Fourth Estate, 2003), 93; further page references appear in parentheses.

40. 'Unsigned Notice', *Scots Observer* (5 July 1890), 181, reprinted in Karl Beckson, ed., *Oscar Wilde: The Critical Heritage* (London: Routledge and Kegan Paul, 1970), 75.

41. Max Nordau, *Degeneration* (London: William Heinemann, 1895).

42. E. M. Forster, *Maurice* (London: Edward Arnold, 1971), 159.

43. Havelock Ellis, 'Commentary', in Radclyffe Hall, *The Well of Loneliness* (London: Jonathan Cape, 1928), quoted in Laura Doan and Jay Prosser, eds., *Palatable Poison: Critical Perspectives on 'The Well of Loneliness'* (New York: Columbia University Press, 2001), 36; further page references from this volume appear in parentheses.

44. Elisabeth Ladenson, *Dirt for Art's Sake: Books on Trial from 'Madame Bovary' to 'Lolita'* (Ithaca, NY: Cornell University Press, 2007), 116.

45. See Neil Addison, *Religious Discrimination and Hatred Law* (London: Routledge-Cavendish, 2007), 290.

2

ANDREW WEBBER

Psychoanalysis, homosexuality and modernism

Was I ill? Have I recovered?
Has my doctor been discovered?
Nietzsche[1]

Gay science?

Psychoanalysis has often been seen as complicit in dominant social constructions and constrictions of homosexuality, and there is certainly some evidence
for this in the classic psychoanalytic texts, from the early works of Freud
onwards. Certain parts of the psychoanalytic institution in some historical
periods have been particularly wedded to such social orthodoxies, the post-war
American school for instance; and even today, theories and practices of psychoanalysis at large are not entirely free of homophobic positions. As a whole, across
its historical and geographical range, psychoanalysis has achieved rather
ambivalent forms of recognition for gay and lesbian sexualities. As in its work
on gender, in the field of sexuality orthodox psychoanalysis at once affords
certain forms of emancipation for alternative models and retains an attachment
to the conventions of the patriarchal culture that such models would challenge.

From the outset, psychoanalysis dared to speak the name of homosexuality, at a time when it was, often violently, unspeakable. Yet the
psychoanalytic modelling of gay sexuality, derived from that which it constructs for gender, imposes discursive constraints of its own. Freudian
psychoanalysis makes homosexuality speak its name in ways that are
coloured by the suppositions of its broader project and constrained by those
of the culture out of which it emerges. If, as Henry Abelove has argued, Freud
resists the pathologization of homosexuality per se, and the assumptions about
the functional viability of homosexuals as both analysands and analysts that go
with this,[2] the Freudian casebook certainly shows a tendency to assume that the
neurotic or the psychotic may have a particular inclination to homosexuality.
Indeed, in his *Three Essays on the Theory of Sexuality* (1905), Freud suggests
that homosexuality (the 'tendency to inversion') is a necessary feature of all

psychoneuroses, adding in 1920 that this should have a 'decisive influence on any theory of homosexuality'.[3] While homosexuality may not in itself be diagnosed as a pathology demanding therapeutic attention for Freud and most of his followers, it is seen as a ready vehicle for particular forms of mental illness, from hysteria and melancholia to paranoia. As such, it all too easily assumes, if only by association, a pathogenic character for the psychoanalytic project.

This chapter will take stock of how psychoanalysis, and in particular its mainstream Freudian version, has treated homosexuality. Psychoanalysis has been styled a 'Jewish science', both by its exponents and, infamously, by its detractors. What is proposed here is to test the leverage to be gained from considering it as a 'gay science', adopting this term freely – or queerly – from Nietzsche. Here I follow a cue from Eve Kosofsky Sedgwick in her reading of Nietzsche in *Epistemology of the Closet*, where she identifies a pervasive vocabulary of potential homosexuality as if from the pages of Proust's *Sodom and Gomorrah*. She rounds off her inventory with 'the "gay"',[4] which is drawn from the translation of Nietzsche's *Die fröhliche Wissenschaft* as *The Gay Science*. The playfully misappropriated term serves as a device to expose the textual closet of Nietzsche's writing.[5] The 'gay' finds subversive expression in the literary excess that marks Nietzsche's 'scientific' discourse, establishing his writings as a key influence for modernist culture. To adapt, or queer, another of Nietzsche's titles – the autobiographical *Ecce Homo* – his writing, however obliquely, displays masculinity as homo-erotically disposed.[6]

Sedgwick resolves the elaborations of the Nietzschean text into a series of versions of the propositions that Freud draws out in his account of the case of Judge Schreber in order to establish a grammar of the intense denial of homosexuality at the core of paranoia.[7] In his *Memoirs of a Nervous Illness* (1903), Daniel Paul Schreber describes an elaborate system of erotic and violent visions, at once personal and cosmic, constructed around a fantasy of becoming a woman in sexual union with God. And in Freud's *Psychoanalytic Remarks on an Autobiographically Described Case of Paranoia (Dementia Paranoides)* (1911), Schreber's paranoid fantasies are seen to reveal the homosexual constitution of this illness. For Sedgwick, the Gothic fantasy world of the memoirs of Judge Schreber, as read by Freud, is a graphic enactment of the potency of homophobia, the paranoid control mechanism produced by 'intense male homosocial desire' as 'at once the most compulsory and the most prohibited of social bonds'.[8] In her reading this is the paranoid desire that informs Nietzsche's profoundly ambivalent attachment to Wagner, but also that which binds the 'gayness' of his writing to a no less ambivalent attachment to Jewishness.[9] It seems that Nietzsche's 'gay science', which is also in some sense a 'Jewish science', prefigures the similarly hybrid condition of psychoanalysis.[10]

Homosexuality certainly figures very significantly in the elaboration of the psychoanalytic project by Freud and his collaborators. Indeed the origins of psychoanalysis can in a sense be understood as having been formed by homoerotic dynamics, a creation of knowledge born out of an erotic attachment between men. The key formative steps of Freud's new science were framed by his charged relationship with the Berlin-based doctor Wilhelm Fliess, and described in the sentimentally heightened correspondence between the two men as if they were rather the product of acts of love than of science. It was to 'private utterances' from Fliess that Freud attributed his claim that the inclination towards 'inversion' should be seen as a constitutive feature of psychoneuroses.[11] The shared theory of universal bisexuality was a mainstay of their passionate collaborative work at the origins of psychoanalysis, as was the assumption that homosexuality figures in all psychoneurotic conditions.[12]

As we have already seen in the example of the case of Schreber, homosexuality is also a key feature of many of the most significant texts of early psychoanalytic literature, texts that indeed stake a claim to being understood as *literature*, as creative science writing. And its presence arguably has an effect on the writing of the texts in question, lending them a tendency towards 'gay writing'. Freud famously cast his case histories as literary, asserting more than once that they read strangely like novellas, rather than carrying 'the serious stamp of science' as he put it in the *Studies on Hysteria* (1895).[13] In this chapter I shall show how the case history acts as a model for creative writing about homosexual conditions. I suggest that the case histories are, in part at least, readable as lesbian and gay novellas, and that they have a particular affinity with some of the popular cultural genres that have been co-opted for more recent lesbian and gay writing: the fairy tale, the detective story and science fiction.[14] If Freud aligned his case histories with the popular nineteenth-century genre of the novella (not simply the short story, as the translation of the *Standard Edition* suggests), then it might be particularly interesting to consider the determining role of both detective story and fantasy or dream narrative in the genealogy of the novella. And this, in turn, may be linked to the particular affinity that those genres have with the writing of homosexuality.

At the same time, this chapter will consider how the fashioning of homosexuality in creative writing responds to psychoanalytic constructions of gay and lesbian sexualities. Its principal references will be drawn from German literature in the era of Freud, and the proposition will be that the texts in question have a special relationship to psychoanalysis that might be called queer. Those modernist texts may also be aligned with the fantasy structures of fairy tale, detective fiction and science fiction. These aspects of fantasy and genre are also evident in much contemporary gay and lesbian writing. To give but one example, Jeanette Winterson's *The Passion* (1997) undertakes a reworking of the fantasy scenario of Mann's modernist fairy tale, *Death in Venice*.

As I have argued elsewhere, the relationship between Freud and the modernist canon can be understood through the figure of the *Doppelgänger*, a Romantic phantom that returned to haunt the culture of modernism and came, in part, to embody its relationship to the new science of psychoanalysis.[15] The figure of the double is paradigmatic for the genres in focus here: a case-history figure that also operates in the speculative worlds of fairy tale, crime writing and science fiction. Freud famously identified his Viennese contemporary, the fellow-doctor and writer of fictions and dramas Arthur Schnitzler, as his uncanny double,[16] and the ambivalent, libidinal investments that characterize that figure can be seen at work in the double-bound dialogues with psychoanalysis across a wide range of the leading modernist writers.

The *Doppelgänger* relation here, in its model form a narcissistically inflected and sexually charged relationship between men, is certainly understandable as queer in its implications. It embodies a particular version of the hom(m)osexual condition, the mirroring of masculinity (doubling *homo* into *hommo*) that Irigaray has seen as constituting the specular regime of patriarchy, its narcissistic power structures.[17] It is a form of attachment to a transgressive form of self-sameness that also marks out the subject who hosts it as separate from heterosexual norms. In its mimicry of that general condition, it also represents its crisis in the form of a paranoid fantasy. The *Doppelgänger* subject, carrying shades of queer sexuality, is always, to borrow the title of a German silent film concerned with homosexuality (and one that doubled as the German title for the Hollywood film *Tea and Sympathy*), 'Other than the others' (*Anders als die Anderen*).[18] As these film references suggest, the double lives in question here also have the potential to transport homosexual life-stories or case histories into the domain of another popular cultural genre, melodrama.

While the *Doppelgänger* is particularly aligned with the sorts of fictions 'between men' that Eve Kosofsky Sedgwick has read for their queer subtexts (Wilde's *Picture of Dorian Gray* serves as a classic case), it also has potential to act as an agent of desire between women. This is shown for instance in the scene from Schnitzler's interior-monologue text *Fräulein Else* (*Miss Else*) (1924), where the protagonist responds to the seductive charms of the alluring young woman that is her image in the mirror. It is an encounter, however, with a logic that seems to be hom(m)osexual in

Irigaray's terms. Else's position in her eponymous text (the 'Miss' here indicates a socially limited entitlement of the young female subject) is to be an object of exchange between men. Her enjoyment of her image in the mirror is derived from her production as object of the voyeuristic male gaze, as she prepares to exhibit herself to Herr von Dorsday, the man who will save her father from ruin for this favour. It seems that Else, constructed as hysteric in her melodramatic case history of a novella, can only step outside of the frame of male desire by miming it. As 'hysteric', her destiny is to be constructed into an iconography of display for the at once diagnostic, or knowledge-seeking, and scopophilic, or pleasure-seeking, male gaze. If this scene from Else's theatre of identifications can be seen as at least potentially a lesbian one, it is one of narcissistic exhibitionism, excluding the other woman and fashioned in a way that might give pleasure to the eye of the heterosexual male. Else, in other words, is subject to the sort of phallocentric pressures that are also brought to bear upon perhaps the exemplary case of hysteria for psychoanalysis, that of (Freud's) Dora. We shall return to that much-reviewed case below.

In what follows, the relationship between psychoanalysis and literary homoerotics will be understood as that between doubles, a relationship of desire mediated through similarity, but also fraught with ambivalence. It remains to be seen whether this special relationship between a scientific discipline and a form of creative writing that are both 'other than the others', non-standard, ultimately functions as emancipatory or pathologizing. The melodramatic case of the hysterical Else, as scripted by the Freud double Schnitzler – the creative writer as a kind of wild analyst in his literary case histories – certainly appears to suggest the latter. The early twentieth-century female subject, Else, is caught here in a particular form of fantasy space: the mirror in the hotel room as narcissistic closet.[19] And the closet, often fitted with both literal and metaphorical mirrors, also features as the recurrent habitat of her male contemporaries in the various texts to be considered here. To recall the warning raised by Sedgwick in her analysis of the elaborate work of aesthetic creativity and constraint, of human knowing and unknowingness, carried out through the framework of the closet, we have to beware of glamorizing what remains at base a structure of forcible limitation for its techniques of self-fashioning.[20] The narcissistic fixation that psychoanalysis attributes to homosexuality may exert a certain effect of glamour, but it is extrapolated into psychical conditions with less glamorous implications, or where any surface appearance of glamour is won at the cost of deep psychological suffering in conditions of hysteria, melancholia and paranoia.

Closet cases

This chapter now considers a sequence of Freud's most high-profile and intensively studied case histories. All have been subject to various revisionist readings, including some from queer critical perspectives. What is offered here is a synoptic review of the casebook, drawing on its implications for gay and lesbian writing and for the criticism that addresses that writing. The case studies are understood as 'closet cases', both hiding and showing the secret life of homosexuality. As ever, the closet is not some autonomous structure freely fashioned by the queer subject, but a function of social networks. It is co-constructed, that is, by the subject's others (also including that significant other, the psychoanalyst). It is accordingly never fully fitting for the subject who is other than those others, but remains relatively heteronomous in its construction. A paradigmatic case would be the 'don't ask, don't tell' policy of the US Armed Forces, as deconstructed by Judith Butler in her *Excitable Speech*, whereby the homosexual subject is under a continuous regime of what she calls, after Agamben, emergency or exception.[21] This state of exception, the authority to legislate beyond the norms of civil law, is as powerful in its coercion as it is contradictory in its logic. And the closeted space of the armed forces (thinkable as coextensive with the dormitory of the barracks or battleship) exposes that coercive logic as operating in less exceptional forms in the social order at large.

The state of exception of the military clause also endorses the general rule; its closet logic likewise extends into more public spaces and their legal and behavioural codes. In Butler's analysis, the clause exposes the paranoia of law in its relationship to homosexuality.[22] It is a transposition, we might say, of the paranoid homophobia at work in the case of Judge Schreber. We might think of the scenario evoked by Sedgwick of a gay judge enacting homosexual laws: in a dramatic crisis for the law, Justice as embodied by the judge comes up before (and is potentially made to come out to) Justice.[23] Schreber as both agent and subject of the law could be imagined in just such a position relative to another case of legislation by exception: Clause 175 of the German penal code, which, from 1871, outlawed sexual relations between men. It is a principle of double-bind from which, for Butler, the jurisdiction of psychoanalysis is also not free, as it illustrates, in part through its own workings, the character of its own epistemological closet.[24]

Sedgwick inserts a sort of textual closet into *Epistemology of the Closet*: a page listing the definitions for 'closet' given by the *OED*, which is separated off from the rest of her text, a discrete place for a sort of private perusal of the system of spaces that the term can denote. In keeping with the logic of the 'closet', this closed off spatial inventory is defined by the fact of 'belonging to or communicating with' a larger space,[25] one which ramifies the implications of its contents (as in Butler's special or exceptional case of and against the US armed forces). The system of meanings provided by the *OED* includes variations with telling implications for the literary closet, not least given that one of the chief types of private room indicated here is that of the writer. This is the closet, then, as a more or less secret place of writing, but one that – according to one of the illustrative sentences supplied by the *OED* – is also susceptible to break-in ('A sudden intruder into the closet of an author').[26] The motives behind such an intrusion into the space of 'private devotion' or of 'secluded speculation' may vary of course,[27] and Sedgwick herself conducts an enlightening, critical form of such intrusion into the writerly closet (also in part an outing of a series of closeted writers).

The strategy of Sedgwick and other queer critical detectives working after her is to make knowable the functions of the closet, functions which can be adopted from the *OED* inventory: to expose the subjection to the other that is at work in the closet in its sovereign form (as 'private apartment of a monarch or potentate'); to revalue the contents of the 'private repository of valuables', revise the catalogue of the cabinet of 'curiosities'; to show that the closet of the writer, the potentate or the collector also relates to pent-up dangers (the closet as 'den or lair of a wild beast'); and to examine its plumbing, showing that it communicates with the more mundane space of the 'closet of ease' or 'water closet' and thereby establishes a conduit between the larger space of habitation and the abject system of the 'sewer',[28] between the social or domestic scene and the obscene. The closet cases considered here show various configurations of these types of spatial construction, not least in identifying the channels between subject and abject, scene and obscene. Sedgwick's interpolation of a dictionary page is reminiscent of Freud's strategy of semantic exploration in his classic essay on *The Uncanny* (1919), and there would indeed be potential to view the closet as a particularly acute definition of the uncanny: that haunting otherness which is concealed at the heart of the private domain or, with recourse once more to the *OED* entry, the '*skeleton in the closet*'.[29]

Fairy tales

For Freud, sexuality in general, and homosexuality in particular, have infantile origins, so that their knowledge structures are intimately linked to the culture of the nursery. This enclosed space of play and reading establishes, we might say, the architecture of the closet. The child, as premature epistemologist of sexuality, sexual difference and reproduction, is a figure of ironically framed identification for the research project of the adult science of psychoanalysis. Thus, from the casework of Freud's early career to the adult fairy tale of Hoffmann's *The Sandman* (1816), as explored through his reading in *The Uncanny*, sexual identity is constructed through the generic conventions of the fairy tale. And homosexuality, as a strange case of human sexuality (at once a universal stage of development and a particular, queer identity), has a peculiar relationship to such tales, their rites of passage and more fixed conditions. Homosexuality is apt to take on both the shape of the valuable and curious secret in the closet and that of the beast, drawing on the ambivalent tension between these two generic conventions.

This fairy-tale logic can be seen at work in two of Freud's classic child case histories: the 'Analysis of a Phobia in a Five-year-old Boy' (Little Hans (1909)) and 'From the History of an Infantile Neurosis' (The Wolf Man (1914)), both of whom are diagnosed by Freud as passing through stages of homosexual identity. Both are cast as infant researchers of (homo-)sexuality, both in quest of sexual curiosities, and both terrorized by a phobic relation to a menagerie of masculine animals that is bound up with that quest. Their imaginative worlds are based upon the fairy tale, most explicitly in the case of the Wolf Man, whose phobia takes root in a picture of a wolf exhibiting itself in a book of fairy tales and is animated by the Grimm tales of *Little Red Riding Hood*, *Reynard the Fox* and *The Wolf and the Seven Little Goats*. These are stories that feature narratives of curiosity and duplicity that end in encounters with the beast in an enclosed space: hiding-places are exposed and the space of protection is uncannily doubled into one of threat. It is the same generic structure as operates in Hoffmann's adult version of the nursery tale in *The Sandman* and is adopted in the cases of Little Hans and the Wolf Man. The protagonists of the case histories enact in imagination the sort of experience that Nathanael, the protagonist of Hoffmann's *The Sandman*, recalls from his childhood, when he hides in a recess in the family home to observe the strange nocturnal experiments conducted by his father and the uncanny Sandman, only to be outed from his hiding-place and exposed to gruesome acts of extortion by the fairy-tale bogeyman. By identification with the nocturnal fantasy scene performed in secret by the two men, the child thus becomes the skeleton in the closet of the family home, that uncanny figure which, to cite the definition of the uncanny that Freud adopts, 'ought to have remained secret and hidden but has come to light'.[30]

The closets of Hans and the Wolf Man are certainly host to versions of the beast that emerge in the Gothic fairy tale of the Sandman. The imagination of the nursery creates uncanny hybrids that are subject to repression and destined to return out of that repression: on the model of the Wolf Man, Nathanael's Sandman also figures as a kind of Owl Man, and Little Hans could be seen as a Little Horse Man. The closets are also fashioned following other of the specifications from the *OED*. For the Wolf Man, it is the closet derived from the private apartment of the sovereign, and converted into a sado-masochistic cabinet, a 'narrow room' in which he as 'heir to the throne' is subjected as a whipping-boy to homoeroticized fantasies of punishment and in particular genital chastisement.[31] This is fantasy in its model version, as described in Freud's essay 'A Child is Being Beaten' (1919), where the punitive agent is the father, drawing on the little boy's masochistic homosexual attachment.[32] For Little Hans, the performance of homosexuality, with the father interpellated as witness, is located in the water closet or 'closet of ease'. As part of his obsessive research into the 'widdler' or 'wee-wee maker', suspended in a protracted phallic stage, Hans establishes a closet for himself, not in the toilet which leads off the lobby of the family apartment, but in the neighbouring dark lumber room. His father reports this as follows:

> Leading out of the front hall there is a lavatory and also a dark storeroom for keeping wood in. For some time past Hans has been going into this woodcupboard and saying: 'I'm going to my W.C.' I once looked in to see what he was doing in the dark storeroom. He showed me his parts and said: 'I'm widdling.' That is to say, he has been 'playing' at W.C. That it is in the nature of a game is shown not merely by the fact that he does not go into the W.C., which would after all be far simpler, but prefers the wood-cupboard and calls it 'his W.C.'[33]

His toilet visits avoid the convenience of the closet of ease and adopt instead this *camera obscura* or dark room dedicated to another function. This, he declares, is 'my closet', a place of secrecy that is nonetheless designed for public exhibition, as he 'plays' water closet. The game in question involves a pantomime of 'wee-wee making', one which allows the young player to make a show of manipulating his penis (the German nicely enough describes the fictional 'wee-wee making' as being *fingiert*, pretended, or more literally, fingered or manipulated).

The choice of the neighbouring dark room for this play-acting for his own pleasure and his father's spectatorial benefit is in keeping with the more general logic of Hans's fantasies and the morbid fears that attach to them. In Freud's analysis, the desires and fears of Little Hans are relayed through a systematic structure, as articulated especially through the transport system. They are thus transposed from horse to wagon through a particular logic of cause and effect; as Lacan points out, the slippage between *wegen* (because of) and *Wägen* (a Viennese form of the plural of wagon or carriage) that Freud notes in Hans's usage indicates a principle of displacement at work in the signification of desire.[34] The wagon is laden with the ambivalent cargo of phobic desire *because* of the horse, to which it is linked, and which also bears an ostentatious penis. Hans's obsession with the penis as 'wee-wee maker' follows a similar metonymic logic (the part of the body for the whole, that part which is defined by its particular function). And the visit to the toilet indicates that the function in question is itself subject to displacement by manipulation into another – that of sexual pleasure through showing and touching. In the public-private space of his closet, Little Hans has the opportunity to make a show of that function, for himself, for his father, but also for the significant other that is 'the professor': the analytic master, Freud, to whom he knows his father will report all aspects of his behaviour, especially as concerns his wee-wee maker. That is, he manipulates himself for an exchange of knowledge between men, one which includes for the adult males the pleasure of seeing, of knowing, and indeed of manipulating, directly or by proxy, the half-open secrets of the closet.

The Wolf Man and Little Hans correspond to a whole series of protagonists in modernist writing whose formative scenes are located in a variety of closet spaces, between private and public exhibition, with more or less explicit indications of homoerotic attachment. There is Kafka's para-psychoanalytic casebook: Gregor Samsa in *Metamorphosis* (1915), transformed in the locked space of his bedroom into a closeted beast; Josef K. in *The Trial* (1925), stumbling upon the sado-masochistic beating scene in the junk room at the bank where he works, one of a sequence of such closet fantasy spaces; the physician in 'A Country Doctor' (1919), whose libido emerges from a pigsty as a rapaciously heterosexual beast but who then gets into bed with his young male patient; or the protagonist of 'Blumfeld: A Bachelor' (1915), who is pursued in his bachelorhood by two strange celluloid balls which fail to stay closeted in his wardrobe. There is the case of Musil's *Confusions of Young Törless* (1906), where homoerotically charged sado-masochistic fantasy scenes are played out in a theatrical hiding-place in the loft of a cadet school, a closet which houses a particular form of bestiality. There are the school-boys of Wedekind's *Spring Awakening* (1891), who – like Little Hans – use a water closet for masturbation but also compete in group sessions in more public spaces. There are the many protagonists of Thomas Mann's narratives whose sexualities are fashioned in forms of closet-theatre and are subject to more or less public forms of outing: most notoriously, Aschenbach in *Death in Venice* (1912) with his grotesquely late spring awakening; or the young Italian subjected to a kiss from the magician in the theatrical cabinet of *Mario and the Magician* (1929); or a more obscure figure from Mann's juvenilia, the protagonist of the early short story 'The Wardrobe: A Story full of Mysteries' (1899), whose morbid travels in the decadent style lead him to an allegorical encounter with a sexually ambiguous wraith in the closet of his boarding-house room.[35] And there are the male counterparts to Fräulein Else from Schnitzler's casebook, ostentatiously heterosexual in performance, but in ways that are nonetheless ambiguous: the young Lieutenant Gustl from the interior monologue novella of the same name, whose male gaze is drawn to female members of the audience at the opera, but whose virility is put in doubt by a phallically charged encounter with an old baker who challenges him to a duel; or the protagonist of *Dream Novella* (1926), whose heterosexual fantasy life takes the form of a series of failures to perform, and who is replaced by a woman as sacrificial victim at the orgy, as though he might have been the primary sexual object of the masked men.[36] The homosocial worlds of modernist writing, and not least of the German modernist canon, are rife with such closet cases, along with their public-private epistemologies and neurotic symptomatologies.

Lesbian detective fiction

If male homosexuality is regularly teased out of its closets by Freud, only to be placed in another form of enclosure in the consultation room, lesbianism is located in a less accessible recess. Freud famously described the mystery of feminine sexuality as a dark continent for the psychoanalytic project of exploration, and lesbianism can be seen as the heart of darkness in this *terra incognita*, a deeply invaginated space for the not always equally intrepid sexual explorer. Or, to adopt another fantasy role with a particular affinity for the psychoanalyst and his casebook, lesbianism remains a resistant, elusive mystery for the psycho-sexual detective.

The detective here is not the queer agent of contemporary lesbian crime fiction, for while Freud can adopt the homosexual position in the elaboration of his project, the lesbian version of it is where such queer performativity as he exercises is blocked. Freud here is the reader and writer of more conventional forms of fiction, as we can see in the case-history-as-novella, *Fragment of a Case of Hysteria* (1901), also known as Dora. As many revisionist readings of the Dora case have shown, Freud is complicit in the construction of his analysand for male desire, unable or unwilling to give her lesbian desire its due. And in his return to Freud, Lacan concerns himself with the question of 'who desires in Dora', asserting that 'the ego of Dora is Herr K.'.[37] The lesbian subject seems unable to have an ego of her own, whether of her own gender or not. This is also one way of reading the ego-relation that Schnitzler's Else performs in her mirror-scene. The feminine image is either there for a narcissistic female subject or a projection of an ego that has been taken over by the male subject of voyeurism. We might say, that is, that 'the ego of Else is Herr von Dorsday', to whom she is required to exhibit herself. While Dora has another woman in the text of her case history, one whom she can at least partner in alternation in what Lacan calls the ballet between four dancers (Frau K., Herr K., Dora's father and Dora herself),[38] Else has only the phantasmatic surrogate of the lovely woman in the mirror. Her literary case history operates under the sort of camouflage that Sedgwick sees in the narcissistic scenarios common to Romantic and modernist writing: 'Not everyone has a lover of their own sex, but everyone, after all, has a self of their own sex.'[39] Under the generically male authorship of the modernist canon, lesbianism seems destined to appear as a second-order duplication of the *Doppelgänger* relations that are constructed between men.

The criminal case of *Fräulein Else*, one of extortion of sexual favours in a deal struck between men (the bankrupt father and the louche voyeur, von Dorsday), belongs, like that of Dora, to a casebook of social crimes and misdemeanours against the person and the psyche of young women in the age of modernism, pointing up the limits to the emancipation that that age fosters. In Frank Wedekind's Lulu plays (*Earth Spirit* (1895) and *Pandora's Box* (1904)), when the eponymous protagonist performs as lesbian in the repertory of a sexual circus which is as much that of her creator as her own,[40] she draws her lover, the Countess Geschwitz, into abjection (Geschwitz connotes sweating) and crime (ending in the murder of both by the hyperbolic phallic agent, Jack the Ripper). And in Alfred Döblin's criminological-cum-sociological study, drawn from a true case, *The Two Girlfriends and their Murder by Poison* (1924), the lesbian lovers, caught in abusive relationships with men, commit a capital crime. Döblin, who is another modernist writer with a close, but also ambivalent relationship to psychoanalysis, presents the case of lesbian crime without any attempt to analyse it.

Dora and Freud's other famous lesbian analysand, in 'The Psychogenesis of a Case of Homosexuality in a Woman' (1920), are not driven to crimes such as those of Döblin's two girlfriends against the men who constrain or violate them. Dora is subjected by Freud to a form of treatment that only mimics the structure of the abuse she has suffered: the analytic detective story turns here on the logic of lock and key. What Dora needs and desires, in Freud's analysis, is the key that is the phallus. It is a form of unlocking treatment that seems to aim at discovering secrets in a case cast from the start as a sort of *roman à clef*, but in fact achieves no access to the secret knowledge of lesbian desire that Dora and Frau K. are seen to share. As much as Freud understands the symbolism of Dora's sexual fantasy life as turning on the jewellery box of her genitals, she retains control of another kind of secret treasure, the sort of 'private repository of valuables' that featured in the *OED* definition of the closet. That closeted desire, where box and treasure are opened up to another such jewel-box rather than a key, can only take the form of a footnote to the case history, as Dora does the only thing she can do, short of criminal action, by breaking off analysis and removing herself from the social relations in which she has grown up. And in the case of the 'homosexual woman', the protest against patriarchal constraint (her father's fury at her walking out with the woman she loves) takes the form of crime against the self in a suicide attempt. This 'crime' may well have also been aimed at the father, but it is interpreted by the analyst in one of his most tendentious, not to say offensive, readings as an enactment of the desire for the father (jumping from a railway embankment in order to 'fall' pregnant – *niederkommen*).[41] Freud's 'novella' here adopts a fictional conceit that shows psychoanalysis in its most paternally identified form and at its most blind to the crimes of the fathers in which the analyst as master detective has a certain stake. It is the paternal transference on the part of the analysand that leads Freud to suggest that this is a case he will never be able to solve, one better suited for a female colleague. Perhaps the case and its analysis would be best elucidated by a lesbian detective with analytic training.

Gay science fictions

If Freud's psychoanalytic project does indeed perform a kind of gay science, one that identifies homosexuality as a key disposition of the fantasies and anxieties that it addresses, and given that it casts the identification of that disposition in the shape of case histories as forms of docu-fiction, we might indeed like to think of his casebook as featuring a series of gay science fictions. In the case histories that have been considered here, systematic knowledge – *Wissenschaft* or *scienza* – is the crux of the analytic study and the creative writing of homosexual dispositions. Little Hans as precocious 'researcher' and Dora in her illicit reading practices are both epistemologists of sexuality, the one adopted as a model student by Freud, the other exploring dark, recessive territory beyond his ken. While Little Hans's antics in the customized water closet can be opened up to view and understood as part of the journey towards mature psycho-sexual knowledge, Dora's lesbian closet and its epistemology remain closed off. Freudian psychoanalysis may in some senses be a gay science, but it is not so able to be a lesbian one.

In the case of Judge Schreber, another figure with a compulsive attachment to the (water) closet, the intercourse between homosexuality and science in a highly speculative form is most fantastically developed. The Schreber memoirs, with their extraordinary visions of counter-worlds, built around a fantasy of submission to a divine super-lover and the penetrating powers of libidinal rays, could indeed be called gay science fiction. And Freud's Schreber Case is intimately identified with the logic of that fiction, identifying in it a model for his own speculative science, and arguably also for his own homosexual fantasy life.[42] The key scene in the memoirs where the Judge describes himself stripped to the waist in front of the mirror, taking pleasure in wearing 'feminine adornments' and imagining himself to have female breasts,[43] raises an interesting speculation: that Schreber, like Schnitzler's Else, may have a closet fantasy life as a lesbian. But this would be an identification that would go too far for the detective Freud and his transferential methods. What all of the 'science fictions' discussed here show is the ambiguous achievement of Freudian psychoanalysis in its opening up of the closet of homosexual desires, a closet that is also, to some extent, built into its own project.

NOTES

1. From 'Dialogue' ('Zwiegespräch'), one of the rhymes from Friedrich Nietzsche, *The Gay Science: With a Prelude in German Rhymes and an Appendix of Songs*, ed. Bernard Williams, trans. Josefine Nauckhoff and Adrian del Caro (Cambridge: Cambridge University Press, 2001), 12.
2. See Henry Abelove, 'Freud, Male Homosexuality, and the Americans', in Henry Abelove *et al.*, eds., *The Lesbian and Gay Studies Reader* (New York and London: Routledge, 1993), 381–93.
3. Sigmund Freud, *Standard Edition of the Complete Psychological Works*, 24 vols., ed. James Strachey *et al.* (London: Hogarth Press, 1953–74), vol. VII: 166.
4. Eve Kosofsky Sedgwick, *Epistemology of the Closet* (Berkeley: University of California Press, 1990), 134.
5. That Nietzsche's own project might have been a form of 'gay science' is supported by Joachim Köhler, in his psychoanalytically informed biography, *Zarathustra's Secret: The Interior Life of Friedrich Nietzsche*, trans. Ronald Taylor (New Haven: Yale University Press, 2002). Köhler suggests that Nietzsche found satisfaction only in the homoerotic world of Sicily, as recorded in the photographs of Wilhelm van Gloeden, and that the superman figure of *Thus Spake Zarathustra* is readable as a kind of homosexual fantasy figure.
6. As Nietzsche records in *Ecce Homo*, the songs that accompanied *The Gay Science*, which were largely written during his stay in Sicily, followed the principle of the Provençal *gaya scienza* in what he calls their 'union' of minstrel and knight. That is, one of the images of manhood on display here is a double one that would certainly be open to homoerotic interpretation. See Friedrich Nietzsche, *Ecce Homo: How One Becomes What One Is*, trans. R. J. Hollingdale (Harmondsworth: Penguin, 1979), 98.
7. Sedgwick, *Epistemology of the Closet*, 161.
8. Sedgwick, *Between Men: English Literature and Male Homosocial Desire* (New York: Columbia University Press, 1985), 91.
9. Sedgwick, *Epistemology of the Closet*, 177.
10. For links between cultural assumptions about the Jewish and homosexual dispositions of decadence around 1900, see Sander L. Gilman, *The Case of Sigmund Freud: Medicine and Identity at the Fin de Siècle* (Baltimore: Johns Hopkins University Press, 1993), 164.
11. The *Standard Edition* (vol. VII: 166) removes the reference to the *private Äußerungen* in its translation of this passage.

12. For the relationship of the Freud–Fliess affair to the discourses of anti-Semitism and homophobia around 1900, see Daniel Boyarin, 'Freud's Baby, Fliess's Maybe: Homophobia, Anti-Semitism, and the Invention of Oedipus', *GLQ*, 2:1 (1995), 115–47.

13. Freud, *Standard Edition*, vol. II: 160. The German can also be understood to mean that the case histories 'should be read as novellas'.

14. See, for example, the gay retellings of traditional fairy stories by Peter Cashorali, the lesbian detective fiction of Sandra Scoppettone and the science fiction and fantasy writing of Nicola Griffith or David Gerrold.

15. See Andrew J. Webber, *The Doppelgänger: Double Visions in German Literature* (Oxford: Clarendon Press, 1996), 316–56.

16. See *ibid.*, 335–6.

17. Irigaray works to release relationships between women from the mediation of this masculine specularization, a construction, as it were, of 'femmosexuality'. See Luce Irigaray, *Speculum of the Other Woman* (Ithaca, NY: Cornell University Press, 1985).

18. Richard Oswald's film, *Anders als die Anderen* (1920), one of the key *Aufklärungsfilme* or films of educational enlightenment from the Weimar period, starred Conrad Veidt as a gay man being blackmailed by an ex-lover. Vincente Minnelli's *Tea and Sympathy* (1956), which was produced under the anti-enlightened strictures of the Hollywood Hays Code, encoded the homosexuality of its protagonist as 'not regular' and 'sister boy'.

19. The hotel room also functions as her dressing- or undressing-room as she prepares for her rendezvous with the scopophilic blackmailer von Dorsday.

20. Sedgwick, *Epistemology of the Closet*, 68.

21. Judith Butler, *Excitable Speech: A Politics of the Performative* (New York: Routledge, 1997), 105.

22. *Ibid.*, 107.

23. Sedgwick, *Epistemology of the Closet*, 77.

24. 'Psychoanalysis not only sheds theoretical light on the tensions between homosexuality and citizenship, but psychoanalytic discourse is itself a textual allegory for how the production of the citizen takes place through the rejection and transmutation of an always imagined homosexuality' (*ibid.*, 108–9).

25. Sedgwick, *Epistemology of the Closet*, 65.

26. *Ibid.*

27. *Ibid.*

28. *Ibid.*

29. *Ibid.* The *Doppelgänger* text taken by Freud to illustrate the uncanny, Hoffmann's *The Sandman*, is certainly open to reading as a case of the sort of queer Gothic paranoia that Sedgwick discusses (see Webber, *The Doppelgänger*, 121–48).

30. Freud, *Standard Edition*, vol. XVII: 225.

31. Freud, *Standard Edition*, vol. VII: 26.

32. Freud, *Standard Edition*, vol. XVII: 175–204.

33. Freud, *Standard Edition*, vol. X: 14.

34. Jacques Lacan, *Le Séminaire IV – La relation d'objet* (Paris: Seuil, 1994), 317–18.

35. While the figure is ultimately shown to be female (or at least, to have breasts), its gender is initially derived from the term *Gestalt* or figure, which happens to be feminine in German.

36. The queer subtext is taken up in Kubrick's film version of the text, *Eyes Wide Shut* (1999), where the protagonist, wandering the streets at night, is challenged as a 'fag' by a group of youths.

37. Jacques Lacan, *Le Séminaire III – Les Psychoses* (Paris: Seuil, 1981), 197.

38. *Ibid*. Lacan overlooks the fifth dancer, Freud himself, who enters transferentially into the formation.

39. Sedgwick, *Epistemology of the Closet*, 161.

40. I borrow the term from Elizabeth Boa, *The Sexual Circus: Wedekind's Theatre of Subversion* (Oxford: Blackwell, 1987).

41. Freud, *Standard Edition*, vol. XVIII: 162.

42. For a critique of Freud's 'queer reading' of Schreber, see Eric Santner, *My Own Private Germany: Daniel Paul Schreber's Secret History of Modernity* (Princeton: Princeton University Press, 1996).

43. Freud, *Standard Edition*, vol. XII: 21.

3

JOANNE WINNING

Lesbian modernism: writing
in and beyond the closet

The closet describes the private, hiding space in which lesbians and gay men who will not admit publicly to their sexual identity either reside or put their dissident sexuality. In his book *Gay New York: Gender, Urban Culture, and the Making of the Gay Male World, 1890–1940*, George Chauncey describes the closet as 'the spatial metaphor typically used to characterize gay life before the advent of gay liberation as well as their own lives before they "came out."' He argues that the origins of the term remain 'obscure' but speculates that its usage derives originally from the notion of 'the skeleton in the closet' and thus evokes the notions of secrecy, shame, abjection and surveillance which all constellate around the concept, as used both in dominant heterosexual culture and by lesbians and gay men themselves.[1] Historically, the term comes into use after the Stonewall riots in New York City in June 1969. Undoubtedly, since the advent of the gay liberation movement the closet has accrued substantial power as a signifier in both cultural and political terms. The metaphor of the closet has been extended by attendant terminology, principally the notion of 'coming out' – now shorthand for a subject's articulation of their sexuality – which derives from the notion of opening the closet door and stepping out into the public world. In contemporary lesbian and gay subcultures, the term has developed so that it now functions as a noun, the 'closet', as well as an adjective which describes subjectivity, 'closeted', and even a taxonomy of different subject-types, amongst others, the 'closet queen', the 'closet case', the 'closet Tommy' and the 'closet dyke'.[2] The plasticity of language here and its usage in lesbian and gay writing represent one possibility for relevant analysis in a collection of essays on lesbian and gay literature. However, my focus in this chapter will be on the closet, the closely implied concept of the secret and the ways in which these concepts encode what I call, following Gaston Bachelard, the dialectics of outside and inside. As Bachelard notes in his discussion of metaphysics, the concepts of 'open and closed ... are thoughts'. If this observation were applied to the closet door, we might note that the metaphor operates most profoundly within our imaginations. Indeed, Bachelard argues, our ideas about being outside or inside are 'experienced by the imagination'.[3] As such, I examine how notions of outside and inside function within the lesbian and gay imaginary and how this might be expressed in our sense of the cultural present and our appraisal of the past. My early focus in the chapter will be on contemporary notions of the closet, examining what I shall call the modern closet and its impact both on lived existence and also on our notions of lesbian and gay history. Then, however, my literary focus will be on early twentieth-century texts by lesbian modernists, whose lives and works predate notions of 'closet' and 'secret' but whose textual representations of lesbian subjectivity articulate compellingly different notions of 'outside' and 'inside' and which, in this sense, profoundly challenge the contemporary obsession with the concept of the closet.

The modern closet

That the closet endures as a pervasive concept in Anglo-American cultural discourses in the early twenty-first century is demonstrated by a recent example from British popular culture. In the trail of publicity surrounding the airing of her popular fashion show *Mary, Queen of Shops* in the summer of 2007, the retail and fashion consultant Mary Portas was treated to the traditional 'naming and shaming' moves by one of the British red-top tabloids, the *News of the World*. Two weeks into the run of the show, the paper ran one of its infamous 'outing' exposés, titled 'Mary, Queen of Shocks' in which the 'TV Shops star' was revealed as 'having an affair with a woman'. One finds in the tenor of the reporting and the 'revelation' of the 'secret' of Portas's lesbian relationship the key terms with which the cultural symbol of the closet is constructed. In the 'Exclusive' article, journalist Dan Wootton typically constructs the paper itself as the truth-finding agency: 'Telly fashion queen Mary Portas left her husband and moved in with her LESBIAN lover, the News of the World can reveal.'[4] The *News of the World* 'Exclusive' was, however, pre-empted by Portas's own shrewd and assertive use of a mid-market tabloid, the *Daily Mail*. In an interview with *Daily Mail* journalist Sarah Sands, published on the day the first episode of the fashion show aired on BBC2 and over two weeks before Wootton's attempt to 'out' Portas, she had already come out about her relationship with another woman. Portas explains to Sands 'I don't want to live a lie', and gives full details of her divorce, her subsequent relationship with the fashion editor Melanie Rickey and her family living arrangements.[5] Perhaps the most interesting element of this relatively well-worn story of the 'outing' of a popular cultural icon is the canniness with which Portas deals with the popular media. The complex imbrication of the 'closet' with the idea of the 'secret' is evidenced in the control Portas manages to obtain over the public consumption of her sexuality by diffusing any potential manipulation by the tabloid press by assertively naming the 'secret' via the media. Portas, who has a formidable career as a retail and branding consultant, is fully cognisant of the effectiveness of her actions. In July 2008, in an *Observer* interview, Portas comments: 'But really there is no big deal, is there? . . . The shock would be . . . what? That I told you? And you already knew anyway?'[6] The 'shock', then, is not that Portas is a lesbian but that there is *no* secret, and thus, by implication, no closet. Perhaps the closet in this story is, after all, just a piece of furniture in which to hang garments, albeit cutting-edge, 'on-season' ones. This subverts the traditional cultural 'script' in which the public figure is outed and shamed both for her sexual 'perversion' and her attempts to keep it hidden. We might say that secrets have become more repugnant than the modes of sexual desire tradition-ally kept in the closet. More recently in contemporary culture, Jacqueline Rose argues, the shaming thing is not the sexuality itself but rather the act of keeping it a secret, of being *closeted*: 'it is not of being homosexual but for *hiding* it that the outed public figure is meant to be ashamed'.[7] Portas's refusal either to keep her 'secret' or be shamed, alongside her culturally savvy 'handling' of the British tabloid press, represents a 'victory' in the sense that she controls the fate of her own 'secret'. Portas refuses to live in what the gay journalist Michael Musto has described as the 'glass closet', 'that complex but popular contrap-tion that allows public figures to avoid career repercussions of any personal disclosure while living their lives with a certain degree of integrity'.[8]

Key elements of the Portas story – her own coming out and the attempted outing by a tabloid – exemplify the ways in which, as Eve Kosofsky Sedgwick argues, the closet is both a 'fundamental feature of social life' and 'a shaping presence' in the lives of lesbians and gay men in contemporary culture.[9] Portas's actions seem to demonstrate Sedgwick's argument that the closet is 'a regime of knowing' (67). Yet, if the closet does indeed have an epistemol-ogy, who is it who holds the knowledge? Who *knows*? Somewhat perversely, Sedgwick notes, Western culture has become increasingly obsessed with the exposure of the secret in the closet, despite the growing lesbian and gay presence within it:

> To the fine antennae of public attention the freshness of every drama of (espe-cially involuntary) gay uncovering seems if anything heightened in surprise and delectability, rather than staled, by the increasingly intense atmosphere of public articulations of and about the love that is famous for daring not speak its name. (67)

Thus *knowledge* is the prized possession of mainstream culture, the knowing of the secret. Conversely, though, the Portas story seems to suggest that knowledge is also in the possession of the sexually dissident. Portas *knew* the traditionally prescribed script about the closet and the British tabloid press and opted to subvert it. In addition, lesbians and gay men possess their own subcultural knowledge about the closet and its functions. The construction of such knowledge is evidenced in the close analysis of the closet undertaken by contemporary lesbian and gay historians and theorists.

Michelangelo Signorile, editor of the American gay magazine *The Advocate*, figures the closet as profoundly harmful to the mental, emotional and physical lives of lesbians and gay men. He describes it as a trans-cultural phenomenon with far-reaching implications:

> The definition of the homosexual closet is the same in Britain, the United States and most countries where homosexuality is feared and loathed. It is a place where gay men and lesbians are forced to live – under penalty of ostracism and, in some cases, even death – since their earliest realization of their sexuality. The anguish and torment that the closet imposes upon its victims is equally universal, transcending cultures and countries.[10]

Signorile articulates a clear political agenda: 'if we are to break down homophobia in our respective countries, the closet, no matter what culture we are part of or what government presides over us, must be broken down' (xvii). His analysis aims to examine the closet in sufficiently close detail that we come to understand its forms, its workings and its effects and then, with this knowledge, 'proceed in destroying it' (xvii). Signorile's strategy, which came to prominence in the 1990s as one of the foremost queer political practices, is the enforced 'outing' of closeted public figures by the gay and queer press. Signorile's rationale is complicated. To 'break down' the closet, the media needs to 'equalize the discussion of homosexuality and heterosexuality' (xv). In the seeming spirit of respect for privacy, 'most of the "responsible" media refuse to reveal public figures' homosexuality' (xv). Yet, Signorile argues, this is driven by a 'homophobic agenda', in which the media come to 'set themselves up as the enforcers of the closet, holding the key and opening the door only when it is to their advantage' (xv). Signorile advocates that the 'outing' of individuals should not only occur when they are involved in 'hypocritical, antigay behavior' but should be used rather as an act of 'liberation' through a kind of equalization and 'a refusal to make special arrangements for the closeted when reporting the news' (xv).

Despite the radical call to arms advanced by the queer politics of the 1990s, critics are still called upon to consider the continuing existence of the modern closet within Western culture. Recalling Sedgwick's argument that the closet is woven profoundly into lesbian and gay subjectivity, Steven Seidman describes the closet as 'a life-shaping pattern of gay concealment'.[11] In his book *Beyond the Closet*, Seidman works to define the way the closet functions in the imaginations and behaviours of contemporary lesbians and gay men. Seidman admits at the outset of his book that in interviewing his subjects in the mid 1990s he expected to be driven by his empirical evidence to 'tell a story of the closet as a condition of social oppression' (7) but he discovers that whilst his interviewees certainly 'spoke of concealing their homosexuality in specific situations or with particular individuals', the 'episodic pattern of concealment' does not correspond to the full historical reality of living out an undisclosed and hidden sexuality as represented by being in the closet (7–8).[12] By contrast with the relatively open and autonomous lives lived by these contemporary lesbians and gay men, Seidman describes 'the heyday of the closet era, between roughly 1950 and 1980', in which coming out publicly as lesbian or gay carried a profound and abiding social, and indeed in the case of gay men, legal sanction (10). In the light of Seidman's work, we might say, the modern closet persists most prominently in the imaginary of contemporary Western culture rather than the lived experiences of lesbians and gay men.

The historical closet and the problems of identification

To what extent, then, do we read the past in terms of modern notions of the closet and the secret? Given my focus on the early twentieth century, this is a crucial question. To what extent can we use these terms and models of signification in an early twentieth-century context? George Chauncey identifies the way in which the concept of the closet pervades our contemporary appraisal of previous historical periods: 'Before Stonewall (let alone before World War II), it is often said, gay people lived in a closet that kept them isolated, invisible, and vulnerable to anti-gay ideology.'[13] There is an implicit value-judgment in the way we interpret the sexual and social behaviours of previous generations: 'While it is hard to imagine the closet as anything other than a prison, we often blame people in the past for not having had the courage to break out of it' (6). Chauncey, undertaking careful historical analysis, argues that it is both 'bracing' and 'instructive' to discover that in fact the term 'the closet' is never used in lesbian and gay writings and documents prior to the 1960s (6).

Chauncey argues that in the years before the Second World War, gay men had other modes of being and very different ideas about secrecy and practices of concealment. Whilst for some 'the personal cost of "passing" was great', the practices of concealment opened up diverse possibilities so that 'many men positively enjoyed having a "secret life" more complex and extensive than outsiders could imagine' (7). These complex but rich experiences of identity and desire meant that the metaphors used by many pre-War gay men were very different from those of the later twentieth century: '[i]ndeed, the gay life of many men was so full and wide-ranging that by the 1930s they used another – but more expansive – spatial metaphor to describe it: not the gay closet, but the *gay world*' (7). This metaphor of a 'world' shapes the usage of the term 'coming out'; taking the cultural practice of a society debutante's 'coming out' as a model, gay men described the practice rather as '*coming out into* what they called "homosexual society" or the "gay world", a world neither so small, nor so isolated, nor, often, so hidden as "closet" implies' (7). The focus is on the possibilities inherent in the creation of a subculture, rather than the limiting notion of a private space – the closet – in which the secret of sexuality must be kept hidden. In this sense, Chauncey's historical work requires us, in the contemporary moment, to think in more detail about the dialectics of outside and inside that pervades our own formulations of sexual identity.

Despite the anachronism, Chauncey argues that contemporary lesbian and gay studies can productively use the closet as 'an analytic category', but he notes that we need to use it 'more cautiously and precisely, and to pay attention to the very different terms people used to describe themselves and their social worlds' (6). The urge to find historical precedents in history has prompted much recuperative work by lesbian and gay scholars and in this sense history itself is figured as a kind of temporal closet in which sexual dissidents in previous eras have been encased. Works such as Neil Miller's *Out of the Past: Gay and Lesbian History from 1869 to the Present* and Duberman, Vicinus and Chauncey's edited collection *Hidden from History: Reclaiming the Gay and Lesbian Past* attempt to reconstruct a history of and for lesbians and gay men.[14] Here the closet and the laudable act of living *outside* it, especially in a past we assume to present even more challenging social circumstances than our own, is considered an act of heroism with which we can identify and of which we can feel proud. In this sense, our historical use of the closet is generative in terms of our own identities. To assimilate famous figures from the past into the lesbian and gay 'community' is to shore up that community by creating a sense of tradition. Typical of this genre of recuperative work, Thom Nickels's book *Out in History* presents a catalogue of famous figures whom Nickels regards as having lived, in some way, 'out'. In his Foreword to the book, the gay novelist and publisher Felice Picano articulates this clearly:

> We know that coming out is a process that enriches us. We also know that reading a GLBT book for the first time is another step that propels you even further into the gay community. Reading Nickels' compendium of short but by no means small biographies of well-known homosexuals and fellow-followers is a third helpful, significant, and enriching step.[15]

Thus we underpin the structures of our own identities even as we look backwards to discover those brave men and women who chose to openly express their sexual dissidence. Yet this is to impose the contemporary model of the closet and the decision to come out on to the biographical details of historical subjects. Indeed, as Picano goes on to acknowledge, 'for the exacting amongst us, the title [*Out in History*] isn't precisely true. Not all of these people were "out" the way many of us are today.'[16]

The majority of the women whom Nickels includes in his collection are key figures from the modernist period.[17] This is not surprising since the movements of modernist art and literature are notable for the unprecedented number of women who were both engaged in aesthetic experimentation and at the same time either living out or representing same-sex desire.[18] In his account of the period Nickels makes the following assertions about the socio-cultural context in which these women found themselves: 'Though intimate friendships between women were commonplace early in the 20th century, women with lesbian or bisexual inclinations were categorized as spinsters or pressured into heterosexual marriages. As a result, many women's self-awareness of lesbian feelings usually occurred later in life.'[19] Whilst his attempt to recognize the specificities of socio-cultural context is important, Nickels still imposes the model of 'coming out' on the biographical narratives of these women. He presupposes that they neither recognized nor even experienced lesbian desire early in their lives, perhaps entering into heterosexual unions or remaining celibate in states of self-ignorance.

In her work on lesbian subcultures in South Dakota in the 1920s and 1930s, the social anthropologist Elizabeth Kennedy admits that whilst gathering empirical evidence from the period she is 'tempted' to use the concept of the closet, but is constantly reminded by one of her main sources that 'neither she nor her friends thought about life in those terms in the past'.[20] Kennedy learns through her interviews that the opposition of outside/inside does not structure lesbian experience in this period. Rather than 'bringing lesbianism into the public' these women were engaged in 'constructing a private world in which lesbianism could flourish' (16). In light of her research Kennedy eschews the model of the modern closet, its imperative of secrecy and the notions of coming out as a liberationary process. This period is markedly different from our own, she argues, in the sense that 'the social dichotomies of heterosexuality and homosexuality were not yet hegemonic. Concomitantly, the closet was not fully institutionalized' (38–9). Kennedy thus institutes the term 'private lesbianism' as the closest phrase she can find to describe these very different circumstances of self-knowledge, sexual desire and self-representation (16).

Closet, silence, text

Eve Kosofsky Sedgwick, following Foucault, makes the case for understanding the act of keeping quiet as an act marked by the notion of the closet and the decision to stay 'inside' it. For Sedgwick, *not* telling, *not* describing one's identity or desire, still represents an articulation of sexuality. As she argues: '[I]n the vicinity of the closet, even what *counts* as a speech act is problematized on a perfectly routine basis. As Foucault says: "there is no binary division to be made between what one says and what one does not say; we must try to determine the different ways of not saying such things."' As such the act of refusing to identify oneself, Sedgwick argues, is worthy of analysis: '"Closetedness" itself is a performance initiated as such by the speech act of a silence – not a particular silence, but a silence that accrues particularity by fits and starts, in relation to the discourse that surrounds and differentially constitutes it' (3). Might the act of creative writing be understood as one specific example of the kind of 'speech act of a silence' to which Sedgwick refers? If it is not quite a perfect fit, can it still be productively interpreted through this model? In what ways might the act of writing challenge the dialectics of outside and inside ('coming out' or 'closet') that we see in the notion of the modern closet? This is perhaps to understand the text in spatial terms and to suggest that textual space might be a space in which a kind of coming out – or self-articulation – might be enacted. In this sense, what might be *put into* words? This is not to invoke the late twentieth-century paradigm of the 'coming-out story', which comes to such cultural prominence in the 1970s and 1980s.[21] It is rather to suggest that the text might represent a third space that undoes the restrictive dialectics of outside and inside which structures our own contemporary thought. For instance, regarding the analysis of the journalist and commentator of modernist Paris Janet Flanner, Terry Castle considers the complex way in which written words can both contain sexuality and convey it in earlier socio-cultural contexts. Castle takes issue with Flanner's biographer Brenda Wineapple for her inability to recognize 'the more sensuous and celebratory aspects of lesbian experience' which Castle sees recorded in Flanner's energetic, vivacious journalistic style. Indeed it is Flanner's words, Castle argues, which enact a kind of self-revelation: 'If, in her magical letters from Paris, Janet Flanner never revealed her sexuality in so many words, what she did share with her readers – her ineradicable, coruscating delight in the world – was in its own way a perfect coming out.'[22]

One of the notable themes in key lesbian modernist texts is the desire or need to write. The 'writer as figure', as well as the 'figure of writing', feature most notably in novels such as Dorothy Richardson's *Pilgrimage* (1913–57),

Virginia Woolf's *Orlando* (1928), H. D.'s posthumously published novels *Paint it Today* (1992), *Asphodel* (1992) and *Her* (1984) and Bryher's *Development* (1920) and *Two Selves* (1923). In these texts, the protagonists come to writing at the same time as they come to resolutions and understandings about their sexual desire and identity. Often, this sexual narrative is encoded *beneath* the coming to writing so that we also see in these texts the self-reflexive recording of the inscriptive acts of their authors. In this way, the text in hand becomes an artefact that inscribes the progress towards both self-inscription and sexual self-knowledge. To some degree, of course, the pre-occupation with writing in these modernist texts functions within the received formulations of modernist concerns with language; however, it *also* acts as an acknowledgement of the need to write 'the lesbian' into existence in autonomous terms, however codedly, at a time when dominant cultural discourses were so keen to write the lesbian's life-history for her.

These experimental modernist novels, in different ways, suggestively evoke the idea of the text as space or container where desire might be put instead of *speaking* it. In a profound way, the lesbian modernists provide particularly resonant examples of the complicated relationship between lived identity and textual self-representation. Amongst the lesbian modernists Thom Nickels introduces in his book, he includes the Imagist poet H. D. What exactly does it mean to include H. D. in a roll-call of those who were 'out in history'? Glossing the complex constitution of her sexual identity, Nickels argues that 'Doolittle's own "discovery" was not actualized until after her 1913 marriage to poet Richard Aldington, which lasted several years.' Nickels notes that 'Doolittle chose not to publish her explicitly lesbian works during her lifetime.'[23] Indeed, between 1921 and 1930, H. D. wrote but suppressed three autobiographical novels, *Paint It Today*, *Hermione* and *Asphodel*, which detail her two principal lesbian attachments.[24] Across the three texts, H. D. first constructs herself fictionally as Midget in *Paint It Today* and then as Hermione Gart in both *Her* and *Asphodel*. Something of the sense of coming out *into* the text is conveyed most succinctly in *Her*, in the formula articulated by Hermione: 'Love is writing.'[25] Susan Stanford Friedman reads this equation of 'erotics and poetics' as a combative refutation of the traditional choices imposed upon the woman writer, a 'radical renunciation of the culturally imposed choice many women artists feel compelled to make, a choice that often fuels narrative movement in women's *Künstlerromane* – the choice to be an artist or a woman, categories culturally constituted as mutually exclusive'.[26] Also, however, H. D.'s complex equation formulates a correlation between lesbian subjectivity and modernist textuality, structurally binding these together so that the figure of writing becomes a coterminous destination with lesbian identity. For Hermione Gart, finding a way to 'put the thing in writing' means repudiating the masculine disconnection of 'love' from 'art' as articulated by her soon-to-be ex-fiancé George Lowndes ('Love doesn't make good art, Hermione') and reconstituting that connection so that she can locate a language in which to record both her own female subjectivity and her desires, most notably her desire for her female lover Fayne Rabb.[27]

To tease these relations between textuality and sexuality out further, I should like to examine the lesser-known modernist patron and writer Bryher. Bryher was one of the most influential and well connected of the female modernist writers of the early twentieth century. Born Annie Winifred Ellerman in 1894, to the British shipping magnate John Ellerman and his common-law wife Hannah Glover, in adolescence she adopted the name of the wildest and most remote of her beloved Isles of Scilly – the suitably androgynous Bryher – and changed it legally by deed poll in 1951. Bryher produced a wide range of writings, including autobiographical fiction, historical novels, poetry and literary and film criticism. She is notable for her contribution to the cultural production of modernism, in both financial and editorial terms. After she encountered the first Imagist collection, *Des Imagistes*, in 1913, the trajectory of Bryher's literary career and allegiances was set; her own endeavours were to find their milieu in the experimental literatures of modernism and the avant-garde writings of the Futurists and the Surrealists. After writing her first piece of precocious criticism, *Amy Lowell: A Critical Appreciation* (1918), Bryher orchestrated a meeting between herself and H. D., which marked the beginning of a lifelong sexual and emotional relationship. Bryher's autobiographical fiction, *Development: A Novel* (1920), *Two Selves* (1923) and *West* (1925), employs a mixture of realism and Imagist prose and represents the complexities of early twentieth-century lesbian subjectivity. Though lesbianism is never overtly named, the novels document the complexities of female masculinity and desire for other women. In addition to her later turn to historical fiction, Bryher also wrote the memoirs *The Heart to Artemis: A Writer's Memoirs* (1963) and *The Days of Mars: A Memoir, 1940–1946* (1972).

In *Heart to Artemis*, Bryher records her lifelong relationship with H. D. in terms which do not speak of the full emotional and sexual register of the relationship. Bryher describes the misery of her 'Victorian' childhood and her desire to escape the confines of her social and familial context. In such circumstances, she notes, 'the young usually fall in love'. She does, she admits, fall in love, but 'with a country, not a person. America was my first love affair.'[28] Developing the metaphor, she describes the country as her 'mistress', because they are both 'perceptive and also inconstant' with each other (60). Bryher notes that she has 'spent a lot of my life trying in small ways to bring Americans and English together' (161). She then attests, with the advantage of hindsight, that whatever she has achieved in life has been 'due originally to an economic fact and to Imagist poetry' (161). The 'proper secondary function' of poets, she writes, 'is to be an ambassador'. Then, somewhat peremptorily, she quotes lines from H. D.'s poem 'Hermes of the Ways'.[29] These lines of poetry, indented and in italics, literally break the text of her prosaic recollections. Their inclusion is made even more enigmatic by the cryptic line with which Bryher follows them: 'I, too, waited for another five years' (161). Given that Bryher is recounting events that took place in 1913, waiting another five years takes her to 1918, the year she meets H. D. and becomes embroiled in the crisis of the pregnant H. D.'s life-threatening encounter with influenza and the birth of her daughter Perdita. Here in the public memoir, America is both symbolized by and acts as a symbol for H. D. herself, to whom Bryher felt that she owed her own life. Bryher goes on to describe the events of 1918, recording the exact date on which she was invited to tea at H. D.'s rented cottage in Zennor, Cornwall – 17 July 1918 – and in her account there can be no doubt of the importance of this relationship:

> I had a friend at last who talked to me about poetry and did not laugh at my meagre attempts at writing ... It was my first real contact with an artist, and H.D. was the most beautiful figure that I have ever seen in my life, with a face that came directly from a Greek statue and, almost to the end, the body of an athlete. (190–1)

Yet the account here is muted. The full terms of this critical event in Bryher's young life, the meeting and falling in love with another woman, are recorded principally as central facts in the life-story of a modernist patron and experimenter. What the memoir omits is the story of affect and desire. These are found elsewhere in Bryher's oeuvre, in the autobiographical novels *Two Selves* and *West*, which map these same years in Bryher's life. In the public space of her memoir, Bryher writes that she is 'ashamed' of *West*, the text in which she fictionalizes H. D. as Helga Brandt (205). Yet it is in the text of *West* that she can articulate the truth about falling in love with 'America': 'when she imagined America in her thoughts she saw it as a place without a past ... Even as the name Helga was new and rich. A spear-shaft ... corn-gold and sun-gold mingled ... with about it something of ice and of the inner heart of a peach. America ... Only an American had bade her live.'[30]

In her autobiographical fiction, Bryher names her pseudonymous heroine Nancy. Nancy's childhood and early adult experience follow Bryher's own very closely. In structure the novels follow the conventions of traditional *Künstlerromane*, yet in both form and content Bryher's novel records the complexities of the coming to identity of a young woman whose body and desires run counter to the dominant culture in which she finds herself. As

Nancy's best friend Doris notes sharply: 'You don't seem to want ... what most girls want.'[31] And indeed Nancy's desire has divided her: 'Something had cleft her from herself. She was two personalities now ... Something, like an axe, had hit her and taught her *to keep hidden in herself*' (295; my emphasis). In her divided state – the 'two selves' of the novel's title – Nancy feels the desperate desire to 'find a friend'. Throughout the narrative, finding 'a friend' comes to figure as the articulation of her desire for an Other who also might understand her own gender difference ('A boy, a brain, that planned adventures and sought wisdom' (183)) and her dissident desires.

> If she found a friend they might shut her up. Everyone, Eleanor, Doreen, Downwood. Because if she had a friend something would burst and she would shoot ahead, be the thing she wanted and disgrace them by her knowledge. Because she would care for no laws, only for happiness.   (288)

Nancy articulates a strong sense of being silenced in *Two Selves*, of living an enforced speechlessness: 'none of the faces passing would have urged her to a sentence could she have stopped them and have spoken' (185). The text sustains an ongoing subtextual commentary on language and difference that is hard not to read as a commentary on the unspeakability of same-sex desire. Nancy understands there is another vocabulary, indeed another way of *knowing*, which is *not* the language of the dominant culture: 'She had never heard words spoken. Real words. Only the headlines of the papers repeated over and over again. Or the phrases of an older generation that had no link with her thought. Never words leaping, shining with meaning, saying a fact' (287). In Bryher's text, as in other lesbian modernist autobiographical fiction, there is an equivalence made between writing and freedom to desire. Nancy frets about her ability to *write*: 'There was something too authentic and too storm-wracked about her emotions for the right word ever to come. And if the right word did not come it would not be good enough to get printed and if it were not printed she would never get a friend' (281).

Development was published by Constable in London in 1920. In *Heart to Artemis*, Bryher describes the editing of the novel. She explains that after the manuscript's submission, the publisher returned it to her asking that she revise it to include a 'happy ending' (193). What this meant, Bryher explains, was actually 'a romantic one' and this she 'indignantly refused to supply' (193). Bryher refuses to provide the desired closure of the traditional heterosexual narrative, yet she fails to note that the next novel in the trilogy, *Two Selves*, does supply a romantic ending in its closing moments, in the dramatic and deeply emotional account of the first meeting with H. D. As the narrative of *Two Selves* draws to a close, Nancy, in a suicidal state, hears from 'the writer' on whom she has pinned her hopes of understanding and is invited to tea. The last moves of the novel use stream-of-consciousness to convey the emotional intensity of the encounter: 'Better not try to find a friend. Better drown under the cliffs. One stab of water and no fear more' (289). Nancy's way to the sea is literally blocked by the cottage in which the writer stays: 'the Phœnician path stopped at a grey cottage that faced the south-blue sea' (289). And there, even before she has met the figure within, she sees that 'familiar yellow covers, French books, were piled at an open window' and recognizes that this writer reads the *same* kind of books, the same *writing*, as she does (289).[32] The narrative concludes as Nancy's desiring gaze falls on the breath-taking body and eyes of H. D. and the opening of a door:

> Better not try to find . . . oh, take a chance on adventure. This was the place. She knocked.
>
> She was too old to be disappointed if an elderly woman in glasses bustled out . . .
>
> A tall figure opened the door. Young. A spear flower if a spear could bloom. She looked up into eyes that had the sea in them, the fire and colour and the splendour of it. A voice all wind and gull notes said:
>
> 'I was waiting for you to come.' (289)

Bachelard asks 'onto what, toward what, do doors open?'[33] And indeed we may well read this opening door at the end of *Two Selves* symbolically, as the opening up of a new space, neither *outside* nor *inside*, in which to act on desire. Here in Bryher's writing, as in other lesbian modernist texts, textual space allows for the articulation of selfhood and desire. This writing constitutes a certain kind of speaking of the self, a speech-act which does not commit the subject to making the difficult choice between what *we* would now describe as staying in the closet or coming out. Thus, the lesbian modernists are not best described as being 'out in history', but rather as writing beyond these categories and envisioning other possibilities and spaces of living and loving altogether.

NOTES

1. George Chauncey, *Gay New York: Gender, Urban Culture, and the Making of the Gay Male World, 1890–1940* (New York: Basic Books, 1994), 6, 374–5, n. 7.
2. For a discussion of homosexuality and the subcultural usage of slang terms, see Jennifer Terry, *An American Obsession: Science, Medicine and Homosexuality in Modern Culture* (Chicago: University of Chicago Press, 1999).
3. Gaston Bachelard, *The Poetics of Space* (Boston, MA: Beacon Press, 1994), 212, 216.
4. 'Mary, Queen of Shocks', *News of the World* (17 June 2007), 38.
5. Sarah Sands, 'I'm Mary, Queen of Shops', *Daily Mail* (31 May 2007).
6. Polly Vernon, 'Rip it up and start again', *Observer Woman* (July 2008).

7. Jacqueline Rose, 'Introduction: Shame', *On Not Being Able to Sleep: Psychoanalysis and the Modern World* (London: Vintage, 2004), 1.

8. Michael Musto, 'We all know which stars are inside the glass closet, so why don't they just come out', *Out* (4 April 2007), http://out.com/detail.asp?id=22392, accessed 4 September 2008.

9. Eve Kosofsky Sedgwick, *Epistemology of the Closet* (Berkeley: University of California Press, 1990), 68. Further references are given in parentheses.

10. Michelangelo Signorile, *Queer in America: Sex, the Media and the Closets of Power* (London: Abacus, 1994), xi. Further references are given in parentheses.

11. Steven Seidman, *Beyond the Closet: The Transformation of Gay and Lesbian Life* (New York: Routledge, 2002), 25. Further references are given in parentheses.

12. Seidman undertook his empirical research between 1996 and 1998. He interviewed 'thirty individuals of different races, classes, genders, and generations' (6).

13. Chauncey, *Gay New York*, 6. Further references are given in parentheses.

14. See Neil Miller, *Out of the Past: Gay and Lesbian History from 1869 to the Present* (London: Vintage, 1995) and Martin Bauml Duberman, Martha Vicinus and George Chauncey, Jr, eds., *Hidden from History: Reclaiming the Gay and Lesbian Past* (London: Penguin, 1991).

15. Felice Picano, Foreword, in Thom Nickels, *Out in History* (Sarasota, FL: STARbooks Press, 2005), xiii.

16. *Ibid.*, xiii.

17. Nickels details the lives of the bookseller Sylvia Beach, Alice Toklas, partner of Gertrude Stein, foremost modernist poet Marianne Moore, modernist novelist Djuna Barnes, modernist poet H. D. and novelist and sometime lover of Virginia Woolf, Vita Sackville-West.

18. The theorization of this correlation between modernism and what we would now call lesbian sexuality presents profound challenges to contemporary critics in terms of definition, not least in whether or not we can even employ the term 'lesbian'. Critics use various terms: lesbian modernism, Sapphic modernism or queer modernism. Key works on modernism and lesbian sexuality include Hugh Stevens and Caroline Howlett, eds., *Modernist Sexualities* (Manchester: Manchester University Press, 2000); Karla Jay, 'Lesbian Modernism: (Trans)Forming the (C)anon', in George E. Haggerty and Bonnie Zimmerman, eds., *Professions of Desire: Lesbian & Gay Studies in Literature* (New York: Modern Language Association of America, 1995), 72–83; Joanne Winning, *The Pilgrimage of Dorothy Richardson* (Madison: University of Wisconsin Press, 2000); Mary E. Galvin, *Queer Poetics: Five Modernist Women Writers* (London: Greenwood Press, 1999); Anne Hermann, *Queering the Moderns: Poses/Portraits/Performances* (Basingstoke: Palgrave, 2000); Shari Benstock, 'Expatriate Sapphic Modernism: Entering Literary History', in Karla Jay and Joanne Glasgow, eds., *Lesbian Texts and Contexts: Radical Revisions* (New York: New York University Press, 1990; reprinted London: Onlywomen Press, 1992), 183–203; Diana Collecott, *H.D. and Sapphic Modernism, 1910–1950* (Cambridge: Cambridge University Press, 1999); Laura Doan and Jane Garrity, eds., *Sapphic Modernities: Sexuality, Women and National Culture* (London: Palgrave Macmillan, 2007).

19. Nickels, *Out in History*, 99.

20. Elizabeth Kennedy '"But We Would Never Talk About It": The Structure of Lesbian Discretion in South Dakota, 1928–1933', in Ellen Lewin, ed., *Inventing Lesbian Cultures in America* (Boston, MA: Beacon Press, 1996), 16. Further references are given in parentheses.

21. See for instance Biddy Martin, 'Lesbian Identity and Autobiographical Difference(s)', in Bella Brodzki and Celeste Schenck, eds., *Life/Lines: Theorizing Women's Autobiography* (Ithaca, NY: Cornell University Press, 1988), 77–103.

22. Terry Castle, *The Apparitional Lesbian: Female Homosexuality and Modern Culture* (New York: Columbia University Press, 1993), 197, 199.

23. Nickels, *Out in History*, 99, 100.

24. See *Paint It Today*, ed. Cassandra Laity (New York: New York University Press, 1992); *Her* (London: Virago, 1984); *Asphodel*, ed. Robert Spoo (Durham, NC: Duke University Press, 1992).

25. H. D., *Her*, 149.

26. Susan Stanford Friedman, *Penelope's Web: Gender, Modernity, H.D.'s Fiction* (Cambridge, Cambridge University Press, 1990), 105.

27. H. D., *Her*, 149, 13. Fayne Rabb is the fictionalized Frances Gregg, whom H. D. met and became involved with in 1908.

28. Bryher, *The Heart to Artemis* (London: Collins, 1963), 160. Further references are given in parentheses.

29. 'Hermes of the Ways' was published in the collection *Sea Garden* (1916). Bryher quotes the concluding stanza of the poem:

> *Hermes, Hermes,*
> *the great sea foamed,*
> *gnashed its teeth about me;*
> *but you have waited,*
> *where sea-grass tangles with*
> *shore-grass.*

See H. D., *Collected Poems, 1912–1944*, ed. Louis L. Martz (New York: New Directions, 1983), 39.

30. Bryher, *West* (London: Jonathan Cape, 1925), 20.

31. Bryher, *Two Novels: 'Development' and 'Two Selves'*, ed. Joanne Winning (Madison: University of Wisconsin Press, 2000), 285. Further references are given in parentheses.

32. The very specific description of these books, 'yellow covers, French books', evokes a certain sexual narrative since, as Sally Ledger notes: 'the yellow dust jacket generally denoted either risqué French fiction or popular novels sold at railway stations.' A yellow cover evokes *The Yellow Book*, the periodical associated with 'aestheticism and Decadence and, after April and May 1895, homosexuality'. See Sally Ledger, 'Wilde Women and *The Yellow Book*: The Sexual Politics of Aestheticism and Decadence', *English Literature in Transition*, 50:1 (2007), 5–26.

33. Bachelard, *The Poetics of Space*, 224.

4

TIM DEAN

The erotics of transgression

> O brilliant kids, frisk with your dog,
> Fondle your shells and sticks, bleached
> By time and the elements; but there is a line
> You must not cross nor ever trust beyond it
> Spry cordage of your bodies to caresses
> Too lichen-faithful from too wide a breast.
> The bottom of the sea is cruel.

A vivid warning about transgression, these lines by the modern American poet Hart Crane conclude the initial poem of 'Voyages', a lyric sequence inspired by his maritime lover Emil Opffer.[1] The penalty for crossing the line here is death, figured as an ineluctable embrace by the sea, whose 'caresses' represent a fatal union. Yet the poem does exactly what it warns against, with its strongly enjambed syntax luring readers across the line before we're aware of the transgression ('but there is a line / You must not cross'). As the heavy caesurae of the stanza's opening lines give way to the enjambment of those that follow, so the innocent, earth-bound identities are overtaken by the dark dissolution of the sea. The boundary that is crossed not only separates one line of poetry from another but also divides shore from sea, innocence from experience, childhood from adulthood and this world from the next. The 'line / You must not cross' thus suggests an ontological limit as well as a formal division.

Since the speaker cautions the 'brilliant kids' not to transgress a boundary that the adult reader seems always already to have crossed, we may infer that the fraught line has something to do with sexuality (the imagery of fondling, frisking and caressing, in conjunction with the 'Spry cordage of your bodies', supports this inference). It is striking that, despite the poem's erotic overtones, neither the children nor the sea are gendered. In subsequent poems of the 'Voyages' sequence and elsewhere, Crane figures the sea as archaically feminine; here it is as if we confront a scene prior to sexual difference. Not only that: by making erotic excess – '*Too* lichen-faithful from *too* wide a breast' – appear indistinguishable from death, the poem evokes a long tradition of imagining sex as potentially fatal. From sexually undifferentiated innocence to deadly excess, the line that demarcates transgression bears an unmistakably erotic charge.

'Transgression has its entire space in the line it crosses', declared Michel Foucault in an essay from 1963 that inaugurated the critical discourse on transgression.[2] He thus identified the paradox whereby transgression, thanks to its functioning most intensively at the moment a line is crossed, must always seek out new limits, new boundaries to push against. This paradox leads to a situation in which, as gay writer Simon Sheppard put it, 'Problem is, transgressions are a dime a dozen these days.'[3] In the decades following Foucault's homage to Georges Bataille, the vocabulary of transgression has permeated academic discourse to such an extent – influencing not just lesbian, gay and queer studies but the humanities and social sciences more broadly – that much of its original force has been blunted. The term itself circulates as something of a cliché and, as one critic suggests, ironically 'transgression has become a safe topic for the progressive intellectual'.[4] Far from pushing the envelope, the critical discourse on transgression has become blandly predictable. I want to suggest that its predictability stems from the loss of transgression's conceptual specificity and that, irrespective of how it has degenerated into jargon in contemporary critical discourse, transgression retains its potency in some marginal literary discourses of the past several decades. In order to support these claims, I examine the development of the concept of transgression in the work of Bataille and Foucault, emphasizing a distinction between the intuitive *idea* of transgression and its significance as a philosophical *concept*. The chapter then turns to two US minority writers, Samuel R. Delany and John Rechy, to assess their literary practices of transgression. Regretfully, I leave aside others – Gloria Anzaldúa, Reinaldo Arenas, William Burroughs, Pat Califia, Dennis Cooper, Sarah Schulman and Matthew Stadler – who would merit discussion in a more expansive treatment of the topic.

With respect to the literary dimension, Foucault made plain that transgression operates at the limit of the speakable, that it tends to resist the grasp of discursive or philosophical language. In perhaps the best-known lines of his essay on the subject, he speculated about the future of transgression:

> Perhaps one day [transgression] will seem as decisive for our culture, as much a part of its soil, as the experience of contradiction was at an earlier time for dialectical thought. But in spite of so many scattered signs, the language in which transgression will find its space and the illumination of its being lies almost entirely in the future.[5]

Foucault discerned the 'scattered signs' of the language of transgression as much in Bataille's literary writings as in his philosophical works – just as Bataille found that language in the fiction of André Gide, Thomas Mann and the Marquis de Sade, as well as in the poetry of Baudelaire and Nietzsche.

Following this emphasis on imaginative literature, we might suggest that the future envisioned by Foucault has become more clearly legible in the sexually transgressive writers who wrote in his wake. Indeed, in the course of an argument about transgression whose full significance I hope to elaborate, Bataille claimed that 'the true nature of the erotic stimulant can only be revealed by literary means, by bringing into play characters and scenes from the realm of the *impossible*'.[6] Pointing to transgression's inseparability from eroticism, he highlighted how literature is a realm of invention, not merely of imitation or reflection, because one can do things 'by literary means' that one cannot do so readily in actuality, owing to the necessity of consent. For Bataille it was ethically imperative that literature push beyond the constraints on sexual practice that customarily are respected in everyday life, even if that entails representations of violence and dismemberment.

Conceptualizing transgression

There can be no possibility of transgression without law, prohibition, limit or taboo. As Foucault put it, 'The limit and transgression depend on each other for whatever density of being they possess: a limit could not exist if it were absolutely uncrossable and, reciprocally, transgression would be pointless if it merely crossed a limit composed of illusions and shadows.'[7] A prohibition or taboo must be breakable, and breaking it must qualify as more than mere theatrics, for transgression to be meaningful. Whenever same-sex erotic activity is explicitly outlawed, as it has been in one form or another throughout much of human history, an air of the transgressive clings to its every representation. With the longstanding prohibitions on sodomy and then, beginning in the nineteenth century, on homosexuality more specifically, came a rich literary tradition of coded depictions that culminated in what might be called the literature of the closet. This literature is exemplified in the fiction of Henry James, Herman Melville, Marcel Proust and Oscar Wilde.[8] The 'love that dare not speak its name' tended to utter 'only a few hints, a few diffused faint clews and indirections'; anything more direct was deemed obscene and risked incurring legal sanction, as Wilde discovered at great cost.[9] When homosexuality is illicit or illegal, the literature of same-sex love always risks transgression.

But what happens when it is no longer illegal, when the age-old prohibitions are lifted? This question is especially pertinent for lesbian and gay literature produced during the period in which homosexuality's social acceptance has increased dramatically. Among other things, the question points to shifting definitions of obscenity that regulate representations of heterosexual, as well as same-sex, eros. Considering canonical European literature that was deemed obscene or pornographic in its time – for example, *Madame Bovary*, *Ulysses* and *Lady Chatterley's Lover* – one cannot help noticing how remote from any charge of transgression such literature appears today. Pornography remains a significant genre for the transgressive, and several of the works I discuss below are unapologetically pornographic. Yet the history of obscenity legislation, at least in the United States, bears witness to a shift from concerns about sexual explicitness to anxiety over representations of non-normative sexualities.[10] Intergenerational sex, sadomasochism, sex involving animals or inorganic objects – all are guaranteed to attract the censor's attention. It is notable that for contemporary obscenity law, as for Foucault in 'A Preface to Transgression', the hetero/homo division is far from the most salient feature when it comes to determining transgression.

Another way of putting it would be to say that lesbian and gay sexualities have no essential or privileged relation to transgression. There is nothing necessarily revolutionary or, indeed, politically progressive about same-sex desires, practices, identities and representations today. Much of the lesbian and gay literature produced after Stonewall has been realist in orientation, seeking to provide recognizable images of ordinary, often middle class, gay men and lesbians discovering their sexuality, finding love and living their lives in ways that readers can easily identify with. One thinks, for example, of the hugely popular fiction of Rita Mae Brown or Armistead Maupin. This literature is not only enjoyable but also valuable for its offering scenes of affirmative identification to readers struggling to find their way out of the closet. It is vital for human diversity that high culture, middlebrow culture and mass culture all furnish narratives that are not organized primarily around heterosexuality.

The literature of transgression is something different. Both Bataille and Foucault assume that transgression is bound up with sexuality, though they have little to say about sexual identity. Foucault invokes sexuality throughout 'A Preface to Transgression' without ever specifying a distinction between heterosexuality and homosexuality, for example. It would be a mistake to attribute this absence to the closet or to the historical moment of the essay's composition, tempting though such possibilities might be in view of French cultural norms and, particularly, Foucault's biography. To understand the lack of sexual specificity in primarily historical or biographical terms would be to overlook how transgression involves an experience of sexuality in which the gender of the partner remains secondary, if not altogether irrelevant. Bataille insists on this point when he remarks that 'the object of desire is the *universe*' or, more abstractly, '*the concrete totality of the real*'.[11] By this Bataille designates not a desire to sexually possess the entire world but the opposite – a desire to lose oneself in the universe through erotic intensity. Such ecstatic obliteration of the self's boundaries is what Crane, describing oceanic dissolution in 'Voyages', figures as 'this great wink of eternity, / Of rimless floods, unfettered leewardings', and again as 'Infinite consanguinity'.[12] When by means of eros the self transgresses its boundaries, the notion of sexual *identity* no longer makes much sense.

It is this experience of ecstatic self-dissolution that Bataille is gesturing towards when he claims that 'love is a kind of immolation'.[13] The marked difference between such an extreme experience and our conventional under-standing of sex or love helps to illuminate the distinction – insisted on by both Bataille and Foucault – between sexuality and eroticism. For both thinkers, it is eroticism (rather than sexuality or sexual identity) that remains inextricable from transgression. Bataille elaborates this distinction in the following way:

> The status of man's sexual activity is surprising: it is not at all forbidden in principle. It is subject to restrictions, of course, but these restrictions leave open an extensive field of possibilities. Whereas the history of eroticism is by no means that of sexual activity allowed within the limits defined by the rules: indeed, eroticism only includes a domain marked off by the *violation of rules*. It is always a matter of going beyond the limits allowed: there is nothing erotic in a sexual game like that of animals. And perhaps eroticism is relatively rare (it is hard to say anything definite on this point due to the paucity of reliable data).[14]

Eroticism is linked to transgression since it is defined by the violation of rules. Bataille's theory of eroticism remains resolutely anti-essentialist (despite its heteronormative bias), insofar as he differentiates eroticism from what is natural in a biological sense and what is cultural in an anthropological sense. Eroticism serves the purposes of neither nature nor culture, but comes into play only when cultural prohibitions are transgressed. Its rarity helps to account for eroticism's appearance in the literary domain, because defying cultural prohibitions is always easier in fantasy than in reality. Nevertheless, it must be acknowledged that, by most standards, its appear-ance in transgressive literature hardly alleviates 'the paucity of reliable data', since few fully credit 'literary' evidence, especially when derived from porno-graphic literature.

Bataille's point is that most sex does *not* violate prohibitions; transgression is not as common as one might suppose. To appreciate how, far from being 'a dime a dozen', transgressions are comparatively infrequent enables us to grasp not only the distinction between sexuality and eroticism but also that between transgression as an idea and as a philosophical concept. Not every-one wishes to cultivate his or her sexuality in pursuit of the erotics of transgression; indeed, there are perfectly valid reasons for not doing so. One might prefer to conserve one's safety, dignity or integrity – all of which transgression puts at risk. Bataille's suggestion that ordinarily sex is not transgressive anticipates Foucault's famous admonition to the advocates of sexual liberation: 'We must not think that by saying yes to sex, one says no to power'.[15] Neither a refuge from power nor a reliable wedge against it, sexual activity is only rarely – and with some difficulty – transgressive in the sense that Bataille and Foucault aspire to locate.

What makes transgression so difficult? Defining eroticism in terms of 'the violation of rules', as Bataille does here, obscures how transgression involves violating not so much rules or social conventions but, more precisely, *taboos*. It is far from a matter of inconsequence to transgress something that one regards as taboo, since taboos radiate a genuinely aversive power. Here Freud's account, in *Totem and Taboo*, is useful for its emphasis on the internal necessity that maintains taboo prohibitions, which, he says, 'have no grounds and are of unknown origin'.[16] Comparing the force of taboos with that of Kant's categorical imperative, Freud differentiates taboo restrictions from religious prohibitions, insisting that 'taboo is older than gods and dates back to a period before any kind of religion existed'.[17] The significance of taboo prohibitions for Bataille and Foucault lies in how taboos also survive the death of God. Believed unquestioningly, taboos wield a power that remains immune to logical argument or enlightened reasoning. One cannot be agnostic or sceptical about a taboo, as one can about a god. As Freud put it, 'no external threat of punishment is required, for there is an internal certainty, a moral conviction, that any violation will lead to intolerable disaster'.[18]

It is not necessary to subscribe to Freud's reductive explanation of all taboos in terms of incestuous desire and the Oedipus complex to see how the 'internal certainty' that characterizes such prohibitions makes transgressing them particularly difficult. With taboos the threat of punishment comes from inside rather than outside the self. Transgressing laws that one regards as unjust, arbitrary or externally imposed (for example, anti-gay legislation) is easy enough; here we observe the difference between transgression and civil disobedience. What is much harder to sustain is any transgression of one's own internal limits. Both Foucault and Bataille suggest that, at the end of the day, transgression does not concern the juridical. Despite the case of Oscar Wilde (and others such as the obscenity trial of Allen Ginsberg's *Howl* in 1957[19]), we cannot grasp the significance of transgression primarily by reference to historically variable legislation about sexuality and its representation.

Understood philosophically, transgression concerns not the law but *the limit* – or what Foucault calls 'the experience of finitude and being'.[20] In his meditation on Bataille, Foucault conceptualizes 'the limit' not only in terms that are fairly synonymous with law (such as prohibition or boundary), but also in the more existential terms of human finitude. Inspired by Bataille's linking of transgression to the sacred, Foucault is curious about what happens to the possibility of transgression after the death of God. With the post-Nietzschean disappearance of a previously stable sense of the infinite, we have lost the limit represented by limitlessness. Human finitude becomes a new kind of problem in a world without the infinite. What remains is a particular sense of the sacred that is encapsulated in the notion of taboo. As Freud notes, *taboo* is a Polynesian word that bears a meaning close to that of the Roman word *sacer*, from which we derive the English *sacred*.[21] But 'taboo' and *sacer* both carry a double resonance that 'sacred' lacks, since the former connote 'unclean', 'forbidden' and 'accursed', as well as 'consecrated', 'holy' and 'exceptional'. It is by exploiting this double significance that Bataille draws the connection between transgression and the sacred, observing that 'what is *sacred* is precisely what is *prohibited*'.[22] Transgression may entail contact with not only the low and impure but also the sacred and holy. In other words, it may entail touching what is supposed to remain untouchable.

To designate something as untouchable – to make it taboo – tacitly acknowledges that somewhere there lurks the desire to touch it ('every horror conceals a possibility of enticement', says Bataille[23]). Yet making something taboo also *intensifies* the desire for it, by erecting a barrier that stimulates the erotic impulse to overcome and transgress the limit. From this perspective, prohibitions may be regarded as soliciting their own transgression rather than as simply forbidding it. Foucault points to this counterintuitive notion when he characterizes the relation between transgression and limit in other than binary or negative terms:

> Transgression, then, is not related to the limit as black to white, the prohibited to the lawful, the outside to the inside, or as the open area of a building to its enclosed spaces. Rather, their relationship takes the form of a spiral that no simple infraction can exhaust ... Transgression does not seek to oppose one thing to another, nor does it achieve its purpose through mockery or by upsetting the solidity of foundations ... Transgression contains nothing negative, but affirms limited being – affirms the limitlessness into which it leaps as it opens this zone to existence for the first time.[24]

Although he defines it by negation (transgression is not this and not that), Foucault insists that transgression itself should be understood as operating affirmatively rather than negatively. Picturing the relationship between transgression and the limit in 'the form of a spiral that no simple infraction can exhaust', Foucault anticipates one of the key images through which later he will re-think the relationship between power and pleasure ('*perpetual spirals of power and pleasure'*[25]). Just as a major contribution of his *History of Sexuality* was to reorient our notion of power as a positive force that induces (rather than just negates) sexual desire, so in 'A Preface to Transgression' thirteen years earlier he was conceptualizing transgression as affirmative and creative rather than as simply oppositional.

Given how Foucault's work has been taken up in queer theory, it is significant that for him transgression does not 'achieve its purpose through mockery or by upsetting the solidity of foundations'. Transgression remains quite distinct from the antifoundationalist theories of parody, mimicry and performativity that came into vogue during the 1990s, in the wake of Judith Butler's *Gender Trouble.*[26] Even as queer theory drew inspiration from Foucault more than from any other philosopher, and even as queer critics spoke incessantly about transgression, Foucault's own account of transgression was quietly forgotten. Academics apparently prefer the Foucault of normalization and its subversion to the Foucault of transgression. This may be because the latter, in claiming that transgression 'affirms limited being', attributes to it a positive ontological status. It is easier to contest the arbitrary limits of historically variable socio-sexual norms than to wrestle with the internal limits that constitute one's own most intimate existence.

Practising transgression

The difference between transgressing internal limits and external limits is dramatized especially vividly in the work of John Rechy. A Chicano writer known for his sexually explicit renditions of the pre-Stonewall demi-monde in New York and Los Angeles, Rechy rose to prominence with *City of Night* (1963) and *Numbers* (1967), novels whose protagonists are hustlers and whose episodic narratives are structured around mostly anonymous sexual encounters. Paradoxical figures with equivocal identities, Rechy's hustlers cultivate their desirability by passing as straight, even as they live by – and for – having sex with other men. Since these figures repeatedly violate not only municipal laws and social norms but their own internal limits, Rechy represents them as outlaws, as walking embodiments of the eros of transgression. 'The promiscuous homosexual is a sexual revolutionary', he writes. 'Each moment of his outlaw existence he confronts repressive laws, repressive "morality."'[27]

Presented as a 'documentary', as closer to truth than fiction, Rechy's *The Sexual Outlaw* offers a post-Stonewall account of cruising that dates from 1977. Despite the themes it shares with *City of Night* and *Numbers*, this manifesto of transgression could hardly have been written a decade earlier, not just because of its boldness in handling the subject-matter but also because it explicitly treats 'the sexual outlaw' as a distinct minority. That conception is the product of the gay liberation movement. 'None more easily prosecuted – even so-called liberals condone his persecution – his is the only minority against whose existence there are laws', Rechy maintains.[28] His claim is that gays, a social minority constituted on the analogue of ethnic and racial minorities, stand at greater risk than other groups because our very existence threatens to transgress long-established laws. Such comparisons with the status of other minorities have generated controversy ever since sexual identities crystallized along the lines of a civil rights model. Rechy's writing captures the historical moment at which it first became possible to think of laws as directed not merely against certain sexual acts that might be performed by anyone, but against particular actors whose actions are coextensive with their political identity.

The Sexual Outlaw appeared shortly after the first volume of Foucault's *History of Sexuality* was published in France, but before it was translated into English. One of the most striking features of Rechy's book stems from its conviction that by saying yes to sex, 'the promiscuous homosexual' says no to power. His 'documentary' seems to exemplify the 'repressive hypothesis' that Foucault had just demolished. It is because Rechy conceives of power primarily in juridical terms, by focusing on 'repressive laws', that he defines his protagonists as outlaws. His conceiving of power in this way is a legacy of the civil rights framework within which homosexuality was constituted as a minority identity in the first place. Thus Rechy provocatively compares the sexual outlaw to Rosa Parks: 'When a courageous black woman in the South refused to move to the back of the bus, that was a revolutionary act – breaking the law in public. When gay people fuck and suck in the streets, that too is a revolutionary act. That's where *we* confront ignorant sex laws.'[29]

And yet *The Sexual Outlaw* also registers how the law actively solicits its own transgression: 'Widespread entrapment – creating the "crime" it insists it wants to curb – gives cops a destructive means of purging latent devils', Rechy argues.[30] Here he refers to the law-enforcement practice of undercover cops soliciting sexual encounters for which they then arrest their consenting participants, whether prostitutes or gay men in public places. His novel *This Day's Death* (1969) explores an incident in which the police entrap a man, Jim Girard, in Los Angeles's Griffith Park, focusing on how his life is mercilessly destroyed by the arbitrary yet nonetheless widely publicized arrest and trial. It can only be because it furnishes an outlet for policemen wishing to engage in homosexual activity without recognizing themselves as gay that the perverse practice of entrapment persists to this day.[31] Rather than as deterring homosexual activity in public, entrapment may be understood as a disavowed form of homosexual activity.

Although Rechy rails with considerable warrant against the injustice of such arrangements, he nevertheless appreciates the degree to which cruisers and the police depend on each other to sustain their desire. At certain times of night, urban locales such as Hollywood Boulevard in Rechy's Los Angeles are populated only by hustlers, their johns and the cops. *The Sexual Outlaw* describes the elaborate manoeuvres that these groups undertake in their dance of mediated desire, where transgression and the law go hand in hand. If, as Bataille suggests, eroticism 'is always a matter of going beyond the limits allowed', then 'repressive laws' and their uniformed agents provide the barriers that augment the lust of Rechy's sexual revolutionaries. It is not only the *law*'s desire that benefits from the intently illicit activities portrayed in his novels.

Towards the end of *The Sexual Outlaw*, Rechy acknowledges another, deeper contradiction. Conceding that sexual revolutionaries feel ambivalence about their own promiscuity, he suggests that 'we're fighting on two fronts – one on the streets, the other inside'.[32] In saying this, Rechy comes close to articulating the insight that Bataille and Foucault expressed more abstractly, namely, that above and beyond its framing in juridical terms, transgression is a matter of 'inner experience' or 'limit experience', an experience necessitating encounter not with external authorities but with the self.[33] His most sustained meditation on this aspect of transgression may be found in *Numbers*, a novel whose plot is organized around a strictly numerical limit that the protagonist imposes on himself in order precisely to transgress it.

Returning to Los Angeles, where he once worked as a hustler, Johnny Rio requires a new motive for his pursuit of as much anonymous sex as can be crammed into his ten-day visit. After seducing his twenty-first trick in Griffith Park, 'the horror that he *is* counting, accumulating numbers aimlessly, strikes his consciousness like a sniper's bullet'.[34] Without any conception of limits, the notion of erotic excess remains meaningless, and so Johnny invents the numerical limit of thirty, based on a 'feverish' calculation:

> I've been away three years. ... If I hadn't left, I would have made it with, say, 300 people in one year. ... In three years 900. ... I'm behind 900. ... How long would it take to catch up?. . . The least I've made it with in one day in the park is three. ... At least three a day ... into 900. ... that's 300. ... I could catch up in 300 days. ... But I came back for only 10 days, and that's exactly how long I'll stay. Ten into 300 – ...
> Thirty.
> That's it!
> *Thirty!*
> That's the goal![35]

This arithmetic evokes the strange persistence of counting in modern pornography, from de Sade's *120 Days of Sodom* to *Dawson's 20 Load Weekend*.[36] Johnny Rio's calculations make plain that the point of counting lies less in the challenge of meeting a quota, no matter how impressive, than in the discovery of a limit grounded in logic or reason – a secular limit. Thus Johnny thinks to himself, 'Now that the game has a winning score, the horror of counting toward no limit – of being swallowed by the Park – is actually gone.'[37] Relief comes neither from experiencing a series of orgasms nor from passing his self-imposed quantitative test, but from acknowledging a limit that somehow truly counts. A limit that counts lends meaning to excess and thereby makes transgression possible.

Numbers ends with Johnny's thirty-seventh trick ('*Thirty-seven!*'), just as *Dawson's 20 Load Weekend* ends with its eponymous star taking his twenty-fourth load of ejaculate on camera. The numerical limit turns out to be arbitrary after all. Far from abating, desire escalates with the accretion of 'numbers' or 'loads'. As Ricardo Ortiz points out, 'Johnny's tricks are named as numbers, as determinate quantitative values which accumulate as the hollow of Johnny's desire expands.'[38] In the final analysis, perhaps it is not desire but something else that motivates the accumulation of numbers. Certainly it is not a quest for sensual pleasure, insofar as Rechy's fiction is distinguished by an almost complete absence of pleasure throughout its narratives of sex.[39] His impulse to transcend the regulative limit of the pleasure principle situates Rechy squarely in the domain of eroticism as defined by Bataille.

The pornographic fiction of African-American writer Samuel R. Delany, in which excess takes many forms that nevertheless usually yield pleasure, represents a more complex case. Delany creates cosmologies in which what would be impossible in our world appears fully plausible, even unremarkable. Irrespective of the genre in which he's working, Delany pictures homosexuality as part of the order of things, rather than as threatening a transgression of them. Thus, unlike Rechy and others, he does not imagine that men having sex together in parks, public bathrooms or movie houses are necessarily revolutionary or transgressive. At the same time, Delany holds no brief for the putative 'naturalness' of homosexuality; what motivates sex among men is neither a biological nor a political imperative but, instead, a search for connection in which bodily contact offers an especially pleasurable means.

In novels such as *The Mad Man* (1994) or *Hogg* (1995), excess takes less quantitative than qualitative forms. It is the *kind* of sex his characters enjoy, not the fact that they have so much of it, that renders Delany's work ostensibly transgressive. For example, during the post-coital moments following a vividly described scene that results in climax for both its participants, the title character of *Hogg* remarks to the narrator:

'I think that was the one we both needed. Always been sort of partial to shit, 'specially my own. But you don't get much of a chance to fuck in your own, less you got a cocksucker who likes a face full of it now and then . . . 'Cause that's the way we're set up, us two. I'm the shit machine, and you're my personal shit bowl and pee pot, right?'[40]

In view of the fondness for excrement, we might note that a number of Delany's characters qualify as 'shit machine[s]' and that they never seem to lack a steady supply of enthusiastic partners ready to join in their scatological play. It is not only excrement and urine (and, of course, semen) but also mucus, sweat, smegma and, in one unforgettable scene, pus from a swollen infected glans that the young narrator of *Hogg* enjoys consuming. When, in the novel's final moments, he muses that 'the best thing out of a dick, no matter how dirty, is the cheese', we appreciate how, given his range of experience, the frame of comparison is unusually broad and therefore the judgment especially considered.[41]

Yet what makes Delany's fiction equivocally transgressive is that his characters rarely seem to struggle with the barrier of disgust that ordinarily prevents consumption of bodily excretions and waste. Either the space of abjection doesn't exist in his fictional worlds or else everything takes place on the far side of its taboo-laden perimeter.[42] Irrespective of how the reader experiences this fiction's scat play, there is little of the frisson associated with taboo-violation in the novels themselves. One never gets the impression that Delany is trying to shock his readers, whether for pedagogical purposes or otherwise. Instead, his scat play constitutes a central part of what Mary Foltz has anatomized as Delany's 'excremental ethic', one in which encounters with waste – whether of the human or the social body – open the self to experiences of pleasure that undo the self.[43] Rather than orienting his practice towards transgression, Delany focuses on all of the ways in which ostensibly rebarbative experiences and persons may yield pleasure.

Enlarging our appreciation of the capacity for pleasure entails acknowledging that it is not only adults who enjoy sex. The transgressive aspect of the scene quoted above is compounded by the fact that *Hogg*'s narrator, characterized here as 'a cocksucker who likes a face full of [shit] now and then', is an eleven-year-old boy. Well below the age of consent, he nevertheless participates with gusto in the erotic exploits of numerous adult men. As Rob Stephenson comments in his introduction to the novel's second edition, 'The unnamed boy who narrates *Hogg* is deliberately fashioned as the opposite of the "corruptible child." He is corruption itself.'[44] Yet, as the novel's central consciousness, this boy is also a wholly sympathetic character who, unlike some of Sade's young narrators, never bemoans his fate. He is the dark twin of all those youthful, ostensibly innocent narrators in the US literary tradition, such as Huckleberry Finn and Holden Caulfield, whose naïve perspective casts an ironic light on the events they narrate. By means of this eleven-year-old narrator, Delany, like other writers of transgressive fiction such as Dennis Cooper or Matthew Stadler, lays siege to our culture's cherished myth of childhood innocence.

Freud – who also went some way towards demystifying the idea of childhood innocence – argued that children fantasize erotic union with their parents, not that they actually want sex with them. Taking matters several steps further, Delany depicts a boy on the cusp of adolescence who not only fantasizes but avidly wants – and repeatedly gets – to partake in group sex, coprophagy and every form of sodomy imaginable with fully grown men. Doubtless it is *Hogg*'s violation of the taboo on intergenerational sex that accounts, at least in part, for Delany's difficulty getting the novel into print. Begun in 1969, around the time of the Stonewall riots, and completed in 1973, *Hogg* remained unpublished until almost a quarter century later, many sympathetic editors having considered it unpublishable despite their professed admiration for it.[45]

This novel's transgression of formal age-of-consent boundaries is compounded by its transgression of the more concrete boundaries of physical consent, in the form of rape, violence and murder. Although the young narrator's volition appears not to have been abrogated, his master makes his living as a rapist-for-hire who evidently relishes his work. The scenes of Hogg and his gang brutally raping various women are much harder to read than the extensive scenes involving consumption of bodily waste. That the narrator relates all these scenes with muted neutrality contributes to the novel's disturbing effect, whereby the *reader* is apt to feel that his or her consent has been tested and possibly transgressed.[46] In thus substantially pushing the limits of the readable, *Hogg* exemplifies Bataille's claim that eroticism manifests itself 'by bringing into play characters and scenes from the realm of the *impossible*'.

Texts such as Delany's *Hogg* or Bataille's pornographic fiction, with their scenes of violence and rape, require us to confront the politics and ethics of the literature of transgression.[47] Given that murder, rape and incest have been central to literary representation since the ancient Greeks, it cannot be a question of whether the depiction of these acts is permissible but of how their depiction is framed. Modern audiences are sufficiently distant from premodern representations of violence not to feel implicated in them; but pornography specializes in minimizing the distance between representation and audience, such that it is hard not to feel implicated in some way or another. If one is not aroused, one is likely to feel disgusted or horrified – or, worse, horrified and aroused at once. Transgressive literature tests the limits not only of social norms but also of its most progressive readers. Content to witness social norms and hierarchies being transgressed, we become much less comfortable when our own limits are infringed upon or violated. Usually the medium of representation, whether word or image, insulates its audience from any such violation (this is part of its appeal). But literary representation also has the capacity to bring us into contact with matters that otherwise would remain untouched, indeed, untouchable (this is partly why it has been censured since Plato). Literature, like sex, is not always 'safe'. The risk of transgressive literature – that it may expose the self to extreme boundary violation – is the source of its erotic power. Such a risk does not need to be politically defensible in order to be experienced as exciting; indeed, the reverse may be true. As with any kind of sexual experience, the erotics of transgression is not for everyone.

NOTES

1. Hart Crane, *The Poems of Hart Crane*, ed. Marc Simon (New York: Liveright, 1989), 34.
2. Michel Foucault, 'A Preface to Transgression', trans. Donald F. Bouchard and Sherry Simon, *The Essential Foucault: Selections from Essential Works of Foucault, 1954–1984*, ed. Paul Rabinow and Nikolas Rose (New York: New Press, 2003), 445.
3. Simon Sheppard, 'Discourse: Dick', in D. Travers Scott, ed., *Strategic Sex: Why They Won't Keep It in the Bedroom* (New York: Harrington Park Press, 1999), 75.
4. Ashley Tauchert, 'Against Transgression', *Critical Quarterly*, 50 (2008), 10.
5. Foucault, 'Preface', 445.
6. Georges Bataille, *The Accursed Share: An Essay on General Economy*, trans. Robert Hurley, 3 vols. (New York: Zone Books, 1993), vol. II: 177, original emphasis.
7. Foucault, 'Preface', 445.
8. See Eve Kosofsky Sedgwick, *Epistemology of the Closet* (Berkeley: University of California Press, 1990).
9. On Wilde's trial, see Ed Cohen, *Talk on the Wilde Side: Towards a Genealogy of a Discourse on Male Sexualities* (New York: Routledge, 1993). The phrase 'the love that dare not speak its name', which featured prominently in the trial, comes from Lord Alfred Douglas's poem 'Two Loves'. The line 'Only a few hints, a few diffused faint clews and indirections' comes from Whitman's poem 'When I Read the Book', in *Leaves of Grass*.
10. See Linda Williams, 'Second Thoughts on *Hard Core*: American Obscenity Law and the Scapegoating of Deviance', in Pamela Church Gibson and Roma Gibson, eds., *Dirty Looks: Women, Pornography, Power* (London: British Film Institute,

1993), 46–61. See also Edward de Grazia, *Girls Lean Back Everywhere: The Law of Obscenity and the Assault on Genius* (New York: Random House, 1992).

11. Bataille, *Accursed Share*, vol. II: 116 and 117, original emphases.

12. Crane, *Poems*, 35 and 36.

13. Bataille, *Accursed Share*, vol. II: 119.

14. *Ibid.*, 124, original emphases.

15. Foucault, *The History of Sexuality: An Introduction*, trans. Robert Hurley (London: Allen Lane, 1979), 157.

16. Sigmund Freud, *Totem and Taboo*, in James Strachey, ed. and trans., *The Standard Edition of the Complete Psychological Works of Sigmund Freud* (London: Hogarth Press, 1955), vol. XIII: 18.

17. *Ibid.*

18. *Ibid.*, 26–7.

19. On *Howl*'s obscenity trial, see de Grazia, *Girls Lean Back*, Chapter 17.

20. Foucault, 'Preface', 449.

21. Freud, *Totem and Taboo*, 18.

22. Bataille, *Accursed Share*, vol. II: 92, original emphases. The Italian philosopher Giorgio Agamben has developed the structural ambiguity of *sacer* in a different, though related, direction. See Agamben, *Homo Sacer: Sovereign Power and Bare Life*, trans. Daniel Heller-Roazen (Stanford: Stanford University Press, 1998).

23. Bataille, *Accursed Share*, vol. II: 96.

24. Foucault, 'Preface', 446.

25. Foucault, *History of Sexuality*, 45, original emphasis.

26. Judith Butler, *Gender Trouble: Feminism and the Subversion of Identity* (New York: Routledge, 1990).

27. John Rechy, *The Sexual Outlaw: A Documentary* (New York: Grove Press, 1977), 28.

28. *Ibid.*

29. *Ibid.*, 71, original emphasis.

30. *Ibid.*, 29.

31. A particularly high-profile case of entrapment involved the closeted Republican senator from Idaho, Larry Craig, who was arrested on 11 June 2007, for soliciting sex from an undercover cop in a toilet of the Minneapolis-St. Paul International Airport.

32. Rechy, *The Sexual Outlaw*, 286.

33. What Bataille means by 'inner experience' and Foucault by 'limit experience' is analysed expertly in Martin Jay, *Songs of Experience: Modern American and European Variations on a Universal Theme* (Berkeley: University of California Press, 2005), Chapter 9.

34. Rechy, *Numbers*, rev. edn (New York: Grove Press, 1984), 190, original emphasis.

35. *Ibid.*, 190–1, original emphases and ellipses.

36. *Dawson's 20 Load Weekend* (dir. Max Sohl, Treasure Island Media, 2004) is a cult classic of bareback moving-image porn produced by the renegade San Francisco pornographer Paul Morris. On the phenomenon of this subculture's pornography, with its commitments to transgressing safer-sex norms and to tabulating the number of 'loads' ingested by bareback 'power bottoms', see Tim Dean, *Unlimited Intimacy: Reflections on the Subculture of Barebacking* (Chicago: University of Chicago Press, 2009).

37. Rechy, *Numbers*, 191.
38. Ricardo L. Ortiz, 'John Rechy and the Grammar of Ostentation', in Sue-Ellen Case, Philip Brett and Susan Leigh Foster, eds., *Cruising the Performative: Interventions into the Representation of Ethnicity, Nationality, and Sexuality* (Bloomington: Indiana University Press, 1995), 62–3.
39. I owe this insight to Kevin Arnold, '"Male and Male and Male": John Rechy and the Scene of Representation', unpublished manuscript.
40. Samuel R. Delany, *Hogg*, 2nd edn (Normal, IL: Fiction Collective 2, 2004), 263.
41. *Ibid.*, 267.
42. See Julia Kristeva, *Powers of Horror: An Essay on Abjection*, trans. Leon S. Roudiez (New York: Columbia University Press, 1982).
43. See Mary Catherine Foltz, 'The Excremental Ethics of Samuel R. Delany', *SubStance*, 37:2 (2008), 41–55.
44. Rob Stephenson, 'Introduction', in Delany, *Hogg*, n.p.
45. See Samuel R. Delany, 'The Making of *Hogg*', *Shorter Views: Queer Thoughts and the Politics of the Paraliterary* (Hanover, NH: Wesleyan University Press, 1999), 298–310.
46. For an acute analysis of the complex readerly experience entailed in navigating *Hogg* (and a generally excellent account of Delany's pornographic novels), see Ray Davis, 'Delany's Dirt', in James Sallis, ed., *Ash of Stars: On the Writing of Samuel R. Delany* (Jackson: University Press of Mississippi, 1996), 177.
47. For Bataille's pornographic fiction, see *Blue of Noon*, trans. Harry Matthews (London: Marion Boyars, 1979) and *Story of the Eye*, trans. Joachim Neugroschal (Harmondsworth: Penguin, 1982).

5

HUGH STEVENS

Normality and queerness
in gay fiction

In 1955 the British journalist and playwright Peter Wildeblood explained in *Against the Law*, an *apologia pro vita sua* he wrote after serving a prison sentence in HM Prison Wormwood Scrubs for homosexual offences, that society should tolerate good homosexuals like himself, but not 'the pathetically flamboyant pansy with the flapping wrists ... corrupters of youth, not even the effeminate creatures who love to make an exhibition of themselves'.[1] Wildeblood's argument for tolerance works by opposing a notion of decent homosexuality, which he believes should be legitimized, to demonized constructions of homosexuality – the elderly predator, the effeminate queen – from which he distances himself. This kind of opposition is precisely the kind of gesture challenged by 'queer' theory and activism.

Although 'queer' became popular as a category in American lesbian and gay politics and scholarship in the early 1990s, the conflicts the term addressed have a long history in lesbian and gay culture. Formerly a term of abuse, 'queer' began to be used by lesbians and gay men to describe themselves. Used as a self-description, queer re-emphasized the dissident and subversive potential of gay and lesbian identities, and embraced elements of sexual culture, such as drag, fetishism, sadomasochism and cruising, which mainstream lesbian and gay politics were seen as disavowing.

In the United States, the homophile movement of the 1950s and 1960s aimed to present lesbians and gay men as decent, well-dressed and professionally respectable citizens in order to make political progress. Groups like the Mattachine Society and the Daughters of Bilitis believed that they needed 'to accommodate themselves to a society that excoriated homosexual behavior', and 'impressed upon their gay constituency the need to adjust to normative standards of proper behavior'.[2] Yet these organizations were often challenged by more militant gay men and women who 'insisted that society had to do the adjusting', and who vocally criticized the movement leadership for attempting to enforce gender conformity.[3] Organizers of demonstrations in this period often insisted on strict dress codes: participants were required to dress in conservative clothing perceived as appropriate to their gender, dresses for women, suit and tie for men.[4]

The gay liberation movement of the 1970s, while reacting against the anodyne image of the homophile movement, was divided between those who thought gay activism should work pragmatically to achieve particular goals, and those who saw homosexuality as valuable in that it radically questioned the social structure and worked against strictures of gender conformity and the privileging of the monogamous couple.[5] Debates were waged, and continue to be waged, not only about what lesbian and gay culture consists of, but also about how this culture should present itself. In 1980 Edmund White described tensions between the politics of normality and the politics of queerness in gay politics. White called the 'political choice' between assimilation and radicalism 'a central disagreement ... a question of principles as much as tactics'. Assimilationists, whom White considered the 'majority', believe 'that most gays are essentially like straights save for the seemingly disturbing but actually neutral matter of affectional preference ... Gay subculture ... is merely defensive, a ghetto created by prejudice and likely to dissolve once gays are integrated into the mainstream.' (The views White deftly outlines found full expression in two jeremiads of the 1990s, Bruce Bawer's *A Place at the Table* and Andrew Sullivan's *Virtually Normal*, both of which rather too neatly demonstrate how the affirmation of normality can also involve the repudiation of queerness. Sullivan and Bawer seem almost to have been invented by the queers they don't want to dine with.[6]) On the other hand, White claimed, 'Radical gays deplore almost everything about this approach. As a strategy, it is dangerously wrong.' Whereas assimilationists, by insisting on the virtual normality of lesbian and gay identities, worked 'at the price of disowning the more bizarre elements in the gay community', radicals 'might say we are only as strong as our most exposed flank ... It does no good to disown questionable elements in gay life; we must defend them.' According to White, 'radicals have no desire to see gays normalized and turned into useful members of the system as it now exists. They believe that gays can serve as a vanguard of a liberation movement that might transform American society into something better, more humane, more equitable, less repressed.'[7]

The AIDS epidemic gave new urgency to these debates, and activism began to challenge assimilationist lesbian and gay politics more aggressively. In March 1990 the activist group 'Queer Nation' was founded in New York. Queer Nation grew out of ACT UP (the Aids Coalition To Unleash Power), the radical, wonderfully effective and theatrical protest organization formed in 1987 with the specific aim of raising awareness of AIDS and challenging homophobia and government inaction.[8] Queer Nation continued ACT UP's agenda of fighting heteronormativity and homophobia, but also challenged the affirmation of normative gay and lesbian identities at the expense of other, more troubling affiliations such as S/M or transgender. Queer political activism insisted on the importance of a coalition of oppositional and unstable differences, rather than the single, reifying difference of homosexual and heterosexual. If the concepts of 'homosexual' and 'heterosexual' were used to demarcate individual identities and, concomitantly, distinct groups of individuals, 'queer', a term which is intrinsically relational (opposing itself to 'normal'), worked to blur the clarity of all dividing lines, and to emphasize the strangeness and instability of sexual identities.[9]

The queer of activism quickly migrated into the academy, and the early 1990s saw a number of foundational works in the new discipline (or anti-discipline) of 'queer theory'. In 1993, Eve Kosofsky Sedgwick's *Tendencies* characterized the present as 'a QUEER time ... the moment of Queer'.[10] Queer theory forged alliances between the new pluralism of queer activism on the one hand and post-structuralist or postmodern critiques of identity on the other. Sedgwick characterized queer theory and politics as 'antiseparatist' *and* 'antiassimilationist', 'relational, and strange' (xii). Queer theory aimed to preserve the radical potential and anger of queer activism, and to avoid what it perceived as the stultifying straitjacket of lesbian and gay identities. It wanted to protest against discrimination on the basis of sexual identity, even though it was suspicious of identity categories, which, as Judith Butler claimed in her influential essay 'Imitation and Gender Insubordination' (1991), 'tend to be instruments of regulatory regimes, whether as the normalizing categories of oppressive structures or as the rallying points for a liberatory contestation of that very oppression'.[11] For Sedgwick, while queer could 'denote, almost simply, same-sex object choice, lesbian or gay', the term was exciting in that it worked 'outward along dimensions that can't be subsumed under gender and sexuality at all', dimensions such as 'race, ethnicity, postcolonial nationality' (8–9).

The term's expansiveness and ambiguity – what Michael Warner calls its 'deliberately capacious way' of suggesting 'how many ways people can find themselves at odds with straight culture'[12] – are both strengths and limitations. In his work on queer theory, Lee Edelman says that he takes 'queers' to be beings who are 'stigmatised for failing to comply with heteronormative mandates'.[13] These ways of thinking about queerness can make it difficult to see who might mobilize under the sign of queer. To be unqueer, how many such mandates do you need to comply with? To be queer, do you need to resist one, some, several or all such mandates? And how much, and how often, do you need to be stigmatized? Will it be sufficient to be at odds with the Pope, or with Evangelical pastor Rick Warren? (As the character Fritz drawls lugubriously in Christopher Isherwood's *Goodbye to Berlin*, 'Eventually we're all queer.'[14] We are getting used to this.) When queer is thus defined, it is unclear just who can lay claim to, or repudiate, a queer identity. In aspiring to embrace a range of oppositional identities, 'queer' can ignore the ways in which some marginalized sexual identities and behaviours are more marginalized, and discriminated against, than others. It can also ignore the extent to which queerness is dependent on context: a monogamous gay couple might seem quaintly normal in London's Soho, but dangerously queer in rural Yorkshire.

This single, umbrella term was overdetermined and over-worked, has acquired some of the monolithic status it aimed to resist, and lost some of the subtlety of other articulations of the politics of sexuality, such as that advanced by Gayle Rubin in her 1984 essay, 'Thinking Sex'. Rubin identified what she called 'hierarchies of sexual value – religious, psychiatric and popular', which separated 'good, normal, natural, blessed' sexuality from that which was perceived as 'bad, abnormal, unnatural, damned'.[15] Rubin identified the multiple ways in which these hierarchies worked, opposing approved and proscribed behaviours and sexualities according to a set of binary oppositions (see Table 1).

Note that the opposed terms in each pairing do not necessarily exclude each other: an individual might, for instance, enjoy sex alone, in pairs *and* in groups. Rubin's schema might help you generate for yourself a tally of points showing how blessed or damned you are (though it fails to account for individuals who are not very interested in sex at all, or, say, for bisexuals, who might be both heterosexual and homosexual, or neither). Add up your blessed points, dear reader, and add up your damned, to arrive at two scores out of twelve. What you do with your test result is up to you.

Table 1

heterosexual	homosexual
married	unmarried
monogamous	promiscuous
procreative	non-procreative
non-commercial	commercial
in pairs	alone or in groups
in a relationship	casual
same-generation	cross-generational
in private	in public
no pornography	pornography
bodies only	manufactured objects
vanilla	sadomasochistic

Whether sexual identity is conceived of as stable or mobile, this array of oppositions suggests ways in which individuals are neither wholly queer nor wholly normal. A radical politics of sexuality might be one which challenges hierarchical thinking and the stigmatizing of 'damned' sexualities, but does not require that those making these challenges should themselves identify with these damned forms. Such a politics would separate the impossibility of leading a life of virtuous normality or absolute queerness from the possibility of broadly challenging hierarchies of sexual value, regardless of the extent to which one's own identity is queer or normal, and from the further possibility of working on specific sexual agendas, such as the legal status of particular sexual acts, the recognition of bisexuality, HIV/AIDS activism, the bullying of kids perceived to be 'queer' (whether 'gay' or gender-dissonant), the rights of sex workers, or the rights of same-sex couples (immigration, inheritance, access to health care, parenting). Just as the limitations of the opposition between homosexual and heterosexual can obscure the plurality and specificity of these agendas, so too can the utopian embrace of queerness. As Leo Bersani wrote in *Homos*, 'It is not possible to be gay-affirmative, or politically effective as gays, if gayness has no specificity.'[16]

Post-Stonewall lesbian and gay fiction, while showing some affinities with queer politics and theory, is difficult to classify as either assimilationist or antiassimilationist. It depends on what books you read, and how you read them. Fiction tells stories; readers respond. 'Yes – oh, dear, yes – the novel tells a story,' as E. M. Forster has it (his campy isolation, with commas and dashes, of 'dear' gives his claim an air of worldly resignation which belies the wit and great pleasures of his own story-telling).[17] Yet stories told in the pages of published fiction (a small and privileged minority of stories) were, until the last decades of the twentieth century, only rarely stories of 'lesbians', 'gay men' or 'homosexuals'. Some of those novels which did tell lesbian stories and gay stories openly were either prosecuted (Radclyffe Hall's *The Well of Loneliness*, D. H. Lawrence's *The Rainbow*) or not submitted for publication (Forster's *Maurice*, which was published posthumously). Many novels – Thomas Mann's *Death in Venice*, André Gide's *The Immoralist*, Proust's *Remembrance of Things Past*, Djuna Barnes's *Nightwood*, the novels of William Burroughs or John Rechy – tell inspiring stories of same-sex desire, but characters in this diverse group of books rarely experience their same-sex desire as 'ordinary'. If queer theory opposed the assertion of normative gay and lesbian identities, then it rarely needs to reproach fiction written before modern queer politics – before the politics of 'coming out' which began in 1969 shortly after the Stonewall riots[18] – for its presentation of queer normalcy. (Even Forster's *Maurice*, that most suburban and conventional of homosexuals, has a cross-class relationship and has to flee to some vaguely located greenwood.)

The tension between assimilationism and queerness which characterizes gay and lesbian culture has not resulted in two stories – a story of the normal gay man or lesbian as opposed to the story of radically perverted queers – but in a plurality of stories. If you read Dennis Cooper's *The Sluts* (2004), for instance, you will find described a world of violent sex with hustlers whose clients post reviews online for other potential clients to read.[19] Characters in novels by Alan Hollinghurst, like *The Swimming-Pool Library* (1988), *The Spell* (1998) or *The Line of Beauty* (2004), enjoy adventurous sex lives but are in most respects conservative rather than radical; cruising and sex in these novels are forms of entertainment, pleasurable diversions rather than acts of resistance.[20] The gay man of Hollinghurst's fiction does not confine his sex life to mono-gamous couplehood, but in other ways he is an establishment figure, wanting to resist the status quo only when the status quo is hostile to homosexuality.

Even those novelists who might be understood as assimilationist are involved in a process of re-making, exploring ethical situations and the difficulty of relationships rather than showing how relationships survive or fall apart to the extent that they conform to, or resist, a pre-existing set of rules or values. Consider the case of David Leavitt, a writer whose humour and irony remind me of E. M. Forster. April, the lesbian folk singer in his novel *Equal Affections* (1989), writes a song called 'Living Together', which celebrates the relationship of her young brother Danny and his lover Walter.[21] Danny and Walter, both lawyers, commute to New York from Gresham, New Jersey, and are members of the town's 'Gay Homeowner's Association' (24), which meets at the Unitarian Church and discusses how homophobia affects their lives. (Mady Kroger knows that the lady who looks at her in the supermarket is thinking, 'What a dyke' (24).) Here is how April introduces her song at gigs: 'Sometimes I think the most political thing a gay man or woman can do is to live openly with another gay man or woman' (25). And her song tells how Danny and Walter have renounced a life of bath-houses and bars for one of lace curtains and commuting:

> *After the years of the baths and the bars*
> *And the one-night stands in the backseats of cars*
> *And the nights we spent with so many different men*
> *It feels so good to come home to you again.*   (24)

Leavitt juxtaposes April's song with a novelistic glimpse of Danny and Walter:

> So: what was it really like, their living together. Danny and Walter are sitting in the living room on a Sunday afternoon, their pants round their ankles, having just watched *Bigger in Texas* on the VCR.   (25)

86

The folksong idealizes, but Leavitt's novel shows a couple of unequal affections ('If equal affection cannot be, / Let the more loving one be me', is Leavitt's epigraph, from W. H. Auden's poem 'The More Loving One'), a couple negotiating sexual boredom. If Danny thinks that the baths and the bars are April's invention, neither of them 'having ever done more than dip his toes in the great, cold, clammy river of promiscuity' (25), his perceptions of Walter are naïve. Walter has secret plans: he wants to 'find someone else – someone fresh and young, as Danny had once been' (78). He has a further secret, a secret life (why else would he be called Walter?[22]) led on computer chatrooms, a world in which men with queer monikers – 'Hot Leather', 'Teen Slave Master', 'don, 17', 'New York Jock', 'Sweatpants' and 'Bulstrode' – arrange to meet each other, or fantasize with each other while typing with one hand (79–80, 133). Bulstrode's pseudonym suggests the world of George Eliot's *Middlemarch*, a world in which married life is fraught with difficulty and conflict. Another work from F. R. Leavis's 'great tradition' of fiction makes its presence felt in *Equal Affections*: Danny's mother, Louise, watches *Women in Love* on cable (presumably Ken Russell's film, scripted by Larry Kramer), and fantasizes over memories of her affair with Tommy Burns, whom she loved more passionately than her husband Nat, a computer scientist. Leavitt gently reminds us that marriage, in English fiction, is critiqued as much as it is celebrated, and his queer characters, no less than the characters of George Eliot or D. H. Lawrence, have to negotiate a world whose guidelines may be inadequate and whose forms may need to be re-created. A gay or lesbian identity is something both given and questioned, fixed and provisional, and so it is both different from and similar to a straight identity, or even a Jewish or Christian identity. Danny's father Nat is having an affair with another woman; and Louise, his mother, dying of cancer, is considering changing faith, abandoning Judaism for Catholicism. And April, who has no interest in Catholicism, has gotten pregnant using a turkey baster and sperm donated by her tall, good-looking gay friend Tom Neibauer. (Hearing this news, Danny is ready with a helpful question: 'has he had an AIDS test?' (129).) Nat, Louise, Danny and April do not form a family which exiles its queer members (if it did, not much of a family would be left), but a family involved in a complex dance (to use a metaphor from Leavitt's first collection of stories, *Family Dancing*) which demands great flexibility from the dancers.

'We're here, we're queer, get used to it,' was Queer Nation's most celebrated chant, a slogan which raises a question about the very future of queerness. If the slogan is successful, how queer will we be once our auditors have acceded to our demands? Leavitt's fiction portrays an America in the process of getting used to queerness. On 31 May 1982, *The New Yorker* published Leavitt's short story 'Territory' (Leavitt was only twenty; this was a remarkable debut). The magazine had begun occasionally to publish stories with gay themes in the late seventies – one notable example is Ann Beattie's brilliant story 'The Cinderella Waltz',[23] a minimalist *What Maisie Knew* in which a little girl copes admirably with a life consisting of weekdays with her mother and weekends with her father and his male lover. Leavitt's story, however, was notable for the specificity with which it described the specialized sexual culture of American gay urban communities. If anyone in 1982 were to walk thirty or so blocks south and a couple of blocks west from *The New Yorker*'s offices on Manhattan's West 43rd Street, they would have encountered the commercial gay scene of Greenwich Village, the 'West Village', centring on Christopher Street, with its bars, saunas (or 'bathhouses'), sex-shops, pornographic cinemas, S&M clubs, gay bookstores, gay restaurants, and a sexual ambience so cruisy that the street itself was a place of close encounters of the intimate kind, a place where you could depend on the kindness of strangers. In *States of Desire*, Edmund White called Greenwich Village 'the gay ghetto . . . the epitome of gay sex the world over' (265). White gave generous, intimate and explicit portraits of New York institutions like the St Mark's Baths (a gay bathhouse) and the Mine Shaft (a gay sex club), and described a milieu in which 'Sex is performed with strangers, romance is captured in brief affairs, friendship is assigned to friends. In this formula, one notices, the only stable element is friendship' (287).

This world and its formula, however, were not customarily represented in the elegant upper-middle-brow pages of *The New Yorker*, in its cartoons, attractive covers (often delightful pictures of Manhattan), its event listings, or, indeed, its writing. Neil, the 23-year-old protagonist of 'Territory', is aware of the erotic potential of 'the scene', but thinks of 'bathhouses and back rooms, enemas and poppers, wordless sex in alleyways' as 'dangers' to be avoided, dangers nevertheless identified for the prestigious magazine's readers.[24] Neil and his lover Wayne visit Neil's mother in her comfortable Northern Californian home, with its swimming pool and its obligatory shirtless and nameless Chicano gardener, just right for drooling over while catching rays. Wayne is Neil's 'lover of ten months and the only person he has ever imagined he could spend his life with' (4), and this is the first time Neil has brought a lover home. Although the gay scene is mentioned, the territory of Leavitt's story is that of domesticity and coupledom.

Leavitt's story, however, does not innocently or unwittingly disparage the erotic territory explored so boldly by gay writers of the 1970s in works such as Larry Kramer's prurient and censorious satire *Faggots*, or Andrew Holleran's rapturous but melancholy *Dancer from the Dance*, two novels published in 1978. Instead, it signals an awareness of where it stands in relation to an urban gay commercial scene and posits that relationship in generational terms. Homosexualities inhabit many 'territories', and these territories relate to each other knowingly, sometimes pleasurably, sometimes anxiously. Four years earlier, when Neil was nineteen, he attended a Gay Pride Parade in San Francisco. Travelling to the city by train the previous evening, he meets Luis, 'a dark-skinned man wearing bluejeans and a leather jacket', a man with a 'thick mustache' (15); he intends to spend only a night with Luis, but this night grows into a year. Luis accompanies Neil to the parade, and in the morning light he 'looked older ... more likely to carry diseases' (15). Neil thinks to himself that 'Luis possessed the peculiar combination of hypermasculinity and effeminacy which exemplifies faggotry' (16). On the parade they meet Neil's mother, who is supporting the Parade as president (natch) of the 'Coalition of Parents and Gays' (16). Neil hopes Mom won't meet his butch but also femme dark faggot friend, and when Luis introduces himself and shakes Mrs Campbell's hand, 'wanted to warn his mother to wash it, warned himself to check with a V.D. clinic first thing Monday' (17). The gap between Neil and Luis can be read in many ways. Is this liberal WASP embarrassed by being linked with Latin Luis, whom he would more comfortably think of as a gardener than a lover? Is the sexually timid youngster made anxious by the older man's sexual experiences, warned against in the pamphlets his well-intentioned mother would distribute to the leather- and denim-clad patrons of San Francisco's 'Bulldog Baths' and 'Liberty Baths' (8)? (According to Randy Shilts, the Bulldog Baths was the 'largest gay bathhouse in the world', and 'something of a legend in sexual circles'.[25] The Bulldog Baths and the Liberty Baths, along with San Francisco's twelve other gay bathhouses, were all closed by law in 1984 in response to the AIDS epidemic.[26] In New York, health officials closed the Mine Shaft and St Mark's Baths late in 1985.[27])

For any reader familiar with American gay culture at the time this story was published, however, Neil's discomfort with Luis would be all too clearly legible. Neil is embarrassed by being seen with a 'clone' – a man adopting a rigid gay style made up of moustache, toned body and a recognizable sexual uniform, the staples of which were blue jeans, tight t-shirts or plaid flannel shirts and the leather jacket. The clone was, among other things, one of the recognizable – not 'closeted' – faces of gayness, which Neil was supposedly marching to celebrate. But Neil, we are told, 'was never proud', and is ashamed of his Luis, whom he takes 'a year to dump' (17).

Neil and Wayne want a life in which they can move from New York to the suburbs and back, cross boundary lines, move between territories. In the 1970s, the erotic city was often seen as antithetical to the suburbs, small towns and the country; the emerald city was where one headed to escape these intolerant spaces. Andrew Holleran opens *Dancer from the Dance* with two 'circuit queens' discussing, in an epistolary exchange, the possibility of gay fiction. 'Gay life fascinates you', one writes, 'only because it is the life you were condemned to live. But if you were a family man going home on the 5:43 to Chappaqua, I don't think you'd want to read about men who suck each others wee-wees!'[28] Neil is embarrassed by such men precisely because his mother has read about them and has TMI (too much information) about what they do; he shudders when he recalls his 'brief and lamentable' experience of the dangers of the gay urban scene, he 'winced at the thought that she knew all his sexual secrets' (8). A mother who accepts her son's homosexuality might also be a mother who has some influence over his adult sexual life. To Wayne's criticism that 'You have this great mother, and all you do is complain. I know people whose mothers have disowned them', Neil replies that 'Guilt goes with the territory' (26). The dream of gay liberation, to remake human relationships without reference to prior heterosexual models, founders in Leavitt's story not because of intolerance, but because of an acceptance which comes with strings attached. The freedom and melancholy of desire give way to the constrictions and bonds of love.

Whereas the characters of Leavitt's fiction avoid what they think of as 'the late-night, cigarette-reeking prowl of the city', a 'rank garden . . . with its brief yet intense gratifications' (*Equal Affections*, 109), Edmund White's writing – both his fiction and his non-fiction – has always celebrated sex, and has never restricted sex to the confines of a relationship. 'We thought having sex was a positive good, the more the better', the narrator of *The Farewell Symphony* (1997) tells us, recalling his life in the 1970s. 'We wanted sexual friends, loving comrades, multiple husbands in a whole polyandry of desire. Exclusivity was a form of death – worse, old hat.'[29] If White celebrates the 1970s, he also imagines and designs the new hats required to chart the ethical and emotional territory of AIDS with great sensitivity. In 1977 *The Joy of Gay Sex*, which White co-wrote with his therapist Charles Silverstein, claimed that 'Gay couples are in an advantageous position for devising new relationships that truly suit their needs.'[30] Living with HIV and AIDS intensifies the need to devise new relationships, just as it makes this devising more difficult.

In White's *The Married Man*, the central character, Austin, a 49-year-old American writer living in Paris, is not married. It is 1989, and Austin is HIV-positive and has already lost several friends to AIDS. Austin meets Julien – the eponymous 'married man' – a young Frenchman who has separated from his wife and is about to be divorced. The title is a tease, making us ask whether Austin too is 'married' in any way. Meeting Julien and forming a relationship with him are processes which throw ethical questions in Austin's way, questions which are not answered in existing statute books, etiquette guides or even by the precedent of common practice. When, for instance, should Austin let Julien know of his HIV status? Before they form a relationship? (But how do we know when a relationship is formed?) Before they have sex? (If one is having 'safe' or 'safer' sex, does one need to tell every sexual partner one's serostatus?) What obligations does Austin have towards his ex, Peter, who lives in New York but whom Austin had promised 'he'd take care of ... if he ever came down with AIDS'?[31] Should Austin also explain this prior obligation, or commitment, before getting involved with Julien?

White's novel doesn't give us any clear answers to these questions. Rather it shows its characters making up the rules as they go along: the rules are provisional, improvised, pragmatic, negotiable. Austin hadn't considered the possibility of Julien himself being positive: how could a 'married man' come into contact with a 'gay' virus, a 'gay' disease? But a doctor, concerned by some of Julien's health problems, angers Julien by suggesting that he should be tested. Julien tests positive, and his symptoms – some unusually persistent acne, a stubborn cough, a susceptibility to flu, a wart on his penis that won't go away – suggest that he may have been positive for some time. Soon Austin, seropositive but asymptomatic, a 'slow progresser', finds himself with a partner and an ex both suffering from AIDS. Austin hopes that Julien and Peter will not be jealous of each other, will allow him to give them both his care and affection.

Austin's hopes are dashed when Peter and Julien fall out with each other in Mexico, where the three men are holidaying together. Regarding himself as 'a product of the unpossessive 1970s', Austin had 'always thought gay men shouldn't pair off in little monogamous units' (100). So he is shocked to find that Peter and Julien's mutual antagonism forces him to make a choice between them. Peter expresses the situation harshly, in terms Austin objects to. When he tells Peter that 'one of you has to compromise and adjust a bit', Peter comes back: 'So it should be *me*, I guess, who adjusts ... since he's your boyfriend and he's *schtupping* you' (152). Peter's 'I guess' is significant, as there do seem to be some rules of priority, but the three men can't agree on them. Just as Leavitt portrays generational differences in attitudes towards promiscuity, White contrasts the older Austin's commitment to open relationships with the two younger men's views on emotional commitment within relationships. Austin feels that the situation is so difficult because Julien 'had bad, heterosexual values. As the new wife he, Julien, assumed he had the right to insist that Austin never talk to the ex-wife, Peter, much less shower the castoff with attentions and presents. Only heterosexuals could be so cruel; among male homosexuals friendships ruled supreme' (170–1). Yet what authority can Austin appeal to, in order to identify and evaluate homosexual and heterosexual values, or to learn what to do if one's multiple husbands or wives do not get along with one another? The 'polyandry of desire' White celebrates in *The Farewell Symphony* proves difficult to realize in *The Married Man*.

Austin reaches for an identity – the idea of a homosexual identity – to help him to evaluate the situation, but *The Married Man* (like queer theory) disrupts attempts to connect identity with values. Questions such as whether gay couples should holiday with one or more exes, or how we care for those who are ill, are questions fiction can pose with great eloquence, as fiction enables the reader to inhabit the situation. And fiction can be valuable not because it answers such questions, but because it leaves them as problems for the reader. There are no consensual answers; this is the way we live now.

If Austin's notions of appropriate gay or homosexual values are challenged by the demands of caring for two loved ones with AIDS, he doesn't consider that he can turn to queer theory for any answers. Queer theory has an unflattering cameo role in the novel. In 1990 Austin returns to the United States to take up a position teaching the history of French furniture at Brown University. His reunion with his *patria* is less than joyful. He finds himself at odds with the values enforced by his employing institution. Some of Austin's female students regard his views on women and history as offensive (131). Another student, hoping to learn about the semiotics of furniture – how to 'deconstruct' a chair or two – drops Austin's course when he learns that Austin is more interested in how furniture is *constructed* (161). Austin's absence from the United States during the 1980s has made him unaware of political and theoretical developments in the American academy. One of Austin's colleagues explains that the most harmful theory is that which

> touches on feminism or queer theory.'
> 'I never needed to *theorize* about being queer,' Austin said, batting his eyes.
> 'Don't for a moment imagine that the fact you actually are queer gives you a leg up ... the idea that their professor is a sexually active being amounts to an admission of rape or at best sexual harassment.'　　　　　(162)

Austin's rebuttal might be taken as the glib remark of someone who embodies the kind of unreconstructed male gay identity queer theory set out to critique, and Austin's (presumably straight) friend's concurrence seems just as unreconstructed. But to dismiss this dismissal is to miss a serious point White is making. Queer theory regards queer as subversive of authority, but here it is equated with academic authority, an authority which Austin's queer or gay *life* subverts. Whereas queer theory is often understood as celebrating the disturbing power of sexuality to undo identity, this fictional exchange posits 'queer' as something so *theoretical* that it evades the actual sexed and sexual body, so that it is hostile to, firstly, a man identifying as 'gay' but not seeing his gayness through the enabling lens of queer theory, and, secondly, an older gay man with a sex life. A similar complaint has been made in a more academic context by Leo Bersani, in his book *Homos*, where he discusses a process he calls 'de-gaying gayness'. 'Queer', Bersani notes, 'repeats, with pride, a pejorative straight word for homosexual even as it unloads the term's homosexual referent ... For oppressed groups to accept the queer label is to identify themselves as being actively at odds with a male-dominated, white, capitalistic, heterosexist culture ... This generous definition puts all resisters in the same queer bag – a universalizing move I appreciate but that fails to specify the sexual distinctiveness of the resistance.'[32] More recently Bersani has written that 'Queer intellectuals are curiously reticent about the sexuality they claim to celebrate.'[33]

Bersani does not say so in quite so many words, but he suggests that part of the reason 'queer' has been so successful within the domain of literary studies is that its amorphous radicalism, its deconstructive deferral or questioning of actual sexual identities, enable one to keep one's eyes averted from the shaming and shameful spectacle of gay men having sex. And while there is a large body of literary writing – gay fiction since the 1970s – in which men are represented as having sex with each other, queer theory has paid this writing surprisingly little attention.

In *The Married Man*, Austin behaves in ways which show little respect for the differences between 'gay' and 'queer'. He has lots of sex with men, not only with his partners but also with men he meets cruising. He and his French lover Julien suffer from the absence of legal recognition of gay relationships: they are seriously inconvenienced because Julien has no rights to reside in the US as Austin's partner, and has no entitlement to medication under Austin's health insurance policy. How retrograde, unchic and unqueer of Austin to think of himself as possessing a 'gay identity' (rather than seeing his queerness as subversive of identity), and to be so normatively masculine as to be bored by drag, even though he enjoys camp telephone calls with his younger friend Gregg, the Daughter who chides Mother Austin as an 'old Stonewaller' and a 'shameless hussy' (47). On the other hand, Austin's cruising, his casual sex with a variety of partners and his *penchant* for sadomasochism all seem to make him queer enough. Austin seems unaware that some queer theory has explained that the acceptability and legitimization of same-sex partnership necessarily accompanies the demonization and legal mistreatment of those who like more casual sex. (Michael Warner, in discussing the 'ethics of queer life', attacks marriage as 'the central legitimating institution by which the state regulates and permeates people's most intimate lives'.[34]) Austin mothers, looks after, shelters and enables his lover Julien and his ex-lover

Peter, and takes dearly beloved basset hound Ajax for walks, all of which seem to make him regressively complicit with family values (not heterosexual or homosexual values) such as mothering, caring, sharing and planning for the future – even though Julien and Peter both die. (Ajax and Austin live.)

Since the 1990s, the term 'queer' has come more and more to be used just as a synonym for gay, and has increasingly been used in connection with male gays rather than lesbians. And just as the term has lost its radical edge, lesbian and gay politics, particularly in the United States, have become increasingly preoccupied with questions of partnership and marriage. *The Married Man*, by showing how a 'subculture-oriented gay' (Bruce Bawer's term[35]) is disadvantaged by the absence of recognition of gay partnerships, also suggests ways in which debates around partnership do not need to conceive of marriage as a lifelong, monogamous or exclusive relationship. Rubin, in 'Thinking Sex', advanced the concept of 'benign sexual variation',[36] but it has proved difficult for lesbian and gay culture to accommodate both those gay men and lesbians who want to form long-term relationships, or to have children, and those who do not want their sexuality to be confined to such relationships, or to form these relationships. I wonder, however, if the opposition between the family and queerness can be sustained. As families get used to queers, queers find they are getting used to the queerness of family.

NOTES

1. Peter Wildeblood, *Against the Law* (1955; Harmondsworth: Penguin, 1957), 13. For a full and stimulating account of the Montagu trials, which imposed prison sentences on Wildeblood, Michael Pitt-Rivers and Lord Montagu of Beaulieu, see Patrick Higgins, *Heterosexual Dictatorship: Male Homosexuality in Postwar Britain* (London: Fourth Estate, 1996).
2. John D'Emilio, *Sexual Politics, Sexual Communities: The Making of a Homosexual Minority in the United States, 1940–1970* (Chicago: University of Chicago Press, 1983), 108–9.
3. Martin Duberman, *Stonewall* (New York: Dutton, 1993), 108. For accounts of dissent within lesbian and gay communities, see D'Emilio, *Sexual Politics*, 114.
4. Duberman, *Stonewall*, 111–12.
5. For accounts of these tensions within gay liberation, see Duberman, *Stonewall*, 215–80, and Dennis Altman, *Homosexual: Oppression and Liberation* (1971; London: Allen Lane, 1974), 109–51.
6. Bruce Bawer, *A Place at the Table: The Gay Individual in American Society* (New York: Simon & Schuster, 1993); Andrew Sullivan, *Virtually Normal: An Argument About Homosexuality* (New York: Knopf, 1995). For a remarkably lucid account of gay conservatism of the 1990s, see Paul Robinson, *Queer Wars: The New Gay Right and Its Critics* (Chicago: University of Chicago Press, 2005).
7. Edmund White, *States of Desire: Travels in Gay America* (New York: Dutton, 1980), 295–6. Further references are given in parentheses.

8. An excellent account of ACT UP is given in Douglas Crimp, *AIDS Demo Graphics* (Seattle, WA: Bay Press, 1990).

9. See Annamarie Jagose, *Queer Theory: An Introduction* (New York: New York University Press, 1996) for a lucid discussion of queer theory and politics.

10. Eve Kosofsky Sedgwick, *Tendencies* (Durham, NC: Duke University Press, 1993), x–xi. Further references are given in parentheses.

11. Judith Butler, 'Imitation and Gender Subordination', in Diana Fuss, ed., *Inside/Out: Lesbian Theories, Gay Theories* (New York: Routledge, 1991), 13–14.

12. Michael Warner, *The Trouble with Normal: Sex, Politics, and the Ethics of Queer Life* (Cambridge, MA: Harvard University Press, 1999), 38.

13. Lee Edelman, *No Future: Queer Theory and the Death Drive* (Durham, NC: Duke University Press, 2004), 17.

14. Christopher Isherwood, *Goodbye to Berlin* (1939; London: Chatto and Windus, 1952), 296.

15. Gayle Rubin, 'Thinking Sex: Notes for a Radical Theory of the Politics of Sexuality', in Henry Abelove, Michèle Aina Barale and David M. Halperin, eds., *The Lesbian and Gay Studies Reader* (New York: Routledge, 1993), 13.

16. Leo Bersani, *Homos* (Cambridge, MA: Harvard University Press, 1995), 61.

17. E. M. Forster, *Aspects of the Novel* (New York: Harcourt, Brace, 1927), 45.

18. See Duberman, *Stonewall*, and David Carter, *Stonewall: The Riots That Sparked the Gay Revolution* (New York: St Martin's Press, 2004).

19. Dennis Cooper, *The Sluts* (2004; New York: Carroll and Graf, 2005).

20. Alan Hollinghurst, *The Swimming-Pool Library* (London: Penguin, 1988), *The Spell* (London: Chatto & Windus, 1998), *The Line of Beauty* (London: Picador, 2004).

21. David Leavitt, *Equal Affections* (London: Penguin, 1989), 24. Further references are given in parentheses.

22. *My Secret Life* is the title of an eleven-volume work of frank (gay, straight and other) pornographic memoirs written by 'Walter' and published in a private edition over a number of years in the 1880s and 1890s. For many years commercial publication of *My Secret Life* was banned; it is now available in a cheap edition from Wordsworth Classics.

23. Ann Beattie, 'The Cinderella Waltz', *The New Yorker* (29 January 1979).

24. David Leavitt, 'Territory', *Family Dancing* (1984; London: Penguin, 1986), 8. Further references are given in parentheses.

25. Randy Shilts, *And the Band Played On: Politics, People and the AIDS Epidemic* (New York: St Martin's Press, 1987), 23.

26. John Brigham, 'Sexual Entitlement: Rights and AIDS, the Early Years', *Law & Policy*, 16:3 (1994), 256.

27. Joyce Purnick, 'City Shuts a Bathhouse as Site of "Unsafe Sex"', *The New York Times* (7 December 1985).

28. Andrew Holleran, *Dancer from the Dance* (1978; New York: Plume, 1986), 14.

29. Edmund White, *The Farewell Symphony* (New York: Knopf, 1997), 246–7.

30. Charles Silverstein and Edmund White, *The Joy of Gay Sex* (New York: Simon and Schuster, 1977), 115.

31. Edmund White, *The Married Man* (2000; London: Vintage, 2001), 10. Further references are given in parentheses.

32. Bersani, *Homos*, 5, 71.

33. Leo Bersani and Adam Phillips, *Intimacies* (Chicago: University of Chicago Press, 2008), 32.
34. Michael Warner, *The Trouble with Normal: Sex, Politics, and the Ethics of Queer Life* (Cambridge, MA: Harvard University Press, 1999), 96.
35. Bawer, *A Place at the Table*, 35.
36. Rubin, 'Thinking Sex', 15.

PART II

Affiliations

6

RUTH VANITA

The homoerotics of travel: people, ideas, genres

If there is some truth to the adage that there are two basic plots – person leaves home, and stranger comes to town – it is even truer that stories about same-sex desire involve selves changed through travel. Protagonists move from the rural to the urban, occasionally from the urban back to the rural, and often from one country to another, in search of more congenial climes and of the hidden self.

When people travel so do ideas. Ideas about same-sex desire have circulated between cultures throughout recorded history and cross-fertilized one another.[1] Opposition to homosexuality often takes the form of blaming other cultures for importing it into one's own supposedly pristine society. As John Boswell points out, this tendency is evident in classical antiquity as well as in medieval Europe; it is much more pernicious and widespread today.[2]

The current wave of globalization, which has had many precursors throughout history, brings a new twist to the debate. LGBT movements in developing countries are frequently seen as manifestations of neo-imperialism, with 'third world' queer people mindlessly imitating 'first world' identities, like 'gay', 'lesbian' and 'homosexual'.[3] This is the left-wing counterpart of the right-wing claim that homosexuality is an import from the 'West'.

In response, some third-world AIDS organizations have picked up American health workers' terms, such as MSM (men who have sex with men), as more politically correct, and have also reinvented local terms, which they claim are more accurate than terms like 'homosexual'. Interestingly, they often apply a word in a local language or a regional identity from one region to the entire country.[4] These efforts to separate national from international identities arise from the unstated assumption that identities can be fixed.

Attempts to pin down cultural difference are doomed from the start. More fruitful, in my view, are attempts to explore interconnections and circulations.

Most scholars would agree that great literature has always depicted identities as multiple, fluid and hybrid. Despite this agreement, the anxious desire to reify identities repeatedly resurfaces. Nationalism, arguably the dominant religion of the twentieth century, provides fertile soil for this anxiety.

But fear cannot stop border crossings, physical, virtual or imaginative. When people cross borders, their identities change. The borders may be between nations, religious communities or linguistic groups. Today, even the most brutal dictatorships find it hard to prevent their citizens from crossing borders over the internet.

Perhaps the most invigorating border crossing is that between past and present. Despite continuities, any culture's past is radically different from its present. Lesbian and gay writers often travel into the past in search of ancestors. Indeed, it is impossible to truly explore a culture without considering its past.

North to south: in search of passion and beauty

Tourism and travel in Europe and America became more widespread in the nineteenth century than ever before. Walter Pater was a pioneer of the narrative that intertwines explorations of cultural difference and of homoeroticism. 'Winckelmann', the last essay in Pater's enormously influential little book *The Renaissance* (1873), outlines what would become a familiar pattern – a man journeying from northern to southern Europe, in search of freedom, male beauty and the intensities of love.

Pater conceives of the European Renaissance as steeped in the homoerotic traditions of the medieval and classical pasts. He celebrates the northern transmission of those traditions by Hellenist scholar Winckelmann, who, Pater argues, influenced Goethe's transformation of modern literature through Romanticism. Pater depicts Winckelmann as travelling physically to Rome but imaginatively to Greece in search of pagan beauty, which he characterized as archetypally male. Pater judiciously quotes Winckelmann's letters in a way that links his intense, often anguished, love for men with his quest for 'some unexpressed pulsation of sensuous life' in 'the buried fire of ancient art'.[5]

Many writers, including Thomas Mann, E. M. Forster and Virginia Woolf, would pick up and play with this pattern of a journey from north to south. Today, 'North' and 'South' often refer to Western Europe and North America versus Asia, Africa and South America. But up to the early twentieth century, these terms more commonly referred to the supposedly sharp divide between northern and southern Europe.

Northerners went south in search of the sun. The brilliant skies of southern Europe, closer to Africa and Asia, beckoned them from the chilly industrialism of Puritan England and Germany to literally and metaphorically hot and fertile vineyards. Southern France, Spain, Italy and Greece all participated in this mystique. Greece, indeed, was part of both Europe and 'Asia Minor', serving as a bridge between past and present as well as between continents.

For northern Europeans, Venice, where Shakespeare's Antonio longs to die for his Bassanio, Byron's 'isles of Greece / Where burning Sappho loved and sung', Rome, where Wilde passionately commemorated the tomb of Keats, 'fair as Sebastian', patron saint of Victorian homosexuals, and Florence, where Robert Browning and Elizabeth Barrett fled from her father's chilly Victorian house, all comprised Keats's 'warm south / Full of the true, the blushful Hippocrene'. Here had flourished the glories of pagan poetry and art, and here were to be found the pleasures of free and passionate love. Often, this love was between members of the same sex.

Wilde's works are saturated in this imaginative continuum – almost every poem, short story and essay dwells on forays into other cultures. His comedies, though set in England, are galvanized by 'Bunburying' people who journey between town and countryside, or return home from long sojourns abroad. Dorian Gray's life is changed by a book about a young Parisian, and it seems fitting that Wilde ended his life in Paris and was buried there.

Katherine Bradley and Edith Cooper, who wrote under the joint pen-name 'Michael Field' and belonged to Wilde's circle, recomposed the north to south journey in a Sapphic key. They travelled extensively through Europe, and their poems display an eclectic pursuit of female beauty and love, transposed from southern Europe to England's green and pleasant land. The seduction poem 'An Invitation' places the lover's room in an imagined 'south':

> Come and sing, my room is south,
> Come with thy sun-governed mouth,
> Thou wilt never suffer drouth,
> Long as dwelling
> In my chamber of the south.
>
> . . .
>
> There's a lavender settee,
> Cushioned for my love and me,
> Ah, what secrets there will be
> For love-telling,
> When her head leans on my knee.[6]

Later in the century, Henry James, who emigrated from America to England, shared a passion for Italy with writer and art critic J. A. Symonds. In 1895, sending Symonds a copy of his essay on Venice, James wrote, 'it seemed to me that the victims of a common passion should sometimes exchange a look'.[7]

Both men were homosexually inclined, although Symonds was relatively more open about this than James.

Self-realization abroad

At the start of the twentieth century, two consummate literary tellings of this story of self-realization through discovery of one's homosexuality in a foreign land were André Gide's *The Immoralist* (1902) and Thomas Mann's *Death in Venice* (1912).[8] While Gide's novel explores the consequences of abandoning morality in favour of unbridled hedonism, Mann's is more narrowly focused on same-sex desire. Throughout his tale of a celebrated middle-aged German author's passion for a beautiful Polish boy, Mann emphasizes the foreignness of the setting in that 'most improbable of cities', Venice.[9] The difference between modern Venice and Munich is emblematized in both natural and cultural forces – the naked sun god who draws attention away from the intellect to the senses, the oppressive sirocco blowing across from Africa and the maze of bridges and alleys where the protagonist, Gustav von Aschenbach, loses himself. Equally important is Italy's cultural ancestor, Greece, where Socrates taught his beloved Phaedrus, and where the reigning deities included Eros; Eos, 'ravisher of youth' (55); Apollo who loved Hyacinthus; and Dionysus, whose revels haunt Aschenbach's dreams.

Far from resisting a passion he knows is 'absurd' (59), Aschenbach embraces his emerging identity. Formerly a rigid moralist, he now delights in anything that seems to undermine 'the bourgeois structure' (61). He wears make-up and hair dye, thus becoming like the grotesque old dandy he had despised on his voyage to Venice. All this is possible only because 'He was alone, he was a foreigner, he was sunk deep in this belated bliss of his – all which enabled him to pass unblushing through experiences well-nigh unbelievable' (63).

The locals deliberately hide from foreign tourists the cholera epidemic raging in the city. When an Englishman reveals the secret to Aschenbach, he neither enlightens Tadzio's family nor leaves Venice. Recalling the foreigner in Munich who had aroused in him 'a lust for strange countries and fresh sights' (74), he rejects the option of returning home to a life of reason.

His death just before Tadzio leaves Venice can be read as punishment for his love, but can also be read as the crowning glory of his life – he has nothing to live for, since he knows that the loving contemplation of beauty is the supreme felicity of existence. In Pater's words:

> And what does the spirit need in the face of modern life? The sense of freedom . . .
> Who, if he saw through all, would fret against the chain of circumstance which
> endows one at the end with those great experiences? ('Winckelmann', 148–9)

International community

Since Aschenbach cannot confide in anyone, his identity remains unchanged in the eyes of the world. In contrast, *The Well of Loneliness* (1928) traces its protagonist Stephen Gordon's progress from isolation on her family estate in the English countryside to joining an international gay community in Paris. Paying tribute to the expatriate homosexual community on the Left Bank, the novel maps another pattern that grows increasingly important in the construction of lesbian and gay identities through the twentieth century – leaving one's own country in order to find community abroad.[10]

The need for gay communion impels Stephen to leave England. Her friend, the gay playwright, Jonathan Brockett, insists that she go to Paris because she is atrophying in London.[11] Compelled to concur with his diagnosis, Stephen terms it a 'queer revelation'.[12] This term is echoed later when she finds happiness with Mary Llewellyn in Paris, and life becomes 'a new revelation' (327).

Hall uses the categories 'invert' and 'abnormal' (242), regardless of people's nationality or race. Stephen's sense of identity as a homosexual gradually emerges once she leaves her much-loved country. Unsure at first whether she feels 'outraged or relieved' that Brockett and his friends in Paris recognize her as one of themselves, she withdraws and immerses herself in work.

After the war, she gains not only a partner but also increased confidence in her new identity. She and Mary attract little attention on the streets, where female couples stroll among male-female couples, while in the air is 'the inconsequent feeling that belongs to the night life of most great cities, above all to the careless night life of Paris' (328). Later, Stephen seeks out gay night life. She and Mary frequent bars where women can dance together; they also host and attend gay parties and musical soirées.

Hall paints an invaluable portrait, from the perspective of an insider, of this international gay community's cultural diversity. Stephen's sympathies are broadened as she learns about other cultures. She and Mary befriend a lesbian couple from the Scottish Highlands, and socialize with American lesbian expatriates. With Wanda, a Polish Catholic, Stephen visits the church of the Sacré Coeur. Adolphe Blanc, a 'gentle and learned Jew' (356), tells her of her duty to write about the injustice gay people suffer; she will act on his words at the book's conclusion. She also hears two African-American heterosexual men sing spirituals, and feels a kinship with them.

Although Hall refers to the gay community, especially the drug addicts and alcoholics in it, as a 'miserable army' (393), she depicts its members as mutually supportive and generous. At home in the English countryside, Stephen thinks she is the only one of her kind, but in Paris, she turns to 'her own kind' (360), and realizes that she is one of millions throughout the world.

Hall depicts this, in the book's last pages, as a turning point in the incipient gay movement for justice. Such a movement can grow only when borders are crossed.

Primeval places

As even more Europeans and Americans began to travel in the early twentieth century, they went further afield. More exotic locales appear in gay fiction. Stephen and Mary become lovers not in France but in Orotava on Tenerife, a Canary Island situated off the African coast. They stay in the oldest villa there, which has walls adorned with old erotic frescoes, as well as 'a veritable Eden of a garden' (309). In this brief idyll, they return to a more 'natural' (317) condition: 'They no longer felt desolate, hungry outcasts' (320).

The lush vegetation is described as an objective correlative for their love, which is termed 'primitive' (317) in the sense of 'primeval'; it is part of 'Creation's terrific urge to create'. Although the local culture is Spanish, they are described as coming together in 'the African night' (311). The memory of 'those African nights' (327) sustains them after they return to Paris.

Here, Hall adumbrates a cluster of ideas that is found at this time in many European and American fictional representations of travel in Africa, Asia and South America. Such travel is represented as pleasurable, liberatory and conducive to discovery of one's self and one's sexuality. From the late nineteenth century onwards, many homosexual and bisexual writers undertook and wrote about such travels – Edward Carpenter in Sri Lanka and India, J. R. Ackerley, Christopher Isherwood and Allen Ginsberg in India, E. M. Forster in Egypt and India, Paul and Jane Bowles in Morocco, Hart Crane and Tennessee Williams in Mexico, Elizabeth Bishop in Brazil – the list could go on for several pages. For some, like Isherwood, these travels were part of a spiritual quest. These travels were part of a larger, still continuing, historical pattern of gay people leaving home for sojourns in places where they feel freer precisely because they are foreigners there. Radclyffe Hall's Barbara puts it succinctly when she pleads with her lover to leave their village in Scotland: 'Jamie, let's go away ... they hate us. Let's go where nobody knows us' (359).

It is important to remember that travellers to Asia and Africa also travelled widely in Europe and America. For instance, Isherwood travelled to Germany, and then moved to the US with Auden (he depicts the isolation of a Britisher in America in *A Single Man*); Forster travelled in Italy and Greece; Bishop lived in Brazil for many years; many Americans, including Natalie Clifford Barney, Romaine Brooks, Gertrude Stein and Alice Toklas, H. D., and later Paul Cadmus, James Baldwin and Patricia Highsmith sojourned or settled in Europe. Rimbaud and Verlaine conducted their tempestuous affair, memorialized in both poetry and prose ('A Season in Hell'), partly in England, and this preceded Rimbaud's later travels in Asia and Africa.

The reverse movement, from Asia and Africa to Europe and America, began later, concurrently with the ironic reversal of levels of tolerance between 'East' and 'West' in the late twentieth century. This movement is in full spate today. With the recent and honourable exceptions of South Africa, Nepal and India, most formerly colonized countries in South and South-East Asia and Africa have retained the anti-sodomy laws introduced by the European colonizing powers. But most European countries and now the USA too have abolished the anti-sodomy laws, and many have also introduced a range of civil rights for gay people. Consequently, a substantial number of Asian and African gay people seek amnesty in the USA, Canada and European countries, on the grounds that they face persecution in their home countries.

Hunted and exiled

The twentieth century was the century of exiled refugees pouring from one country or continent into another. The Holocaust is the enduring image of such exile, but it was preceded and succeeded by many waves of such unwilling boundary crossers. This century also saw an increasing number of writers hounded for their works, and as gay writers became more visible, they suffered greatly in this respect. Wilde, who died as the century began, was the archetype of such suffering.

Ironically, the trial of *The Well of Loneliness* enacted the persecution the novel documented, thus confirming its central thesis. Throughout the book, Hall uses images of hunted animals to symbolize the victimization of defenceless homosexuals. English literature has a long and honourable history of critiquing the hunt, by juxtaposing it with the oppression of women, children, prisoners and other wretched of the earth. William Wordsworth's 'Hartleap Well' and Thomas Hardy's *Tess of the d'Urbervilles* are among the more famous examples. Hall was among the first to explicitly connect the image to the persecution of gay people.

Stephen is an avid hunter, but one day, after her father's death, she suddenly identifies with the fox as a 'solitary creature' hunted by 'ruthless, implacable, untiring people' (123), and then experiences an almost mystical epiphany: 'she perceived that all life is only one life, that all joy and all sorrow are indeed only one, that all death is only one dying' (125). Much later, the misery of a drug-addicted young gay man reminds her of the fox and her own thoughts about it: 'It's looking for God who made it' (394). This perception illuminates the dark underside of Paris's international community, or of gay exiles and refugees anywhere. Their border crossings and assumption of international identities are not chosen but forced, and they suffer irreparable losses, as Stephen suffers the loss of her ancestral home.

'I have no country'?

At the beginning of the twentieth century, a number of artists and writers across the world, who were supporters of colonized countries' struggles for national independence, developed an aspiration towards internationalism. In India, Tagore critiqued narrow nationalisms, and Suryakanta Tripathi 'Nirala', arguably the greatest twentieth-century Hindi-language poet, described 'ekdeshiya' (uni-national) writing as 'inherently narrow'.[13] He claimed that interaction between literary traditions caused them to shine 'like the many beautiful colors of the rainbow in the rays of one sun'.[14]

In England, members of the Bloomsbury group, most of whom were homosexual or bisexual, forcefully enunciated an internationalist position. Virginia Woolf, for example, claimed, 'as a woman, I have no country. As a woman I want no country. As a woman my country is the whole world.'[15]

Such utopian yearnings, though, were haunted by the spectres of colonialism and imperialism.[16] Forster was famously to remark in 1939, 'if I had to choose between betraying my country and betraying my friend, I hope I should have the guts to betray my country'.[17] But his last novel, *A Passage to India* (1924), which emblematizes this aspiration in the homoerotic friendship of the Englishman Fielding and the Indian Aziz, concludes with the two men's separation. They want to be friends, but larger forces obtrude. Although both Fielding and Aziz marry women, their relationship is the thread running through the book, and evolves as the thematic centre. Their separation indicates how hard it is for what Forster termed 'Love, the Beloved Republic' to survive the tensions created by imperialism. Forster dedicated *Passage* to Ross Masood, the Indian he loved unrequitedly for years. This was a time when ideas about homosexual identity were being exported from one country to another. While this created connections, it also spawned fears, many of which are still alive today.

Imports and exports

In north India, male homoerotic subcultures had flourished in pre-colonial cities and been celebrated by major poets.[18] But in the late nineteenth century, British-educated nationalists, both on the right and on the left, who had internalized Victorian homophobia, claimed that homosexuality was imported into India by 'Westerners' – either Europeans or West Asian Muslims. This myth still thrives in India today. Ironically, it was in fact not homosexuality but homophobia in its modern form that was imported into India via British education and law.[19]

The first public debate in north India around homosexuality and its representation in literature was also a debate about 'West' versus 'East'. It was sparked off in 1927 by the publication of a collection of short stories on male homosexuality, entitled *Chocolate*.[20] The author, a firebrand nationalist, Pandey Bechan Sharma, with the pen-name 'Ugra' (Extreme), claimed that despite the anti-sodomy law introduced by the British in 1860, homosexuality was widespread in all strata of Indian society, and that his stories were written to expose and denounce it. However, his opponents claimed that the stories titillated readers with depictions of beautiful boys and lovers' encounters, and were therefore obscene. Ugra, who never married, was suspected of homosexuality, and there is evidence that male homosexuals were delighted by the book's publication. The first edition sold out in a week.

Ugra depicts groups of sophisticated young men, both Hindu and Muslim, who enjoy the pleasures of the city, and most of whom acknowledge the attractions of other males. 'Chocolate', the title of the collection and of one of the stories, is a term they use both for their desires and for the objects of those desires. While suggesting that male–male desire is a Western import, this term also normalizes that desire by indicating that Western tastes are an ineradicable part of modern Indian identity. One of the most widely available consumer items in India, chocolate is so indigenized as to have become a Hindi word, but is nevertheless non-Indian in origin. Hence the term works against Ugra's narratorial denunciations of homosexuality.

Ugra's homosexual characters are proud of their hybridity. They defend their desires by expounding a hedonist philosophy, derived from both ancient Greek and medieval Indian thought: 'Truth must be respected wherever it is. Beauty alone is truth. So whether the beauty is a woman's or a man's, "I am a slave of love"' (49). They also claim an illustrious ancestry, with hybrid sources, Eastern and Western, Hindu and Muslim. In the title story, a homosexually inclined character quotes the renowned Urdu poet Mir Taqi Mir's homoerotic love poetry but also looks to the West for inspiration. The censorious narrator reports, '[H]e told me, on the basis of an English book, that even Socrates was guilty of this offence. He said that Shakespeare too was a slave of some beautiful friend of his. He spoke of Mr Oscar Wilde as well' (39).

Ugra uses a range of terms for homosexuality, and these too are drawn from different cultures. Among them are older indigenous words like *sarvabhogi* (taking pleasure in or consuming everything) and *ranginmijaz* (of colourful temperament),[21] popular pejorative terms like *laundebaaz* (boy fancier) and poetic words in local dialect like *paatalpanthi* (followers of the path of *paatal*, a rose or trumpet flower). Ugra's writings were widely attacked by

Hindi litterateurs. One reason was that he dared depict homosexuality as a heady mix of different cultural traditions from West and East.

Anxiety and transformation

Suniti Namjoshi, the first openly lesbian Indian writer, moved from India to Canada and then to England. From its inception, her work draws on Indian as well as European literary traditions to engage with post-colonial and diasporic anxieties about Western identities. A number of her animal figures, from the blue donkey and the one-eyed monkey to the tiger and the dragon, suggest the fear and hostility that prevail between heterosexual and homosexual, East and West, men and women.[22] While acknowledging these conflicts as real, she also deconstructs identities to reveal convergences across national and other boundaries.[23]

The Conversations of Cow, a fantasy novel, is her most sophisticated exegesis of the question of identity.[24] The protagonist, Suniti, and the object of her pursuit, the eponymous Cow, constantly metamorphose yet remain recognizable. Cow is Goddess, woman and animal; this is normal in an Indian context where one may be reborn as an animal, many Gods have an animal vehicle, some Gods take an animal form and most animals are worshipped, but it appears outrageous in a Western context. While Suniti, with her Western education, is agitated by identities that fluctuate, Cow is equally comfortable as an Indian lesbian and a white heterosexual man.

Namjoshi draws on Hindu philosophy to undo everyday categories. In Hindu thought, Kama is one of the four aims of human life, and represents the third stage before the final one of Moksha or liberation. One interpretation of this is that when all desires are fulfilled and one has nothing left to desire, one reaches liberation. Namjoshi's Cow resonates with a number of Hindu narratives, recalling both the mythological cornucopian cow Surabhi, who produces an endless stream of milk, and Kamadhenu, the cow who fulfils all desires. *Kama* means desire, and *dhenu* means cow. Bhadravati, the lesbian cow, both fulfills Suniti's desires and also liberates her from prejudices and unreal categories. Evoking the Hindu idea that all living beings are manifestations of the divine, Cow becomes a symbol for dissolving cultural differences, like those of gender, race, nationality and sexuality.

When Suniti is perplexed by Cow's rapid transformations, Cow reassures her – 'It's all right ... identity is fluid. Haven't you heard of transmigration?'[25] – thus pointing to ancient Indian versions of apparently new Western ideas. When Suniti is not persuaded, Cow expresses a desire that many people who are categorized as deviant may have experienced, 'All I ever wanted ... was to be an ordinary animal' (32).

In the closing peroration, Namjoshi draws on another Indian devotional practice, that of invoking a God by hundreds of names. She uses this linguistic strategy to displace gender and cultural difference, much as Monique Wittig and Jeannette Winterson use the first-person pronoun. The protagonist invokes Cow as all who have appeared in the narrative, including Westerners and Indians, living and imagined beings, humans and nonhumans, men and women, straight and gay, concluding, 'O Cow who manifests herself in a thousand shapes and a thousand wishes' (121–2).

Namjoshi thus returns us by many routes to a modern version of the *Bhagavad Gita*'s claim that a wise person sees the one in the many, and the many in the one. The novel concludes with the return of Cow, which makes Suniti 'feel so very, so extraordinarily happy' (124). She decides that she likes Cow in all her incarnations, and finds even her heterosexual white male persona 'wholly engaging' (125).

Sweet dualities[26]

Crossing boundaries involves meetings, encounters and sometimes dualities. A love relationship is one kind of duality, and as international relationships become increasingly common, identities are transformed at the most visceral levels. As Edmund White remarks, 'a love affair between foreigners is always as much the mutual seduction of two cultures as a meeting between two people'.[27]

In *The Married Man*, White's most extended examination of such a mutual seduction, the American protagonist Austin falls in love with a Frenchman, Julien, and part of the attraction is that the relationship represents 'a total immersion into France' (67). As in Henry James's novels, this has mixed results for Austin's identity. Julien has a French disdain for sexual identities, which shakes Austin's sense of himself as a gay man; he becomes distanced from his gay friends and from America, which appears more and more like a foreign country to him.

The limitations of identity politics become evident when Austin is accused of political incorrectness at the American university where he teaches. American liberal tolerance of homosexuality is scathingly revealed as shallow and xenophobic; Austin's colleagues do not warm to Julien and him, because they are not 'the sort of dotty, aging gay couple an academic community likes'. As Julien's health declines, they travel to Venice and Morocco; here, White pays tribute to Gide, Mann and Bowles, and perhaps to James Baldwin's *Giovanni's Room*, one of the earliest novels about a transatlantic gay relationship.

A kind of relationship less often examined is that between expatriates from two different countries who settle down together in a third. Such was the relationship between American Natalie Barney and Englishwoman Renée Vivien, both of whom settled in France, and later between short story writer Katherine Mansfield and Ida Baker. Mansfield came from New Zealand and Baker from Burma to a finishing school in London, where both later relocated. Though Mansfield had earlier had an intense affair with Maata, a Maori classmate, her unfinished manuscript 'Maata' records her lifelong partnership with Baker, whom she termed her 'wife', and who coexisted, not always happily, with Mansfield's husband, the literary critic Middleton Murry.[28] More recently, Namjoshi and her partner, Gillian Hanscombe, explore their relationship in a poetic dialogue, *Flesh and Paper*, which touches on their life as expatriates from two former colonies (India and Australia) who lived in Canada and England.

Travelling genres

Another way cultural identities mingle is when genres are translated and rewritten in cultures other than their native ones. Marilyn Hacker's villanelles and Adrienne Rich's *ghazals* come to mind. The *ghazal* is a particularly interesting case, because of its conventions in its native languages, Persian and Urdu, where lover and beloved always take the masculine grammatical gender. This is so even when a woman is the addressee. The convention lends itself especially well to male–male relationships, and renders unnecessary the kind of subterfuge that poets in English resorted to for centuries, using the 'I-you' format to avoid revealing the beloved's gender.

From the late nineteenth century onwards, Indian nationalist critics launched campaigns to purify literature in several Indian languages. The *ghazal* came in the line of fire; Urdu critics denounced it as decadent. Fortunately, it proved resilient and still flourishes, but the homoeroticism endemic to the genre was purged or disguised, and the male–male convention was gradually replaced by a male–female convention. Twentieth-century Urdu poets, like Josh Malihabadi and Firaq Gorakhpuri, widely known to be homosexual, wrote in the male–female mode.[29] From the late nineteenth century onwards, Rekhti, a sub-genre of early nineteenth-century Urdu poetry, which contained explicit descriptions of female–female relationships, was suppressed in India as obscene.[30]

The recuperation of same-sex conventions in the English-language *ghazal* is, therefore, an example of how cross-cultural travellings shift the identities not only of individuals but even of genres. If the encounter with British colonialism heterosexualized the *ghazal*, the encounter with Western gay identities enables a recuperation of same-sex desire. Where Agha Shahid Ali draws on his own identity as an Indian Muslim to write in the *ghazal* form (interestingly, English allows him to disguise the homoerotic content of his work by avoiding third-person pronouns), Adrienne Rich, an American half-Jewish lesbian, writes *ghazals* that are explicit about female–female amours.

Citizens of the world

Today, many writers, especially from the developed world, emigrate, move freely across borders, live in more than one country and obtain dual or triple citizenships. Their quest may be for foreignness itself, for the special creative urge triggered by exposure to different cultures and histories. Many others, from Asian and African countries, are still forced into exile, fleeing either outright persecution or more subtle forms of discrimination.

France has retained its status as a site favoured by gay writers, despite or perhaps because of its literary climate where many openly homosexual writers refuse to identify as 'gay' or attend gay literary conferences.[31] Marilyn Hacker's sonnet sequence *Love, Death and the Changing of the Seasons* records a relationship lived out in Manhattan and Paris.[32] Edmund White's *The Married Man* is based on his own life. American David Sedaris light-heartedly recounts his experiences with his partner in France.[33]

Greece, too, whose past contributed so centrally to shaping modern gay identity, retains its allure. For two decades James Merrill and his partner David Jackson spent part of each year in Greece, and Merrill's poetry, which, like Forster's fiction, develops a poetics of place, often evokes Greek life and Greek men. Merrill and Forster also had in common an admiration of Greek homosexual poet C. P. Cavafy, whom Forster brought to the English-speaking world's attention and three of whose poems Merrill later translated.[34]

A forerunner of today's globe-trotting gay writers was the peripatetic Ronald Firbank, who often wrote a novel set in a real or imaginary foreign land while himself living in another foreign land; he travelled around Spain, Italy, the Middle East and North Africa; Venice was one of his favourite cities.[35] European and American gay writers today, because of their privileged position, are increasingly able to identify with more than one nationality. However, writers of Asian, African or Latin American origin, whether straight or gay, who live in the 'West', tend to write only or largely about their countries of origin or about ethnic diasporas.

Vikram Seth is an exception; he writes not only with the ease but with the loving knowledge of an insider about China, England and America as well as India. As *A Suitable Boy* demonstrates, not least by its wide popularity among readers in India, he is one of the foremost imaginative chroniclers of modern Indian life. But his masterpiece, *The Golden Gate*, which Gore Vidal called 'the great California novel', nowhere suggests his Indianness, and predictably came in for some criticism on this score.[36] Its portrait of a gay relationship between a bisexual older man and a tormented young gay Catholic reveals how certain feelings cross times, places and sexual orientations, for example when one man must stretch out his hand in the darkness to his roommate, making the first move and thus risking rejection.

Seth's lyric poems excel in working out variations on the theme of unrequited or semi-requited love, the age-old, even central, preoccupation of European as well as Indian lyric poetry. In his first collection, *Mappings* (1981), Seth play-fully wonders how his bisexuality fits into identity categories: 'In the strict ranks / of Gay and Straight / what is my status? / Stray? or Great?'.[37] *Mappings* features explicit love poems about men ('Guest', 'Even Such') and women ('Time-Zones'), rendering somewhat futile the years of media speculation about his sexuality that followed. The media imagined that he first came out on a radio talk-show in the late 1990s, or even later, when his mother mentioned his bisexuality in her autobiography, or still later, when he was the lead signatory to an open letter calling on the Indian government to repeal the anti-sodomy law instituted by the British.[38] His 'coming out' has had to be repeated again and again.

From the start, Seth favoured the time-honoured 'I-you' form in his lyric love poems, most of which avoid gendering the beloved. One reason this form has, throughout history, been so popular is that it allows anyone, regardless of gender, to identify with both lover and beloved, and it also allows the poet to get to the heart of the matter by exploring universal rather than gendered emotion.

In his introduction to his *Collected Poems*, first published by Penguin India in 1995, Seth suggests that an author's national identity is ultimately irrele-vant to writing: 'I see myself as Indian ... But ... [T]he wish to write about anything is such a rare and mysterious feeling that it is pointless to preempt or constrain it by notions of subject or geography or genre'.[39]

The next generation of writers, born and bred in the internet patch, often bypasses the question altogether. The protagonist of *Kari*, a graphic novel published in India in 2008 by Amruta Patil, lives in Bombay, and is in love with a vanished non-Indian called Ruth.[40] Going by her appearance and preoccupations, Kari could as well live in New York or London, as many readers of the book do. Elements of Indian life (the house cleaner, for instance) appear without being marked as exotic in any way, as do the many signs of international identity. No sexual identity terms are used, but Kari's butch baby dyke ways are quite evident, visually and in words.

As the world shrinks, gay people are indeed everywhere, both in life and literature, popping up in the most remote places and unlikely settings. This frenzied travelling, however, should not obscure that journeying for which it

is a metaphor, and which, fittingly, travel-shy poets like Emily Dickinson and
Mary Oliver have best evoked:

> One day you finally knew
> what you had to do, and began,
> though the voices around you
> kept shouting
> their bad advice –
> . . .
> But little by little,
> as you left their voices behind,
> the stars began to burn
> through the sheets of clouds,
> and there was a new voice
> which you slowly
> recognized as your own,
> that kept you company
> as you strode deeper and deeper
> into the world,
> determined to do
> the only thing you could do –
> determined to save
> the only life you could save.   (Mary Oliver, 'The Journey')[41]

NOTES

1. For example, by erecting statues of his dead lover Antinous throughout the empire, Roman Emperor Hadrian publicly idealized male–male love in regions unused to such idealization. Another example is the translation of the fourth-century *Kama Sutra*, including its chapter on male–male sex, by nineteenth-century Europeans like Richard Burton.
2. John Boswell, *Christianity, Social Tolerance and Homosexuality* (Chicago: University of Chicago Press, 1980), 52.
3. For detailed analyses of this debate, see my essay, 'A Rose by Any Other Name: The Sexuality Terminology Debates', in Ruth Vanita, *Gandhi's Tiger and Sita's Smile: Essays on Gender, Sexuality and Culture* (New Delhi: Yoda Press, 2005), 60–9.
4. For example, in India, the word *koti*. See Lawrence Cohen, 'The Kothi Wars: AIDS Cosmopolitanism and the Morality of Classification', in Vincanne Adams and Stacy Leigh Pigg, eds., *Sex in Development: Science, Sexuality and Morality in Global Perspective* (Durham, NC: Duke University Press, 2006), 269–303.
5. Walter Pater, *The Renaissance* (Oxford: Oxford University Press, 1986), 118.
6. Michael Field, *Underneath the Bough: A Book of Verses* (London: George Bell, 1893), 80–2.
7. Daniel Mendelsohn, 'The Passion of Henry James', *New York Times* (9 May 2008). In 1884, James had written a story, 'The Author of Beltraffio', based on Symonds's problems with his wife over his homosexuality.

8. In *Thomas Mann: Eros and Literature* (Berkeley, CA: University of California Press, 1997), Anthony Heilbut analyses Mann's diaries, which were unsealed in 1975, and which establish his homosexual inclinations.

9. Thomas Mann, *Death in Venice, Tristan, Tonio Kröger*, trans. H. T. Lowe-Porter (translation 1928; Harmondsworth: Penguin Modern Classics, 1955), 24.

10. There were several precursors of this expatriate gay–lesbian community, for example, the circle around Harriet Hosmer and Charlotte Cushman in mid-nineteenth-century Rome. See Martha Vicinus, *Intimate Friends: Women who Loved Women 1778–1928* (Chicago: University of Chicago Press, 2004).

11. Terry Castle, in her *Noël Coward and Radclyffe Hall: Kindred Spirits* (New York: Columbia University Press, 1996), suggests that Brockett may be modelled on Coward.

12. Radclyffe Hall, *The Well of Loneliness* (London: Virago Press, 1982), 234.

13. 'Sahitya ki Samtal Bhumi' (1926) in *Nirala Rachanavali*, ed. Nandkishor Naval (New Delhi: Rajkamal Prakashan, 1983), vol. v: 156–61, 156.

14. 'Navin Sahitya aur Prachin Vichar' (1929) in *Nirala Rachanavali*, vol. v: 441–3, 441.

15. Virginia Woolf, *Three Guineas* (1938; London: Harcourt Brace & Co., 1966), 109.

16. See Leela Gandhi, *Affective Communities: Anti-Colonial Thought, Fin-de-Siècle Radicalism, and the Politics of Friendship* (Durham, NC: Duke University Press, 2006).

17. E. M. Forster, 'What I Believe', *Two Cheers for Democracy* (1938; New York: Harcourt Brace, 1951), 68.

18. See Ruth Vanita and Saleem Kidwai, eds., *Same-Sex Love in India: Readings from Literature and History* (New York: St Martin's Press, 2000), especially 119–25, 161–8, 175–83.

19. *Ibid.*, 194–205.

20. For a more detailed account and analysis of the controversy and a translation of the text, see Ruth Vanita's translation of and introduction to Pandey Bechan Sharma Ugra, *Chocolate and Other Writings on Male-Male Desire* (New Delhi: Oxford University Press, 2006).

21. See Pandey Bechan Sharma Ugra, *About Me*, translated and with an introduction by Ruth Vanita (New Delhi: Penguin, 2007), 64. For *ranginmijaz* as a term for homoerotic inclination, see Vanita and Kidwai, *Same-Sex Love in India*, 192.

22. For an analysis of the homoerotic implications of these animals, see Ruth Vanita, *Sappho and the Virgin Mary: Same-Sex Love and the English Literary Imagination* (New York: Columbia University Press, 1996), chapter 9, 'Dogs, Phoenixes and Other Beasts: Nonhuman Creatures in Homoerotic Texts'.

23. See Anannya Dastupta, '"Do I Remove My Skin?": Interrogating Identity in Suniti Namjoshi's Fables', in Ruth Vanita, ed., *Queering India* (New York: Routledge, 2002), 100–10.

24. For a more extended analysis of this text, see Ruth Vanita, '"I'm an Excellent Animal": Cows at Play in the Writings of Bahinabai, Rukun Advani, Suniti Namjoshi and Others', in her *Gandhi's Tiger and Sita's Smile*, 290–310.

25. Suniti Namjoshi, *The Conversations of Cow* (London: The Women's Press, 1985), 32.

26. Borrowed from Gillian Hanscombe and Suniti Namjoshi, 'And There's You and Me, My Sweet Duality', *Women's Studies International Forum*, 24:3 (2001), 401–8.

27. Edmund White, *The Married Man* (London: Chatto & Windus, 2000), 66.

28. See George Wickes, *The Amazon of Letters: The Life and Loves of Natalie Barney* (New York: Popular Library, 1978); Claire Tomalin, *Katherine Mansfield: A Secret Life* (Harmondsworth: Penguin, 1988).

29. See Vanita and Kidwai, *Same-Sex Love in India*, 201.

30. See Ruth Vanita, *Love's Rite: Same-Sex Marriage in India and the West* (New Delhi: Penguin, and New York: Palgrave-Macmillan, 2005), Chapter 8, 'Married Among Their Companions: Female-Female Unions in Pre-Modern Erotica', 246–80.

31. See Edmund White, 'Out of the Closet, On to the Bookshelf', *New York Times Book Review* (16 June 1991).

32. Marilyn Hacker, *Love, Death and the Changing of the Seasons* (1986; London: Onlywomen Press, 1987).

33. David Sedaris, *Me Talk Pretty One Day* (Boston: Back Bay Books, 2001).

34. C. P. Cavafy, *Three Poems*, trans. James Merrill (Westchester, PA: Aralia Press, 1987).

35. See Miriam Benkovitz, *Ronald Firbank: A Biography* (New York: Knopf, 1969); James Merritt, *Ronald Firbank* (New York: Twayne, 1969).

36. Vikram Seth, *The Golden Gate* (New York: Random House, 1986); *A Suitable Boy* (New Delhi: Penguin, 1993).

37. Vikram Seth, *The Collected Poems* (New Delhi: Penguin, 1995), 46.

38. Sheela Reddy, interview with Vikram Seth, 'It Took Me Long To Come To Terms With Myself. Those Were Painful Years', *Outlook India* (2 October 2006); 'Sex, Lives, and no Videotape, and Transformative Grief', Up Front Radio, 30 December 2005; Leila Seth, *On Balance* (New Delhi: Viking, 2003).

39. Vikram Seth, *Collected Poems*, xv.

40. Amruta Patil, *Kari* (New Delhi: HarperCollins, 2008).

41. Mary Oliver, *Dream Work* (1986; New York: Atlantic Monthly Press, 2000), 38–9.

7

KATHRYN BOND STOCKTON

The queerness of race and same-sex desire

Intercourse and rubbing, or talking and crossing

The rub between 'race' and 'same-sex desire', as two concepts hotly contested yet frequently wedded, powerfully plays out its frictions in literature. Novels and films are capacious enough, as are poems, to show how fraught is the place where race and queerness cross – between groups of people, inside specific groups, or in individuals – and cross, moreover, at odd, oblique angles. Always, one wonders: what is the logic of how they join? Fictional texts immediately thicken these explanations, forging 'nonce taxonomies' (new, specific, one-time namings) as they help us theorize through the lure of details.[1]

A highly credentialled 'Negro' doctor, played by Sidney Poitier in 1967, in *Guess Who's Coming to Dinner*, becomes a black queer hustler depicted in 1993 by the actor Will Smith. The means of this startling transformation is *Six Degrees of Separation*, John Guare's 1990 play, written in the midst of the AIDS epidemic, in the early period of queer theorizing.[2] With its spare, staccato lines ('It's awful'; 'I am shaking'; 'You brought this thing into our house!'), its verbal patter (mixing ideas about revolution with Broadway showtunes) and its obvious theme of art as beholden to colour (a 'burst of color asked to carry so much'), *Six* shows queerness cannily haunting its mainstream model.[3]

Guess Who's Coming to Dinner (dir. Stanley Kramer) won Oscars in 1968 for depicting liberal parents (Spencer Tracy and Katharine Hepburn) coming to terms with their white daughter's marriage to a Negro doctor (Sidney Poitier). *Six Degrees of Separation* (dir. Fred Schepisi, 1993), playing on *Guess*, shows a black homosexual's intrusion into a wealthy liberal family by posing as their children's friend from boarding school and, invitingly, as the straight son of Sidney Poitier. The ultimate goal of this boy is embrace (later, adoption) by white wealthy parents. Thus *Six Degrees* simply makes explicit what, from the standpoint of contemporary struggles surrounding gay marriage, gay adoption and gay childhood, retrospectively looks like the spectral presence of homosexuality in *Guess Who's*. For in the latter film, set in San Francisco just before Stonewall, resistance to interracial marriage has signs of gay struggles to come: the shock of seeing a black–white passionate kiss in public view; the expectation of acceptance from liberals; the sad realization that even liberal parents need time to adjust to the less-than-happy sight of their newest relation; the parents' confession that they 'never thought that such a thing could happen' in their family; and, of course, the 'problem' of children, since children of 'mixed marriages' will be 'mixed' themselves, thus guaranteeing more children queered by colour. Since *Six Degrees* injects a gay protagonist into its playful engagement with *Guess*, the earlier film looks even more like it has phantom meanings alongside its focus on race relations.

Both films, moreover, call out white liberals for what they don't (fore)see. Responding to the children they did not see growing (either in their families or in the larger culture) is a belated task for liberal parents. No wonder these parents are birthed by their children in reverse, learning to *become* who they say they've been. Ironically, then, the black child-intruder reveals that liberal parents in one respect occupy the structural position of the 'gay' child: they are becoming themselves on delay. Protogay children, as we know, cannot be seen by the public to be 'gay' until they are no longer children. The paradigm for liberal whites in *Guess* and *Six* is this: they cannot be 'liberal' in the eyes of others until a situation makes them seem illiberal – some event, that is, which illuminates their potential prejudice and thus, paradoxically, gives them a chance to overcome intolerance and demonstrate 'enlightenment'. This strange period of re-negotiation lets them 'be' (really, become) who they say they 'are', even though they haven't been themselves until now.

Just as importantly, Guare's aggressive encroachment on *Guess*, like his black homosexual's invasions, shows how attempts to 'assume' identities may reveal intrusions of narratives on narratives. Indeed, *Six Degrees's* black homosexual, posing as Poitier's mannerly son, is at last unmasked. He is the creation of a white gay boy – who, in shaping this black hustler, would like to have himself seen through the figure of the cultured black straight son of Sidney Poitier: an acceptable and visible civil rights icon. Yet, *Six Degrees* does not come to climax with all family members (save the family maid) sitting down to dinner, as they do in *Guess*. Rather, in *Six*, the gay protagonist does what Poitier never did in the earlier film. He splits a marriage instead of making one. That is, he breaks a mirror. He makes the split in the echoing selves of liberal intellectual and liberal intellectual fully apparent, against all odds. The mother of the family he's been invading ends by saying, of her husband, his 'father': 'We're a terrible match.' *Coitus interruptus* in white liberal thinking is this film's intercourse, by its end.

Further setting the stage for this chapter, offering crossings no less dense, we could explore the layered depictions in the documentary *Paris is Burning* (dir. Jennie Livingston, 1990), portrayals that could be layered with depictions from the documentary *Southern Comfort* (dir. Kate Davis, 2001), a decade later. One storyline of *Paris is Burning* shows poor black and Latino men who might like to be, not just encounter, wealthy white women. This sex change is hard to achieve – an assumption of identity that weds impossibilities (though Michael Jackson nearly made this switch). One engaging interviewee tells the camera: 'I want to be a . . . rich white woman.' Yet a different person – Pepper Labéja, a 'legendary mother', who plans to keep her penis – reasonably muses that life as a woman might be even worse than life as a drag queen. In fact, in *Paris* an obvious earnestness (a wish for new realities) meets acknowledged ironies (a settling for 'realness'), for where queer campiness meets a people-of-colour inventiveness, one feels the rub between queer camp and a more straight-faced aesthetic creativity. Even more strikingly, *Paris* creates a new kind of woman. Here are truly phallic mothers. Each *has* the phallus while dressing to *be* it, fiercely supporting her own phallus precisely by being the beautiful woman who is meant to prop up phallic power.[4] These phallic women are clearly self-propping, though they are also propped up by 'children' (gay fashionistas) who deem them 'mothers'. That is, they are mothers not by birthing babies but by winning contests at gay fashion balls.

In *Southern Comfort* one steps outside the more usual depictions of trans-sexuals as male-to-female and urban in their dwellings. Following the lives of F to M transgendered whites in rural Georgia, one finds a trans-man who is dying of ovarian cancer ('the last part of me that's female is killing me'), while being cared for by a trans-woman, who proves to be, at least in some ways, the kind of woman the men in *Paris* would like to be: white, pampered, financially secure and touched by fame (through *Southern Comfort*). The class and racial components of this setting are even more engaging than the movie's questions of queerness. Crossing one's gender may result in shifting one's racial context – or in intensifying racial effects. The F to M men end up resembling and sharing interests – guns, hunks of meat, styles of dress, though not politics – with the Georgian men, the 'bubbas' of their town, who are Ku Klux Klan. Trans-men, then, can find themselves hailed by the very people who would organize to hurt them.

Hailing whom you hurt, even lethally wounding yourself in a fatal case of misrecognition, lies at the heart of David Henry Hwang's drama *M. Butterfly* (1988). As David Eng explains, the putatively straight, Western, white pro-tagonist of Hwang's play kills himself with supposed honour, committing seppuku, in an apparent bid to sustain his heterosexual, colonial fantasies, which he renders in this peroration: 'There is a vision of the Orient that I have.

Of slender women in chong sams and kimonos who . . . are born and raised to be the perfect women . . . It is a vision that has become my life.'[5] Although this French diplomat has been having relations with a diva he believes is female, not a male Chinese, and even though in a fateful moment the diva's penis is revealed to him, he performs suicide in order to straighten out his 'mistake'. Just before dying, he 'don[s] the robes of the forsaken Japanese geisha Cio-Cio San' (from Puccini's 1904 *Madama Butterfly*) and applies thick white makeup, as he prepares to conduct his act in whiteface.[6] Or, as Eng concludes: 'Gallimard [the diplomat] is forced to counter the disrobed diva with a transvesting act of his own: now that Song [the diva] is publicly the man, Gallimard must publicly become the woman.' This strange act preserves 'the psychic integrity' of Gallimard's desperate 'farce', which, despite its pretzel twists, rests on pedestrian colonial desires.[7]

These are complications for 'race' and 'queerness' by the end of the twentieth century. And despite the tease of their near-symmetries, there is no fully symmetrical, mirrored relation between 'queerness' and 'race'. Their linguistic binds and conceptual fields can be quite distinct. Rather, what we find is what I have conceived of as a set of 'switchpoints' between these domains.[8] I think of switchpoints, at least in part, in railroad terms, according to which a 'switch' is 'a movable section of railroad track' used to transfer 'a train from one set of tracks to another'; or, in electrical terms, 'a device used to open, close or divert an electric current'; or, in the general sense of a switch as 'a shift or transference, especially if sudden or unexpected'.[9] This term can refer to a connection between two signs – for example, 'black' and 'queer' or 'queer' and 'Asian' *and their sets of connotations* – where something from one flows towards the other, lending its connotative spread and signifying force to the other, illuminating it and intensifying it, but also sometimes shifting or adulterating it. One could thus explore, as I have sought to do, the stigmatized 'skin' of some queers' clothes; the description of blacks as an 'economic bottom'; and the ways in which blacks and queers (and, of course, queer blacks) have intersected through sufferings from AIDS – crossings depicted by literary texts in sophisticated ways.[10]

Moreover, dictionaries show that 'queer' and 'black', for instance, are linguistically elastic but historically narrow. 'Black' is an adjective (designating colour, mood, degree of hope) that may potentially apply to any noun. (This is not the case with 'Chicano/a' or 'Asian'.) 'Queer' in its general signification (meaning 'strange') may append itself to anything. Yet, in what we might call their congealed forms, these fluid terms have been hardened by historical use into nouns (blacks and queers) that trail debasements and contaminations dramatically behind them. 'Black' and 'queer' illustrate a basic feature of any meaning-making: the 'contamination' of any word's meaning by other meanings it also allows. It is now difficult to use the word 'queer' to mean only 'strange', without a listener or reader thinking 'homosexual'. The word's most group-specific definition ('[Slang for] homosexual: term of contempt or derision') contaminates its more general spread, congealing into 'homosexual'. Many queer theorists have fought this freezing – but not, intriguingly, its contaminations. Queer theorists (including Eve Kosofsky Sedgwick, Lee Edelman, Joseph Litvak, Lauren Berlant, Michael Warner, Carolyn Dinshaw and Carla Freccero) have tried to reinstate 'queer' as 'strange', to break against any scripted identities for 'gays' or 'homosexuals' – to break with congealment, as it were. And yet, in a sense, they would willingly, gladly spread contamination. They would make supposedly 'normal' sexualities confess their strangeness, and thus their queerness, lending 'normal' sex a whiff of their slang. (The phrase 'queer straights' illustrates this point.)

As for 'black', there's a nearly opposite dynamic. It is as if the word's more general meanings – 'totally without light', 'soiled', 'dirty', 'disgraceful', 'harmful', 'full of sorrow or suffering', 'disastrous', 'sullen or angry' and 'without hope' – threaten to swamp its group-specific definitions, which sound, by comparison, more benign: 'designating . . . any of the dark-skinned traditional inhabitants of sub-Saharan Africa, Australia, or Melanesia or their descendants in other parts of the world; by, for, or about black people as a group'. The range of contaminating significations sticking to 'black', even so, has led, in rather remarkable fashion, to politically sensitive forms of congealment on the part of anti-racist advocates. I am referring to the call to stop using any negative general meanings of 'black' altogether ('this is a black day', 'the outlook is black'), so as to cleanse the sign. The urge, in this case, is to foster freezing without contamination – to foster the use of a pure group sign for a people's identity.

Granted, there are prominent black queer theorists whom we might interpret as pushing to read 'black' as a sign for loss of boundaries or the queerness of death. But if 'black' spreads in these studies, it generally does so on the back of 'queer'. Sharon Patricia Holland, for instance, in her Epilogue ('"I'm in the Zone": Bill T. Jones, Tupac Shakur, and the (Queer) Art of Death') to *Raising the Dead: Readings of Death and (Black) Subjectivity*, argues that 'our proximity to death as human beings . . . might mark the queer space in us all because the possibility of an impending death is something we all share'; one page later, she states that 'the space of death is marked by blackness and is therefore always already queer'.[11] Similarly, in *Black Gay Man*, Robert Reid-Pharr suggests that 'the homosexual, like the Jew, becomes in late-twentieth-century Black American writing a vehicle by which to express the omnipresence of black boundarylessness'.[12] For Reid-Pharr, black gay men epitomize the 'border crossing and boundarylessness that has so preoccupied contemporary Black American intellectuals', and suggest 'that there is no normal blackness, no normal masculinity to which the black subject, American or otherwise, might refer'.[13] To be sure, 'gay', in Reid-Pharr's thinking, is making 'black' spread beyond the bounds of normativity. But what is the range of black border crossing? Just how far does 'black boundarylessness' extend itself? Even E. Patrick Johnson's clever use of 'quare' – his grandmother's Southern dialect for 'queer', which would seem to blacken this Irish word for 'strange' – appears to be on behalf of specificity, one that sticks to 'black'.[14] As he and Mae G. Henderson explain: 'we want to *quare* queer – to throw shade on its meaning in the spirit of extending its service to "blackness"'.[15]

These are the matters that make the intercourse of 'race' with 'queerness' a difficult, but also lush, form of talk. Now we should explore what other kinds of talking surround these crossings – and what other signifiers, or raced identities, have emerged in lesbian/gay/queer fictions.

Harlem Renaissance, black and blue

Why are 'gay voices' of the Harlem Renaissance hard to hear, if they exist? Although Henry Louis Gates, Jr has said that the movement 'was surely as gay as it was black', the neglect of this doubleness has been legendary.[16] What, however, does it mean to engage it? How does one listen for the strains of queerness running through poems whose bluesy collisions can almost always reduce to race? Do the details of writers' lives demand that we find doubled meanings in their work? Should the goal be 'varied and nuanced gay readings', 'sexually dissident' formulations or the excavation of 'haunting possibilities'?[17] Should the use of 'gay' be dropped in favour of 'same-sex interested' writers? As Christa Schwarz explains, claiming certain 'Renaissance writers as "gay" makes sense only on a very general level of discussion'. Schwarz contrasts, for instance, the 'affirmative gay identity' of Richard Bruce Nugent, and 'his unapologetic portrayal of men-loving men', with the 'more subdued' pitch of Countee Cullen's 'gay voice'.[18]

Less ambiguous when these writers were writing was the coding of Harlem. (The Renaissance ran from the early 1920s to the mid 1930s.) 'Negro capital of the world', Harlem was not just the residential centre of black life then, but also the 'sexual pleasure center' of Manhattan and the nation. It represented 'the racial segregation of vice', insofar as it provided an 'outrageous' and 'safer alternative' 'for those seeking same-sex encounters' in the city.[19] Even so, its 'single, unifying theme' was 'explicit sexuality', not sexual orientation, and thus it was for tourists 'the epitome of the forbidden', offering what amounted to 'show nights for ... Nordics'.[20] Which is not to say that some magical tolerance blanketed Harlem in those years. The black bourgeoisie, which stressed morality and sought respectability, targeted migrants and 'lower-class' blacks as the source of deviance; the black newspapers ran headlines that read 'Are Pansies People?' and 'Will the Plague Spread?'; and leaders like W. E. B. Du Bois responded to writings like Claude McKay's novel, *Home to Harlem*, by saying, 'for the most part [it] nauseates me, and after the dirtier parts of its filth I feel distinctly like taking a bath'.[21] In part in response, 'several artists, including [Wallace Thurman], Nugent, Hughes, Aaron Douglas, and Zora Neale Hurston, formed the provocatively named Niggeratti', offering to Harlem and the nation 'a brand new nigger', as Hughes put it.[22]

Nugent and Hughes make a striking pair. In his 'Smoke, Lilies and Jade' (1926), a tumbling, dreamy, mind-in-slipstream story of a racially unspecified man, Nugent pens the first openly homoerotic writing by a black author. The story, which first appeared in the short-lived periodical *Fire!! A Quarterly Devoted to the Younger Negro Artists*, is liquid, hypnotic and mysterious, as it unwinds in strings of ellipses. Gently rolling memories of death are the waves the protagonist rides to his cyclical, conscious act of lying abed, doing nothing, blowing blue smoke: 'was all life like that . . . smoke . . . blue smoke from an ivory holder'; 'he blew a cloud of smoke . . . but soon the moon would rise and then he would clothe the silver moon in blue smoke garments'.[23] Here are echoes of Lord Henry Wotton, the sybarite from Oscar Wilde's famous novel, *The Picture of Dorian Gray*, who, in a 'studio filled with . . . the heavy scent of . . . lilac', 'from the corner of the divan of Persian saddle-bags on which he was lying, smoking . . . innumerable cigarettes . . . could just catch the gleam of . . . blossoms . . . [on] branches [that] seemed hardly able to bear the burden of a beauty so flame-like as theirs'.[24] And, indeed, from the smoky, bluesy island of his bed, Nugent's nineteen-year-old would-be Wildean artist (who, unlike Lord Henry Wotton, had 'spent his last five cents' and was 'hungry' (1)) recalls meeting Beauty, a flame come to life. The latter, speaking Spanish, enters into the blueness of night and the 'blue thoughts' of Nugent's young man: 'the stranger knew the magic of blue smoke also'. 'Alex called him Beauty . . . long they lay blowing smoke and exchanging thoughts . . . he felt a glow of tremor . . . and they talked and . . . slept' (3). Held in that ellipsis, between 'talked' and 'slept', may be an action forbidden to be named – or perhaps not. From here, Alex moves between Beauty and Melva, a female lover, in his dreams, but not before he pauses and 'his eyes wandered . . . on past the muscular hocks to the firm white thighs . . . the rounded buttocks . . . then the lithe narrow waist . . . strong torso and broad deep chest . . . grecian nose with its temperamental nostrils . . . and it was Beauty' (4). The beauty of blue may be homosexual, but also bisexual; it may be interracial, but also unspecified, even if someone is speaking Spanish.

Still, Nugent seems positively reckless, or open, or flaming, in comparison to the puzzling Hughes – which may explain, in part, the dense fascinations that surround 'Langston'. Hughes is an icon of historical hiddenness, whether or not he had things to hide. For he's been taken by many to be lying just beneath the sliding surface of his words. Hence, the sly quotation by Nugent of Hughes, making the words of Hughes play a part in 'Smoke, Lilies, and Jade', where Nugent writes: 'a few lines of one of Langston's poems ... Somewhat like Ariel Somewhat like Puck Somewhat like a gutter boy Who loves to play in muck. Somewhat like Bacchus Somewhat like Pan And a way with women Like a sailor man' (3). Mythical, airy bad-boyishness, with strains of manliness, touches down in muckiness and escapes homoerotics (does it really?) in the image of a seaman. What does it mean that Hughes liked sailors, adored his time at sea, recalled it in writing in Whitmanesque tones, at least at times? We can't really know. His poem 'Young Sailor' reveals no more than the playful grandiosity he locates in his subject and a *carpe diem* that comes with the sea. 'Port Town', however, is cleverly crafted so that the author shares, of all things, a prostitute's voice, beckoning seductively and shading into a valentine not quite meant to be believed:

> Hello, sailor boy,
> In from the sea!
> Hello, sailor,
> Come with me!
> Come on drink cognac.
> Rather have wine?
> Come here, I love you.
> Come and be mine.[25]

The other side of this momentary brio is the evaporative quality of love, disappearing almost before it is known, since the reader enters when it's already vanished:

> Last night I dreamt
> This most strange dream,
> And everywhere I saw
> What did not seem could ever be:
> *You were not there with me*!   ('Dream', 97)

Hughes's aptly named 'Desire' speaks to this evanescence most directly – as if the act of grasping lust has made desire escape, leaving nakedness to the room alone:

> Desire to us
> Was like a double death,

> Swift dying
> Of our mingled breath,
> Evaporation
> Of an unknown strange perfume
> Between us quickly
> In a naked
> Room.   (90)

Then there are poems that spotlight strangeness (beyond the 'strange dream' and 'strange perfume' above) by making it materialize in a range of forms:

> In times of stormy weather
> She felt queer pain   ('Strange Hurt', 84)

And sorrow poems take these feelings further into cryptic lands of pain, as in 'Island':

> Wave of sorrow,
> Do not drown me now:
> I see the island
> Still ahead somehow.   (78)

But who is there for him?

No wonder Isaac Julien could find in Langston Hughes an emblem of burial, a barrow of blues, suggesting desires that never did die but had to push against the (dangers of) light. In *Looking for Langston* (1989), Julien's experimental film about the poet, Hughes is given a lively wake, and Julien imagines what the Harlem Renaissance is still yielding in the age of AIDS. With its sirens, funerary ornaments, campy, solemn angels and smoky incense; its beautiful corpse (Julien as Hughes, resting in a coffin); its tuxedoed black gay males (with a pair of lesbians) frozen on the dance floor, then put into motion; and its mingling of Nugent's 'Smoke' (Beauty is black, his head cradled in a naked lap) with the AIDS poems of Essex Hemphill ('this nut might kill, this kiss could turn to stone'), Julien is undoubtedly creating, in the words of José Muñoz, 'a grand and glowing mythotext', 'revisionary history that meditates on queer cadences ... [in] Hughes' life and work', and 'a complicated transhistorical dialogue' that puts Hemphill in touch with Nugent, Robert Mapplethorpe with James Van Der Zee, while also 'layering ... different gay spaces' around the central icon.[26] As David Marriott rightly puts it: 'Black gay desire does exist in *Looking for Langston*, but as an enigma, as the enigmatic encounter with a look in which desire withdraws as soon as it shows itself, destined to depart' – just as we saw in Hughes's own poems.[27] What does it mean, then, that we end this film with Hughes himself exclaiming: 'Sun's arisin': this is goin' to be my song; I could be blue, but I been blue all night long.'[28]

Ties that bind, unbind: Chicano/a family exiles

Unburial – what Julien seems to seek for Hughes – can be exilic, nonetheless. The act of unburying one's own self, especially in writing, while one is living, can promise exile. John Rechy and Cherríe Moraga make, in this respect, an unexpected pair. They gauge escape – into experimental sexual lives – by their exiles from their mothers, illuminating destinies of unmarked racialities.

I say 'unmarked' because Rechy famously spurned being read for any racial specificity attached to him – unlike Moraga. Both, nonetheless, offer a version of the labyrinthine, subtle snaking of a racial signifier through one's life – and, in their cases, through a brown mother ghosting their lives, even hiding inside of words that do not at all signify her. This could be a browning of Freudian theory: returning to your mother who signifies a colour you are destined to relate to, fitfully, (un)consciously. And yet, Rechy, son of a surly Scottish father and a beloved Mexican mother, saw himself as heir to writers as diverse as Faulkner, Lorca, Poe, Euripides, Stein, Baldwin and Emily Brontë.[29] And, indeed, *City of Night*, long considered a 'modern classic' since it appeared in 1963, has been largely seen as a sexual tour de force, as the definitive, fictional account, written directly from Rechy's life, of male hustling on both coasts, and, so memorably, in Times Square. Here is the 'youngman', as he is called, with New York as 'symbol of my liberated self', with Times Square as 'an electric island floating on a larger island', 'magnet for all the lonesome exiles', 'shadowy figures' with 'malehungry looks', striking a range of hustler poses: 'youngmanoutofajob butlooking; dontgiveadamnyoungman drifting; perennialhustler easytomakeout; youngmanlostinthebigcity pleasehelpme-sir'; also 'a mixture of jazz, joint, junk sounds'.[30] 'But like a possessive lover', says the narrator, 'or like a powerful drug – it lured me' (30). Here is the inverse of film theory's fascination with the spectator-as-voyeur, as a Peeping Tom, looking into the lit window of the moviescreen to ogle women-as-visual-pleasure. In this theatre, every Peeping Tom is self-involved, trying to score with his back to the screen, 'swallowed instantly by that giant wolfmouth of dark at the opening of which the dreamworld of a certain movie is being projected: the actors like ghosts from an altogether Different world' (31).

And there's a different Different world. Threading through these tales, only intermittently and often momentarily, are Mexican memories: 'Crazily Im remembering a Mexican kid song: "Let it rain, let it rain, Virgin of the Cave"' (25). And at times powerfully, there is his mother: 'The figure of my Mother standing by the kitchen door crying, watching me leave, hovered ghostlike over me' (31). These, we realize, are the two poles of *City of Night*: his Mexican mother, 'a beautiful woman ... who loves me fiercely and never once understood about the terror between me and my father', and other figures now wanting him, drifters like 'the merchant marine ... from a recent Voyage to somefarwhere' (14, 21–2). One can read this novel as the story of how racialized memories of a mother and place (El Paso) become unspoken references for the 'exiled exiles' Rechy is drawn to – not because causal connections are there to be read in terms of race or class, but precisely because, adumbrated, they remain unguessed. *City of Night* begins in El Paso, with a dying dog, a violent father, 'my mother's blind carnivorous love' and the 'seeds of ... rebellion' planted 'somewhere in that plain of childhood' (12). In ways unspecified, these seeds take root in 'the alluring anarchic world' of male hustling. Only later, in 1984, in his author's introduction, does Rechy tell us that he wrote the book in 'my mother's small house': '"You're writing a beautiful book, my son," [my mother] told me' (xiii).

No less intensely, Moraga's story pivots on the axis of her mother in *Loving in the War Years* (1983/2000). Moraga is a moon, as she states in metaphor, to her brother's sun. Pale and 'exiled into the darkness of the night', 'writing in exile', she is even like the Aztec moon, 'severed into pieces in the war against her brother', he who as a male receives his mother's love unreservedly, as she gives it without measure.[31] The metaphor of moon illuminates two facts: Moraga's exile into whiteness (she is fair-skinned, passing for white); and her exile into her desires (knowing the 'danger of putting ... "lesbian" and "Chicana" together on the same page' (iii)). No wonder Moraga, at twelve years old (who, at ten, 'knew she was queer', 'making up stories' about her being a 'sailor/savior of ... French women'), dreams of lying in a hospital bed: '[My] breasts are large and ample. And below my stomach, I see my own cock, wildly shooting menstrual blood totally out of control. The image of the hermaphrodite' (ix, 107, 110). She was 'bleached and beached', she succinctly says (50). And betrayed – by the very woman (her Chicana mother, married to an anglo) who has inspired Moraga's love of women: 'What kind of lover have you made me, mother / *so in love* / with what is left / unrequited' (8); 'the gash sewn back into a snarl / would last for years' (52).

Can Moraga untie this bind? Perhaps paradoxically, being in love with an illiterate, wounding mother with dark skin, Moraga becomes an assimilating, light-skinned, educated writer, whose mother-infused-woman-love (which looks riddled with betrayals) poignantly returns her to Chicana contexts: 'when I finally lifted the lid to my lesbianism, a profound connection with my mother reawakened in me', alongside 'empathy for my mother's oppression', since 'in this country, lesbianism is poverty' (44). So, she writes, 'I am a white girl gone brown to the color of my mother speaking for her' (52). Still – therefore? even so? – 'I long to enter you like a temple' (82).

Rituals awry: queer Asian conflicts

In Deepa Mehta's film *Fire* (1996), the entry into a woman's 'temple' is required. Palaces and tombs, moreover, are the bookends to the love of women: their severe disappointments in men – symbolized, intriguingly, by the Taj Mahal – and their fragile escape with each other (will it just be exile?) after their reunion at a sacred tomb – the burial place for a Sufi saint – from which they will alight, at the film's end. This cunning framework holds the rarity of South Asian women stepping into the signifieds of 'lesbian', while, as Gayatri Gopinath suggests, *Fire* is 'part of … [the] project of decentering whiteness' by critiquing the 'Euro-American paradigms' *Fire* both evokes and circumvents.[32] In fact, *Fire* dramatizes how the signifiers of 'race' and 'culture' are hard, if not impossible, to disentangle.

Perhaps not surprisingly, this deck is stacked. Using specific South Asian signifiers, *Fire* creates conditions for its women that would make any pair of females want each other: one arranged marriage undermined by a husband's devotion to his guru, leading to his celibacy; the other marriage arranged around a husband's Chinese-but-American-sounding mistress he will not forsake; all while the wives are expected to present themselves purely for their husbands' use, which includes their husbands' not touching them, even not desiring them. Thus, the utter cruelty of these women's purity. That is to say, if director Deepa Mehta would make Indian women's mutual sexual adoration visible and plausible, especially to other than 'Western eyes', she must find a wedge with which to open purity to its own brutalities, while making beautiful what would otherwise signal perversity. Hence, her film is a pretty prison flick, burnishing the surface of nearly every image and her protagonists' visual pleasure, so that the camera's gaze *does* objectify, oddly to surprising feminist effect, each woman's beauty. *Fire*, that is, makes us wonder what two women, immured in their 'prison' – middle-class homelife with its requirements of a wife's purity (and two husbands who don't want them) – could do for sex but have it together. Add to this mix: a dour and mute mother-in-law that the women wait on continually (hand and foot, since she is bedbound) and the family servant who, when alone, masturbates to videos in full sight of the aging mother – that is, before the servant is discovered by the women, after which discovery he exposes *them*. This film's signifying field is full. It slips meanings inside signifiers that cannot convey them – though we *see* their lack of conveyance – and it layers provocative signifiers onto meanings we thought we knew.

Unthinkability, as we learn in Gopinath's *Impossible Desires*, has been more the mode of Asian women's queerness and same-sex desire. And, to be sure, when *Fire* hit theatres in Indian cities, after a two-year run at film

festivals held in India, Europe and North America, feelings exploded over
what the public (might think it) was seeing. Violent activists from the Shiv
Sena, a militant wing of the Hindu Right, assaulted both cinemas and movie-
goers, claiming that the scene of the women having sex 'is a direct attack on
our Hindu culture and civilization' (157) by the West. As Gopinath informs
us, even a prominent feminist author, Madhu Kishwar, berated the Canadian
Indian director, Deepa Mehta, saying, 'I wanted to ignore [the film] as an
exercise in self-flagellation by a self-hating Hindu and a self-despising
Indian – a very common type among the English educated elite in India'
(132). No doubt what these voices were responding to was the extent to
which the film *recruits* Hindu mythology – its treasured signifiers – for its
depictions of its protagonists, Radha and Sita. Gopinath explains: 'In Hindu
mythology, Radha is the consort of the god Krishna, who is famous for his
womanizing; together Radha and Krishna symbolize an idealized, transcendent heterosexual union'; 'Sita, the heroine of the Hindu epic *Ramayana*,
proves her chastity to her husband, Ram, by immersing herself in fire, and
thus represents the ideal of wifely devotion and virtue' (141). Clearly, Mehta
bends these stories by having Radha and Sita peel off from their respective
myths and, in essence, elope with each other, after Mehta's Radha (not the
myth's Sita) emerges unscathed from a kitchen fire that proves the purity of
her *desire*. And yet, crucially, these signifiers, 'their eroticizing of a particular
aesthetic of Indian femininity', a 'queer femininity ... at odds with conventional Euro-American "lesbian" histories' in their whitened forms, step outside, in Gopinath's view, the Western understandings that the Hindu Right
feels it detects (154–5). Just as crucially, the yardstick in these arguments –
Hindu nationalist culture – is not itself pristine, as we learn from Ratna
Kapur, in *Erotic Justice: Law and the New Politics of Postcolonialism*.
Kapur emphasizes how many aspects of Indian culture and sexuality – especially 'women's sexual purity' – were 'reshaped and reconstituted' through
the British 'colonial encounter'.[33] '[T]he paradox is that both sexuality and
nationalism as they emerged were simultaneously Western, but not' (54).
Moreover, 'just as the emerging Indian nationalist bore the mark of
Western conceptions of nationalism, so too did the reconstituted space of
Indian sexuality bear more than a slight resemblance to Victorian sexuality';
even so, in a rich contradiction, Indian women's sexual chastity came to stand
for the 'purity of Indian culture' and 'its superiority to the culture of the
Empire' (54). Fighting this battle in reverse, unpurifying Indian culture from a
different angle, Indians arguing for gay and lesbian rights, says Kapur, claim
that the *Kama Sutra*, which began to be compiled in the early 4th century AD,
'contains an entire chapter on homosexual sex as well as on lesbian sex' (83).
No wonder *Fire*, then, accumulated layered, warring meanings as it circulated

'within India, within the South Asian diaspora, and within film festival circuits and theatres in Europe and North America.'[34]

Fire even offers figures for its warrings and its layers. The masturbating servant is a brilliant switchpoint where two Victorian meanings cross each other and also intersect with Indian purity. In the British Victorian novel, there is no figure more crucial for the maintenance of the family's hymen, its sense of boundedness and self-protection from the penetration of any impropriety, than the family servant, who has the job of controlling the entrance and exits of visitors.[35] That *Fire*'s servant is a masturbator – a Victorian symbol of perversion, which has become by now a sign of health in Western contexts – indicates that cultures, like families and signs, are extremely porous and can't avoid intercourse (or at least a rubbing) with their own outsides. Through the masturbator, we are viewing contaminating motions, as we watch the traffic of significations at cultural switchpoints. Moreover, since the viewer of *Fire* sees the mother – the aging symbol of 'Mother India', as it were – having to watch the masturbating servant pleasure himself with video porn, while she madly rings her bell (since she's mute) in vigorous protest, we see how signifiers gather layered meanings. A simple ring that once meant 'I am hungry', 'I need water', 'please attend to my needs', now can mean unheard of things like 'a man is masturbating in my room' or, even later, 'two devoted wives are dancing with each other and acting in love'. Only the viewer watches these meanings accrue and build on top of each other, showing Mother India with no claims to purity in the signifiers that speak for her (which, even earlier, were never fully, purely discernible). Just as striking as the changing bells are the signifiers *Fire* is densely layering onto Western lesbian sexuality. Here a particular stroking of the hair, a certain way of escaping to a balcony and talking at its ledge – never mind a scene of hopscotch kissing, an act of licking sweat from a leg and a parody of Bollywood dancing – indicate that new kinds of feminine women (not in the mould of Western 'femmes') are turning sexually to each other.

One last image gathers this chapter in its entirety: the celibate husband, head in hands, playing and replaying as if it were a film the image of the women (the two of them in bed) he now carries as a sign inside him. This is an intercourse he cannot avoid. Neither can we, since via fiction, a fictional film, we have the Hindu-celibate-husband-replaying-the-scene inside ourselves. This is an intercourse open to talking.

NOTES

1. The phrase 'nonce taxonomies' is Eve Sedgwick's, from *Epistemology of the Closet* (Berkeley: University of California Press, 1990), 23.

2. This first section on *Guess* and *Six* is drawn from my book, *The Queer Child, or Growing Sideways in the Twentieth Century* (Durham, NC: Duke University Press, 2009).

3. John Guare, *Six Degrees of Separation* (New York: Vintage, 1990), 3, 14, 49.

4. For his exposition of the differential positions of 'having' and 'being' the phallus, see Jacques Lacan, 'The Meaning of the Phallus', *Feminine Sexuality: Jacques Lacan and the École Freudienne*, ed. and trans. Juliet Mitchell and Jacqueline Rose (New York: Norton and Pantheon Books, 1985), 83–4.

5. Quoted in David L. Eng, *Racial Castration: Managing Masculinity in Asian America* (Durham, NC: Duke University Press, 2001), 138.

6. Eng, *Racial Castration*, 138.

7. *Ibid.*

8. For the original and longer version of these arguments, see Kathryn Bond Stockton, *Beautiful Bottom, Beautiful Shame: Where 'Black' Meets 'Queer'* (Durham, NC: Duke University Press, 2006), 27–33.

9. All definitions in this chapter are from the *American Heritage Dictionary*, College Edition, unless otherwise specified.

10. For extended examples of these crossings in literary texts, see Stockton, *Beautiful Bottom*.

11. Sharon Patricia Holland, *Raising the Dead: Readings of Death and (Black) Subjectivity* (Durham, NC: Duke University Press, 2000), 179–80.

12. Robert Reid-Pharr, *Black Gay Man: Essays* (New York: New York University Press, 2001), 15.

13. *Ibid.*, 103.

14. E. Patrick Johnson, '"Quare" Studies, or (Almost) Everything I Know about Queer Studies I Learned from My Grandmother', in E. Patrick Johnson and Mae G. Henderson, eds., *Black Queer Studies: A Critical Anthology* (Durham, NC: Duke University Press, 2005), 126.

15. Johnson and Henderson, 'Introduction: Queering Black Studies / "Quaring" Queer Studies', in *Black Queer Studies*, 7.

16. Henry Louis Gates, Jr, 'The Black Man's Burden', in Michael Warner, ed., *Fear of a Queer Planet* (Minneapolis: University of Minnesota Press, 1993), 233. See also A. B. Christa Schwarz, *Gay Voices of the Harlem Renaissance* (Bloomington: Indiana University Press, 2003); Eric Garber, 'T'aint Nobody's Bizness: Homosexuality in 1920s Harlem', in Michael J. Smith, ed., *Black Men / White Men: A Gay Anthology* (San Francisco: Gay Sunshine, 1983), 7–16; Alden Reimonenq, 'Countee Cullen's Uranian "Soul Windows"', in Emmanuel S. Nelson, ed., *Critical Essays: Gay and Lesbian Writers of Color* (New York: Harrington Park-Haworth, 1993), 143–66; and Gregory Woods, 'Gay Re-readings of the Harlem Renaissance Poets', in Nelson, ed., *Critical Essays*, 127–42.

17. Schwarz, *Gay Voices*, 3.

18. *Ibid.*, 143.

19. Kevin J. Mumford, *Interzones: Black/White Sex Districts in Chicago and New York in the Early Twentieth Century* (New York: Columbia University Press, 1997), 85, and Schwarz, *Gay Voices*, 9.

20. Schwarz, *Gay Voices*, 11, 10, and Langston Hughes, quoted in Schwarz, *Gay Voices*, 9.

21. W. E. B. Du Bois, 'Two Novels', review of *Passing* by Nella Larsen and *Home to Harlem* by Claude McKay, *Crisis* (June 1928), 202.
22. Schwarz, *Gay Voices*, 34.
23. Richard Bruce Nugent, 'Smoke, Lilies and Jade', 2–3. Accessed online, on 18 June 2008, at http://userpage.fu-berlin.de/~wilker/harlem/smokelilies.htm. Ellipses in original. Further references are given in parentheses.
24. Oscar Wilde, *The Picture of Dorian Gray* (New York: Penguin, 1985), 23.
25. Langston Hughes, *Selected Poems of Langston Hughes* (New York: Knopf, 1979), 71. Further references are given in parentheses.
26. José Esteban Muñoz, *Disidentifications: Queers of Color and the Performance of Politics* (Minneapolis: University of Minnesota Press, 1999), 58, 59, 61, 73.
27. David Marriott, *Haunted Life: Visual Culture and Black Modernity* (New Brunswick, NJ: Rutgers University Press, 2007), 113.
28. It should be noted, as Marriott tells us, that, 'objecting to the film's homosexual content, [George] Bass [Hughes's literary executor] and the Hughes estate twice blocked the screening of *Looking for Langston* in the United States while withdrawing permission for the use of Hughes's poems in the film's soundtrack' (*ibid.*, 116).
29. John Rechy, 'Introduction', *City of Night* (New York: Grove Press, 1984), x.
30. Rechy, *City of Night*, 20, 21, 30, 32. Further references are given in parentheses.
31. Cherríe Moraga, *Loving in the War Years: Lo Que Nunca Pasó Por Sus Labios* (Cambridge, MA: South End Press, 2000), iii. Further references are given in parentheses.
32. Gayatri Gopinath, *Impossible Desires: Queer Diasporas and South Asian Public Cultures* (Durham, NC: Duke University Press, 2005), 11. Further references are given in parentheses.
33. Ratna Kapur, *Erotic Justice: Law and the New Politics of Postcolonialism* (London: Glasshouse Press, 2005), 54. Further references are given in parentheses.
34. Gopinath, *Impossible Desires*, 158.
35. For a discussion of these dynamics, see Kathryn Bond Stockton, *God Between Their Lips: Desire Between Women in Irigaray, Brontë, and Eliot* (Stanford, CA: Stanford University Press, 1994), 232–7.

8

RICHARD CANNING

The literature of AIDS

This chapter considers the breadth, volume, diversity and appeal of works of literature in English which have engaged with the medical syndrome AIDS – Acquired Immune Deficiency Syndrome – since the first evidence of its spread in 1981. It cannot hope to be representative in terms of the global impact of the AIDS epidemic for a simple reason. Though the scale of HIV/AIDS in many non-Western societies is far greater than in Europe or America, non-Western literary and cultural manifestations of AIDS have been scarce. Equally, though many non-English cultures have seen an impressive, substantial body of AIDS-related literature emerge, I have focused on texts written or made in English. With the exception of a few French, Italian and Spanish authors and filmmakers – Cyril Collard, Hervé Guibert, Pier Vittorio Tondelli, Ferzan Ozpetek, Pedro Almodovar and Juan Goytisolo – non-English texts have had a small circulation, rarely being translated or distributed in the English-speaking world.

This relative invisibility holds true for works in English published in countries outside the USA, UK, Ireland and Canada, such as South Africa, Australia or New Zealand. For reasons of space, I have restricted myself mostly to British and American texts in a number of genres, which illustrate key tendencies, and to some lesser-known or untypical works, as well as to some critical and theoretical responses, both to the syndrome and to its cultural representations. After sketching the biomedical context for this discussion, I start, however, with the contemporary dearth of representations of AIDS in culture, examining how the epidemic has become distanced from us today by way of becoming historicized. Next I consider the much larger phenomenon of 'AIDS culture' in the English-speaking world. I have singled out a substantial body of AIDS literature written by non-Caucasian authors, as this material has often been overlooked, and diverges in particular emphases and approaches from its 'white' counterpart.

There is no room here to gloss the many distinct, sometimes contentious medical terms and concepts relating to AIDS. A number of shorthand terms may suffice. This author accepts the prevalent scientific view of how the syndrome works on the body. An initial transmission of the Human Immuno-Deficiency Virus (HIV, one of a group of so-called 'retroviruses') – through blood, semen or another bodily fluid – causes a weakening of bodily immunity which, without medical intervention, is likely to get worse. Consequently, there is the probability that 'HIV-related illnesses' and 'AIDS-related conditions' (ARCs) may proliferate, often proving cumulatively debilitating or fatal. This trajectory can – in many cases, but far from all – be arrested, even prevented, by various 'combination therapies' – combinations of antiretroviral drugs that mutually interact – which have been increasingly prescribed to affected parties since the late 1990s.[1]

The relationship between AIDS and gay sexuality has had a vexed history since symptoms emerged in a number of sexually active gay men, mostly in the United States, in the late 1970s and early 1980s. One of the syndrome's early names – GRID, or Gay-Related Immune Deficiency – reflected its purported provenance, though early sufferers from beyond this supposed risk group – women, children, intravenous drug users, those receiving contaminated blood products – may have exhibited HIV- and AIDS-related symptoms without their being identified.

An estimated 33 million people worldwide are currently said to be 'living with HIV'. Though new transmissions – at something like 7,500 per day – remain a major concern, the UN today argues against generalizing over modes of transmission and risk groups or behaviours.[2] Since 2005 its global strategy has been to target campaigns aimed at preventing the spread of HIV at three groups 'most at risk': 'sex workers, men who have sex with men and injecting drug users'.[3] These three categories identify risk groups according to behaviour rather than identity (or sexual identity). However, the term 'men who have sex with men' points to two contemporary truisms: firstly, there are greater risks of HIV transmission involved in certain sexual acts commonly, but not exclusively, engaged in by men with other men (specifically, anal intercourse without prophylaxis); secondly, many men having sexual relations with other men do not consider themselves to be gay, homosexual or queer. Even here, we must be cautious. While the UN notes that 'in virtually all regions outside of sub-Saharan Africa, HIV infections have disproportionately affected injecting drug users, men who have sex with men, and sex workers', an entirely different model of transmission persists in sub-Saharan African countries, where most new infections may be ascribed to heterosexual sex.[4] The UN concludes that '"Knowing your local epidemic" remains critical to effective prevention efforts.'[5]

In a sense, cultural responses to AIDS constitute a 'local epidemic' in themselves. The huge quantity of novels, memoirs, films, dramas and collections of verse has never come close to reflecting the diversity of the epidemic's affected populations, in respect of geography, race, gender, age, class or sexuality. Many practical factors account for this. Most obviously, the time, energy and material circumstances needed for a writer to produce material may simply not be available. For film, funding opportunities – and related contingencies – have clearly been key. For broadcast and theatre works, censorship and self-censorship have intruded. Globally, the publishing industry has hardly encouraged writing on AIDS. Moreover, one factor might reasonably be considered nearly universal, in inhibiting the free production and expression of creative responses to HIV/AIDS: shame. Whether we think of AIDS as a syndrome affecting the individual, or an epidemic affecting populations, it has been a phenomenon with which few have wished to be linked, whether at the level of macro-politics (President Reagan's notorious long silence) or the reading patterns of the individual (Western publishers 'know' that books about AIDS, unlike those about cancer and other hazards to health, cannot sell).

Today, since the discovery of antiretroviral therapies and their use in treatments, starting from around 1997, we face an unnatural calm, even silence, in respect of 'cultural AIDS'. Globally the epidemic tenaciously endures, even thrives, yet it is too rarely in evidence in the stories we hear about, read, watch or witness. Paradoxically, although there have been fewer fatalities, the number of HIV-infected people in most Western populations has risen significantly, whilst their presence in Western cultural narratives – from soap operas to stage plays and beyond – has diminished sharply. HIV/AIDS threatens to become a non-story.

Since the beginning of the twenty-first century, just a handful of creative responses to this entirely new context for the epidemic has appeared. As I wrote in 2007, 'Armistead Maupin's *The Night Listener* (2000) and *Michael Tolliver Lives* (2007) are still virtually alone in considering the impact of the new drug treatments on how PWAs live.'[6] *Michael Tolliver Lives* highlighted a formal problem: describing the experience of quotidian living, however unexpected, in a way that is compelling. Living on HIV medications can often be relatively undramatic. Women characters with HIV are an even scarcer phenomenon than (usually gay) male PWAs; a single example, perhaps, appearing in the fiction of the last decade in America, in Shannon Burke's *Safelight*.[7] In the memoir genre, one of the only accounts of combination therapy treatment has been *My Pet Virus* (2006) by Shawn Decker, heterosexual and a self-proclaimed 'thinblood [haemophiliac] positoid [HIV-positive] with a sick sense of humor'.[8] Neologisms abound in AIDS literature.

It is tempting to consider that we may be experiencing nothing more than a time delay – that many works are 'in the wings', or gestating in people's minds, as they first come to terms with the new circumstances. After all, this was the case with 'early AIDS'; politicians were castigated for their silence, but within affected subcultures, those individuals who had something to say or write were far outnumbered by those who – initially, at least – did not. This was remedied in a five-year period of intense cultural activity, between around 1992 and 1997, a whole decade into the Western epidemic. Contrastingly, since the year 2000 there has been a remarkable statistical decline in AIDS cultural consciousness, and, as I shall argue, those few works which do appear are more prone to historicize the epidemic – that is, return to the days of uncertainty with the hindsight of a post-treatment consciousness – than to describe it as an ongoing reality.

Hollywood has apparently simply done its duty, with *Philadelphia* (1994) its sole prominent foray into AIDS.[9] Since 2000, just one studio title – Craig Lucas's *The Dying Gaul* (2005), adapted from his own play of that name – has extensively considered the epidemic.[10] In this film, scriptwriter Robert is offered a huge sum if he will change a semi-autobiographical script – 'The Dying Gaul', about his relationship with a now-deceased partner – into a story featuring only heterosexual characters. As Jeffrey – the studio executive chasing the script – puts it,

JEFFREY: You want to reach as many people as possible with the universal human ... truth about these two characters. One of whom is a Person With Aids ...
   Now: Don't. Say. Anything. Until – Okay:
   Hold all my calls. Most. Americans. Hate. Gay people. They
hear it's about gay people, they won't go.
ROBERT: What about *Philadelphia*?
JEFFREY: *Philadelphia* is a movie about a man who hates gay people, period. And it's been done ...
   Now if we make Maurice a woman with AIDS, and let's face it, heterosexuals are getting AIDS in disastrous numbers ... we'll give you one million dollars for your script.[11]

The excerpt suggests how conservative notions of the cinema marketplace have conditioned that industry's engagement with the subject – as with homosexuality itself. It was certainly true, in earlier years, that film dramas concerning HIV/AIDS featured an improbable proliferation of stories about women threatened with infection through their (often unwitting) involvement in bisexual relationships. Wives or girlfriends discovered, through their own unexpected HIV-positive status, the sexual secret of their spouses.[12] Such stories remained very rare in reality, but embodied mainstream society's fear of the epidemic 'leaking out' from the perceived risk groups.

Jeffrey's summary of *Philadelphia* usefully reminds us of that film's coyness in representing gay sex, as well as its blatant efforts to appeal to various market constituencies – in foregrounding the court battle between a homophobic, heterosexual black lawyer (played by Denzel Washington) and an ambitious female lawyer, for example. *Philadelphia*'s publicity featured no mention of homosexuality or AIDS, but used healthy images of Tom Hanks, the dying, white gay man, and his counsel, played by Washington, separated by a judge's gavel. The imagery suggested the centrality of the theme of race, as well as the script's faithful adherence to the familiar format of the courtroom drama.

By the time *The Dying Gaul* got made, Lucas's arguments concerning industry prejudice may have looked somewhat outdated. Doubtless they were informed by his own struggles with director Norman René to make the first important AIDS film, *Longtime Companion* (1990),[13] a work justly acclaimed by one of its stars as 'virtually bereft of sentimentality'.[14] Meanwhile, however, Tony Kushner's two-part epic stage and, later, film spectacular *Angels in America* – a 'gay fantasia on national themes' – was hardly shy of gay content or political bite, played to large audiences across the world, and proved a commercial success on celluloid for cable broadcaster HBO in 2003.[15] There had been another conspicuous 'crossover' success: Michael Cunningham's novel *The Hours* (1998), which interwove an HIV/AIDS storyline with another concerning Virginia Woolf, and was awarded both the 1999 Pulitzer Prize for Fiction and the PEN/Faulkner Award for Fiction.[16] It subsequently became an acclaimed film scripted by David Hare.[17]

Still, as Daniel Mendelsohn has noted, Kushner's pair of plays – set in the period where only hazardous, experimental and largely ineffectual treatments were available, and then only to a select few – had inevitably acquired an aura of the historical once their film version was aired.[18] Mendelsohn argued that the arrival of treatments against the syndrome, although far from a cure or a vaccine, afforded the HBO audience of *Angels in America* a sort of patina of immunity. On balance too – particularly on screen – *The Hours*'s complex narrative structure contained, even diminished the tragic aspect of its HIV-positive character's circumstances. Compare Cunningham's own adaptation of his earlier AIDS novel *A Home at the End of the World* (2004), which simply required an all-but-total abandonment of the one character's demise.[19] Even those who recall the entirety of the history of AIDS, and participated in it, may feel disconnected today from such 'historic' narratives. As novelist Sarah Schulman – author of *People in Trouble* (1990) and *Rat Bohemia* (1995), the two most vivid novelistic accounts of political activism in early AIDS-ravaged New York – has acknowledged: '[t]he world before protease inhibitors is clearly The Past, emotionally for me now … It has ceased to be a continuum.'[20]

In the United States and the United Kingdom, as in other English-speaking countries and in France, the statistical majority of literature about AIDS has been written by and about Caucasian gay men, invariably middle class. Early on, in particular, women sufferers and drug users died much more quickly of HIV/AIDS illnesses; non-white voices took time to emerge, presumably reflecting a longstanding distance from commercial outlets. However, there is now, indisputably, an impressive and substantial body of writing by non-white American authors concerning AIDS.

One rare early fictional example was Samuel Delany's science-fiction novel *Flight from Neveryon* (1985), among the first works of fiction to address the syndrome, invoking historical 'plague' narratives to illuminate its unfolding.[21] Later, in *The Mad Man* (1994), Delany again found new territory, writing in a self-conscious 'Disclaimer' that the novel was 'not a book about "safe sex"'.[22] Indeed, Delany's narrator, John Marr, opens this unfettered account of a highly sexed life with the words:

> I do not have AIDS. I am surprised that I don't. I have had sex with men weekly, sometimes daily – without condoms – since my teens, though true, it's been overwhelmingly … no, more accurately it's been – since 1980 – *all* oral, not anal.[23]

In the intervening years, Larry Duplechan's *Tangled Up in Blue* (1989) and Steven Corbin's *Fragments that Remain* (1993) both related African-American experiences of the syndrome. In 1997, Sapphire's novel *Push* was acclaimed for its articulation of the struggles of a young African-American single mother, infected with HIV through drug use.[24] Thomas Glave's O. Henry Award-winning story 'The Final Inning' (1997) showed the complex faultlines between African-American and gay identities, and how these continue to ensnare the reputation of one closeted sufferer from AIDS after his death.[25]

Arguably, non-white voices became especially articulate in poetry and memoirs. The Indian doctor Abraham Verghese produced one of the most memorable and moving accounts of dealing with AIDS, stigma and the challenges of biomedicine in his *My Own Country* (1994).[26] Rafael Campo, a gay Cuban expatriate also practising in AIDS biomedicine, has written extensively about the epidemic in his verse, and in *The Poetry of Healing* (1997) provided us with one of the most incisive accounts of the consolations of literary creativity as a means of coming to terms with the acute sensations of loss and powerlessness in the face of the ravages of

AIDS.[27] In particular, Campo pays tribute to the redemptive capacity in formal verse construction, since

> The poem is a physical process, is bodily exercise: rhymes become the mental resting places in the ascending rhythmic stairway of memory. The poem perhaps is an idealization or a dream of the physical – the imagined healthy form. Yet it does not renounce illness; rather, it reinterprets it as the beginning point for healing.[28]

Campo's sentiments here illuminate not only his own poetical talents, but the accommodation of this subject into highly formal versification in other verse, such as (the white English) Thom Gunn's late suite of poems concerning AIDS, which formed part of the collection *The Man with Night Sweats* (1992).[29]

Among other non-white voices, Essex Hemphill's anthology *Brother to Brother* (1991) featured a wealth of autobiographical and poetical responses to the syndrome, including work by Assoto Saint, Walter Rico Burrell and Craig G. Harris. *Sojourner* (1993) was a volume exclusively dedicated to African-American responses to AIDS. *Gary in Your Pocket* (1996), the posthumously published journals of Gary Fisher, a young African-American student stricken down by AIDS at the age of 32, includes some of the most moving testimonials to the frustration of losing one's health.[30]

Such works, naturally, have taken their place in the chronological unfolding of 'AIDS literature' in the USA and UK. This unfolding was an especially tardy and uneven affair. The first years of the epidemic – 1981–5, the period covered by the bestselling but extremely flawed popular history of AIDS, Randy Shilts's *And the Band Played On* – saw a time lag.[31] Very few AIDS literary works appeared in the midst of the unfolding disaster, as those people closest to it struggled to comprehend, to care, to bury their dead and to look after their own health. Exceptions included Paul Reed's *Facing It: A Novel of A.I.D.S.* (1984), almost certainly the first novel to handle the syndrome; Robert Chesley's play *Night Sweat* (1984), presumed to be the first play on the subject; and Armistead Maupin's *Tales of the City* novels.[32] Maupin's long-established fiction series, written to order and appearing weekly in the *San Francisco Chronicle*, can lay claim to the first mention of GRID/AIDS in printed fiction in 1982, though the novel in which it appeared became the book *Babycakes* (1984) two years later; it was, however, only in *Significant Others* (1987) and still more fully in *Sure of You* (1989), that gay character Michael Tolliver experienced the syndrome itself, rather than the universal fear and panic concerning it.[33]

A distinctive feature of Samuel Delany's early novel, *Flight from Neveryon*, was its inclusion of commentaries by the characters, criticizing the book's author for various purported omissions, as Kermit does here:

'I'm sorry, Leslie, but that's precisely what he *doesn't* do!' ... 'He doesn't capture – or "document," to use his word – the feel of the gay community between '82 and '84, when he was apparently writing his story and the AIDS coverage was at its height.'

Delany cannily anticipated the ways ongoing debates and concerns about the cultural representation of various identities in American society would inform writings concerning the AIDS epidemic. It is ironic, therefore, to find Delany 'allowing' his own characters their scepticism, since it has mainly been white-authored accounts of AIDS – invariably concentrating on a peer group of relatively wealthy, white gay men – which have been criticized in such terms.

Craig Lucas, reflecting on the cast of characters he came up with for *Longtime Companion*, in part concedes the point, calling them 'a rag-tag army of middle-class, often-complacent, self-involved gay men'.[34] But he went on to insist on the verisimilitude of his film, in that such figures were typical of those first to organize to fight the epidemic. Nevertheless,

[I]n addition to the audiences who found these things eye-opening, there were also those who had waited to see *their* experience of the epidemic represented on screen (including I.V.-drug users, activists as well as gay people from all walks of life, many without health insurance and what they perceived to be the social advantages of the characters in *Longtime Companion*). For these, when the movie did not coincide with their expectations, there was often real dismay and anger.[35]

One collection of critical essays concerning 'AIDS literature' enshrined such concerns in its title: *Confronting AIDS through Literature: The Responsibilities of Representation*.[36]

Instead of criticizing any creative work's failure to reflect all of the many diverse experiences of the epidemic, however, it makes more sense to acknowledge just how AIDS arrived in Western societies, proliferating in already complexly stratified, discrete and distinct subcultures and communities. While individual works reflect such social stratification, their characters are still capable of invoking universal opinions, feelings and preoccupations. For example, the fear which debilitated many writers from engaging with HIV/AIDS at the outset would subsequently become a defining trope in early AIDS literature.

Fear permeates no text more than the most significant and influential early AIDS drama, Larry Kramer's *The Normal Heart*, first staged in 1985.[37] Its boisterous, sensational run at the Public Theatre in New York coincided with a domestic drama about the syndrome, conceived and performed in different (i.e. non-confrontational) terms: William Hoffman's *As Is*.[38] However, Kramer's friend Andrew Holleran captured the most salient historical analogy for the proliferation of ignorance and fear first, in an article entitled 'Journal of the Plague Year' (1982). Some of Holleran's regular essays on AIDS from gay literary magazine *Christopher Street* would be collected in 1988's *Ground Zero*. Holleran abandoned a novel concerning the epidemic – though impressive parts, published as shorter fiction, survive, such as 'Ties' (1985), 'Friends at Evening' (1986) and 'Lights in the Valley' (1990).[39] He was rare in finding a way to document how scapegoating and prejudice would inform opinions within the affected communities, as well as those outside; there is no idealization in his accounts. In 'Friends at Evening', Holleran's Ned suddenly announces that 'Africa is what killed them . . . We are infected with a disease that got started in the garbage dump of a slum in Zaire.'[40] Ned imagines the epidemic as particularly unAmerican in its apparent refutation of values of freedom and of libertarian social and sexual mores. Yet such projections, tempting as they may have been, lead Ned and others nowhere helpful, and his tone merely pre-empts the frankly racist approach to the epidemic's spread adopted in Shilts's *And the Band Played On*.

By 1985, there would also be two AIDS films from America – *Buddies* and (for television) *An Early Frost* – though two more subversive and compelling treatments were released the following year.[41] Stuart Marshall's *Bright Eyes* (1986) was an imaginative polemic made for Britain's Channel 4; still more impressive was the low-budget US drama *Parting Glances* (1986), directed by Bill Sherwood, which managed to feature the syndrome as experienced by a single gay man without sensationalization, exaggeration or cliché.[42] While many early works showed how AIDS affected a particular stratum of urban, sexually active, invariably white gay men, Susan Sontag's story 'The Way We Live Now' (1986) did just the opposite, diversifying as well as universalizing our experiences of fear, hopelessness and loss in the wake of AIDS.[43]

Sontag's tale narrates the fortunes of one HIV-positive gay man through a dialogue of contestation, prioritization, correction and argument acted out by twenty-six of the subject's familiars. Consequently, the sense of impotence in the sick individual could be implied without being openly stated, and Sontag's nuanced inclusion of ideological undercurrents within the exchanges intelligently explored how contentious the language around AIDS would become. As Paula Treichler trenchantly put it, alongside the biomedical epidemic, an 'epidemic of signification' was occurring.[44] The understandable and necessary scientific study of risk groups and behaviours which might identify the agent(s) of the syndrome and help contain its spread simultaneously created a set of assumptions and a socio-cultural symbolism which Sontag would further contest in her essay *AIDS and its Metaphors* (1989).[45]

By this moment, meanwhile, Randy Shilts's sensationalistic history of the epidemic, teeming with inappropriate instances of hindsight, had seized the

Western popular imagination. For tens of thousands of readers, this would be their first – perhaps sole – engagement with AIDS in any form beyond broadcasting and newspaper journalism. James Miller has argued persuasively that *And the Band Played On* amounts to 'a symphonic opus of public oppression and private suffering', as well as 'a coherent cautionary tale set in a sleazy slum-world writhing with green monkeys, bicentennial sailors, and exotic bathhouse bugs'.[46] Douglas Crimp spoke for many in considering the effect of *And the Band Played On* 'pernicious', but its impact was arguably largely irreversible, bound up as it was with a general cultural need for a simple, straightforward 'narrative' of AIDS – one full of readily identifiable instances of good and evil conduct, smart and less smart thinking.[47]

Some writers responded to the pejorative, homophobic implications of accounts such as Shilts's directly.[48] Others sought to humanize the experience of those closest to the syndrome, which Shilts had failed to do with his sensationalist portrait of the purported prime and original transmitter of HIV, French-Canadian Gaetan Dugas, so-called 'Patient Zero'. Notably, American author Edmund White and Englishman Adam Mars-Jones collaborated on a collection of shorter fiction, *The Darker Proof* (1987).[49] White and Mars-Jones first agreed that no story would name the syndrome. Even the volume's subtitle referred to '*stories from a crisis*', not a syndrome, epidemic or plague. Their example was followed by several other writers, including Robert Ferro, whose *Second Son* (1988) would feature conclusive symptomatology indicating AIDS, but never its name.[50]

Both Mars-Jones and White saw in the story form an opportunity to escape the apparently unavoidable narrative development of any credible 'AIDS story'. As White put it,

> We wanted to show the human side of this experience. We chose the story as a form, rather than the novel, because the novel has an inevitable trajectory to it. That is, you begin healthy and end sick and dead. We wanted to get into and out of the subject matter in a more angular and less predictable way.[51]

Others benefited from the capacity and porousness of the story form. Before himself becoming incapacitated by AIDS, Allen Barnett produced a remarkable story collection, *The Body and its Dangers* (1990), all but one of whose stories concerns the syndrome.[52] Rebecca Brown's collection *The Gifts of the Body* (1994) grew out of the author's experiences caretaking for AIDS patients, offers impressions of the medical challenges facing the HIV-positive subject, and portrays the diverse ways carers and patients interact, and fail to interact.[53]

I have made much of the relative stasis attending creative engagements with AIDS since 1997. The situation is rather comparable in critical writing.

Though I have mentioned a good number of the most significant voices of scholarship already, Steven Kruger's monograph *AIDS Narratives* remains the single most important study of creativity and the epidemic, and it appeared in 1996.[54] A fuller and up-to-date account of the subject would have space to consider in detail a number of important novels: Christopher Davis's *Valley of the Shadow* (1988), Carole Maso's experimental novel-memoir *The Art Lover* (1990), Christopher Coe's *Such Times* (1993), Dale Peck's *Martin and John* (1993), Scott Heim's *Mysterious Skin* (1995), Mark Merlis's *An Arrow's Flight* (1998) and Edmund White's *The Married Man* (2000).[55] The most recent monograph on 'AIDS literature' in English is Jacqueline Foertsch's *Enemies Within: The Cold War and the AIDS Crisis in Literature, Film and Culture* (2001).[56]

Outstanding memoirs include David Wojnarowicz's *Close to the Knives: A Memoir of Disintegration* (1991), the book that gets closest to finding a distinct narrative voice to reflect gay men's anger at the epidemic and its political ramifications, Mark Doty's lyrical account of loss, *Heaven's Coast* (1996), Fenton Johnson's equally moving *Geography of the Heart* (1996) and the British Oscar Moore's collected newspaper columns, *PWA: Looking AIDS in the Face* (1996).[57] British filmmaker Derek Jarman's AIDS writings – particularly *Modern Nature* (1991) and *At Your Own Risk: A Saint's Testament* (1992) – have real impact, as does the script/audio track of his monochromatic film *Blue* (1994).[58] Even Paul Monette's *Borrowed Time* (1988) and *Becoming a Man: Half a Life Story* (1992), for all their sentimentality, have a claim to endurance, so evident are the wretched circumstances of their composition.[59] Poetry concerning AIDS that will endure is to be found in two *Poets for Life* anthologies (1989 and 1997), as well as in volumes by Rafael Campo, Thom Gunn, Tim Dlugos (*Powerless* (1996)), Rachel Hadas's brilliant anthology *Unending Dialogue: Voices from an AIDS Poetry Workshop* (1991) and especially Mark Doty – the collections *My Alexandria* (1993) and *Atlantis* (1995) in particular.[60]

Two last selections illustrate how much more is to be done with the subject of AIDS. Both undertake the scarce, complicated but vital tasks of re-examining 'historical' (pre-treatment) AIDS and making connections between that world and our own. Alan Hollinghurst's Booker Prize-winning novel account of Britain during the Thatcher years, *The Line of Beauty* (2004), offers a thorough and sustained account of the emergence of AIDS in the mid to late 1980s, but refuses the epidemic even a walk-on role until the novel's last pages.[61] Hollinghurst – who had written about the syndrome both directly in *The Folding Star* (1994) and indirectly in *The Swimming-Pool Library* (1988) – has his narrator appear to dispatch the subject airily, rather as his protagonist Nick might do.[62] The reality, however, is that it is only

English conversational protocol that has rendered AIDS *hors-texte*. An immi-
nent HIV test strikes Nick first as 'another solemn thing, and even more
frightening than it need have been for not being talked about'.[63] But
Hollinghurst's narration subsequently brilliantly foreshadows the revelation
of Nick's HIV-positive status to him, leaving him to know – or seemingly
know – that he will be told he is infected, but not to anticipate how he will
react, or whether he will survive. In the closing paragraphs, an isolated Nick
succumbs to 'a sort of terror' as:

> It came over him that the test result would be positive. The words that were said
> every day would be said to him, in that quiet consulting room whose desk and
> carpet and square modern armchair would share indissolubly in the moment . . .
> He tried to rationalize the fear, but its pull was too strong and original. It was
> inside himself, but the world around him, the parked cars, the cruising taxi, the
> church spire among the trees, had also been changed. They had been revealed.[64]

The phrase 'It came over him' might give the reader pause: is Nick's
presentiment genuinely proleptic, or an imaginative phantom – one that
might disappear as peremptorily as the tenure of Mrs Thatcher in 10
Downing Street? Hollinghurst subtly shows how AIDS as syndrome, as
epidemic, as prospective threat, as fear, and as day-to-day reality cumulatively constitutes a series of highly unstable, mutually dependent, mutually
modifying ciphers. AIDS affords a sort of 'revelation', ultimately – one
which may even be of the 'beautiful' kind (the novel's final word). But
that is only within the context of the novel itself, and only to the momentary – and plausibly delusional – consciousness of one character. After all,
the political seam of the novel shows Nick to have been taken in, both
figuratively and literally, by Thatcherites and Thatcherism. Another Book,
of course, also ends in Revelation – one on whose account much of the
prejudice, stigmatization, incomprehension, scapegoating and silencing that
has filled both *The Line of Beauty* and Western discourse concerning AIDS
has been generated. These phenomena have deep and enduring consequences today – including in the 'present' of Hollinghurst's implied reader –
which a narrative as intelligent and self-aware as that of *The Line of
Beauty* can illuminate.

Simon Lovat's comparatively unknown story 'Juba' (2008) concerns
Luther's coming to terms with the loss of his lover.[65] The death occurred a
decade ago, yet Luther is all too aware of its consequences attending his
ongoing life. This realization mimics our global circumstances, since
Luther's own dedication to the cause of alleviating third-world poverty and
disease is explicitly related to his own loss. Lovat articulates a rare poignancy
by exploring a deeply felt and credible personal situation in which society's

'good news' – combination therapy treatments – provide only a bitter after-taste in the wake of loss:

> To return home was to face the past, was to face the absence of Thomas. It was true, one never got over the death of a lover. One might learn to cope with it, but the gap still remained . . . Lying in bed at night he sometimes thought of people who had lost their entire family in a war, as so many of his parents' generation had done, yet still managed to carry on . . . poor Thomas had missed the advent of the new chemical therapies – the ones that actually worked – by only a matter of months.[66]

Where Hollinghurst grounds the spread of HIV in Britain in the political climate which accompanied it, Lovat manages something equally rare – he points to the epidemic's wider, unfamiliar realities even as he articulates Luther's highly individual experience of the syndrome at home. Without forcing the comparison, Lovat compares Luther's personal sense of remaining at odds with those around him – homo- and heterosexual – on account of his loss, with the disjunctive relationship between third-world countries – with their imperfect, partial and incomplete administration of anti-AIDS treatments – and the more successful, comprehensive and positive-sounding Western talk of HIV/AIDS as a manageable, if chronic condition. This itself, inevitably, involves a narrative simplification of the huge variety of experiences of combination therapy treatments. That in itself must be a ripe subject for the next generation of works of AIDS literature.

NOTES

1. For more on the enduring scepticism concerning these truths, see my 'Introduction' to Richard Canning, ed., *Vital Signs: Essential AIDS Fiction* (New York: Carroll & Graf, 2007), xi–xlvii.
2. UN press release on data from the UNAIDS 2008 report on the global AIDS epidemic, http://data.unaids.org/pub/GlobalReport/2008/080725_GR08_press release_en.pdf, accessed 31 October 2008.
3. *Ibid.*
4. *Ibid.*
5. *Ibid.*
6. See the 'Introduction' to Canning, ed., *Vital Signs*, xxiv. Armistead Maupin, *The Night Listener* (New York: HarperCollins, 2000) and *Michael Tolliver Lives* (New York: HarperCollins, 2007).
7. Shannon Burke, *Safelight* (New York: Random House, 2004).
8. Shawn Decker, *My Pet Virus: The True Story of a Rebel without a Cure* (New York: Tarcher, 2006), 6.
9. *Philadelphia* (1994), directed by Jonathan Demme.
10. *The Dying Gaul* (2005), directed by Craig Lucas.

11. Craig Lucas, 'The Dying Gaul', *The Dying Gaul and Other Screenplays* (New York: Alyson, 2008), 19–20.

12. See *Mensonge (The Lie)* (1992), directed by François Margolin; *Intimate Contact* (1987), directed by Waris Hussein; *Boys on the Side* (1995), directed by Herbert Ross; *A Mother's Prayer* (1995), directed by Larry Elikann. Other films concerning heterosexual HIV transmission include *Les nuits fauves (Savage Nights)* (1993), directed by Cyril Collard; *Kids* (1995), directed by Larry Clark; and *Todo sobre mi Madre (All About My Mother)* (1999), directed by Pedro Almodóvar.

13. *Longtime Companion* (1990), directed by Norman René; Lucas's screenplay is in his *Dying Gaul and Other Screenplays*, 227–321.

14. Mary-Louise Parker, 'On Craig Lucas and *Longtime Companion*', in Lucas, *Dying Gaul and Other Screenplays*, 226.

15. Tony Kushner, *Angels in America: Part One: Millennium Approaches* (New York: Theatre Communications Group, 1993); *Angels in America: Part Two: Perestroika* (New York: Theatre Communications Group, 1994); *Angels in America* (2003), directed by Mike Nichols.

16. Michael Cunningham, *The Hours* (New York: Farrar, Straus and Giroux, 1998).

17. *The Hours* (2002), directed by Stephen Daldry.

18. Daniel Mendelsohn, 'Winged Messages', *The New York Review of Books*, 51:2 (12 February 2004).

19. *A Home at the End of the World* (2004), directed by Michael Mayer.

20. Sarah Schulman, *People in Trouble* (New York: Dutton, 1990), *Rat Bohemia* (New York: Dutton, 1995) and 'Through the Looking Glass', in Edmund White, ed., *Loss within Loss: Artists in the Age of AIDS* (Madison, WI: University of Wisconsin Press, 2001), 14.

21. Samuel Delany, *Flight from Neveryon* (New York: Bantam, 1985).

22. Samuel Delany, *The Mad Man* (New York: Masquerade Books, 1994), xiii.

23. *Ibid.*, 7.

24. Larry Duplechan, *Tangled Up in Blue* (New York: St Martin's Press, 1989); Steven Corbin, *Fragments that Remain* (Boston, MA: Alyson, 1993); Sapphire, *Push* (New York: Vintage, 1997).

25. Thomas Glave, 'The Final Inning', *Whose Song? and Other Stories* (San Francisco, CA: City Lights, 1997); reproduced in Canning, ed., *Vital Signs*, 265–92.

26. Abraham Verghese, *My Own Country: A Doctor's Story of a Town and its People in the Age of AIDS* (New York: Simon & Schuster, 1994; in the UK, this book first appeared as *Soundings*).

27. Rafael Campo, *The Other Man Was Me: A Voyage to the New World* (Houston, TX: Arte Publico, 1994), *What the Body Told* (Durham, NC: Duke University Press, 1996), *The Poetry of Healing: A Doctor's Education in Empathy, Identity and Desire* (New York: Norton, 1997).

28. Campo, *The Poetry of Healing*, 166–7.

29. Thom Gunn, *The Man with Night Sweats* (London: Faber and Faber, 1992).

30. Essex Hemphill, ed., *Brother to Brother* (Boston, MA: Alyson, 1991); B. Michael Hunter, ed., *Sojourner: Black Gay Voices in the Age of AIDS* (New York: Other Countries Press, 1993); Gary Fisher, *Gary in Your Pocket: Stories and Notebooks of Gary Fisher* (Durham, NC: Duke University Press, 1996).

31. Randy Shilts, *And the Band Played On: Politics, People, and the AIDS Epidemic* (New York: Penguin, 1987).

32. Paul Reed, *Facing It: A Novel of A.I.D.S.* (San Francisco, CA: Gay Sunshine Press, 1984); Robert Chesley, *Night Sweat, a Romantic Comedy*, in his *Hard Plays, Stiff Parts: The Homoerotic Plays of Robert Chesley* (San Francisco, CA: Alamo Square, 1990). I am indebted to the following website for its chronology of early cultural responses to AIDS: www.artistswithaids.org/artery/AIDS/AIDS. html, accessed 21 August 2008.

33. Armistead Maupin, *Babycakes* (New York: Harper & Row, 1984), *Significant Others* (New York: Harper & Row, 1987) and *Sure of You* (New York: Harper & Row, 1989).

34. Steven Drukman, 'Craig Lucas on "Movie-Land"', in Lucas, *The Dying Gaul and Other Screenplays* (New York: Alyson, 2008), x.

35. *Ibid.*, x.

36. Judith Laurence Pastore, ed., *Confronting AIDS through Literature: The Responsibilities of Representation* (Champaign: University of Illinois Press, 1993).

37. Larry Kramer, *The Normal Heart* (New York: Plume, 1985).

38. William Hoffman, *As Is* (New York: Vintage/Random House, 1985).

39. Andrew Holleran, *Ground Zero* (New York: William Morrow, 1988); revised and reissued as *Chronicle of a Plague, Revisited: AIDS and its Aftermath* (New York: Da Capo, 2008); 'Ties', in Michael Denneny, Charles Ortleb and Thomas Steele, eds., *First Love/Last Love: New Fiction from Christopher Street* (New York: Putnam, 1985), 206–15; 'Friends at Evening', in George Stambolian, ed., *Men on Men* (New York: Plume, 1986), 88–113, revised for republication in Canning, ed., *Vital Signs* (New York: Carroll & Graf, 2007), 1–28; 'Lights in the Valley', in George Stambolian, ed., *Men on Men 3* (New York: Plume, 1990), 321–39.

40. Holleran, 'Friends at Evening', in Canning, ed., *Vital Signs*, 19.

41. *Buddies* (1985), directed by Arthur J. Brennan, Jr; *An Early Frost* (1985), directed by John Erman.

42. *Bright Eyes* (1986), directed by Stuart Marshall; *Parting Glances* (1985), directed by Bill Sherwood.

43. Susan Sontag, 'The Way We Live Now', *The New Yorker* (24 November 1986).

44. Paula Treichler, 'AIDS, Homophobia and Biomedical Discourse: An Epidemic of Signification', in Douglas Crimp, ed., *AIDS: Cultural Analysis, Cultural Activism* (Cambridge, MA: MIT Press, 1988), 31–70. Crimp's anthology is still the most essential gathering of cultural criticism concerning AIDS.

45. Susan Sontag, *AIDS and its Metaphors* (New York: Farrar, Straus and Giroux, 1989).

46. James Miller, 'AIDS in the Novel: Getting it Straight', in James Miller, ed., *Fluid Exchanges: Artists and Critics in the AIDS Crisis* (Toronto: University of Toronto Press, 1992), 257.

47. Douglas Crimp, 'How to Have Promiscuity in an Epidemic', in Douglas Crimp, ed., *AIDS: Cultural Analysis, Cultural Activism*, 43–82; 46. For other criticisms of Shilts's reporting, style, use of source material and narratorial mode, see Jeff Nunokawa, 'All the Sad Young Men: AIDS and the Work of Mourning', in Diana Fuss, ed., *Inside/Out: Lesbian Theories, Gay Theories* (New York: Routledge, 1991), 311–23; Ellis Hanson, 'Undead', in Fuss, ed., *Inside/Out*, 324–40; Miller, 'AIDS in the Novel'; Paul Morrison, 'End Pleasure', *GLQ*, 1:1 (1993), 53–78; Simon Watney, 'Politics, People and the AIDS Epidemic', *Practices of Freedom: Selected Writings on HIV/AIDS* (Durham, NC: Duke University Press, 1994);

Judith Williamson, 'Every Virus Tells a Story', in Erica Carter and Simon Watney, eds., *Taking Liberties: AIDS and Cultural Politics* (London: Serpents Tail, 1989), 69–80.

48. See my discussion of Shilts and creative responses to his book in the 'Introduction' to Canning, ed., *Vital Signs*, xxv–xxxv.

49. Adam Mars-Jones and Edmund White, *The Darker Proof: Stories from a Crisis* (London: Faber and Faber, 1987; revised and expanded edn, London: Faber and Faber, 1988).

50. Robert Ferro, *Second Son* (New York: Crown, 1988).

51. Kay Bonetti, 'An Interview with Edmund White', *Missouri Review*, 13:2 (1990), 97.

52. Allen Barnett, *The Body and its Dangers* (New York: St Martin's Press, 1990).

53. Rebecca Brown, *The Gifts of the Body* (New York: HarperCollins, 1994).

54. Steven Kruger, *AIDS Narratives: Gender and Sexuality, Fiction and Science* (New York: Garland, 1996).

55. Christopher Davis, *Valley of the Shadow* (New York: St Martin's Press, 1988); Carole Maso, *The Art Lover* (San Francisco, CA: North Point, 1990); Christopher Coe, *Such Times* (New York: Harcourt Brace, 1993); Dale Peck, *Martin and John* (New York: Farrar, Straus and Giroux, 1993; in the UK, the novel was published under its author's preferred title, *Fucking Martin*); Scott Heim, *Mysterious Skin* (New York: HarperCollins, 1995); Mark Merlis, *An Arrow's Flight* (New York: St Martin's Press, 1998; published in the UK as *Pyrrhus*); Edmund White, *The Married Man* (New York: Knopf, 2000).

56. Jacqueline Foertsch, *Enemies Within: The Cold War and the AIDS Crisis in Literature, Film and Culture* (Champaign: University of Illinois Press, 2001).

57. David Wojnarowicz, *Close to the Knives: A Memoir of Disintegration* (New York: Vintage, 1991); Mark Doty, *Heaven's Coast: A Memoir* (New York: HarperCollins, 1996); Fenton Johnson, *Geography of the Heart* (New York: Scribner, 1996); Oscar Moore, *PWA: Looking AIDS in the Face* (London: Picador, 1996).

58. Derek Jarman, *Modern Nature* (London: Century, 1991) and *At Your Own Risk: A Saint's Testament* (London: Hutchinson, 1992); *Blue* (1994), directed by Derek Jarman.

59. Paul Monette, *Borrowed Time* (New York: Harcourt Brace, 1988), *Becoming a Man: Half a Life Story* (New York: HarperCollins, 1992).

60. Michael Klein, ed., *Poets for Life* (New York: Crown, 1989); Michael Klein and Richard McCann, eds., *Things Shaped in Passing: More 'Poets for Life'* (New York: Persea Books, 1997); Tim Dlugos, *Powerless: Selected Poems, 1973–90* (London: Serpents Tail, 1996); Rachel Hadas, *Unending Dialogue: Voices from an AIDS Poetry Workshop* (London: Faber and Faber, 1991); Mark Doty, *My Alexandria* (Champaign: University of Illinois Press, 1993), *Atlantis* (New York: HarperPerennial, 1995).

61. Alan Hollinghurst, *The Line of Beauty* (London: Picador, 2004).

62. Alan Hollinghurst, *The Folding Star* (London: Chatto & Windus, 1994), *The Swimming-Pool Library* (London: Chatto & Windus, 1988).

63. Hollinghurst, *The Line of Beauty*, 484.

64. *Ibid.*, 501, 500.

65. Simon Lovat, 'Juba', in Peter Burton, ed., *A Casualty of War: The Arcadia Book of Gay Short Stories* (London: Arcadia, 2008), 195–208.

66. *Ibid.*, 199.

9

HEATHER LOVE

Transgender fiction and politics

'Very well – what is this love we have for the invert – boy or girl? It was
they who were spoken of in every romance that we ever read . . . They go
far back in our lost distance . . . They are our answer to what our
grandmothers told us love was, and what it never came to be; they, the
living lie of our centuries.'[1]

This meditation on the curious appeal of the invert is addressed by Doctor
Matthew O'Connor to the lovelorn Nora Flood in Djuna Barnes's 1937 novel
Nightwood. *Nightwood* is generally read as a classic in lesbian and gay
literature, and for good reason. The object of Nora's 'miscalculated longing'
is the faithless Robin Vote, who has abandoned her to wander the Paris
underworld and, ultimately, to take up with another woman, involving
Nora in a lesbian triangle. O'Connor is familiar with the homosexual demi-
monde, and in particular with the Paris *pissoirs* where he cruises other men.
Though *Nightwood* is full of representations of same-sex desire, it would be
possible to describe it not as a novel of homosexuality but rather as a novel of
gender variance. In an earlier scene, Nora goes to the Doctor's room to seek
advice and finds him lying in bed 'in a woman's flannel nightgown' (79),
wearing a blond curly wig and heavy makeup. The doctor explains his taste
for cottaging with reference to a bungled act of reincarnation: 'I've turned up
this time as I shouldn't have been', he says, and muses that 'in the old days I
was possibly a girl in Marseilles thumping the dock with a sailor' (90–1). We
might want to see Nora's desire for Robin as something other than same-sex
desire: her declaration that she 'chose a girl who resembles a boy' prompts the
Doctor's meditation on the allure of the invert.

In representations of the boyish Robin and the cross-dressing O'Connor,
and in philosophical meditations on the 'third sex', *Nightwood*'s focus is as
much gender variance as it is homosexuality. In this sense, we might read
Nightwood not as a lesbian or gay classic but as a transgender classic.
Nightwood takes us 'far back in our lost distance' – to a time when the
distinction between sexual and gender transgression was not as secure as
now. Although this distinction is self-evident to many today, homosexuality
across history has been seen just as often as a form of gender as a sexual
practice defined by object choice.

Distinguishing transgender existence from homosexuality and transvestism requires a sharp line drawn between gender and sexuality. This distinction developed in the twentieth century. Sigmund Freud lays the groundwork for it in his *Three Essays on the Theory of Sexuality* (1905) when he describes the distinction between sexual object and sexual aim. But, as George Chauncey argues in *Gay New York*, this distinction was not solidified in American culture until mid century.[2] Before homosexuality was understood primarily as a matter of object choice, it was understood both in popular and medical contexts as gender variation. Late nineteenth- and early twentieth-century sexologists such as Richard von Krafft-Ebing, Karl Ulrichs, Magnus Hirschfeld and Edward Carpenter did not have an account of same-sex desire; rather, they framed such experiences as gender inversion, and included the testimony of individuals who felt that they were born in the 'wrong' body.

The term *transgender* emerged in the last few decades as a way to describe a range of gender embodiments and practices, some of which are bound up with same-sex sexuality. Versions of the word began appearing in the late 1960s and the contemporary transgender movement began in the early 1990s.[3] According to the editors of the collection *Transgender Rights*, the definition of the term began to settle around 1995 and is 'now generally used to refer to individuals whose gender identity or expression does not conform to the social expectations for their assigned sex at birth'.[4] While 'transgender' is sometimes understood as an umbrella term encompassing all forms of gender variance, it is also used more specifically – to indicate, for instance, gender transition without surgery or hormones, or a specific commitment to living between the sexes. 'Transgender' can overlap with other terms such as transsexual, cross-dresser, transvestite and drag king and drag queen. It is sometimes used to refer to butch and femme lesbians as well as effeminate gay men; it can be used to describe people who choose to live outside the two-gender system, identifying as both male or female, or neither. The term can be used by people who prefer to use transgender pronouns for themselves, or no pronouns at all. (Common transgender pronouns are *s/he* (pronounced *shu-hee*) and *ze*, and the possessive pronoun *hir* (pronounced *here*).) It is occasionally used to refer to people in the intersex community (people born with an anatomy that is not easily categorized as male or female), and it can also be used to refer to a range of cross-cultural gender variance (Brazilian *travesti*, Native American two-spirit, Indian *hijras*, the *xanith* of the Arabian peninsula and the 'female husbands' of west Africa[5]). Transgender has been an important political and critical tool because it draws attention to the shared element of gender variance in all of these practices and forms of embodiment. As such, it offers an alternative to lesbian and gay frameworks that would read many cross-gender practices as versions of homosexuality (often as undeveloped or pre-modern versions). In addition, it offers a powerful term for a coalitional politics based on opposition to gender discrimination and compulsory gendering.

'Transgender' is a contested term: many people who use it to describe themselves mean quite different things, and it is regularly used to describe people who would never understand themselves in this way. Most lesbian and gay movements, publications and community centres in the United States now include transgender people at least nominally, often in the form of a 'T' appended to existing acronyms (as in the example 'LGBT' or Lesbian Gay Bisexual Transgender), yet questions remain about how fully integrated trans people really are in such organizations. There have been territorial struggles over representations of transgender people between the trans community and the lesbian and gay community. The most spectacular of these was over Brandon Teena, the transgender youth murdered with two friends in Nebraska in 1993, and whose story was represented in the popular film *Boys Don't Cry* (1999). While the trans community unequivocally claimed Brandon as one of their own, Brandon was identified in some gay and lesbian media as a lesbian forced to adopt a male gender style in a homophobic rural environment.

It is not self-evident that a volume dedicated to lesbian and gay literature should include a chapter on transgender literature. Contemporary lesbian and gay subjects tend to understand many forms of gender variance as part of the pre-history of modern homosexuality, but transgender and transsexual critics are returning to this archive to claim it as part of a transgender history. Perhaps no one has been so influential in this rewriting of history as Leslie Feinberg, the trans activist, novelist and historian who has spearheaded the movement for transgender awareness. In *hir* important 1992 pamphlet, *Transgender Liberation: A Movement Whose Time Has Come*, and the subsequent book *Transgender Warriors: Making History from Joan of Arc to Dennis Rodman*, Feinberg offered a strong rewriting of the history of gender variance, claiming a proud ancestry across time and across cultures. In addition to Feinberg's work, there is currently a publishing boom in memoirs, autobiographies, novels and critical works dealing with transgender themes.[6]

Establishing a transgender tradition means addressing the crucial distinction between literature about transgender people and literature by transgender people. Transgender individuals have long exerted a fascination for non-transgender people – as symbols of transgression, enlightenment or degeneration, transgender people have done hard representational labour in the annals of Western literature. We might look back as far as the Greek myth of Tiresias, the blind prophet who spent seven years of his life as a woman, and was asked to settle a bet between Zeus and Hera about whether men or women have more pleasure in sex. While Tiresias' double nature is associated with wisdom, it also makes him a spectacular figure and an object of fascination in a way that is potentially troubling. With the rise of a movement for transgender rights, transgender people have begun to author their own stories and to challenge the traditional frameworks through which they have been represented. Still, the voyeurism that has characterized so many historical representations of transgender people is still with us today. The tendency to see gender-variant individuals as freaks, while perhaps most fully realized in the infamous Jerry Springer Show, runs through more sober and sympathetic representations as well.

Fantastic transformations of gender have a long history in Western literature. In the twentieth century, there is probably none better known than Virginia Woolf's account of the male-to-female transformation of her fictional hero Orlando. The early twentieth century is closely associated with the emergence of a queer literary canon, but it was also an era deeply fascinated with gender transgression and transformation. In *Orlando: A Biography* (1928), Woolf traces the life of an Elizabethan courtier who lives until the end of the First World War. At the moment of transformation, Woolf writes,

> Orlando had become a woman – there is no denying it. But in every other respect, Orlando remained precisely as he had been ... The change seems to have been accomplished painlessly and completely and in such a way that Orlando herself showed no surprise at it. Many people, taking this into account, and holding that such a change is against nature, have been at great pains to prove (1) that Orlando had always been a woman, (2) that Orlando is at this moment a man. Let biologists and psychologists determine. It is enough for us to state the simple fact; Orlando was a man till the age of thirty; when he became a woman and has remained so ever since.[7]

Orlando's change is quite unlike the transformations – slow, difficult, often physically painful – that are represented in many transgender narratives. Retrospective readings of the novel as a coded love-letter to Vita Sackville-West suggest a reason why the rendering of this transformation is fantastic, not material: Orlando's sex-change is not the focus of the novel, but rather a device that allows Woolf to write about lesbian desire and spin out a revisionist feminist history of England.

Radclyffe Hall's novel *The Well of Loneliness*, also published in 1928, has been more influential than *Orlando* in the history of transgender representation. Although the novel is generally understood as a classic in lesbian literature, its masculine hero Stephen Gordon does not see herself as a woman and does not see her relationships with women as same-sex. When

Stephen is caught in an affair with a married woman, her mother disowns her. In a painful scene of confrontation, Stephen counters her mother's accusations of immorality and perversion with a claim that, for her, loving women is natural:

> 'If I loved her the way a man loves a woman, it's because I can't feel that I am a woman. All my life I've never felt like a woman, and you know it – you say you've always disliked me, that you've always felt a strange physical repulsion . . . I don't know what I am; no one's ever told me that I'm different and yet I know that I'm different.'[8]

Stephen Gordon claims her 'difference' not as a matter of sexuality but as a matter of gender; moments later, when she discovers the sexological texts hidden within her father's office, her identity as a congenital invert is confirmed. In his important reading of the novel, Jay Prosser finds evidence of a transsexual imaginary in the novel. Stephen's desire to be a man is powerfully material: she experiences what would now be called 'gender dysphoria', and imagines maiming or rending her body in a way that Prosser associates with a desire for sex-reassignment surgery.[9]

While novels like *The Well* and other narratives of inversion offer transgender narratives *avant la lettre*, it is not until the latter half of the twentieth century that self-conscious transgender and transsexual literatures emerge. Several developments at mid century led the way for this development: advances in the technology for sex-reassignment surgery; early groups of cross-dressers, transsexuals and transvestites began to meet and circulate newsletters; and the public acknowledgement of transsexuals was increased with the media coverage of figures such as Christine Jorgenson. As is clear from these examples, it is the transsexual community that is most visible during these years; very soon, this burgeoning movement would face hostile opposition not only from the general public but also from the feminist and lesbian-feminist movements, particularly in the work of Mary Daly, Germaine Greer and Janice G. Raymond. In *The Transsexual Empire: The Making of the She-Male* (1979), Raymond claimed male-to-female transsexuals were raping women's bodies. While this argument is now notorious, it set the tone for many feminist appraisals of the trans community in the period.[10] Representations of transsexual existence such as Gore Vidal's 1968 novel *Myra Breckenridge* did not help matters. Vidal's MTF heroine is a hypersexual and hyperviolent woman whose feminism consists in raping men and destroying their masculinity; this camp superhero is a mouthpiece for a gay male sensibility, and offers little insight into trans existence on its own terms.

An important book in countering such attacks on transsexuality was Jan Morris's 1974 memoir, *Conundrum*. At the time of her transition, Morris was a well-known journalist and travel writer in Britain; as James Morris, she had served in the Army, travelled widely, even climbed Mount Everest as a correspondent for *The Times*. The memoir famously begins with Morris's account of her first memory: 'I was three or perhaps four years old when I realized that I had been born into the wrong body, and should really be a girl. I remember the moment well, and it is the earliest memory of my life.'[11] Morris's conviction that she ought to have been a girl never wavered, even when, as a young man, she married and had children. At the end of the narrative, she remarks that she is often asked if she has regrets; her response is unequivocal: 'I do not for a moment regret the act of change. I could see no other way, and it has made me happy' (168).

Conundrum offers a partisan record of the experience of being both a man and a woman. Morris recalls some moments of being in a male body and in all-male company with intense pleasure. In a description of the experience of climbing Everest, she writes: 'The male body may be ungenerous, even uncreative in the deepest kind, but when it is working properly it is a marvelous thing to inhabit ... I look back to those moments of supreme male fitness as one remembers champagne or a morning swim' (82). Morris describes the 'subtle subjection of women' (150) that pervades everyday life, and makes her the object of condescension and derogation in almost all public settings. Still, despite such drawbacks, she describes her intense joy in being a woman, and her 'conviction that the nearest humanity approaches to perfection is in the persons of good women ... it is into their ranks, I flatter myself, if only in the rear file, if only on the flank, that I have now admitted myself' (173).

Although she describes some attraction to both men and women, the memoir as a whole does not deal extensively with sexuality. Morris describes her early life as characterized by necessary sublimation, but that is not the only reason that sex does not play a larger role in the narrative. *Conundrum* is essentially a spiritual autobiography; although the description of her actual physical change of sex is quite material ('between 1964 and 1972 I swallowed at least 12,000 pills, and absorbed into my system anything up to 50,000 milligrams of female matter' (105)), the ultimate focus is Morris's soul, and her lifelong quest to achieve spiritual completion. Moreover, Morris wishes to resist current misunderstandings of the transsexual as a transvestite (someone who derives sexual pleasure from wearing the clothes of the opposite sex) or as a homosexual manqué. She writes that transsexualism 'is not a sexual mode or preference. It is not an act of sex at all. It is a passionate, lifelong, ineradicable conviction, and no true transsexual has ever been disabused of it' (8).

Ultimately, Morris chooses not to resolve the mystery of her condition; she never explains why she is transsexual, and expresses scepticism about all the usual explanations (genetic, social, psychological). She remarks that in her early years she 'approach[ed] her problem existentially, and ... assume[d] that it was altogether of itself, *sans* cause, *sans* meaning' (169). In a telling anecdote, she describes having her bag searched in Russian customs while she was in the process of writing her memoir; the officer, glancing at the manuscript, commented 'Ah, a psychological novel, I see' (171). *Conundrum* is emphatically not a psychological novel; Morris treats her younger self with respectful tact. She writes, 'For me an enigma lies at the root of my dilemma, and I am content to leave it so; others may hope for a more exact diagnosis, and would prefer me to worry the problem further still, pursuing its echo down the paneled corridors of psychiatry, or looking for its shade in the halls of social science' (170). Morris presents the story of her life not merely as an example of a social or psychological problem, but rather as a quest, 'sacramental or visionary' – not a case study but, as she says, an epic (170).

Written two decades later, and after the birth of an explicitly transgender movement, Leslie Feinberg's autobiographical novel *Stone Butch Blues* also narrates a quest for completeness.[12] Jess Goldberg is a masculine woman who grows up in working-class Buffalo, comes out in the butch–femme bar scene, gets surgery and takes hormones to live as a man, and ends up living between the sexes. Not only does *Stone Butch Blues* depart from the transsexual narrative of *Conundrum*, it is also set in a very different social milieu. Morris describes the decline in social status that accompanied her transition; as a woman, Morris is no longer able to spend time in the all-male club to which she had earlier belonged, but she maintains many of her social contacts in the world of the arts and journalism. By contrast, *Stone Butch Blues* describes the trials of a woman who grows up in conditions of economic deprivation. Jess is partly motivated to have surgery and take hormones by economic pressure, and her transition takes her from one position of social insecurity (working-class butch) to another (working-class transgender person).

Feinberg is the person most identified with the transgender movement, and *Stone Butch Blues* is certainly the work of fiction that has had the most influence on its development. The novel recounts several decades in the history of the gay, lesbian and transgender community. When Jess first appears in the bars, she is a young butch with little sense of herself or of a community. The drag queens, butches and femmes (many of them pros, or prostitutes) she meets take care of her and induct her into a way of life, teaching her how to dress, how to approach women and how to avoid police harassment. 'Stone' in the title *Stone Butch Blues* refers primarily to Jess's identification as a stone butch – namely, a woman with a masculine gender style who takes an active role sexually and refuses to be touched genitally. But the term also refers more broadly to an emotional state, to being hardened as a result of stigma, harassment and violence – especially sexual violence. When Jess has sex for the first time, her lover Angie remarks that she has already been hardened by such experiences. After Jess makes love to her, Angie says

> 'I just wish I could make you feel that good. You're stone already, aren't you?' I dropped my eyes. 'Don't be ashamed of being stone with a pro, honey. We're in a stone profession.'   (73)

Throughout the novel, butches and femmes share an erotic and emotional identification based on a particular response to violence. Although Jess is male-identified throughout her life, she relates to femmes through a shared self-understanding as stone.

The bars change radically in the late 1960s when feminist and gay liberation begin to emerge. Eventually this collective movement for rights would lead to a decline in police harassment and brutality, but the immediate results are more mixed. Not only is police harassment stepped up in the immediate aftermath of Stonewall (135), but Jess finds herself at odds with the ideology of the new movement. The new centre of gay, feminist and lesbian life is no longer the bars – it is the college campus. Middle-class lesbians carve out a community and a way of life in part by distinguishing themselves from 'old school' working-class butches and femmes. This class shift has profound consequences in terms of gender: while the bar butches and femmes of the 1950s and 60s might be understood as transgender, the lesbian-feminists who headed the movement in the 1970s clearly understood themselves as women, and saw butch–femme life as a betrayal of feminist solidarity.

Jess registers this transformation not only at the level of community but also in her personal life. Her girlfriend Theresa, at first sceptical, becomes involved in the new movement. When Theresa asks Jess if they can put a 'Sisterhood – make it real' poster up on their wall, Jess says, 'You're really getting into this women's lib stuff, aren't you?'

> 'Yeah,' she said, 'I am. I'm realizing a lot of things about my own life – about being a woman – that I never even thought about until the women's movement.'
>
>   I listened to her. 'I don't feel it so much,' I told her. 'Maybe because I am a butch.'
>
>   She kissed my forehead. 'Butches need women's liberation, too.'
>
>   I laughed. 'We do?'
>
>   Theresa nodded. 'Yes, you do. Anything that's good for women is good for butches.'   (138)

Although their conversation is still playful and romantic, the faultline that opens at this moment will ultimately break up their relationship. Jess is at home in the butch–femme community, but she does not identify as a woman, nor see her desire for femmes as 'same-sex desire'. This scene shows the two distinct movements that will emerge from gay liberation and the women's movement: a gender-normative model of gay and lesbian life, defined by sexual object choice, and the beginnings of a transgender movement, defined by gender variance.

As the butch–femme community collapses and Jess has a harder time finding community and finding employment, she decides to start passing as a man: she has top-surgery and begins taking hormones. While at first it looks as though Jess's trajectory will be transsexual, she feels even more isolated when passing as a man, and ends up quitting hormones and living between genders.[13] While Jess is more comfortable in her body than before, she misses the community of the bars and the comfort of femmes. The difficulty of her position between sexes – without names, without categories – is dramatized in a scene when Jess decides to take a motorcycle ride across the border into Canada. At the bridge, she realizes that she will not be able to make it through customs:

> I couldn't cross the border. I had no valid ID in case I was pulled over at customs. I opened my wallet and looked at my ID. Birth certificate, drivers license. They were all clearly marked female. How could I get ID as a male? . . . I felt like a nonperson. (175)

In this scene, Feinberg shows the material costs of living between genders – outside the law, and without social recognition.

Stone Butch Blues is the story of Jess's attempt to find a home: in her body, in a community and in the world. Throughout the book, this quest is lived out materially as Jess tries to make a domestic space that will shelter her and reflect the full complexity of her being. Although these attempts are frustrated again and again, the ending of the novel is somewhat hopeful. After moving to New York, Jess befriends Ruth, a transgender person who lives across the hall in her apartment building. Beyond this community of two, Feinberg gestures towards the possibility of a larger collective trans community. One day Jess stumbles onto a gay rights rally in Greenwich Village, and takes the stage to call for a more inclusive queer community, one that would make room for gays, lesbians and transgender people: 'Couldn't the *we* be bigger?' she says. 'Isn't there a way we could help fight each other's battles so that we are not always alone?' (296).

Feinberg's 2006 novel *Drag King Dreams* takes up where *Stone Butch Blues* leaves off.[14] The central characters in the book are almost all transgender, but the narrator Max Rabinowitz – not Jess Goldberg, but with recognizable traces of Leslie Feinberg – is still searching for a sense of community.

While transgender people have gained more recognition, they still struggle against violence, misrecognition, racism, isolation and the ravages of capitalism. Along with these pressing daily challenges, they feel despair and paranoia in the wake of 9/11. The novel is set in New York City and New Jersey during the beginning of the Iraq war, and it offers a blistering critique of US militarism and imperialism. Max does not identify as male or female but rather as something in between. A secular Jew, *ze* is deeply anti-Zionist, and makes common cause with the Arab and Muslim immigrants in *hir* neighbourhood. Still, Max is haunted by memories of *hir* working-class mother, and *ze* covers the walls of *hir* apartment with excerpts from Yiddish poems and sayings. Feinberg gestures towards a political community that, at its most expansive, might include victims of US imperialism, workers, gays and lesbians (who are regularly referred to as 'family' in the book), disabled people and everyone along the very wide gender spectrum that the novel represents: cross-dressers and their lovers, FTMs and MTFs, aggressives, femmes, drag people, boyz, bois, trannies, two-spirits and other genderqueers.[15]

The novel indicates Max's gender very sparsely. While we understand that Max is a female-born person who has transitioned into a masculine gender and embodiment, explicit statements about *hir* gender occur very rarely – we learn most of what we know from contextual clues. The clearest indication of Max's assigned gender at birth is at the end of the novel, when *ze* and many of *hir* friends are arrested at a march that is protesting the war, roundups of Muslims in the US and transphobic violence. In the last line of the novel, the police address the narrator as 'Maxine Rabinowitz'. This final revelation of Max's given identity recalls other novels that feature a first-person narrator of ambiguous gender – such as Jeannette Winterson's *Written on the Body* – but the transgender specificity of Max's story makes it quite distinctive. Max is not a cipher: *hir* gender is complex, multilayered and deeply material, more like the palimpsest of Yiddish poems scratched into the wall than the blank beneath. Max is transgender, not androgynous; *ze* bears the marks of transgender visibly, and in a way that makes *hir* a target.

Since the 1990s, transgender people have received increasing media attention, with profiles of transgender men, women and youth receiving prominent profiles in the *New York Times* and elsewhere. There has also been a modicum of recognition for the movement for transgender rights. Jackie Kay's 1998 novel *Trumpet* offers an example of the kind of thoughtful renderings of transgender life that have emerged recently. *Trumpet* is loosely based on the story of the jazz trumpeter Billy Tipton, who lived as a man for many years, and was only discovered to have been born female after his death.[16] The novel describes the history, music and intimate life of Joss Moody, a black Scottish trumpeter who lived as a man. It begins after Joss's death and offers a sustained meditation on grief and memory. Joss's widow and his son sift through their memories of him; while Millie knew of Joss's birth-identity before they were married and kept his secret, his son Colman finds out only after the fact, and feels both betrayed and unmanned.

The structure of the novel highlights the problem of framing transgender lives. Each chapter of *Trumpet* is narrated from a different perspective, and the book includes many voices, including a letter to the editor from a transvestite organization. In Millie's intimate memories, Joss is her husband and her lover. Colman's memories swerve between admiring recollections of his father and distanced appraisals of him as a freak. The most distanced appraisal of Joss's life is the doctor who performs the medical exam on Joss's corpse; after she undresses the body, she alters the death certificate: 'She crossed "male" out and wrote "female" in her rather bad doctor's handwriting.'[17] Even more damaging than this clinical perspective, however, is that of the novel's true villain, a journalist named Sophie Stones. Sophie's relationship to Joss (whom she consistently refers to with a female pronoun) is purely exploitative; she plans to ghost write a book by Colman, exploiting his grief to tell a sensational story of 'big butch frauds'.[18]

Jeffrey Eugenides's 2002 Pulitzer-winning novel *Middlesex* shows some of the same attention to the conditions of transgender representation as *Trumpet* does. Eugenides's novel is narrated from the perspective of a second-generation Greek American hero who is intersex. The product at one generation remove of an incestuous union, the hero is born and raised as a girl, Calliope Stephanides, but at age 14 begins living as a boy (Cal). In the opening paragraph of this sprawling, satirical family chronicle, the narrator introduces himself with the phrase 'I was born twice', rewriting the famous first line of *David Copperfield* ('I am born.'). Outlining the circumstances of his double birth, he offers an alternative introduction: 'Or maybe you've seen my photograph in chapter sixteen of the now sadly outdated *Genetics and Heredity*. That's me on page 578, standing naked beside a height chart with a black box covering my eyes.'[19] This image of our narrator, pictured in a dusty textbook as a mere specimen, offers a sad commentary on the standard representation of intersex people. Eugenides promises to bring to bear the humanizing resources of the novel to counteract the pathologizing force of medical science.

Middlesex also engages – if ironically – intersex activism. Describing his self-imposed isolation, Cal writes,

> A word on my shame. I don't condone it. I'm trying my best to get over it. The intersex movement aims to put an end to infant genital reconfiguration surgery. The first step in that struggle is to convince the world – and pediatric

endocrinologists in particular – that hermaphroditic genitals are not diseased . . . But we hermaphrodites are people like everyone else. And I happen not to be a political person. I don't like groups. Though I'm a member of the Intersex Society of North America, I have never taken part in its demonstrations. I live my own life and nurse my own wounds. It's not the best way to live. But it's the way I am.   (106)

While this passage might be understood again as an attempt to humanize the figure of the intersex person, showing the narrator's distance from the strait-jacket of an imposed identity category, the passage reduces the humanity of the narrator in other ways. As in the rest of the book, the narrator describes himself as a hermaphrodite, a term that many intersex people have rejected because of its association with a history of stigma. The narrator rejects the notion of intersex as a disease, takes an overt stand against shame and mentions activism against mandatory genital manipulation surgery; at the same time, being intersex is described as a wound, a term that invokes associations with shame and disease and offers a specific reminder of the material cost of surgery. Such meditations might be understood as empathetic efforts to represent the ambivalence of an intersex person, but they also recall a tradition of spectacular representations of 'the hermaphrodite'. Hermaphroditism in *Middlesex* is often described as a metaphorical condition of twoness or self-division. In the end, immigration emerges as a deeper concern than gender, and intersex existence appears a symbol of divided heritage rather than a focus in its own right.[20]

The recent publication of anthologies, novels and non-fiction works dealing with the situation of transgender and intersex children and teenagers shows not only a new public acceptance of transgender issues but also the critical importance of dialogue about the challenges that trans youth face. Many of the fiercest gender battles are fought on the bodies of newborn infants, elementary school children and adolescents – it is during childhood that the violence of making gendered individuals imposes itself with greatest force. Julie Anne Peters addresses these difficulties with great sensitivity in her 2004 novel *Luna*. Narrated by the younger sister of a transgender high school student, *Luna* treats both the difficulties of being trans (and, in this case, in the closet) and of being intimate with someone who is. In protecting her brother Liam (who at night becomes Luna), Regan shares in his secret, and is isolated from her parents and her peers.

Peters deals sensitively with Liam/Luna's transgender existence. Speaking in Regan's voice, Peters uses male pronouns for Liam and female pronouns for Luna, often switching within the same scene as Liam shades into Luna and back. Regan's observations of the falseness of Liam's pose as a boy are particularly striking. She describes Liam sitting stiffly in his male clothes, look-ing miserable, only half-alive. At night, when Luna comes into Regan's room to try on clothes and plan for the future, she comes to life. After comparing 'before' and 'after' shots of a post-op MTF that Luna has met online, Regan reflects on the sad fact that Luna is still trapped in a false identity:

> Teri Lynn's other face. Her false face. It wasn't the difference between male and female that struck me so much as the change in demeanor, the attitude, the confidence. Teri Lynn, the male, seemed to be another person altogether. A dead person, the way Liam appeared sometimes. Sad, vacant. The other Teri Lynn, the real one, had blossomed and sprung to life. The way Liam broke free when he morphed into Luna.[21]

In *Luna*, Peters offers a sensitive account of the experience of a transgender adolescent, clearly distinguishing Liam/Luna's experience from homosexual-ity and portraying the violence of compulsory gender. It is heartening that Peters, as a lesbian author, is able to capture the specificity of transgender experience so well. For while there has been a rise in awareness of transgender issues in the lesbian and gay community, the relationship is still not an easy one. Some critics, looking at the history of the development of lesbian, gay, trans and queer identities have drawn attention to a troubling dynamic: they have noted that with the increasing acceptance of gays and lesbians, the stigma of marginal sexualities has shifted to those whose gender visibly departs from the norm.

Eve Kosofsky Sedgwick considers this shift, along with the pressure on gender nonconforming children, in her essay 'How to Bring Your Kids Up Gay'. She notes, as many others have, that the demedicalization of homo-sexuality coincided with the medicalization of transgender. In 1980, the Diagnostic and Statistical Manual of Mental Disorders was published for the first time without an entry for homosexuality; but this was the same year that it included an entry for 'Gender Identity Disorder'. Sedgwick considers the theoretical 'advance' in queer studies that has allowed critics to consider gender and sexuality separately. While conceptually this is an important distinction, she worries that it will not account for the complex ways in which gender and sexuality are bound up with each other. 'To begin to theorize gender and sexuality as distinct though intimately entangled axes of analysis has been, indeed, a great advance of recent lesbian and gay thought. There is a danger, however, that that advance may leave the effemi-nate boy once more in the position of the haunting abject – this time the haunting abject of gay thought itself.'[22]

Paying attention to the complex interaction of sexuality and gender is crucial in working towards real coalition between lesbian and gay and transgender movements. In the era of gay mainstreaming, gender deviance is increasingly stigmatized. Shannon Price Minter traces the historical roots of this phenomenon in his essay, 'Do Transsexuals Dream of Gay Rights?', when he argues, 'In an important sense, the mainstream gay rights movement defined itself and emerged as an organized political and legal movement by embracing an explicitly non-transgender, or gender-normative, model of gay identity.'[23] Across the course of the twentieth century, transgender individuals were the most 'obvious', stigmatized members of the LGB community; gender deviance has often been linked to non-dominant class and race identities as well. In his book *Imagining Transgender*, David Valentine sees in the emergence of the category of transgender an attempt to purify and 'straighten' gay identities. He writes: 'I would argue, then, that "transgender," while it has been generated by individuals who so identify, is also an effect of the historical development of privatized homosexual identity . . . "Transgender" by its categorical implication of visible gender variance, and its association of "overtness" and the street, confers stability on the gender of (especially white and middle-class) gay men and lesbians.'[24]

This dynamic continues to play out today and to have profound material and political consequences. In 2007, for instance, the US House of Representatives passed a bill to protect lesbians, gays and bisexuals from employment discrimination (the Employment Non-Discrimination Act, or ENDA), but transgender people were dropped from the original version of the bill. While the LGBT rights organization the Human Rights Campaign claimed that they would not support ENDA without transgender inclusion, in the end they reversed their position to support a diminished version of the bill. It is clear that organizations such as HRC can move ahead more quickly if they cut ties to their most vulnerable constituencies. But if we are to build a truly inclusive and just movement for gender and sexual rights, it is crucial that we recall the centrality of gender outsiders to lesbian and gay history, and make space for the emergence of an independent transgender movement.

NOTES

1. Djuna Barnes, *Nightwood* (New York: New Directions, 1937), 136–7. Further references are given in parentheses.
2. George Chauncey, *Gay New York: Gender, Urban Culture, and the Making of the Gay Male World, 1890–1940* (New York: Basic Books, 1994).
3. See Susan Stryker, *Transgender History* (Berkeley, CA: Seal Press, 2008), 123.
4. Paisley Currah, Richard M. Juang and Shannon Price Minter, 'Introduction', in Currah, Juang and Minter, eds., *Transgender Rights* (Minneapolis: University of Minnesota Press, 2006), xiv.

5. For a critique of the use of such cross-cultural examples in transgender literature and activism, see Evan B. Towle and Lynn M. Morgan, 'Romancing the Transgender Native: Rethinking the Use of the "Third Gender" Concept', *GLQ: A Journal of Lesbian and Gay Studies*, 8:4 (2002), 469–97.

6. Leslie Feinberg, *Transgender Liberation: A Movement Whose Time Has Come* (New York: World View Forum, 1992); Feinberg, *Transgender Warriors: Making History from Joan of Arc to Dennis Rodman* (Boston, MA: Beacon Press, 1996). The history of transgender autobiography is a long one, and it includes work by such prominent figures as Christine Jorgenson, Renée Richards and Jan Morris. For contemporary examples of the genre, see Deirdre N. McCloskey, *Crossing: A Memoir* (Chicago: University of Chicago Press, 1999), Jennifer Finney Boyle, *She's Not There: A Life in Two Genders* (New York: Broadway Books, 2003), Daphne Scholinski with Jane Meredith Adams, *The Last Time I Wore a Dress: A Memoir* (New York: Riverhead Books, 1997) and Max Wolf Valerio, *The Testosterone Files: My Hormonal and Social Transformation from Female to Male* (Berkeley, CA: Seal Press, 2006). For a discussion of the genre of transsexual autobiography, see Jay Prosser, *Second Skins: The Body Narratives of Transsexuality* (New York: Columbia University Press, 1998), especially Chapter 3. For important critical works on transgender (many of which combine analysis with personal memoir and reflection), see Prosser, *Second Skins*; Stryker, *Transgender History*; Currah, Juang and Minter, eds., *Transgender Rights*; Kate Bornstein, *Gender Outlaw: On Men, Women, and the Rest of Us* (New York: Vintage, 1995); Jamison Green, *Becoming a Visible Man* (Nashville, TN: Vanderbilt University Press, 2004); Riki Anne Wilchins, *Read My Lips: Sexual Subversion and the End of Gender* (Ithaca, NY: Firebrand Books, 1997); David Valentine, *Imagining Transgender: An Ethnography of a Category* (Durham, NC: Duke University Press, 2007); Julie Serano, *Whipping Girl: A Transsexual Woman on Sexism and the Scapegoating of Femininity* (Berkeley, CA: Seal Press, 2007); Judith Halberstam, *Female Masculinity* (Durham, NC: Duke University Press, 1998); Joanne Meyerowitz, *How Sex Changed: A History of Transsexuality in the United States* (Cambridge, MA: Harvard University Press, 2002) and Susan Stryker and Stephen Whittle, eds., *The Transgender Reader* (New York: Routledge, 2006).

7. Virginia Woolf, *Orlando: A Biography* (1928; New York: Harcourt Brace Jovanovich, 1956), 138–9.

8. Radclyffe Hall, *The Well of Loneliness* (1928; New York: Anchor Books, 1990), 201.

9. See Prosser, *Second Skins*, Chapter 4.

10. Raymond writes, 'All transsexuals rape women's bodies by reducing the real female form to an artifact, appropriating this body for themselves.' Janice G. Raymond, *The Transsexual Empire: The Making of the She-Male* (1979; New York: Teachers College Press, 1994), 104. Also see Mary Daly, *Gyn/Ecology: The Metaethics of Radical Feminism* (Boston, MA: Beacon Press, 1978) and Germaine Greer, *The Female Eunuch* (London: MacGibbon and Kee, 1970).

11. Jan Morris, *Conundrum* (1974; New York: New York Review of Books, 2002), 3. Further references are given in parentheses.

12. Leslie Feinberg, *Stone Butch Blues* (New York: Firebrand, 1993). Further references are given in parentheses.

13. For a discussion of Jess's transgender trajectory that distinguishes it from a transsexual narrative, see Prosser, *Second Skins*, Chapter 5.
14. Leslie Feinberg, *Drag King Dreams* (New York: Carroll & Graf, 2006).
15. For a critical anthology that focuses on a similarly expansive view of transgender or genderqueer, see Joan Nestle, Claire Howell and Riki Wilchins, eds., *GenderQueer: Voices from Beyond the Gender Binary* (Los Angeles: Alyson, 2002).
16. For an excellent biography of Tipton, see Diane Wood Middlebrook, *Suits Me: The Double Life of Billy Tipton* (New York: Mariner Books, 1999).
17. Jackie Kay, *Trumpet* (New York: Vintage, 1998), 44.
18. Another novel that deals with a historical example of cross-living is Patricia Duncker's *James Miranda Barry* (published under the name *The Doctor* in the United States: New York: Echo Press, 1999).
19. Jeffrey Eugenides, *Middlesex* (New York: Picador, 2002), 3. Further references are given in parentheses.
20. The use of Cal's gender in this novel is reminiscent of many other literary treatments of the hermaphrodite. One might think for instance of Henri de Latouche's *Fragoletta*, Theophile Gautier's *Mademoiselle de Maupin*, Honoré de Balzac's *Sarrasine* and *Seraphita*, Julia Ward Howe's *The Hermaphrodite*, Thomas Pynchon's *V* or Angela Carter's *The Passion of New Eve*. See also Michel Foucault, ed., *Herculine Barbin: Being the Recently Discovered Memoirs of a Nineteenth-Century French Hermaphrodite* (New York: Pantheon Books, 1980).
21. Julie Anne Peters, *Luna* (New York: Little Brown, 2004), 126.
22. Eve Kosofsky Sedgwick, 'How to Bring Your Kids up Gay', *Tendencies* (Durham, NC: Duke University Press, 1993), 157.
23. Shannon Price Minter, 'Do Transsexuals Dream of Gay Rights?', in Currah, Juang and Minter, eds., *Transgender Rights*, 150.
24. Valentine, *Imagining Transgender*, 64.

PART III

Literary traditions

10

JODIE MEDD

Encountering the past in recent lesbian and gay fiction

Then and now

In what has become an iconic moment in gay history, Oscar Wilde, on trial for 'acts of gross indecency' between men, eloquently defined and defended 'the Love that dare not speak its name' through historical citation:

> 'The Love that dare not speak its name' in this century is such a great affection of an elder for a younger man as there was between David and Jonathan, such as Plato made the very basis of his philosophy, and such as you find in the sonnets of Michelangelo and Shakespeare. It is that deep, spiritual affection that is as pure as it is perfect. It dictates and pervades great works of art like those of Shakespeare and Michelangelo, and those two letters of mine [to Alfred Lord Douglas], such as they are ... It is beautiful, it is fine, it is the noblest form of affection.[1]

Aligning his alleged criminality with the greatest names in Western civilization, Wilde knew the uses to which the past could be (re)made to sustain a queer present. Indeed, such historical and mythological allusions were variously employed by nineteenth- and early twentieth-century writers like Walter Pater, John Addington Symonds, Edward Carpenter and E. M. Forster to signal, code and defend male same-sex desire. Similarly, female writers of the period such as Renée Vivien, Natalie Barney and Michael Field (Katherine Bradley and Edith Cooper), and modernist poets H. D. and Amy Lowell, reference the life and work of Sappho, the celebrated ancient poet of Lesbos from whom the terms Sapphist and lesbian were derived. Resisting turn-of-the-century constructions of homosexuality as criminal, pathological, diseased and corrupting, these invocations of the past shaped an alternative sense of collective identity formation and belonging through historical affiliation.[2] The 'shame' of the Love that dare not speak its name was countered by the legitimating 'pride' of historical belonging.

Neither simple nor uncritical, these queer historical (re)turns demonstrate an attachment to the past as a resource for negotiating the complexities of queer experience in the present, and convey the interfusion of history, desire, identity and community, four highly debated terms in queer studies. In this context, Stuart Hall's formulation is particularly apt: 'Identities are the names we give to the different ways we are positioned by, and position ourselves within, the narratives of the past.'[3] This chapter starts from a positional 'narrative of the past' informing contemporary queer identity in the West: the sense that the late nineteenth and early twentieth centuries constitute a critical period in historical formations of (homo)sexual identities. It explores how selected lesbian and gay authors since the late 1980s have engaged with the Victorian and modernist past. This focus on how well-known contemporary writers represent a key historical period reveals a range of complex and variable approaches to the past. Indeed, these texts offer distinct models of queer literary engagement with history, where the past may function as a structure of pedagogy, an inspiration for future transformation, a literary template for addressing past and present queer issues, a source of narrative pleasure that transforms established genres while imagining occluded sexual desires and cultures, and an imaginative playground for destabilizing temporality and subjectivity.

Pedagogies of the past: encountering the history of injury

Alan Hollinghurst's first novel, *The Swimming-Pool Library*, self-consciously looks backward and forward in gay history. Published in 1988, it is framed as Will Beckwith's nostalgic reminiscence about his lost youth in 'the far-off spring of 1983', but also proleptically mourns a larger, collective loss by anticipating the coming of AIDS.[4] As the novel unfolds, it also gazes back across the century to the decades preceding and leading up to the reforms that loosened state control of gay sex in Britain. Indeed, Will is reluctantly educated into understanding how the homophobic past matters to his sexually liberated present. Evoking the conflicted 'history of injury' that constitutes queer experience, the novel demands engagement with the past while acknowledging its discomforting implications for the present.[5]

Young, wealthy, attractive and libidinous, Will is simultaneously an heir to his grandfather's fortune and peerage, and the beneficiary of decades of legal change and gay activism, allowing him the 'constant leisure' (81) to pursue sexual encounters with men. As many critics have noted, Will's 'last summer' of erotic licence presages the close of a sexual era in gay history:

> My life was in a strange way that summer, the last summer of its kind there was
> ever to be. I was riding high on sex and self-esteem – it was my time, my *belle*

époque – but all the while with a faint flicker of calamity, like flames around a
photograph, something seen out of the corner of the eye. (3)

That 'faint flicker of calamity' obliquely signals both the historical inevit-
ability of AIDS and the waning of Will's own *belle époque* of 'sex and self-
esteem' as he discovers his complicity in an oppressive queer past of which he
had been blithely unaware and which challenges his carefree self-indulgence
as a leisured aristocrat and sexually liberated gay man.

Will encounters Lord Charles Nantwich, an octogenarian 'queer peer' (85)
whose collapse in a public lavatory obliges Will to abandon his cottaging to
resuscitate him. Meeting again at another cruising spot, the Corinthian
('Corry') Club pool, Will is 'drawn' to the eccentric man, speculating that
he 'might have a distracting story to tell' (28). In fact, Charles wants *Will* to
tell his story, by writing a biography of Charles's queer life over the century.
Finding 'the prospect of the Nantwich book' both 'alluring' and 'oppressive'
(85), Will explores Charles's diaries, discovering a simultaneously alluring
and oppressive history. Directly quoting the diaries Will reads, the novel
creates 'a fragmentary secondary narrative that Hollinghurst interleaves
through the framing story'. This 'double narrative' draws a series of parallels
between the men, inviting, resisting and complicating relationships between
the gay past and present.[6]

Initially Will admits his 'irresistible elegiac need for the tenderness of an
England long past' prompts him to enter 'with spurious, or purely aesthetic
emotion into' Charles's archive; however, he discovers that the past offers
unsettling correspondences while refusing nostalgic identifications (122). Will
finds that 'despite its period', Charles's diary 'spoke for me too', in an
unexpected 'fore-echo of my own life' (129). Both members of Britain's
white male elite, Will and Charles share a similar but historically differentiated eroticization of racial, social and class difference. Will's multicultural
cross-class London sex-tourism unevenly parallels Charles's adoration of
Sudanese youth while a 1920s colonial administrator in Africa. Charles's
deepest attachment is to Taha, a houseboy who returns to England as his
servant, marries and fathers a son. While Charles is in prison in the 1950s on
charges of homosexuality, Taha is killed by a gang of racists. First described
by Charles as 'a supple, plum-black sixteen' (206), Taha poses a fraught
parallel with Arthur, a seventeen-year-old Afro-Caribbean man with whom
Will has, as he says, 'a crazy fling with all the beauty for me of his youngness
and blackness' (31). Will's unapologetic 'stricken devotion' (187) for black
male bodies sits in uneasy tension with what he dismisses as Charles's outdated 'trying kind of nature-worship thing about blacks' (178). As the novel
works this parallel, it asks us to (re)consider the relationship between the

racial erotic fantasies and power structures of Charles's colonial past, and those of certain gay white sexual cultures in Will's present.[7] Similarly, while accompanying Charles to a private porn movie set, Will is disturbed to find the actors are staff from Charles's club, including Abdul, the cook Will 'fancied ... crazily' for his 'high, haunted African brow, and ... high, rolling African ass' (187). When Abdul poses in a fur coat, the scene's primitivism both entices and offends Will: 'With his scarred black skin inside the thick black fur he struck me, who adored him for a moment, like some exquisite game animal, partly skinned and then thrown aside still breathing. I excused myself for the lavatory, tiptoed to the front door; but then slammed it behind me' (188).

We (and Will) eventually learn Abdul is Taha's son, orphaned by the racism that killed his father. This history of violence is revisited when Will is gay-bashed by skinheads outside Arthur's council flat. Attacking Will for being a 'Fuckin' nigger-fucker' (173) while stamping beneath their Doc Martens a rare copy of Ronald Firbank's *The Flower Beneath the Foot*, the gang inaugurates Will into the history of injury that accompanies and often over-whelms the Firbankian decadence of the queer past. With his 'vandalised' face (183), Will temporarily loses his narcissistic identity founded on sexual desirability, but gains a sense of gay community forged through homophobic suffering, an identification compounded when his best friend is entrapped and arrested for sexual solicitation (echoing Charles's arrest in the 1950s): 'James's experience, like mine with the skinheads, made me abruptly self-conscious, gave me an urge to solidarity with my kind that I wasn't used to in our liberal times' (223).

Just as this urge to collective historical identification arises, however, Will's relation to the queer past is further troubled with the final revelation of Charles's diary – that Will's own grandfather, Denis Beckwith, Director of Public Prosecutions in the 1950s, led a 'crusade to eradicate male vice' (260) through 'brutal purges' (253) of male homosexuality, and was personally responsible for Charles's imprisonment.[8] 'Buil[ding] his career on oppression' (264), Beckwith was promoted to the House of Lords, securing the peerage, status and fortune that underwrite Will's life of leisure and sexual adventure. As both victim and beneficiary of historically entrenched homophobia, Will is caught in an impossibly ambivalent relation to the gay past. Feeling 'so stupid and so ashamed' he contritely searches for Charles but finds Abdul, who reveals himself as Taha's son and then anally penetrates Will with 'a thrilling leisured vehemence' over a chopping table (260, 262). Rendering him 'gur-gling with pleasure and grunting with pain', this pornographic scene of retributive violence conveys Will's complicated positioning in intertwining colonial, racial and homophobic histories of injury (262).

Newly aware of 'the power and the compromise' in which he 'had unthinkingly been raised' (268), Will concludes he cannot write Charles's biography. 'All I could write now', he tells Charles, 'would be a book about why I couldn't write the book' (281). Indeed, *The Swimming-Pool Library is* the book about why he couldn't write the book. His eyes now opened to the 'blind spot' (279) of queer history that preceded him, Will sees he is not as immune from the gay past as he had assumed; yet he can neither vaguely 'enter into' this history with elegiac longing nor directly identify with it in queer solidarity. By exploring how writing the gay past is alluring, oppressive and ultimately impossible, *The Swimming-Pool Library* insists on the traumatic but necessary process of encountering the history of injury that has formed – and even benefited – present queer identities.

Romancing the past: 'patterns of the possible' for healing the history of injury

Described by David Halperin as 'arguably the most important work of gay male historical fiction since ... *The Swimming-Pool Library*',[9] Jamie O'Neill's *At Swim, Two Boys* (2001) is set near Dublin in 1915–16, with its action climaxing in the 1916 Irish Easter Rising. Strategically invoking a heroic and romanticized national past to heal the homophobic injuries of history, the novel narrates Jim Mack's coming-of-age as he falls in love with another boy while awakening to the revolutionary cause of Irish nationalism. O'Neill describes *At Swim* as an attempt to reconcile the apparent split between his own national and sexual identities: 'Often when people would ask me "Are you Irish?" I'd say, "No, I'm gay" and I'd wanted to try to square that apparent circle. I wanted to write a book about two boys falling in love, about finding each other and their own country, the country they would fight for. And the question was, Is the love of Ireland very different from loving an Irish man?'[10] O'Neill's novel returns to a time when both modern gay identity and modern Irish national identity were in formation, mapping one onto the other. A gay romance, the novel also romances the redemptive possibilities of the past, particularly by appropriating and queering structures of nationalism.

Jim's gay/national *Bildung* develops in relation to Doyler Doyle, an impoverished former schoolmate, and Anthony MacMurrough, a disgraced Irish aristocrat. Doyler's bold talk of nationalism, socialism and the Irish language inaugurates Jim's national consciousness, while their friendship inspires a profound but unnameable devotion. Consequently, Jim adopts the rhetoric of heroic nationalism and self-sacrificing fraternal comradeship to articulate his love for Doyler. Meanwhile, Jim is also befriended by MacMurrough, who has returned to his family's estate after his incarceration in London for a homosexual affair. Bitter, disgraced, cynical and libidinally restless, MacMurrough converts his initial lusty regard for Jim into a tender protectiveness, encouraging Jim's growing love for Doyler. Healing the loss, suffering and shame inflicted by the homophobic history of injury, MacMurrough finds redemption in his mentorship of Jim and his own renewed nationalism.

With Jim's nascent political and sexual identities fed equally by Doyler's stories of Irish nationalism and MacMurrough's Hellenic tales of homoerotic heroism, the novel overtly 'cross[es] the codes of Irish identity and gay identity, making each into a figure for the other'.[11] In fact, Scrotes, an elderly academic who died in prison beloved by MacMurrough and now offers him ghostly advice, proposes that the Irish revival of history, myth and language provides a model for Jim's gay *Bildung*:

> Help these boys build a nation their own. Ransack the histories for clues to their past. Plunder the literatures for words they can speak. And should you encounter an ancient tribe whose customs, however dimly, cast light on their hearts, tell them that tale; and you shall name the unspeakable names of your kind, and in that naming, in each such telling, they will falter a step toward the light.[12]

As Scrotes's advice to 'ransack the histories' and 'plunder the literatures' figures history as a resource to be strategically exploited and re-imagined, the novel explores uses of the past for building a queer 'nation of the heart' (329). Metafictionally aware of the discursive fallibility of historical narratives, it nevertheless endorses their transformative value in the present. For example, Jim seems naïvely to ingest tales of national, political and personal heroism, even as one story contradicts or discredits another; however, he proves his savvy in reading historical fictions, for when he is told that these stories are unreliable or even invented, he not only already knows this, but he also *does not care*. Historical fallibility 'doesn't signify' (507) to him; what matters are the intimacies that are formed and the identities that are imagined through historical retellings. As MacMurrough observes, Jim grasps 'instinctively ... that more than stories, they were patterns of the possible' (607). Similarly, Scrotes acknowledges that Ireland's idealized pre-colonized past relies on 'fabulous claims' and questionable comparisons, but that is of 'no matter' for 'the struggle for Irish Ireland is not for truth against untruth ... The struggle is for the heart' (329), just as MacMurrough's stories of Greek love are admittedly 'not nearly the same' as modern homosexuality (328), but they can still inspire a new queer 'nation of the heart'. In this way, O'Neill's novel incorporates and transcends postmodern scepticism about historical 'truth' to consider how the *transmission* of fictions of the past may support present and future political transformation, an idea enacted through its own historiographic status.

Indeed, while acknowledging its convincing Irish historical atmosphere, critics find that the novel anachronistically 'imposes' contemporary post-Stonewall notions of gay sexuality 'upon its depiction of the past'[13] and fails to 'historicize sexual subjectivity itself' or to provide 'a historically and culturally specific Irish experience of gay desire'.[14] These criticisms point to ongoing debates in queer historiography over historicizing sexuality without importing contemporary paradigms into the past. However, given *At Swim*'s metafictional awareness of historical appropriations, I do not read it as purporting to full historical authenticity; instead, it knowingly 'ransacks' the past to transmit an emotionally engaging *fiction* to imagine or inspire queer futures. The novel's historiographic struggle is not for 'truth against untruth', but for the hearts of its historical characters and present readers, romancing the (queer) present through its (queer) romance with the past.

Rewriting modernism: opportunities of the literary past

While *At Swim, Two Boys* romances Irish national history and *The Swimming-Pool Library* considers the twentieth century's history of injury, another queer return to the past involves rewriting historically significant fictional texts. Undoubtedly, the most famous example in contemporary gay fiction is Michael Cunningham's *The Hours* (1998), which updates Virginia Woolf's *Mrs. Dalloway* by transposing it to modern-day New York City, while also imaginatively returning to the scene of Woolf's writing. Placing lesbian and gay characters at the centre of its reworking of a canonical novel, *The Hours* uses the literary past to narrate the queer present.

Three distinct but related narrative strands chart a day in the life of three women: Virginia Woolf composes *Mrs. Dalloway* in Richmond in 1923; Laura Brown surreptitiously reads *Mrs. Dalloway* to escape from the feminine mystique of suburban Los Angeles, 1949; and Clarissa Vaughn, a lesbian living in Manhattan's West Village at the 'end of the twentieth century',[15] mimics the character Mrs. Dalloway as she prepares a party for Richard, a brilliant gay author dying of AIDS. The novel focuses on the historically embedded possibilities and limitations of these women's lives, including the realm of same-sex desire, which subtends Clarissa's own identity in *Mrs. Dalloway*. The transposition of *Mrs. Dalloway* from 1920s London to contemporary Manhattan indulges in a 'what if' play of sensibility – what if Clarissa had lived in our queer present, with the freedom to pursue her relationship with Sally, and choose a career rather than capitulate to the heteronormative necessity of marriage? What if, rather than sharing just one kiss when they were eighteen, in 'the most exquisite moment of [Clarissa's] whole life',[16] they had shared an eighteen-year relationship?

While *The Hours* provides Mrs. Dalloway's contemporary counterpart with such expanded options, Clarissa still questions her choices, and still memorializes a transgressive kiss as her 'missed opportunity' of youth (97) – in this case, her kiss with Richard, which defies their homosexual identities for a heterosexual, and ultimately impossible, desire.

Granting Clarissa Vaughn the sexual and social freedoms that are denied to not only Clarissa Dalloway, but also Virginia Woolf and Laura Brown, *The Hours* nevertheless refuses an easy progressivist vision in which the present trumps the past. Clarissa experiences profound moments of estrangement and alienation from her 'empty and arbitrary' domestic comforts (92), and nurses some of the greatest doubts and regrets in the novel. She is subject to negative judgments from within the queer community – including the revived version of Miss Kilman, here a queer theorist 'despotic in ... her endless demonstration of cutting-edge, leather-jacketed righteousness' (23) who regards Clarissa contemptuously for her respectable homonormativity: 'queers of the old school, dressed to pass, bourgeois to the bone, living like husband and wife' (160). With quick semi-satirical strokes, Cunningham adopts Woolf's free indirect style of interior narration to present queer characters' competing opinions of one another. Similarly, Cunningham's rewriting finds in its precursor an opportunity for addressing a particular structure of feeling regarding AIDS in America at the century's end.[17] *The Hours* aligns Richard, an acclaimed writer whose mind has been 'eaten into lace by the virus' (55), with Septimus Smith, a shell-shocked veteran who was once an aspiring poet, implicitly comparing the incalculable cultural losses of the First World War and the AIDS epidemic. Physically surviving their respective battles but mentally ravaged and finally driven to suicide, Richard and Septimus uncomfortably remind their contemporaries of the irreparable damage caused by the century's catastrophic events. In appropriating *Mrs. Dalloway* to compare key stages of Anglo-American feminism and address contemporary American queer culture and the vagaries of desire, *The Hours* attests to the continuing relevance of Woolf's modernist text while staging a decisively queer intervention into the literary past.

Lesbian historical fictions: 'the sort of history we can't really recover'

While contemporary gay and lesbian identities share a history of homophobic suffering, the historiography of same-sex desire is diacritically marked by gender. Greater historical documentation, awareness and representation of men in general provide more widely archived and recognized traditions of male same-sex practices, as we have seen with Wilde's eloquent self-defence of 'the Love that dare not speak its name', and the stories of Greek love and Irish comradeship that inspire Jim. Further, as demonstrated by Hollinghurst, O'Neill and even Wilde's famous martyrdom, knowledge of the history of injury relies on existing archives of laws, trials, public scandals and ruined reputations – all dominantly oriented towards men – through which such a history can be traced. In contrast, with much of women's experiences undocumented in public records and traditional archives, histories of female same-sex desire often lack the resources through which the past can be remembered and understood in the present. While Sappho has long been claimed within lesbian genealogies, she is only one figure compared to the many historical sources and traditions available to gay male culture. That her poetry survives only in fragments and her biographical details are obscure attests to the fragmentary and occluded history of female same-sex desire itself. Accordingly, lesbianism in Western cultural traditions has been characterized as 'apparitional' by Terry Castle. That is, Castle argues, the lesbian has been 'ghosted' or 'derealized' by the Western imagination while having a 'peculiar cultural power ... to "haunt" us'.[18] Only recently have more scholars explored the subtle history of female homoerotic desires, relations and structures of identity. This research carefully theorizes and debates women's sexual historiography, even considering how the very concept of lesbianism confounds phallocentric systems of signification and eludes historical representation.

Accordingly, in a survey of 'popular realist lesbian historical novels' from the 1980s and early 1990s, Laura Doan and Sarah Waters observe an 'impulse towards the tracing of an erotic genealogy' and recovering a 'lesbian tradition' in response to 'the suppression or absence of lesbian activity from the historical record'. While such novels provide 'empowering and consolatory fantasies' that answer 'the angers and anxieties provoked by lesbians' marginalized' representation, they tend 'simply to insert a mirror-image of a contemporary lesbian into an earlier historical period', and may suppress sexual and historical complexities, such that 'the past ... emerges ... as an erotic and political continuum through which alterity can be mystically overridden'.[19] Notably, Sarah Waters herself has transformed lesbian historical fiction since her first novel in 1998, complicating the genre and expanding its readership.

'A different path' through 'all the classic scenarios and tropes'

Arguably the best-known British lesbian novelist since Jeanette Winterson, Sarah Waters founded her literary career upon queer engagements with the past. Her historical novels have earned critical accolades and impressive commercial success; two were adapted into successful BBC television productions. Convincing in their period detail and atmosphere, her first three novels engage with literary genres specific to their Victorian settings. They particularly invoke 'the secret life of sexuality' of the 'Other Victorians' identified in Steven Marcus's groundbreaking book of that title. Indeed, gender, sexuality and 'other' cultural arenas that were 'not part of the Victorians' official consciousness of themselves' have attracted ongoing research in recent decades.[20] Waters's fiction reflects this interest in the 'other' Victorian past, representing transgressive sexuality in the form of same-sex desire, pornography and prostitution, as well as women's experiences in prisons and madhouses, and as servants, hysterical spinsters, spiritualists and music hall performers. Adapting established literary genres to write the period 'then' as we have come to understand it 'now', Waters draws upon conventions and styles of the Victorian novel to address 'what did *not* get into the Victorian novel, what was by common consent or convention left out or suppressed'.[21]

Waters thus combines the familiar form and content of Victorian literature with the recent interest in the 'Other Victorians' to tell her lesbian stories. Indeed, her comment that in *Fingersmith* she was 'appropriating all the stuff I most love about 19th-century fiction for a lesbian agenda' applies to all three of her first novels.[22] Informed by her academic background in Victorian studies and a critical awareness of her contemporary position as a lesbian writer, her novels 'exploit ... the literary and cultural paradigms of a period Waters knows well enough to ventriloquize and thus to test' while 'embody[ing] and bring[ing] to vivid life episodes in the history of sexuality'.[23]

Although not overtly self-referential, Waters's fiction critically engages with history and narrative, leading many critics to consider it historiographic metafiction,[24] arguing, for example, that in 'remain[ing] resolutely silent on its own fictionality', Waters's fiction strategically critiques through re-enacting 'history's obscuration of its own narrativity'.[25] Exploiting the familiar pleasures of Victorian conventions – Gothic elements, narrative suspense, sensational twists and turns of plot, domestic melodrama, Dickensian characters, picaresque adventure, gritty gas-lit London – Waters manipulates them to shape 'lesbian' narratives.[26] As Waters has said of *Fingersmith*, 'I wanted to take all the classic scenarios and tropes of sensation fiction and to take a different path through them, pursuing lesbian attraction, and making them mean different things.'[27] Repurposing the 'classic scenarios and tropes' of Victorian fiction to articulate female same-sex passion, Waters also acknowledges the historical differences and discursive limits of such desires and identities in the past.

Waters's debut, *Tipping the Velvet* (1998), is narrated by Nancy Astley who undergoes a sexual *Bildung* as she moves through various late Victorian cultures and sexual subcultures. The picaresque coming out story appeals to present lesbian identities, with Nancy ultimately embracing a confident identity as a 'Tom'. At the same time, her story explores a range of socially and class-differentiated contexts in which female sexual desires and identities may have been manifested in the past. Historicizing female sexuality, Waters also takes strategic historical liberties. Admitting to 'pinch(ing) for women' what is known of male homosexual subcultures of the 1890s[28] while relying on period terms such as 'tommistry' more than might be historically accurate, Waters explains, 'Part of the project of that book was not to be authentic, but just to imagine a history – to imagine the sort of history that we can't really recover.'[29] This comment speaks as much to the historical as to the contemporary concerns of Waters's fiction.

Waters's next two novels, *Affinity* (1999) and *Fingersmith* (2002), both counterpose two female narrators with one another. As they are set progressively further back in the nineteenth century, the terms of female same-sex representation become less direct than in *Tipping the Velvet*, according to the discursive limitations of the period, while the dual narrations and unexpected twists of plots and desires further complicate the novels' sexual representations. Both novels also subtly acknowledge the processes of erasure through which female sexuality becomes a history 'we can never really recover'. *Affinity* thematizes the ideological split in which men write the official history of male public accomplishments, while it is assumed 'all women can ever write ... are "journals of the heart"'.[30] But we find that Margaret, a middle-class spinster who plans to write an account of Millbank's prison for women, not only records in her journal the unknown lives of the incarcerated women she visits (information relevant to women's history now), but also documents her obsessive desire for one of the inmates. When the journal becomes the means through which Margaret's desire is betrayed and double-crossed near the end of the novel, she burns it and contemplates suicide. Unlike Charles Nantwich who wants his private papers made into a public biography of his queer life, here Margaret's spinsterly sense of propriety and shame prompts her to destroy her diary, rendering her queer past inaccessible to future historians.[31] In *Fingersmith*, a passion between two women that traverses sensational plots of deception and disinheritance is finally put to paper when one protagonist becomes a professional writer and fills her pages, as she tells her lover, 'with all the words for how I want you'.[32] This record of their desire, however, takes the form of an erotic novel to profit from the male-dominated pornography market. Imagining these women's re-appropriation of the pornography trade as both a means of income and a testament to their passion, the novel encourages us to re-think the meanings, uses and resonances of Victorian pornography beyond its assumed circulation by and for men, and suggests that the archive of lesbian experience may exist where we least expect it.

Ultimately, Waters avoids the pitfalls of earlier lesbian historical fiction through her knowing manipulation of genre and history. Partaking in Victorian literary conventions and constrained by their historicity while still psychologically complex, the narrators inhabit the literary and cultural past while soliciting identification from present readers, without simply mirroring contemporary lesbianism. Further, the novels explore the uneven ways in which female sexuality is discursively shaped, represented and occluded according to class, place and social position, while raising histor-iographic questions about our ability to access the 'lesbian' past. Waters's fiction thus allows for the pleasures of literary identification and historical curiosity, but at the same time maintains a sense of historical and literary alterity.

History without boundaries

While the writers I've discussed engage with particular historical periods, other novelists rupture temporal conventions to write a queer history without boundaries as they destabilize identity, gender, sexuality and desire. Virginia Woolf's 1928 novel *Orlando* provides a canonical model of this queer repre-sentational strategy. Woolf's playful fantastical mock 'biography' of Vita Sackville-West disregards temporal boundaries and somatic coherence to expand identity possibilities. Orlando's indeterminate and multiple identities that extend over centuries, across genders and through a range of careers, costumes and experiences convey the plurality of subjectivity itself: 'all the selves we have it in us to be'; 'these selves of which we are built up, one on top of another, as plates are piled on a waiter's hand'.[33] Such a model of fluid and multiple subjectivity has implications for categorizations of sexual and gender deviance, in Woolf's time and our own. At a time when non-heteronormative desires and identities were censored in literature while undergoing discursive elaboration in sexology and psychoanalysis, Woolf's fantastical (ab)use of history created a space for imagining and writing lives beyond the bounded categories of identity and desire prevalent in her contemporary moment.

Orlando's playful modernist engagement with history and identity antici-pates the queer postmodern fiction of Jeanette Winterson. A pioneering British lesbian novelist, Winterson debuted in 1985 with *Oranges Are Not the Only Fruit*, a semi-autobiographical coming out story of Jeanette, whose lesbian desire results in her exile from her fundamentalist religious commu-nity. Incorporating fairy tales, legend, the Bible and fantasy, the novel also metatextually reflects upon history as a form of storytelling that is as powerful as it is unreliable. Musing that '[p]eople like to separate storytelling which is not fact from history which is fact. They do this so that they know what to believe and what not to believe', Jeanette sees historical claims as underwriting oppressive regimes: 'buil[ding] an empire and [keeping] people where they belong[]', while also acting 'as a means of denying the past'. Jeanette's commentary prefaces her account of the church's intervention to exorcize her 'unnatural passions', positioning her own story as a corrective to the dominant narratives that would deny, demonize or exorcize the queer past.[34]

Winterson's next two major novels move away from contemporary narrative and towards fantastical historical fiction, continuing to reflect on history, gender, sexuality and identity. With *The Passion* (1987) set in Napoleon's Europe in the early 1800s, and *Sexing the Cherry* (1989) set primarily in seventeenth-century England, and both referencing specific historical events and figures, these novels inhabit only to confound the terms of history. Indeed, history becomes an imaginative playground for Winterson's texts where, much like *Orlando*, historical 'fact', fantasy and fairy tale intermix, gender and desire vacillate and identities and realities multiply. Unlike other lesbian historical fictions, Winterson's novels are not concerned with locating coherent lesbian identities in the past. Rather, her overt historiographic metafictions invoke only to destabilize the concepts of history upon which historical fiction ostensibly relies, while concomitantly rupturing notions of coherent subjectivity upon which certain forms of gender and sexual identity politics rely.[35] Thus, while we've seen other contemporary authors return to the Victorian and modernist past as a time when queer subjectivities were under consolidation, Winterson reaches further back in history to 'the founding moments of modern subjectivity itself', with an interest in disrupting and unravelling 'the regime of the coherent, Cartesian subject'.[36] In this way, her fiction evidences 'not a quest for a unified and coherent essentialized self but a consistent willingness to explore multiple and fragmented fictions of identity, that is, to engage in endless speculation'.[37] This exploration critically questions sexuality and gender, so that even as these novels and their characters resist sexual categorization, their continual disruption of heteronormative gender codes, sexual desires and bodily possibilities have been interpreted as 'virtually lesbian' or a form of 'lesbian postmodern' critique.[38]

The giantess Dog-Woman from *Sexing the Cherry*, for example, has received attention as a woman who 'exceeds and ironizes normative femininity' through her excessive size and heroic strength.[39] Her unsatisfying heterosexual encounters comically diminish male phallic power: her huge vagina swallows up the genitals of one man, while she takes literally another man's appeal to put his 'member' in her mouth, 'biting it off with a snap', only to be 'disgusted by the leathery thing' and feed it to her dog.[40]

The Dog-Woman is just one of the four main narrators in *The Passion* and *Sexing the Cherry* who disrupt bodily and behavioural boundaries of conventional gender and sexuality. The dual narratives – each novel has male and female narrators – present multiple points of view that resist conventional gender and sexual categorization, and are populated by characters whose bodies cross cultural codes of gender. In *The Passion* Villanelle inherits the webbed feet that are the exclusive domain of boat*men* in her family: 'There never was a girl whose feet were webbed in the entire history of the boat-men.'[41] The dictates of 'history' here are ultimately unreliable. When she falls in love with a woman while cross-dressing as a young man, she speculates, much like *Orlando*: 'And what was myself? Was this breeches and boots self any less real than my garters?' (65–6). Jordan, the Dog-Woman's foundling son in *Sexing the Cherry* whose exterior sea journeys with the real historical explorer John Tradescant overlap with his interior, imaginative explorations, also cross-dresses to be 'free of the burdens of [his] gender', discovering women's hidden discursive realm: 'In my petticoats I was a traveler in a foreign country. I did not speak the language' (26–7). Jordan also sails into the novel's feminist revisions of fairy tales and myths that subvert the hetero-normative premises of founding narratives. Indeed, as a number of critics have noticed, Jordan's journeying across the real and the fantastic, the geo-graphic and the psychic, the literal and the metaphorical, and the 'foreign' countries of gender both within and without conveys Winterson's own jour-neying across history, genre, gender, sexuality and identities in her philoso-phical historical fictions.[42]

The final section of *Sexing the Cherry* further collapses boundaries of history and identity when the Dog-Woman's and Jordan's seventeenth-century narratives are inexplicably joined, or echoed, by two narrators from the present. This grafting of periods and narrators – following the figure of plant grafting from the novel's title – accords with Winterson's eschewing of linear temporality and coherent subjectivity. In Jordan's words: 'The inward life tells us that we are multiple not single, and that our one existence is really countless existences holding hands like those cut-out paper dolls, but unlike the dolls never coming to an end.' His next image uncannily recalls *Orlando*: 'Our lives could be *stacked together like plates on a waiter's hand*. Only the top is showing, but the rest are there and by mistake we discover them' (90, my emphasis). The unnamed contemporary female narrator simi-larly regards her spirit as not 'single' but 'multiple': 'Its dimension will not be one of confinement but one of space. It may inhabit numerous changing decaying bodies in the future and in the past' (130). It is precisely through this expansive and plural sense of time, subjectivity and embodiment that Winterson's historical novels, like *Orlando*, allow for a range of sexual and gender experiences, desires, bodies and identifications unbounded by the 'limiting paradigms' of heteronormativity.[43]

Now and then

Historians researching sexualities of the past have actively debated the terms, meanings and challenges of queer historiography. Questions about what and how we know, read, write, conceptualize, understand and *feel* about sexual histories and their relation to our contemporary moment continually inform and animate the challenges of doing the history of (homo)sexuality today. These scholars are intensely self-conscious about their own relation to their historical subject, attuned to how the constructions of the sexual past matter and mean to the politics and communities of the present. Lesbian and gay politics recognize the value of charting historical genealogies for the purpose of community building and identity formation, while cautioning that historical claims to a 'unified queer "heritage"' can obscure differences within both the past and the present.[44]

As this chapter demonstrates, these same questions and conflicts inform present queer literary engagements with the past. These novels are keenly aware of the compelling and unresolvable problematic of knowing, thinking, imagining, feeling, reading and writing the (queer) past. From the impossibility of writing gay history to the 'patterns of the possible' that the past offers for future identities; from the effects of the homophobic history of injury to the pleasures in queer engagements with literary and cultural history; from struggles over historical truth to struggles for the heart; from the traumatic revelations of the gay archive to the creative imaginings of an undocumented lesbian past 'that we can never really recover'; from looking to the past to consolidate a coherent homosexual identity in the present to exploring the plurality of sexual communities and identifications in any one historical moment, to even rupturing the very notions of history and subjectivity, these novels variously (re)turn to, turn away from and even overturn history in their queer (re)writings of the past. Just as queer historiography is not only concerned with historical knowledge but also with the emotional, political and personal investments in and implications of encounters with the past, so too are these novels' historical engagements variously nostalgic, romantic, ironic, traumatic, appropriative, subversive, satiric, strategic and recuperative in response to a past that is complexly figured as injurious, inspiring, enabling, alluring, oppressive, intractable, flexible, unreliable and even immaterial to its characters and readers. These are not just differences or contradictions: they are lessons. For as these novels represent the complexity of sexualities in history while recognizing how various pasts inhabit and inform the present, they remind us of the very discontinuity and 'historical difference within the present itself'.[45] Perhaps most importantly, they demonstrate that while encounters with queer history may be highly fraught and debated, it is precisely through engaging in these historiographical struggles that queer politics of identity, non-identity, community, belonging and difference continually take shape in the present and will continue to change shape in the future.

NOTES

1. H. Montgomery Hyde, *The Trials of Oscar Wilde* (New York: Dover, 1926), 201.
2. For an extended discussion of such invocations of history, see Christopher Nealon, *Foundlings: Lesbian and Gay Historical Emotion before Stonewall* (Durham, NC: Duke University Press, 2001).
3. Stuart Hall, 'Cultural Identity and Diaspora', in Patrick Williams and Laura Chrisman, eds., *Colonial Discourse and Post-Colonial Theory: A Reader* (New York: Columbia University Press, 1994), 394. Scott Bravmann uses this quotation as a fitting epigram to the opening chapter of his *Queer Fictions of the Past* (Cambridge: Cambridge University Press, 1997).
4. Alan Hollinghurst, *The Swimming-Pool Library* (1988; London: Vintage, 1998), 48. Further references are given in parentheses.
5. In *Bodies that Matter: On the Discursive Limits of 'Sex'* (New York: Routledge, 1993), Judith Butler refers to the homophobic 'history of injury' that constitutes queer subjectivity (223). In *Feeling Backward: Loss and the Politics of Queer History* (Cambridge, MA: Harvard University Press, 2007), Heather Love develops this notion of 'historical injury' as a central concept for queer relations to the past.
6. Richard Dellamora, *Apocalyptic Overtures: Sexual Politics and the Sense of an Ending* (New Brunswick, NJ: Rutgers University Press, 1994), 174, 181.
7. For further analyses, see David Alderson, 'Desire as Nostalgia: The Novels of Alan Hollinghurst', in David Alderson and Linda Anderson, eds., *Territories of Desire in Queer Culture: Refiguring Contemporary Boundaries* (Manchester: Manchester University Press, 2000), 29–48; James N. Brown and Patricia M. Sant, 'Race, Class and the Homoerotics of *The Swimming-Pool Library*', in John C. Hawley, ed., *Postcolonial and Queer Theories: Intersections and Essays* (Westport, CT: Greenwood, 2001), 113–27; and Brenda Cooper, 'Snapshots of Postcolonial Masculinities: Alan Hollinghurst's *The Swimming-Pool Library* and Ben Okri's *The Famished Road*', *Journal of Commonwealth Literature*, 34 (1999), 135–57.
8. Hollinghurst bases Lord Nantwich's experience not only on actual homosexual 'purges' in the early 1950s, but on a specific case in which the Director of Public Prosecutions targeted Lord Montagu for prosecution.
9. David Halperin, 'Pal o' Me Heart', *London Review of Books* (22 May 2003), 32.
10. Jamie O'Neill, 'Interview', *Gay Community News* (Ireland) (September 2001).
11. Halperin, 'Pal', 32.
12. Jamie O'Neill, *At Swim, Two Boys* (London: Scribner, 2001), 329. Further references are given in parentheses.
13. Michael C. Cronin, '"He's My Country": Liberalism, Nationalism, and Sexuality in Contemporary Irish Gay Fiction', *Éire-Ireland*, 39:3–4 (2004), 250–67, 266.
14. Halperin, 'Pal', 32–3.

15. Michael Cunningham, *The Hours* (New York: Picador, 1998), 9. Further references are given in parentheses.
16. Virginia Woolf, *Mrs. Dalloway* (1925; Oxford: Oxford University Press, 2000), 30.
17. See Christopher Lane, 'When Plagues Don't End', *Gay and Lesbian Review*, 8:1 (2001), 30–2.
18. Terry Castle, *The Apparitional Lesbian: Female Homosexuality and Modern Culture* (New York: Columbia University Press, 1993), 7.
19. Laura Doan and Sarah Waters, 'Making Up Lost Time: Contemporary Lesbian Writing and the Invention Of History', in David Alderson and Linda Anderson, eds., *Territories of Desire in Queer Culture: Refiguring Contemporary Boundaries* (Manchester: Manchester University Press, 2000), 12–28.
20. Steven Marcus, *The Other Victorians* (New York: Basic Books, 1964), 100–1.
21. *Ibid.*, 104–5.
22. 'Her Thieving Hands', interview with Sarah Waters, www.virago.co.uk/author_results.asp?SF1=data&ST1=feature&REF=e2006111617063697&SORT=author_id&TAG=&CID=&PGE=&LANG=en, accessed 2 June 2008.
23. Mark Wormald, 'Prior Knowledge: Sarah Waters and the Victorians', in Rod Mengham and Philip Tew, eds., *British Fiction Today* (London: Continuum, 2006), 187.
24. Linda Hutcheon defines and elaborates on the genre of historiographic metafiction in *A Poetics of Postmodernism* (New York: Routledge, 1988).
25. Marie-Luise Kohlke, 'Into History through the Back Door: The "Past Historic" in *Nights at the Circus* and *Affinity*', *Women: A Cultural Review*, 15:2 (2004), 153–66, 156.
26. See Stephania Ciocia, '"Queer and Verdant": The Textual Politics of Sarah Waters's Neo-Victorian Novels', *Literary London: Interdisciplinary Studies in the Representation of London*, 5:2 (September 2007), www.literarylondon.org/london-journal/september2007/ciocia.html, accessed 28 April 2008.
27. Waters, 'Her Thieving Hands'.
28. *Ibid.*
29. Linda, 'A Chat with *Tipping the Velvet* Author Sarah Waters', 24 October 2002, quoted in Ciocia, '"Queer and Verdant"', n. 4.
30. Sarah Waters, *Affinity* (1999; New York: Riverhead Books, 2000), 70.
31. For a related reading, see Kohlke, 'Into History through the Back Door'.
32. Sarah Waters, *Fingersmith* (London: Virago, 2002), 547.
33. Virginia Woolf, *Orlando* (1928; Oxford: Oxford University Press, 1992), 294–6.
34. Jeanette Winterson, *Oranges Are Not the Only Fruit* (1985; London: Vintage, 1991), 91–2, 103.
35. For a developed reading of Winterson in relation to lesbian historical fiction, see Doan and Waters, 'Making Up Lost Time'.
36. Lisa Moore, 'Teledildonics: Virtual Lesbians in the Fiction of Jeanette Winterson', in Elizabeth Grosz and Elspeth Probyn, eds., *Sexy Bodies: The Strange Carnalities of Feminism* (London: Routledge, 1995), 106.
37. Laura Doan, 'Jeanette Winterson's Sexing the Postmodern', in Laura Doan, ed., *The Lesbian Postmodern* (New York: Columbia University Press, 1994), 149.

38. Moore, 'Teledildonics', 108; Doan, 'Jeanette Winterson's Sexing the Postmodern', 153.
39. Moore, 'Teledildonics', 120.
40. Jeanette Winterson, *Sexing the Cherry* (1989; Toronto: Vintage Canada, 2000), 37. Further references are given in parentheses.
41. Winterson, *The Passion* (1987; London: Penguin, 1988), 51. Further references are given in parentheses.
42. See for example Cath Stowers, 'Journeying with Jeanette: Transgressive Travels in Winterson's Fiction', in Mary Maynard and June Purvis, eds., *(Hetero)sexual Politics* (London: Taylor and Francis, 1995), 139–58.
43. Doan and Waters, 'Making Up Lost Time', 24.
44. Nealon, *Foundlings*, 6. For a full discussion of the political and cultural differences that can be obscured when history functions as an argument for unified queer identities, see Bravmann, *Queer Fictions of the Past*.
45. David Halperin, *How to Do the History of Homosexuality* (Chicago: University of Chicago Press, 2002), 18.

11

JANE GARRITY AND TIRZA TRUE LATIMER

Queer cross-gender collaboration

This chapter reflects on a rarely acknowledged aspect of 'lesbian and gay literature': the production of literature by gay men and lesbians working in some form of collaboration. Terry Castle, in *Kindred Spirits*, a biography of the friendship between Noël Coward and Radclyffe Hall, observes that 'since Stonewall, our perceptions of the gay and lesbian past have been deeply shaped – too deeply shaped – by intellectual separatism: by the assumption that male and female homosexual cliques have little to do with one another and represent different subcultural traditions ... Yet the history of homosexual creativity is full of vibrant cross-gender relationships.'[1] Queer cross-gender bonding – whether experienced as camaraderie, siblinghood, creative partnership, business partnership, marriage, hero worship or some combination of the above – has been a central component of lesbian and gay culture formation (and indeed culture formation *tout court*) throughout the twentieth century. It has marked the histories of literature, art, music, dance, fashion and architecture in ways that remain virtually unexplored. Lesbian and gay male couples, trouples and groups produced and circulated portraits of each other; they offered each other literary tributes in a range of genres (homage, *roman à clef*, translation, preface, introduction and book-jacket blurb); they cross-fertilized one another's imaginations; they co-authored manuscripts; they collaborated in the production of theatrical events; they lobbied for and underwrote one another's publications; they championed one another in critical reviews and interviews; they archived one another's letters, telegrams and postcards; they edited and published one another's correspondence and collected works; they ruptured with the tabloid flair of Hollywood lovers or suffered private agonies of rejection that left poignant literary traces. They mourned each other's deaths like family and often acknowledged these kinships as the most significant emotional, creative and intellectual connections of their lives.

   Here we propose to explore the creative dynamics of lesbian and gay inter-relationality, focusing on key examples from early twentieth-century

France, England and America. In some cases, although not all, the work we discuss openly affirms non-normative sexuality. The study takes into its sweep representatives of the early twentieth-century literary and artistic vanguard: Gertrude Stein and her gay male entourage, and the Bloomsbury group (Vanessa Bell, Duncan Grant, Virginia Woolf, Lytton Strachey and Dora Carrington). In addition to illuminating a number of culturally significant but historically eclipsed relationships, we have the ambition of complicating separatist stereotypes of homosexuality by calling attention to gay men and lesbians whose intimate dialogues contributed importantly to the production of twentieth-century culture.

Gertrude Stein and her gay male circle

When we think of Gertrude Stein and her famous First-World-War era salon, we imagine Stein and her partner Alice B. Toklas immersed in an artistic milieu that included now canonical male figures such as Pablo Picasso, Henri Matisse, Guillaume Apollinaire and Ernest Hemingway. The circle that formed around Stein after the Armistice, however, has left a fainter trace upon the historical record. Between the two World Wars, Stein cultivated mutually advantageous relationships with a cosmopolitan network of gay and bisexual men – including the choreographer Frederick Ashton, photographer Cecil Beaton, painter Christian Bérard, author and composer Paul Bowles, composer Aaron Copland, author René Crevel, historian Bernard Faÿ, novelist and editor Charles Henri Ford, painter Marsden Hartley, author Bravig Imbs, photographer George Platt Lynes, editor Georges Maratier, editor Robert McAlmon, art critic Henry McBride, painter Francis Rose, painter Pavel Tchelitchew, composer Virgil Thomson, painter Kristians Tonny, author Samuel Steward, novelist/photographer Carl Van Vechten and author Thornton Wilder, among quite a few others. This artistic circle constituted a veritable aristocracy of taste with Stein, of course, as the sovereign.[2] No doubt aware of the historical significance of these relationships, Stein preserved the hundreds of letters that she received from these male admirers (many of whom wrote to her on a weekly basis).

Stein also created abstract literary 'portraits' representing several of the members of this sexually dissident entourage. A selection appeared in a 1930 volume titled *Dix Portraits* (Ten Portraits), published by the heterosexual poet and editor Georges Hugnet in collaboration with Tonny's lover Georges Maratier. Of the ten artists featured, five were bisexual or gay. The book was organized into three sections. Stein's original English texts appeared in the first section of the book. The second section contained a portfolio of illustrations penned by Picasso, Tchelitchew, Bérard, Tonny and another member of

Stein's interwar circle, Eugene Berman. These drawings pictured the ten men portrayed by Stein: Picasso, Apollinaire, Erik Satie, Tchelitchew, Thomson, Bérard, Fay, Tonny, Hugnet and Berman. The portraits mediated between the volume's first and final section, which provided a French translation of Stein's texts composed by Hugnet with the assistance of Thomson. Bérard created a portrait of Stein to be used as the frontispiece for the first 100 signed copies of the publication's modest 250 print run. A collector's book from the outset, this edition targeted an elite transatlantic readership conversant with trends in literature, music and art. *Dix Portraits* has received relatively little critical attention, yet it demonstrates the collaborative dimension of careers typically considered in isolation. It shows, too, the interdisciplinary and cosmopolitan relational dynamics that characterized the modernist scene in France during this period. Of equal importance, the venture evidences Stein's awareness of the role that representational reciprocity plays in the formation of artistic vanguards.

Although it doesn't ostensibly depict the author, this select gallery of literary and visual portraits contributed to the formation of Stein's image as both a preeminent voice and an important arbiter of modernism. These literary and visual portraits, upon Stein's authority, located Stein's lesser-known gay male protégés – Tchelitchew, Bérard and Tonny – in Picasso's artistic lineage, while placing Thomson in the historical trajectory of Satie (one of the most successful composers of the early twentieth century). Not long after the book's publication, Thomson composed a portrait of Stein for violin, as if to repay the honour in kind. There were other rewards for Stein, however; publication of this volume indicated her central position within a (self-ratifying) artistic elite.

Stein collaborated repeatedly with several of those portrayed in *Dix Portraits*. She undertook a 'translation' – which turned out to be more like a poetic interpretation – of Hugnet's surrealist reverie, *Enfances*. As Bravig Imbs recounts, Stein's willingness to collaborate with Hugnet 'was paying Georges a great honor, for she had never translated any foreign literature before . . . Gertrude said the sensation of translating was very strange – that it was like writing in the mirrored reflection of oneself.'[3] Given Stein's narcissistic investment in the project, it is not surprising that her intervention failed to advantage Hugnet's contribution. Since she and Hugnet could not agree about whose name should appear first on the publication's cover, Stein published her text under the title *Before the Flowers of Friendship Faded Friendship Faded* (1933). Hugnet abandoned the project of a bilingual volume containing both his original poem and Stein's 'translation', publishing his poem separately the same year. In a letter to Thomson, he confessed that he could not hold his own in conversation with Stein: 'Vraiment j'ai des amis trop forts pour moi' ('I really have some friends who are too strong for me').[4]

Hugnet's acculturation as a French heterosexual male may have heightened his sense of humiliation in the contest with Stein.

Stein's collaboration with Thomson proved less fragile. Perhaps a kind of sexual solidarity paved the way for less ego-bruising working relations. This partnership began in 1927 when Thomson produced a score for Stein's text 'Capital Capitals', which he repeatedly performed both privately and publicly to audiences in Paris, Boston and New York. Not only did these performances render homage to Stein, they also, by virtue of Thomson's association with the experimental writer, enhanced his own reputation as an important modern composer. 'A French composer, one Henri Cliquet-Pleyel, having heard today our Capitals is enthusiastic', he wrote to Stein in 1928. 'Wants to give in early January a joint concert of his and my works ... Would you [come and] read for ten minutes from your works?' Towards the end of the letter Thomson's voice, whether consciously or not, takes on an ingratiatingly imitative lilt. 'Or better still', he cajoles, 'write a short perhaps *conférence sur la musique* or a ditty about *me and Music* or about *Me and Virgil* or a soi-disant anything you like and why not? And isn't it a pleasant idea and it would be given in the salle de la Mairie du 10eme in the rue Drouot and I hope you will be inspired to collaborate and your collaboration would make it awful impressive and we would all profit.'[5] Indeed, they did all profit and Stein was motivated to engage in a subsequent collaboration with Thomson, which famously yielded the opera *Four Saints in Three Acts*, a modernist tour de force composed, conducted, choreographed, produced and promoted by gay men who wore their reverence for Stein's writing like a badge of distinction.

This operatic production would create a sensation when it opened at Hartford, Connecticut's Wadsworth Atheneum in February of 1934. Thomson's score once again provided a musical medium for Stein's cadences. The opera challenged cultural norms in ways that could today be described, like Stein's writing, as queer.[6] It featured an all black cast recruited with the assistance of Carl Van Vechten, whose dalliances with men he picked up in the gay bars of Harlem were an open secret. Alexander Smallens, whose lover Marc Blizenstein would compose the sensational socialist opera *The Cradle Will Rock* during the same decade, conducted the orchestra. The opera also featured the stylish choreography of London's Frederick Ashton (a gay cultural icon) and a fanciful dramatic scenario by Thomson's lover Maurice Grosser. Florine Stettheimer, salon hostess to this circle, fashioned the costumes and sets largely out of materials such as pink cellophane and ostrich feathers. Thomson, for one, relished the campy aesthetic. He described the sets, in a letter to Stein penned during rehearsals, as being 'of a beauty incredible, with trees made out of feathers and a sea-wall made out of shells and for the procession a baldacchino of black chiffon and branches of black ostrich plumes, just like a Spanish funeral'.[7]

In anticipation of the opening, Thomson performed solo renditions for select guests in the parlours of culture brokers such as Van Vechten. One important patron, Mabel Dodge Luhan, proclaimed that 'if performed [*Four Saints*] would do to opera what Picasso did to Kenyon Cox, nobody could ever listen to [traditional] opera again'.[8] Thomson wrote to Stein from New York about the mounting interest in her work resulting from their collaboration, 'I've been interviewed, caricatured, written about, talked about and entertained ... All agree my music makes you palatable to otherwise-not-having-anys.'[9] While the opera was in rehearsal out in Hartford, Thomson did everything possible to create a buzz around the opening. To this end, he again presented 'Capital Capital' to concert audiences in New York, reporting to Stein, 'Capitals a swell success. N.Y. talks of nothing else since three days. Audience roared with laughter during and bravos afterwards. Critics charmingly confused. Some thought it a good joke some a bad joke and one or so got quite angry.'[10]

The opera, Thomson assured her, was to be an even bigger success, drawing trainloads of cultivated New Yorkers and Bostonians to Hartford. Indeed, months in advance, the city's top hotels were already booked to capacity. With this triumph on the horizon, Thomson envisioned the joint publication of the *Four Saints* score and libretto. An argument with Stein over the terms, however, caused a rift in their friendship. Thomson proposed a 2/3–1/3 split of any profits from the publication, arguing that the composition of his musical score represented a disproportionate share of the joint labour. Stein insisted upon a 50–50 division of the proceeds, however, to which Thomson responded indignantly. His letter to Stein reveals frustrations that had been building during the course of their transatlantic collaboration.

If the only reason for holding to a 50–50 division ... is the commercial value of your name, I should like to protest that although your name has a very great publicity value as representing the highest quality of artistic achievement, its purely commercial value, especially in connection with a work as hermetic in style as the Four Saints, is somewhat less, as I have found in seeking a publisher for our various joint works, although I have (with some difficulty) found a publisher for other works of mine. Moreover, it is not the value of your name or the devotion of your admirers ... that is getting this opera produced, but my friends and admirers, Mr. Austin [Wadsworth Atheneum director] and Mr. Smallens, Florine [Stettheimer] and Maurice [Grosser] who are all giving their services at considerable expense to themselves, and a dozen other friends who are contributing $100 or more each to Mr. Austin's costly and absolutely disinterested enterprise. The value of your name has never produced any gesture from these people, whereas every one of them has on other occasions manifested his interest in my work by creating commercial engagements for me and by offering me further collaborations with himself. And dear Gertrude, if you knew the resistance I have encountered in connection with that text and overcome, the amount of reading it and singing it and praising it and commenting it I have done, the articles, the lectures, the private propaganda that has been necessary in Hartford and in New York to silence the opposition that thought it wasn't having any Gertrude Stein, you wouldn't talk to me about the commercial advantages of your name.[11]

Thomson's tirade reveals not only the stressful interpersonal aspect of the collaboration with Stein, but also the extent to which the production of *Four Saints* involved a whole community of (predominantly gay male) participants that included key figures such as, in addition to Thomson himself, Ashton, Grosser, Smallens and A. Everett ('Chick') Austin.

In the end, Thomson capitulated to Stein. The collaboration, if a strain on their relationship, proved advantageous to both parties. Weeks before the opening, Thomson sent Stein a stack of clippings referencing the event along with a note reporting

everything about the opera is shaping up so beautifully ... that the press is champing at the bit and the New York ladies already ordering dresses and hotel rooms. Carl [Van Vechten's] niece has taken a Hartford house for the opera week. Rumors of your arrival are floating about and everybody asks me is she really coming and I always answer that it wouldn't surprise me. Certainly if everything goes off as fancy as it looks now, you would be very happy to be here and to see your opera on the stage and I would be very happy to see it with you and your presence would be all we need to make the opera perfect in every way.[12]

Stein did not attend, however. And although she doubtless revelled from afar in her success on the American scene – and reaped its benefits a year later when she toured the US and was greeted as a celebrity – she acknowledged no particular debt to those who had helped to put her on this map. Austin, for one, had 'ruined himself' absorbing the costs of the lavish *Four Saints* production.[13] In a letter to Stein's Paris agent, Thomson complained, 'Miss Stein ... has never taken the troubles to thank him, or anybody else connected with the production, nor did she even wish us well by cable at either of our openings.'[14] Bypassing Thomson, Stein had sought remuneration for her role in the production via the intermediary of her Paris agent. Thomson responded to the agent, 'I beseech you to impress upon her that Austin will pay us (as he will pay his other creditors) and that he deserves even at present only gratitude from us.'[15] This exchange should be viewed in the context of a behavioural pattern that Stein formed in relation to her collaborators. She supported their ambitions and happily participated in their artistic projects, but only until they became too famous and threatened to eclipse her, or, on the contrary, failed to achieve sufficient renown to reflect well on her. Collaborating with Stein required negotiation skills that few possessed. Her only enduring collaboration, in fact, was her partnership with Toklas, who laboured to become Stein's indispensable ego accessory. To this end, Toklas served Stein as secretary, hostess, manager, editor, publisher, promoter, archivist and, after the author's death, literary executor.

Queer Bloomsberries

Bloomsbury's broad challenges to conventions of sexuality and gender are vividly captured by the oft-quoted moment when Lytton Strachey, while pointing to the stain on Vanessa Stephen's white dress in the drawing room of 46 Gordon Square, notoriously inquired: 'Semen?' Virginia Woolf recounts this watershed moment in her memoirs, capturing both Strachey's role in revolutionizing Bloomsbury's sexual attitudes and the group's enthusiastic embrace of sexual impropriety:

> With that all barriers of reticence and reserve went down. A flood of the sacred fluid seemed to overwhelm us. Sex permeated our conversation. The word bugger was never far from our lips. We discussed copulation with the same excitement and openness that we had discussed the nature of good.[16]

The space of linguistic liberation that Woolf describes in this 1922 reminiscence, 'Old Bloomsbury', was enabled by their brother Thoby Stephen's circle of gay Cambridge friends, who first began to congregate with the Stephens sisters at Gordon Square in 1905. The 'society of buggers' (Bloomsbury's favoured word for homosexuals) eventually grew to include Strachey, John Maynard Keynes, Adrian Stephen, Saxon Sydney-Turner, David ('Bunny') Garnett and Duncan Grant (a cousin of Lytton Strachey who did not attend Cambridge). In her memoir Woolf identifies the sexual nonconformity of these gay and homosexually inclined men (several of whom established long-lasting relationships with women later in life) as the sexual vanguard, ushering in frank talk about 'copulation', indecency, and 'the love affairs of the buggers'.[17] Virginia and Vanessa's intimacy with the erotic exploits of gay Bloomsbury members – particularly Strachey and Maynard Keynes – contributed to the sisters' sense of revolutionary experiment in which '[e]verything was going to be new; everything was going to be different. Everything was on trial.'[18] Of the two, Vanessa was 'the out-and-out winner' when it came to brandishing her verbal freedom with 'erotic bravado'.[19] We see evidence of this in a 1914 letter to Keynes, where Bell delightfully writes about his 'pleasant afternoon buggering' young men and imagines his 'bare limbs intertwined with [another] and all the ecstatic preliminaries of sucking sodomy ... How divine it must have been'.[20] Here, Bell is clearly titillated by male homoeroticism, demonstrating how female enthusiasm for subversive homoerotic practices contributed to the sexual radicalization of Bloomsbury.[21] As the illegal, the taboo and the banned became the subjects of private jokes, gossip and conversation – Bell remarked that 'one can talk of fucking and Sodomy and sucking ... without turning a hair' – Bloomsbury challenged public convention and produced novels, political tracts and artwork that resisted the dominant culture.[22]

One of the most artistically productive and erotically subversive challenges to decorum was Bell's lifelong personal and professional relationship with the artist Duncan Grant. Bell herself was not gay, but she can be viewed as *queer* to the extent that she embraced unconventional sexual arrangements, delighted in gender parody and expressed enthusiasm for non-normative conceptions of gender and sexuality; moreover, she genuinely appeared to be at home among gay men at a time when homosexuality was still illegal. We know that she enjoyed bucking conventional norms of gender and sexual propriety, as when she cross-dressed as a boy and played charades with Duncan and Mary Hutchinson (her husband's lover) on the words 'sodomy' and 'passion'.[23] Her description, in a letter to Grant, of throwing pots with Roger Fry is suffused with sexually rebellious naughtiness: 'the feeling of the clay rising between one's fingers is like the keenest sexual joy!'[24] We see further evidence of this ethos of rebellion in a 1914 letter to Grant, where Bell responds to the criticism lobbied against his iconoclastic and playful depiction of 'Adam and Eve' (which features Adam in a handstand) by linking aesthetics and sexuality: 'of course your Adam and Eve is a good deal objected to, simply on account of the distortion and Adam's standing on his head ... I believe distortion is like Sodomy. People are simply blindly prejudiced against it because they think it abnormal.'[25] Here, Bell associates artistic innovation – 'distortion' – with homosexuality, seeing the moral prejudices against each as a form of cultural blindness. In art and in life, she opposed all forms of censorship and took great pleasure in flouting conventions. According to Bell's biographer, Frances Spalding, '[h]er largeness of mind ... allowed homosexuals to gossip freely in her presence ... [and she] proposed the creation of a libertarian society with sexual freedom for all'.[26]

While married to Clive Bell, Vanessa had had an affair with Roger Fry (who was also married at the time) before falling in love with Duncan Grant, who at the time had been erotically involved and living with her brother, Adrian Stephen. The complicated, intimate, sexually ambiguous relationship between Vanessa Bell and Duncan Grant lasted for the rest of Vanessa's life despite his subsequent affairs with men.[27] The first of Duncan's lovers whom

Bell incorporated with unorthodox ease was David Garnett ('Bunny', as he was familiarly known), the man who would eventually marry Grant's and Bell's daughter, Angelica.[28] This unusual ménage clearly existed outside of the conventional framework of romantic relationships. In a letter to her husband, Clive, Bell writes: 'I am now alone with the two young men so you see we're three and I suppose I ought to feel *de trop*. But I can't say I bother about it much. After all if you have your nights together it seems to me your days can be spent *à trois*. Don't you think so?'[29] Although Frances Spalding speculates that this triangulated relationship was harder on Vanessa than this quote would suggest, we also know that during this period Bell's 'painting had never blazed with such assurance'.[30] As she walked the tight-rope of a queer *ménage à trois*, Bell experimented with non-representational art and produced some of her boldest figurative work, such as the audacious and jarring chrome yellow, red and pink portrait of the poet and actress Iris Tree. As the triangulated relationship between Bell, Grant and Garnett became more emotionally difficult for Vanessa, she painted 'The Tub' (1918), which features a nude female figure standing next to a circular tub, above which stands a vase with three flowers – two yellow and one red – perhaps, as Spalding speculates, visually encoding her autobiographical pre-occupation with their triumvirate.[31]

This tempting biographical reading is at odds, however, with Bell's interest in post-impressionist style and her desire to transcend life and highlight form, and it also does not account for the unique artistic partnership that existed between Duncan and Vanessa.[32] The two produced art both together and alongside one another for fifty years and were among the progenitors of formalism in England during the period of high modernist activity. They served as co-directors (along with Roger Fry) of the Omega, an extraordinary workshop-cum-showroom venture that was started in 1913 and sought to popularize the influence of post-impressionism on interior decoration by selling furniture, textiles and domestic objects that incorporated abstract design, bright colour and spontaneity. The Omega scorned the Edwardian taste for pastel shades and matching hues and instead utilized bold, uncon-ventional colour combinations and embraced an anti-refinement aesthetic that sought to embellish everyday objects with some form of surface decora-tion. Christopher Reed identifies in Omega design 'Bloomsbury's connection of aesthetic and sexual rebellion', and certainly Grant's irreverent portrayal of 'Adam and Eve' (discussed above) is one salient example.[33] We also vividly see this idea of uninhibited pleasure and rebellion reflected in a letter from Bell to Fry, where she makes note of Duncan's 'intense admiration for the Duchess of Devonshire's footman who was the most exquisite creature he had ever seen' and then goes on to discuss how she and Grant have 'decided to . . . paint really indecent subjects. I suggest a series of copulations in strange attitudes and have offered to pose ... We think there ought to be more indecent pictures painted.'[34] Bell's reference to 'indecent pictures' brings to mind the explicitly homoerotic content of some of Duncan Grant's work, but the threat of indecency speaks more generally both to Bloomsbury's embrace of homosexuality and to the Omega's investment in an aesthetic that was considered by the public to be eccentric, flamboyant and distinctly ahead of its time. For example, Richard Shone observes that many visitors to the Omega were scandalized by the use of bright colours, seeing this practice, in conjunction with spontaneity of treatment, as a sign of 'decadence, dreadful taste and every kind of loose behavior'.[35]

This juxtaposition of art and immorality reminds us not only of Grant and Bell's private embrace of an unconventional sexual arrangement, but of what Reed refers to as Bloomsbury's larger 'participation in the burgeoning sexual subculture of the Twenties' which challenged prevailing cultural norms.[36] This was the decade in which Virginia Woolf, in her correspondence to Jacques Raverat, notes that a number of 'young men ... tend to the pretty and the ladylike, for some reason, at the moment. They paint and powder, which wasn't the style in our day at Cambridge.' She goes on to inquire: 'Have you any views on loving one's own sex? ... All the young men are so inclined.'[37] Like Bell, Woolf is clearly drawn to the beautiful young gay men who intersect with and comprise Bloomsbury's social network during this period, but she also 'felt excluded by the cult of silly effeminacy, of queeny camp, which characterized the gay circles she knew' even though two of her dearest friends – Strachey and Grant – were queer.[38] Hermione Lee argues that Woolf was unable to grasp the utility of feminization for homosexuals who censored themselves in public and needed to act effeminate in welcoming gay circles, and while this may be the case, it's also true that homoeroticism between women is not a topic that was celebrated by the group. Woolf describes a conversation with E. M. Forster in her 1928 diary: 'He said he thought Sapphism disgusting: partly from convention, partly because he disliked that women should be independent of men.'[39] Of course, we know that Woolf was as fascinated by lesbianism as she was by male homosexuality, and her subversive 1928 romp through history, *Orlando*, was conceived as a love-letter to the 'violently Sapphic' Vita Sackville-West, with whom Woolf was physically intimate.[40] Neither woman defined herself as a lesbian, but sapphists (like 'buggers'), were clearly a part of Bloomsbury's extended circle of friends. Dorothy Todd, the lesbian editor of British *Vogue* from 1923 to 1926, showcased several of Grant's and Bell's decorative interiors commissioned by some of Bloomsbury's more eminent members.

The entwined sexual and artistic relationships of the Bloomsbury group are reflected in other queer cross-gender collaborations, such as Lytton Strachey's triangulated relationship with Dora Carrington, a bohemian, bisexual 'crop-head' who won a scholarship to London's Slade School of Art in 1910 but was ambivalent about the craze for post-impressionism which followed Roger Fry's famous exhibition at the Grafton Galleries that same year. Nonetheless, in 1914 she joined Fry's Omega Workshops and produced tiles as well as woodcuts for the Hogarth Press, but her decorative work was praised at the expense of her painting and Fry discouraged her from pursuing a career as a serious artist.[41] It was during this period, while visiting society hostess Ottoline Morrell at Garsington Manor in 1915, that Carrington met Strachey and soon became involved in a devoted if complicated seventeen-year relationship that was based upon a series of shifting triangulations. As Strachey continued to have affairs with men, Carrington fell in love with Ralph Partridge, an Oxford friend of her brother, Noel, who for a time assisted Leonard Woolf at the Hogarth Press. When Carrington married Partridge in 1921, the three honeymooned in Venice together and then shared a home. Strachey wryly observed: 'everything is at sixes and sevens – ladies in love with buggers and buggers in love with womanisers, and the price of coal going up too. Where will it all end?'[42] We see Bloomsbury's embrace of an alternative domesticity in the *ménage à trois* of Strachey, Carrington and Partridge, but what we also see is evidence of a creative, cross-gender relationship that fostered Strachey and Carrington's artistic practice. Although Strachey was more physically attracted to Partridge, he loved Carrington and his emotional and intellectual commitment was to her.[43] In contrast to Roger Fry, who had pronounced her work slight and did not give her paintings serious attention, Strachey admired Carrington's work unreservedly and encouraged her to exhibit her paintings – something she was loath to do – and offered to support her with an annual salary of £100 so she could spend more time on her art.[44] No letter exists to indicate Carrington's response, but we do know that she continued to experience financial difficulties as she simultaneously worked on unfulfilling decorative projects and devotedly kept house for Strachey.

Carrington and Strachey influenced one another's work, but not without gendered consequences; her role as de facto housewife conflicted with her ability to paint without interruption, and it arguably contributed to Bloomsbury's reluctance to take her art seriously. Carrington herself conveys her discomfort with this dynamic in a letter to Gerald Brenan, her intermittent lover, which underscores the contradictions at work in her role as artist-cum-housemaid: 'Clive Bell and Mrs. Hutchinson came here last weekend. They aren't my style. Too elegant and 18th cent. French; for that's what they try to be ... I had to make their beds, and empty chamber pots because our poor cook Mrs Legg can't do everything and that made me hate them, because in order they should talk so elegantly, I couldn't for a whole weekend do any painting and yet they scorned my useful grimy hands.'[45] Where Vanessa Bell was able to distance herself from the quotidian through servants, Carrington (with the assistance of one live-in servant) was willingly absorbed by housekeeping through her devotion to Strachey; although both women loved homosexual men and painted domestic scenes and objects, Carrington's 'grimy hands' inevitably put Strachey's needs first – at considerable expense to her own art. Strachey was happy to let Carrington manage their home – first the Mill House at Tidmarsh and subsequently Ham Spray near Hungerford – but he was reassuring when Bloomsbury members disparaged her work. In a 1920 letter to Carrington, he writes: 'I rather felt that [Vanessa and Duncan] were not quite perfect critics – they tend to want you to be like them, and not like yourself – which is really the only thing it's worth anyone's while to be.'[46]

Carrington was not well known as a painter during her lifetime, did not sign her works and rarely exhibited them, but when she finally did begin to show her work it was only at Strachey's insistence. She sold nothing at the London Group exhibition in 1920, but her portrait of 'Lady Strachey', Lytton's mother, caused such a stir within Bloomsbury that, as Carrington put it, 'when they heard I had captured her as a model, Roger, Duncan, and Vanessa then stormed the castle, and asked her to sit for them'.[47] Carrington painted other figures who were tangentially connected to Bloomsbury, such as her portrait of 'E. M. Forster' (c. 1924–5) which now hangs in the National Portrait Gallery, but one of her most famous paintings is the 'Portrait of Lytton Strachey' (1916), which depicts the author lying in bed, reading. Just as Strachey influenced and supported Carrington, she in turn played the central role of confidante and intimate partner to the brilliant homosexual writer. Strachey finished *Eminent Victorians* (1918) – published to enormous critical acclaim – and *Queen Victoria* (1921) when he was involved with Carrington, and it was arguably the 'love and security and confidence she gave him [that] made possible his extremely successful writing career'.[48] To reduce Carrington to the role of Strachey's handmaid is to misread the emotional complexity of their queer relationship, for although the relationship was, according to most accounts, platonic, Carrington described her love for Strachey as the most 'all absorbing passion' of her life.[49] We might ask: to what extent did Carrington's or Strachey's role as companionate muse influence artistic output, and was each person's work a discrete product of solitary inspiration or a feature of collaborative inspiration?

It is clear that queer cross-gender collaborations within Bloomsbury pervaded the modernist milieu in ways that current constructions of literary and visual history tend to overlook or occlude. One reason that these collaborations have been marginalized is perhaps because they do not fit conventional understandings of erotic 'couplings', or perhaps because of what Christopher Reed argues is the 'persistence of an anti-domestic critical standard' within modernism.[50] In other words, Bloomsbury's adherence to domestic ideals such as cohabiting, collaborating on artwork and producing decorative household goods runs counter to prevailing assumptions of artistic accomplishment within mainstream modernism.[51] Yet it is precisely this conjunction of domesticity and non-normative cross-gender collaborations that influenced Bloomsbury's interventions in modernist cultural production. For example, during the 1920s and 1930s Grant and Bell received many decorative commissions that resulted in what Reed characterizes as delightfully 'campy' interiors for gay men, such as Raymond Mortimer and Angus Davidson, who were drawn to Bloomsbury through their associations with Grant.[52] The queer sensibility of this interior-design work was in high demand and was popularized by not only *Vogue* but also the *Studio* and *Architectural Review*, as well as Dorothy Todd and Raymond Mortimer's *The New Interior Decoration* (1929). Also during this period, Grant and Bell designed sets, scenery and costumes for the theatre and the ballet – including work for Frederick Ashton, the gay choreographer – and accepted a china commission to create twelve hand-decorated dessert plates featuring scenes from Virginia Woolf's gender-bending *Orlando*, as well as a commission for fifty decorated plates that resulted in fanciful and sometimes facetious depictions of famous women of history – from Sappho to 'Miss 1933'.[53] Through such playfully imagined historical revisionism and use of ironic distance, Grant and Bell fused old and new sensibilities and transgressed high and low culture in a way that signalled the influence of the homoerotic.

Conclusion

Most extant analyses of writing couples and collaborators have focused on sibling intimacies (such as Dorothy and William Wordsworth), conjugal literary couplings (such as Elizabeth Barrett and Robert Browning, or Sylvia Plath and Ted Hughes) or artistically productive same-sex relationships (such as 'Michael Field', the authorial identity adopted by Katherine Bradley and Edith Cooper, or Vita Sackville-West and Virginia Woolf).[54] Queer cross-gender collaborations have been marginalized perhaps because they do not fit conventional understandings of erotic 'couplings', or perhaps because a pronounced emphasis on individual achievement in Western narratives of cultural production has valorized the notion of an implicitly heterosexual solitary genius at the expense of more diverse kinds of textual and visual interactions.[55] While collaborative and collective practices have periodically revitalized the art and literature of the modern era, often precisely in the name of social critique, few scholars have devoted serious thought to this subject.[56] This chapter underscores the far-reaching effects of sexuality on writing partnerships and collaborative visual practices, seeking to show how historically grounded, heterogeneous understandings of queer cross-gender collaborations can provide new frameworks for reconceptualizing not only queer culture, but cultural production more broadly.

NOTES

1. Terry Castle, *Noël Coward and Radclyffe Hall: Kindred Spirits* (New York: Columbia University Press, 1996), 11.
2. Susan Sontag remarks that 'since no authentic aristocrats in the old sense exist today to sponsor special tastes, who is the bearer of this taste? Answer: an improvised self-elected class, mainly homosexuals, who constitute themselves as aristocrats of taste.' Sontag, 'Notes on Camp', *Against Interpretation* (New York: Anchor/Doubleday, 1990), 290.
3. Bravig Imbs, *Confessions of Another Young Man* (New York: Henkle-Yewdale House, 1936), 285.
4. Virgil Thomson, letter to Gertrude Stein dated September 1928. Beinecke Rare Book and Manuscript Collection, Yale University (hereafter BRBMC), Gertrude Stein and Alice B. Toklas Papers, YCAL MSS 76, Box 127, folder 2773.
5. *Ibid.*
6. Nadine Hubbs, in *The Queer Composition of America's Sound: Gay Modernists, American Music, and National Identity* (Berkeley and Los Angeles: University of California Press, 2004), discusses Stein's libretto for this opera as 'queer abstraction', highlighting the text's evasion of conventional meaning and the queer expressive potential of such an evasion.
7. VT, letter to GS dated 6 December 1933. BRBMC, Gertrude Stein and Alice B. Toklas Papers, YCAL MSS 76, Box 127, folder 2774.
8. VT, letter to GS dated 21 February 1929. BRBMC, Gertrude Stein and Alice B. Toklas Papers, YCAL MSS 76, Box 127, folder 2774.
9. *Ibid.*
10. *Ibid.*
11. VT, letter to GS dated 9 June 1933. BRBMC, Gertrude Stein and Alice B. Toklas Papers, YCAL MSS 76, Box 127, folder 2774.
12. *Ibid.*
13. *Ibid.*
14. VT, letter to Bradley dated 6 March 1934. BRBMC, Gertrude Stein and Alice B. Toklas Papers, YCAL MSS 76, Box 127, folder 2774.
15. *Ibid.*
16. Virginia Woolf, *Moments of Being*, ed. Jeanne Schulkind (New York: Harcourt Brace, 1985), 195–6.

17. *Ibid.*, 196.

18. *Ibid.*, 185, 196.

19. Frances Spalding, *Vanessa Bell* (New Haven and New York: Ticknor & Fields, 1983), 238.

20. Regina Marler, ed., *Selected Letters of Vanessa Bell* (New York: Pantheon Books, 1993), 163.

21. Christopher Reed, *Bloomsbury Rooms: Modernism, Subculture, and Domesiticity* (New Haven: Yale University Press, 2004), 52.

22. Marler, ed., *Letters of Vanessa Bell*, 163.

23. Spalding, *Vanessa Bell*, 146.

24. Marler, ed., *Letters of Vanessa Bell*, 162.

25. *Ibid.*, 154.

26. Spalding, *Vanessa Bell*, 134.

27. Frances Spalding reads Bell's relationship with Grant in terms of a maternal complex, arguing that because 'Vanessa's maternal feelings . . . played a dominant role in her life' Duncan presented no 'threat' as a lover: 'Like many homosexuals, he was extremely close to his mother and had preserved a streak of juvenile irresponsibility. This, combined with their six-year difference in age, perhaps enabled Vanessa to look on him as a younger brother or even son' (*Vanessa Bell*, 127–8). This reading both pathologizes male homosexuality and reduces Bell's ambiguous sexuality to a caricature.

28. Angelica was born on Christmas in 1918, and although Duncan was the biological father, Clive consented to pretend to the world, and to Angelica herself, that he was her father. Katie Roiphe persuasively argues that 'the ruse smacked of precisely the Victorian hypocrisy that [Vanessa] had spent her life breaking down in both her art and her household'. Paradoxically, Roiphe writes, 'there was an element of Victorian tact required to maintain the thoroughly bohemian household, with all of its perversities'. See *Uncommon Arrangements: Seven Portraits of Married Life in London Literary Circles 1910–1939* (New York: Dial Press, 2007), 167–8.

29. Spalding, *Vanessa Bell*, 141.

30. *Ibid.*, 142.

31. See *ibid.*, 171. We do know that Bell had earlier painted her still life, 'Iceland Poppies', based on triplicates during the period when she was suffering intense jealousy over her sister Virginia's flirtation with her husband, Clive. In 'Iceland Poppies' there are three still-life objects, three bands running across the background and three flowers – two of which are white and slightly separated from the third, which is painted red. See *ibid.*, 82.

32. Tony Tree speculates that Bell's triangular composition may have 'just as much to do with the traditional pyramidal compositions that Bell would have been taught to employ as part of her training at Cope's School of Art, the Royal Academy Schools and, briefly, at the Slade'. See Tree's 'Iceland Poppies: A Photographer's View', *Canvas: News from Charleston*, 20 (October 2007), 5. In one of Bell's rare statements on visual aesthetics, in a 1913 letter to Leonard Woolf, she talks about the 'strong emotion' that is evoked by 'the forms and colours' – as opposed to the subject-matter – in a work of art. See Spalding, *Vanessa Bell*, 126.

33. Reed, *Bloomsbury Rooms*, 144.

34. Spalding, *Vanessa Bell*, 98.

35. Richard Shone, *The Art of Bloomsbury* (Princeton: Princeton University Press, 1999), 104.
36. See Reed, *Bloomsbury Rooms*, 231.
37. Virginia Woolf, *The Letters of Virginia Woolf*, vol. III: *1923–1928, A Change of Perspective*, ed. Nigel Nicolson and Joanne Trautmann (London: Hogarth Press, 1977), 155.
38. Hermione Lee, *Virginia Woolf* (New York: Alfred A. Knopf, 1997), 605.
39. Virginia Woolf, *The Diary of Virginia Woolf*, vol. III: *1925–1930*, ed. Anne Olivier Bell (London: Hogarth Press, 1980), 193.
40. Virginia Woolf, *Letters*, vol. III: 155–6. Vita Sackville-West was married to Harold Nicolson, and both shared their affairs with one another (his exclusively with other men, and hers primarily with other women). See Karyn Z. Sproles, *Desiring Women: The Partnership of Virginia Woolf and Vita Sackville-West* (Toronto: University of Toronto Press, 2006), 4.
41. Gretchen Holbrook Gerzina, *Carrington: A Life* (New York: W.W. Norton, 1989), 68–9.
42. Paul Levy, ed., *The Letters of Lytton Strachey* (New York: Viking, 2005), 444.
43. Although Strachey and Partridge grew to love one another and call each other 'dear' and 'darling' in letters, there is no evidence to support speculation of an affair between the two. Gerzina, *Carrington: A Life*, 154–5.
44. *Ibid.*, 280. Julie Anne Taddeo reads Carrington in terms of 'female subservience' and argues that '[n]either partner considered Carrington the intellectual equal of Strachey'. See her *Lytton Strachey and the Search for Modern Sexual Identity: The Last Eminent Victorian* (New York: Harrington Park Press, 2002), 105, 99.
45. David Garnett, ed., *Carrington: Letters and Extracts from her Diaries* (London: Jonathan Cape, 1970), 152.
46. Gerzina, *Carrington: A Life*, 162.
47. Garnett, ed., *Carrington*, 170.
48. Gerzina, *Carrington: A Life*, 303.
49. *Ibid.*, 167.
50. Reed, *Bloomsbury Rooms*, 5. Bette London argues that 'the dominant model of spousal collaboration that defines most cross-gender writing arrangements' tends to relegate women to 'the roles of helpmeet and amanuensis'. She argues that cross-gender collaborations are 'even more resistant to recognition' than the female literary partnerships that she examines. See *Writing Double: Women's Literary Partnerships* (Ithaca, NY: Cornell University Press, 1999), 19–20.
51. Reed, *Bloomsbury Rooms*, 2–6.
52. See *ibid.*, ch. 14. See also Reed's 'Design for (Queer) Living: Sexual Identity, Performance, and Décor in British *Vogue*, 1922–1926', *GLQ*, 12:3 (2006), 377–403.
53. See Reed, *Bloomsbury Rooms*, 265.
54. See, for example, Marjorie Stone and Judith Thompson, eds., *Literary Couplings: Writing Couples, Collaborators, and the Construction of Authorship* (Madison: University of Wisconsin Press, 2006).
55. Marjorie Stone and Judith Thompson argue that traditional 'constructions of cross-gender writing couples ... cast one partner as more dominant, innovative, or significant than the other (typically the male partner) ... or show how parallel gender binaries are often imposed on same-sex couples and collaborators'. *Ibid.*, 18.

56. One notable exception, a collection edited by Whitney Chadwick and Isabelle de Courtivron, *Significant Others: Creativity and Intimate Partnership* (London and New York: Thames & Hudson, 1996), explores creative partnerships among both writers and artists in essays that examine the creative dynamics of both same-sex and opposite-sex partnerships (although not cross-gender queer collaborations).

12

RICHARD R. BOZORTH

Naming the unnameable: lesbian and gay love poetry

In any survey of love poetry in English, poets as varied as Shakespeare, Walt Whitman, Gertrude Stein, W. H. Auden and Adrienne Rich could hardly be excluded. Yet to consider gay and lesbian love poetry as a category in itself is to face hard questions. Some are of a conceptual order that queer studies has long contended with. Knotty problems, for example, arise on recognizing the social constructedness of sexual identity categories. So, we might ask, what justification can be made for calling Shakespeare 'gay', since he wrote centuries before the 'invention' of modern homosexuality?[1] Or we might consider whether lesbian and gay male literary production share more with each other than not, given the historical differences in the experiences of gay men and lesbians. How much sense does it make to group W. H. Auden together with Audre Lorde, even though both wrote powerful love poetry? Further questions would enter into any thoughtful effort to consider the nature of lyric expression – for example, how exactly *does* the lyric 'I' relate to the authorial subject? How is intentionality related to poetic meaning in erotic contexts? Surely these are important in considering, say, Christina Rossetti's quite popular and, to our ears, intensely homoerotic 'Goblin Market'. And what about love, anyway? What sense of 'love poetry' includes not just Shakespeare's sonnets to the young man but Allen Ginsberg's sado-masochistic prayer 'Please Master'? Critical pluralism can be a virtue, but it leaves us in the awkward position of Mr Sorley, the 'more advanced' missionary in E. M. Forster's *A Passage to India*. He is willing to concede that monkeys may go to heaven, but pushed by the Hindu Professor Godbole to consider the limits of salvation (what about plants? bacteria? mud?), he feels compelled to draw a line: 'We must exclude someone from our gathering, or we shall be left with nothing.'[2]

While a rigorous category of 'gay and lesbian love poetry' may be artificial, it is a matter of historical fact that a variety of texts have been read as gay and lesbian love poetry, as anthologies from recent decades show. This chapter considers some of the most influential and representative love poetry written and read by gay men and lesbians since the time of Shakespeare. Without offering a comprehensive survey – which is not possible in a single essay – it situates the formal and discursive qualities of this work in relation to its most salient cultural and sexual-political contexts. At the same time, it explores how a number of persistent challenges and the literary strategies for dealing with them have continued to animate the writing of same-sex love in English: above all, pressures involved with verbal art motivated by the proverbial 'love that dare not speak its name'. Precisely because same-sex desire in the West has historically occasioned intense moral, social and philosophical scrutiny, gay and lesbian love poetry has routinely engaged with such interrogation, even as it has manifest motives that have generated love poetry since Sappho: literary ambition, sexual seduction, praise, lament, celebration, complaint. When Auden wrote 'O Tell me the truth about love', he was not only voicing a sentiment that has motivated love poetry of all kinds.[3] He was also doing what gay and lesbian poets have often done under the pressures of social marginality and the closet: using love poetry to reflect upon the 'truth' about 'love' itself.

The cultural stakes of gay love poetry became dramatically public on the cusp of the era of modern sexual politics, during the second trial of Oscar Wilde. In late April 1895, as Wilde was undergoing cross-examination, the prosecution read aloud 'Two Loves', a poetic allegory written by Lord Alfred Douglas and published a few months earlier. Wilde was asked, in regard to the final verse, 'What is the "Love that dare not speak its name"?' He replied:

> 'The Love that dare not speak its name' in this century is such a great affection of an elder for a younger man as there was between David and Jonathan, such as Plato made the very basis of his philosophy, and such as you find in the sonnets of Michelangelo and Shakespeare. It is that deep, spiritual affection that is as pure as it is perfect ... It is in this century misunderstood, so much misunderstood that it may be described as the 'Love that dare not speak its name', and on account of it I am placed where I am now. It is beautiful, it is fine, it is the noblest form of affection. There is nothing unnatural about it. It is intellectual, and it repeatedly exists between an elder and younger man, where the elder has intellect and the younger man has all the joy, hope, and glamour of life before him. That it should be so, the world does not understand. The world mocks at it and sometimes puts one in the pillory for it.[4]

These sentences (to which the audience in the courtroom reportedly responded with cheers) have assumed quasi-mythic status: like the drag queens rioting outside the Stonewall Inn in 1969, they are a gesture of defiance against persecution. Provoked by the reading of a poem about gay love in the courtroom, Wilde rejected Victorian opprobrium and the shame

Douglas allegorized in his poem. Far from being unspeakable and unnatural – the crime of 'gross indecency' with which he was charged; the sin of sodomy 'not to be named among Christians' – such love, he asserted, was continuous with the nobility and spirituality at the core of Judeo-Christian culture.

Wilde was also expressing one motive of lesbian and gay love poetry: the drive to put such love into language – to speak it in the face of forces that would make it *unspeakable* in every sense. This political impulse is one of the most persistent in gay and lesbian love poetry even at its most personal, as when Adrienne Rich addresses her lover in 'Twenty-One Love Poems': 'show me what I can do / for you, who have often made the unnameable / nameable for others, even for me'.[5] Wilde's invocation of Western tradition, however, was not telling the whole truth. It was a tactical recasting of his prosecution as persecution by philistines, and a tendentious construction of literary tradition. From the lyrics of the Greek anthology to the writing of Walt Whitman, homoerotic love poetry had long been concerned with the physical as much as the metaphysical – with 'singing the body electric', in Whitman's words, as well as with exploring eros as a mode of intellectual and spiritual affection. In fact, notwithstanding Wilde's idealizing speech, the complex relations between body and spirit not only shaped Plato's exploration of the ethical, emotional and philosophical implications of eros in the *Symposium*, but tensely animated Shakespeare's sonnets, as well as some of the most influential poetry of same-sex love down to Wilde. His emphasis on beauty and the soul – keywords in the Aestheticist movement – and his invocation of Plato resonate with the homoerotics associated in the late nineteenth century with 'Greek love'.[6] Whether or not the (homo)sexual coding was apparent to the court, Wilde was not so much taking a courageous stand against unspeak-ability as exploiting it to speak sexuality and the body as subtext.

In this he was heir to lyric procedures used by writers of same-sex love poetry for centuries. Shakespeare's sonnets constitute the iconic precedent, and they have occasioned critical and sexual-political contestation since at least the mid seventeenth century. Others – most notably Richard Barnfield – had adapted the pastoral mode descending from Virgil, which offered a safely Arcadian realm for expressing homoeroticism between social peers.[7] But Shakespeare wrote in the Petrarchan tradition (itself indebted to Platonism), which had developed by his time into a sophisticated tool for exploring the psychological unfolding of desire for an unattainable beloved. Even so, Shakespeare's sonnets are quite unusual. Despite his centrality in literary history and the status of his sonnets as paradigmatic love lyrics, no other sonnet sequence includes lyrics addressed both to a man and to a woman, much less the implication (as in 144) that the two have jointly cuckolded the poet.

A variety of responses have arisen to deal with the fact that Shakespeare's first 126 sonnets address a young man, including unapologetically altering masculine pronouns to feminine ones. Until recent decades, critics at best remained agnostic about the sexual overtones of the first 126 sonnets, but took the sexual directness of the sonnets to the 'dark lady' (127–54) as certifying Shakespeare's sexual bona-fides. At worst, the absence of historical evidence for the nature or existence of the relationship to the young man could be used to dismiss the issue from consideration.[8] But for poets as varied as Alfred Tennyson, W. H. Auden and Adrienne Rich, Shakespeare's sonnets have offered a paradigmatic example: a lyric sequence exploring the erotic, psychological and emotional unfolding of same-sex love.

Although the authority for the numbering of the sonnets is debatable, they do seem to form a meaningful sequence, and this structure and the sexual charge of their language are the most important things to see about them as same-sex love lyrics. The most notorious locus of debate on this score is sonnet 20, which marks a major turning point. The first seventeen, notwith-standing some bawdy language, do not address the young man as the poet's love object, instead functioning as advice poems. In urging the young man to marry, they recall Diotima's argument, in Plato's *Symposium*, that bodily beauty is immortalized through procreation: the young man's surpassing physical beauty must be preserved in a son. With sonnet 18 ('Shall I compare thee to a summer's day?'), this argument disappears. The young man's beauty will instead be preserved in Shakespeare's poetry: 'So long as men can breathe or eyes can see, / So long lives this, and this gives life to thee'.[9] Sonnet 20 opens in this vein, as a poem in praise of the young man's beauty – 'A woman's face with Nature's own hand painted / Hast thou, the master-mistress of my passion'.[10] But this conceit of androgyny generates an assertion in the last six lines that begs as many questions as they purport to dismiss:

> And for a woman wert thou first created,
> Till Nature as she wrought thee fell a-doting,
> And by addition me of thee defeated,
> By adding one thing, to my purpose, nothing.
> But since she pricked thee out for women's pleasure,
> Mine be thy love, and thy love's use their treasure.

At the literal level, the lines deny the poet's sexual interest: 'love's use' will belong physically to women, but higher, metaphysical 'love' will belong to the poet. While many have gratefully found grounds here for rejecting any sexual element in the love outlined in the subsequent 106 sonnets, this denial of sexual interest comes in a poem that links the young man's physical beauty to his character (which does not fare so well in subsequent sonnets, in fact). The mini-etiology myth of lines 8–12 does a number of things. It offers a comic justification for Shakespeare's attraction: how could he *not* fall in love, since Nature herself did when she created the young man as a woman? Alas, seeing the poet as a rival, Nature won the contest by giving the young man a penis. But while the sexual word-play flippantly suggests indifference to the young man's genitalia, it also implies that the poet *has* been thinking about the young man's 'thing' and what it is for. Not for Shakespeare, apparently, but for women. But for women, not because the young man's physical beauty needs to be immortalized through procreation, but because that's whose 'pleasure' he was designed for. (This is, we should note, a model of *perversion*: by traditional Christian standards, pleasure was not a moral use of sex.) What, we might ask, are *words* designed for? In this poem, not for saying 'one thing' but for taking verbal pleasure in saying many things about the young man's thing, including the sexual pleasure it can give. The word-play also includes 'purpose' (like 'point' and 'will', sometimes used by Shakespeare with phallic innuendo). If the young man's thing is not to Shakespeare's purpose, words for the young man's thing certainly are.

To attend to these overtones is to suspect that the denial this poem offers masks something more complex, that poetic art and verbal wit serve erotic pleasure. And to read this way is to do just what Shakespeare invites in sonnet 23. 'As an unperfect actor on the stage, / Who with his fear is put besides his part', he is unable to speak what he feels: 'I ... forget to say / The perfect ceremony of love's rite'.[11] The metaphor of stage-fright foregrounds this and the other sonnets as performances calculated to produce certain effects. If one effect of sonnet 20 is to attune us to sexual innuendo, we are likely to hear it now, when the poet compares his nervousness to 'Some fierce thing replete with too much rage, / Whose strength's abundance weakens his own heart': an image hard *not* to read in phallic terms, as if the poet's inhibition in person is a matter not of lack but of an impotence born of excessive desire. The closing couplet offers a directive: 'O learn to read what silent love hath writ: / To hear with eyes belongs to love's fine wit.' To 'hear with eyes' means, one might say, to read between the lines – to read for what is unsaid but implied, doing with our imagination what we do with our hearing: listening for sensory and sensual intimations of the unspeakable.

The most elaborate openly 'gay reading' of the sonnets, Joseph Pequigney's *Such Is My Love*, argues that they narrate a love affair including sexual consummation.[12] Even without concluding as much, a careful reader is faced with explaining what the sexual language is doing and what the sequence is implying. In sonnet 87 the opening verses express a resignation we can read as a conventional Petrarchan posture of unworthiness, or as something much more viciously ironic: 'Farewell, thou art too dear for my possessing, / And like enough thou know'st thy estimate'.[13] 'Possessing' may or may not imply actual sexual intimacy, but the possibility lurks within the sonnet's exploration of the young man's 'estimate', which has apparently increased in his own eyes. His love is a gift that the poet must now return, as it depended on 'misprision' – the young man's misjudgment of the poet's worthiness of his love. The sonnet ends with a couplet equally poised between compliment and insult: 'Thus have I had thee as a dream doth flatter, / In sleep a king, but waking no such matter.' This may suggest that the 'dream' of love flattered the poet with a false sense that he was worthy of the young man's love, or more bitterly, that the poet awoke from love to realize the young man was unworthy of such fealty. Either way, to 'have' was not to 'have' after all. But do the lines imply that sexual having was not real having? Or is sexual having, and then being left, a metaphor for being emotionally used and then abandoned? The latter would certainly fit with the implication of many sonnets that this has been an emotionally 'dear' (costly) relationship for the poet, fraught with anxiety and jealousy over unrecipro-cated desire. From this point of view, the sonnets to the young man read like a queering of conventional Petrarchism. The unattainability of the beloved – whether from lack of interest or from fear of same-sex love – generates idealization and then erotic and emotional frustration, in which sexual innuendo disturbingly infects the language of praise for the beloved's beauty.[14]

Whether or not Shakespeare's sonnets record an actual sexual relationship, their model of analytical inwardness has been a stimulus to later poets writing about same-sex love. From this point of view, cultural constraints on speak-ability appear to do several things. They may force the encoding of sexuality in semantic innuendo and figurative implication, as some have concluded happens in Shakespeare. But perhaps as important, such constraints can provoke formal artifice for exploring the psychological, emotional and ethical complexity of same-sex love, and poets as varied as Alfred Tennyson, Gerard Manley Hopkins, Emily Dickinson, Auden, Stein and Hart Crane have pur-sued this route. In this regard, the sexuality of Shakespeare's language, whatever it says about Shakespeare himself, reflects an attitude that informs lesbian and gay love poetry to the present day, notwithstanding Wilde's assertions of intellectual and spiritual purity: sexual desire and the body exist on an erotic continuum with emotional and moral life.

It should not, therefore, be surprising that some of the most famous poetry in the nineteenth century gives spiritual love such a homoerotic cast. The reception of Christina Rossetti's 'Goblin Market' as a Christian fable suitable for children owed a great deal to her reputation as a poet of unimpeachable propriety, and its allegory of temptation, fall, sacrifice and redemption dramatically portrays Christian morality in a form consonant with normative Victorian acceptance of sentimental female friendships: 'What a friend we have in Jesus' is rendered as

'There is no friend like a sister'.[15] To recognize the sexual cast of temptation in the poem, however, is to see that Rossetti also offers an analysis of patriarchal sexuality. Once a girl buys and tastes the goblin men's fruit, she will die: virginity is her only asset, and once lost, death on the marriage market must follow. From this angle, the poem's story of Laura's resurrection implies a contradiction between Christian forgiveness and Victorian sexual moralizing. But Rossetti's radicalness consists even more in her eroticization of language – the endless lists of fruit, succulently elaborated, offer a childlike pleasure in quantity and texture, a verbal deliciousness that mutates gradually into something like oral/aural sex. The poem's climax, when Lizzie comes back from suffering Christ-like scourging by the goblins, resonates erotically for any reader who recognizes the sexual subtext of the goblins' fruit:

> She cried, 'Laura,' up the garden,
> 'Did you miss me?
> Come and kiss me.
> Never mind my bruises,
> Hug me, kiss me, suck my juices
> Squeezed from goblin fruits for you,
> Goblin pulp and goblin dew.
> Eat me, drink me, love me;
> Laura, make much of me.[16]

Authorial intentionality is hard to sort out here, but the intensity of these lines makes it almost beside the point. As metaphor, they depend on the physical as a vehicle for a metaphysical tenor perfectly in line with Anglican theology about the incarnation, crucifixion and Eucharist. But as the acting out of gendered human love – Rossetti's moral that 'there is no friend like a sister' – these lines render same-sex love simultaneously physical and spiritual, and in this, their verbal sensuality is not just decorative but expressively erotic. The gender logic is inescapable: sexual connection with males is exploitative and destructive, while sexual connection with a sister is redemptive.

In the otherwise quite different love poetry of Tennyson and Emily Dickinson, Victorian acceptance of sentimental friendship provided latitude for erotic expression that can be just as surprising today as that of 'Goblin Market'. Tennyson's great elegy *In Memoriam, A. H. H.* (1850), while garnering fame that brought him an appointment as Britain's Poet Laureate, did challenge some readers with hints of unnatural affection for his friend Arthur Hallam,

> My Arthur whom I shall not see
> Till all my widow'd race be run,
> Dear as the mother to the son,
> More than my brothers are to me.[17]

While echoes of David's lament for Jonathan, or Gilgamesh's for Enkidu – ancient topoi of homoerotic grief – gave Tennyson conventional formulations of loss, the physicality of his grief is another matter. Sensory memories of Hallam's voice, hand and kiss all haunt *In Memoriam*. If the poem's power comes in part from the poignancy of these moments, its fame was probably enabled by Tennyson's reticence before erotic depths:

> I sometimes hold it half a sin
>> To put in words the grief I feel;
>> For words, like Nature, half reveal
> And half conceal the soul within.[18]

This is a characteristic moment, in which revelation and concealment themselves govern lyric expression: is the 'sin' that words reveal the soul or that they conceal it? Should he say more or less? Tennyson's gradual reassertion of faith involves, on the one hand, a sense that Hallam's spirit lives on, transfigured into a fearlessly doubting, heroic, Christ-like embodiment of the 'greater man' that humanity is evolving into. In this we see another version, perhaps, of the Platonic movement of the *Symposium*, whereby love of the body is transcended by love of the soul, the physical by the spiritual. If the appeal of this poem to its Victorian audience came in part from its portrayal of heroic grieving, it is also, arguably, the process whereby Tennyson could 'conceal the soul' by sublimating effeminate grief into normative masculine faith.[19]

Despite Tennyson's almost unrivalled stature in Victorian poetry, the figures of Emily Dickinson and Walt Whitman have proven more politically and aesthetically useful for later gay and lesbian love poets. Adrienne Rich has written extensively about Dickinson, instancing her as an exemplar of 'the lesbian continuum': the 'range – through each woman's life and throughout history – of woman-identified experience', and 'many more forms of primary intensity between and among women, including the sharing of a rich inner life, the bonding against male tyranny, the giving and receiving of practical and political support'.[20] In Dickinson's case, the privacy and domesticity of her existence have produced much critical debate. Her intense relationships with Kate Anthon and Sue Gilbert, eventually her sister-in-law, generated a considerable body of letters and poetry, and these have come to seem more important than the relationships with males that earlier critics emphasized.[21] For earlier critics, Rich observes, the hermetic quality of so much of her poetry gave rein to speculations about a male 'Master' as her love object, and to critical deprecation of her artistic eccentricity and naïveté. But for lesbian poets, Dickinson has become an example of empowered subjectivity, because of her courage to explore the boundaries of consciousness and the split between the social and private selves in poetry that challenges conventions of poetry and gender.[22]

Whitman has achieved a similar stature, although his influence on later gay poets has become clear only in recent decades. He himself was partly responsible, given that he cleansed successive editions of *Leaves of Grass* of some of their homoeroticism, and by the end of his life he seems to have felt the need to protect his reputation from dangerous interpretations.[23] Like Tennyson, he had sometimes made poetic capital out of the tension between reticence and revelation, as in *Calamus* 44:

> Here the frailest leaves of me, and yet my strongest lasting,
> Here I shade, and hide my thoughts, I myself do not expose them,
> And yet they expose me more than all my other poems.[24]

Nevertheless, *Calamus* explicitly represents itself to 'all who are, or have been young men' as an effort 'To tell the secret of my nights and days, / To celebrate the need of comrades'.[25] In 'The Base of All Metaphysics', Whitman linked his philosophy of 'adhesiveness', as he called it, to the ancient erotic tradition of the *Symposium*: 'Yet underneath Socrates I clearly see, and underneath the divine I see, / The dear love of man for his comrade, the attraction of friend to friend'.[26] But for Whitman, love of comrades had a political potential that others, like Wilde, were less interested in. Much of his importance for later gay poets came from his prophetic lyric mode, in which several kinds of liberation are interwoven: that of the poetic line and rhythm from constriction by prosodic convention, a verbal liberation from poetic diction and reticence about the body and sex, physical liberation of the body from sexual repression, and all these things with a vision of progressive American freedom. Part of his influence has also come from his exploration of homoeroticism infusing the modern cityscape as much as the conventional landscape of pastoral – wonderfully memorialized by Ginsberg in 'A Supermarket in California' (1955). The possibility of becoming intimate with the stranger – available in the city and through mass publication – creates Whitman's characteristic posture as a love poet, turning the reader from stranger into friend and comrade. In *Calamus* 3 (1860) – 'Whoever you are holding me now in hand' – the physical touch of the book and the voicing of words are proffered as media of erotic contact between poet and reader:

> Here to put your lips upon mine I permit you,
> With the comrade's long-dwelling kiss or the new husband's kiss,
> For I am the new husband and I am the new comrade.
> Or if you will, thrusting me beneath your clothing,
> Where I may feel the throbs of your heart or rest upon your hip,
> Carry me when you go forth over land or sea;
> For thus merely touching you is enough, is best,
> And thus touching you would I silently sleep and be carried eternally.[27]

These lines invite the reader into a physical brotherhood of American 'adhe-siveness', and for gay love poetry his revolutionary significance lay less in his poetic commemorations of a single beloved, as in Shakespeare or Tennyson, than in his celebration of erotic possibility and freedom as essential to a spiritually and socially meaningful love.

Whitman's full stature as a gay poet became clear only well into the twentieth century, when he inspired Ginsberg's aggressive openness about his politics and sexuality in works like *Howl* (1956), and then an outpouring of sexually explicit gay poetry in the wake of Stonewall. This poetry should be seen not only as testimony to the sexual revolution of the 1970s but also as the fruition of Whitman's faith in the unashamed public expression of gay love. That it took so long reveals something about the fortunes of gay and lesbian poetry in the period of modernism, from the time of Wilde to the middle of the twentieth century. Two of the most influential modernist writers, Gertrude Stein and W. H. Auden, wrote important love poetry, and Hart Crane was much inspired by Whitman. But partly because of the formalist, anti-biographical bias of the New Criticism, and partly because Crane, Stein and Auden reflected in their different ways modernism's embrace of difficulty, the significance of their sexuality for their love poetry was often ignored or overlooked until much later.

Only with the 1979 publication of Robert K. Martin's groundbreaking *The Homosexual Tradition in American Poetry* did Crane's debt to Whitman as a gay poet achieve full critical recognition.[28] Crane's most powerful poetry about gay love – the sequence 'Voyages' – follows the trajectory of a love affair. His syntactic difficulty and devotion to complex symbolism, much inspired by T. S. Eliot, seem often to serve as a tactic for negotiating the closet. Nonetheless, as Martin and others have argued, the climax of 'Voyages' is not just powerfully sexual but homosexual, in its portrayal of anal intercourse and orgasm:

> And so, admitted through black swollen gates
> That must arrest all distance otherwise, –
> Past whirling pillars and lithe pediments,
> Light wrestling there incessantly with light,
> Star kissing star through wave on wave unto
> Your body rocking![29]

These lines link lovers to each other and to the sea and cosmos, and they celebrate not just a yearning for but an actuality of love overcoming the isolation that so much of Crane's poetry wrestled with. Not permanently: 'Voyages' grapples with the departure of the lover and end of the relationship. In this, we see him facing something that other gay male poets, especially, have perennially struggled with: if social realities make belief in romantic permanence impossible, what is the meaning of love? There is in 'Voyages', as in much of Crane's writing, a strong elegiac strain, and Crane strives for a kind of consolation sought often in gay love poetry. This is a Platonic and Aestheticist struggle towards a faith that bodily beauty, although experienced only temporarily in sex, may signify something transcending change, towards which the end of 'Voyages' points: 'The imaged Word ... the unbetrayable reply / Whose accent no farewell can know'.

Although Stein and Auden, like Crane, used modernist experimentation in ways that had much to do with the pressures of the closet, both had public careers in the way that Crane never lived to see. Both tested the boundaries of speakability in their work, and what Edward Mendelson has said of the later Auden applies also to Stein: eventually, Auden's poetry was 'leaving his secrets hidden in plain sight' for those readers who chose to notice.[30] Stein famously did so in *The Autobiography of Alice B. Toklas* (1933), but in her poetry, the intertwining of her life with Toklas is equally evident, though transposed into the medium of linguistic play, as in 'Lifting Belly' (1917):

> Lifting belly is a credit. Do you care about poetry?
> Lifting belly in spots.
> Do you like ink.
> Better than butter.
> Better than anything.
> Any letter is an alphabet.
> When this you see you will kiss me.
> Lifting belly is so generous.[31]

Stein's linguistic playfulness – semantic, phonemic, grammatical – is partly a strategy for distancing readers conditioned by conventional poetic and erotic expectations, a poetic self-closeting. But it is also, quite contradictorily, completely revealing: its refusal of convention and its pleasure in exploring the sensual textures of language make it a public erotic performance of lesbian love.[32]

It has become increasingly apparent since his death that Auden's writing was deeply shaped by relationships with other men and his wrestling with the personal and political meanings of gay love.[33] In his earliest poetry, up to the mid 1930s, an alluringly obscure idiom, prompting a generation of imitators, allowed his concerns with desire to be seen through the lens of his interests in leftist politics and psychoanalysis; the role of his sexuality was largely sidestepped. Like Crane, the young Auden was affected by modern pathologizing models of homosexuality, and his poetry tended to express fatalism about love. His most famous love poetry was written after he adopted a more accessible style in the mid 1930s, including a number of sonnets inspired by Shakespeare, and maybe the most famous gay love poem of the century, 'Lullaby' (1937). At a time when Auden was already regarded as the leading younger poet in Britain, the second-person address enabled readers to imagine either a male or a female beloved. But the poignancy of 'Lullaby' comes from its grappling with the tension between a visionary eroticism and a disenchantment that reflected Auden's view of homosexuality as incompatible with permanent love:

> Lay your sleeping head, my love,
> Human on my faithless arm;
> Time and fevers burn away
> Individual beauty from
> Thoughtful children, and the grave
> Proves the child ephemeral:
> But in my arms till break of day
> Let the living creature lie:
> Mortal, guilty, but to me
> The entirely beautiful.[34]

The soothing rhythm of these lines conveys an eroticism credited in the next stanza to a 'vision' from Venus of 'supernatural sympathy'. As a poem about, in effect, a one-night stand, it reflects Auden's sense as a gay writer of the spiritually erotic, and not just sexual, potentialities in an ephemeral encounter. At the same time, eroticism is complicated by a scepticism that deeply informed his writing of love: there is something deceptive about the beauty of love and of poetry. This 'Lullaby' speaks honestly but 'faithless[ly]' to a lover who is 'mortal' and 'guilty', and whose childlike, innocent beauty can be envisioned only because he is not awake – in any sense – to hear these words. Auden's writing about love throughout his career was driven by his sense that beauty is not truth, nor truth beauty, in poetry or in life. These attitudes informed his frequent articulations in his later poetry of the sacredness of reticence, even as he chronicled the emotional contradictions of his long-term relationship with Chester Kallman. The love that dare not speak its name became, after Auden's return to Christianity in the 1940s, love whose mysterious truth can never be adequately captured in art, but also, paradoxically, a love that goes without saying, and in his greatest love poetry – works like 'In Praise of Limestone' (1948), 'Dichtung und Wahrheit: An Unwritten Poem' (1959) and 'The Common Life' (1963) – the unspeakability of eros is inseparable from that of agape.

Among lesbian poets, Adrienne Rich remains the most influential writer of recent decades, and her work has offered a paradigmatic instance of introspection into lesbian love. Her essay 'Compulsory Heterosexuality and

Lesbian Existence' (1980) provided a way of opening up politically and historically a lesbian-feminist tradition of writing, and her ongoing concern with the psychological and political stakes in speaking the truth about lesbianism has informed not just her prose but also her love poetry.[35] This is immediately and powerfully clear in her 'Twenty-One Love Poems', which chronicles a love affair in the modern city. The first poem challenges the beloved – and the reader – 'to grasp our lives inseparable / from those rancid dreams' of 'cruelty' and suffering that reach from the patriarchal unconscious to infect contemporary lesbian life. For Rich, the difficulty of love comes not merely from without: 'these are the forces they had ranged against us, / and these are the forces we had ranged within us, / within us and against us, against us and within us'.[36] Left unresolved is the relation between the truth of erotic experience in itself and the relationship more broadly. In the midst of the sequence is Rich's '(FLOATING POEM, UNNUMBERED)', where she asserts that 'Whatever happens with us, your body / will haunt mine'.[37] It is a moment in which the explicitly personal carries, necessarily, a feminist political force – it is Rich's own act of publicly naming lesbian sex in defiance of patriarchal pressures of silencing. Like the gay male love poetry of Crane, Auden and Whitman, it asserts a transcendent eternal value in erotic ecstasy: 'your strong tongue and slender fingers / reaching where I had been waiting years for you / in my rose-wet cave – whatever happens, this is'. At the same time, precisely because 'this' 'floats' above the sequence as a whole, its separateness from those 'forces' ranged against lesbian eros also signifies its inability to overcome them. The sequence ends with a turn away from the city to a mythic Stonehenge: 'a woman. I choose to walk here. And to draw this circle' (86). This is an image of sacred completion, in love and in poetry. But it is not a physical refuge for two lovers, 'nor any place but the mind / casting back to where her solitude, / shared, could be chosen without loneliness'. What Rich projects here is an ideal space both public and private, personal and political, where love is a 'solitude / shared' between poet and reader.

For lesbian-feminist poets from the 1970s on, most notably Audre Lorde and Judy Grahn, this dedication to sharing lesbian love poetically has carried real political urgency. For gay male poets like Robert Duncan and Harold Norse, Whitman and Ginsberg have been presiding spirits of erotic freedom, but the preoccupation with aesthetic form in the work of Auden and his heirs has been indispensable for interrogating this liberation. These twin impulses are particularly evident since the advent of AIDS, which has challenged the post-Stonewall celebration of sexual freedom and pleasure. The elegiac mode of Tennyson, Whitman and Crane has governed much of this writing, most famously in Thom Gunn's *The Man with Night Sweats* (1992). Perhaps the poet who weaves together most powerfully the various threads of gay poetic tradition is Mark Doty, whose work shows the influence of Auden and James Merrill, with their conscious devotion to poetic craft and the metaphysics of artifice and beauty, but also of Whitman, Crane and Frank O'Hara. Doty's verse frequently concedes the inadequacy of the pleasures of art and life to tame sickness, death and loss. Poems like 'Sweet Machine', 'Lilacs in NYC' and 'Mercy on Broadway' do not look for elegiac consolation so much as embrace the rawness of urban existence – street music, fashion, thugs and skater-boys – in rendering the complexity of eros in the age of AIDS. With a sense shared by so many contemporary lesbian and gay poets that personal love is inevitably political, Doty's 'Mercy on Broadway' grapples with the cheap but still compelling allure of life in the capital of gay capitalism, with 'its hundred thousand ways to say *Hey*' (112). But at the heart of this ode to New York City is a fierce honesty about the erotic life of the survivor:

> I've been lucky, I've got a man
> in my head who's spirit and ash
> and flecks of bone now, and a live one
>
> whose skin is inches from mine.
> I've been granted this reprieve,
>
> and I'll take whatever part
> Broadway assigns me.[38]

Doty manipulates line-breaks and imagery with a wit both fearlessly chilling and invigorating, mixing the dead body of one lover with that of another 'live one', his 'skin' erotically, dangerously 'inches from mine'. To love the pleasures of being alive amidst the tawdry, unrelenting appeal of fashion and bodies on Broadway is, as Doty's poem is relentlessly aware, to be deeply implicated in the very desire that enabled death and the plague. But to 'drink this city street's / ash and attitude, scorch and glory' is to risk the pleasures and beauties without which poetry and love would not happen.

NOTES

1. For the philosophical basis of such debates, see John Boswell, 'Revolutions, Universals, and Sexual Categories', *Salmagundi*, 58–9 (Fall 1982 to Winter 1983), 89–113.
2. E. M. Forster, *A Passage to India* (New York: Harcourt, 1927), 49.
3. W. H. Auden, 'Some say that love's a little boy', *The English Auden: Poems, Essays, and Dramatic Writings 1927–1939*, ed. Edward Mendelson (London: Faber, 1977), 231.
4. 'From the Transcripts of the Second Trial [of Oscar Wilde]', in Byrne R. S. Fone, ed., *The Columbia Anthology of Gay Literature* (New York: Columbia University Press, 1998), 341.

5. Adrienne Rich, Poem IX, 'Twenty-One Love Poems', *Adrienne Rich's Poetry and Prose*, ed. Barbara Charlesworth Gelpi and Albert Gelpi (New York: Norton, 1993), 81.

6. See Linda Dowling, *Hellenism and Homosexuality in Victorian Oxford* (Ithaca, NY: Cornell University Press, 1994).

7. See *The Affectionate Shephearde* (1594) and *Cynthia, with Certain Sonnets* (1595), in Richard Barnfield, *The Complete Poems*, ed. George Klawitter (Selinsgrove: Susquehanna University Press, 1990).

8. See, for example, Stephen Booth's comment that 'Shakespeare was almost certainly homosexual, bisexual, or heterosexual', in William Shakespeare, *Shakespeare's Sonnets*, ed. Stephen Booth (New Haven, CT: Yale University Press, 1977), 548–9. More usefully, see Stephen Orgel's 'Introduction' to William Shakespeare, *The Sonnets: Updated Edition*, ed. G. Blakemore Evans (Cambridge: Cambridge University Press, 2006), 11–19. Oscar Wilde's story about a fictional theory of the sonnets, 'The Portrait of Mr. W. H.', in Oscar Wilde, *The Complete Shorter Fiction*, ed. Isobel Murray (Oxford: Oxford University Press, 1979), is an early queer interpretation of Shakespeare's sonnets.

9. Shakespeare, *The Sonnets*, ed. Evans, 35.

10. *Ibid.*, 36.

11. *Ibid.*, 38.

12. Joseph Pequigney, *Such Is My Love: A Study of Shakespeare's Sonnets* (Chicago: University of Chicago Press, 1985); see also Bruce R. Smith, *Homosexual Desire in Shakespeare's England: A Cultural Poetics* (Chicago: University of Chicago Press, 1991).

13. Shakespeare, *The Sonnets*, ed. Evans, 70.

14. See W. H. Auden, 'Introduction', in William Shakespeare, *The Sonnets*, ed. William Burto (New York: Signet, 1964), xxxv.

15. Christina Rossetti, 'Goblin Market', *Selected Poems*, ed. C. H. Sisson (Manchester: Carcanet, 1984), 97.

16. *Ibid.*, 94–5.

17. Alfred Tennyson, *In Memoriam A. H. H.*, *Tennyson's Poetry*, ed. Robert W. Hill, Jr (New York: Norton, 1971), 125.

18. *Ibid.*, 122.

19. See Jeff Nunokawa, '*In Memoriam* and the Extinction of the Homosexual', *ELH*, 58 (1991), 427–38.

20. Rich, 'Compulsory Heterosexuality and Lesbian Existence', *Adrienne Rich's Poetry and Prose*, ed. Gelpi and Gelpi, 217.

21. See Rich, 'Compulsory Heterosexuality'; Martha Nell Smith, *Rowing In Eden: Rereading Emily Dickinson* (Austin, TX: University of Texas Press, 1992).

22. See Rich, 'Vesuvius at Home: The Power of Emily Dickinson', *Adrienne Rich's Poetry and Prose*, ed. Gelpi and Gelpi, pp. 177–95.

23. When John Addington Symonds, having been in correspondence with him for some twenty years, enquired directly in 1890 about the sexual implications of the Calamus poems, Whitman rejected such 'morbid inferences' and asserted that he had fathered six children. See Walt Whitman, *The Correspondence of Walt Whitman*, ed. Edwin Haviland Miller, 6 vols. (New York: New York University Press, 1978), vol. v: 72–3.

24. Walt Whitman, *Leaves of Grass*, ed. Sculley Bradley and Harold W. Blodget (New York: Norton, 1973), 131.
25. *Ibid.*, 113.
26. *Ibid.*, 121.
27. *Ibid.*, 116.
28. Robert K. Martin, *The Homosexual Tradition in American Poetry* (Austin, TX: University of Texas Press, 1979). See also Thomas Yingling, *Hart Crane and the Homosexual Text: New Thresholds, New Anatomies* (Chicago: University of Chicago Press, 1990).
29. Hart Crane, 'Voyages III', *The Complete Poems and Selected Letters and Prose of Hart Crane*, ed. Brom Weber (New York: Anchor Books, 1966), 37.
30. Edward Mendelson, *Later Auden* (New York: Farrar, Straus and Giroux, 1999), 450.
31. Gertrude Stein, 'Lifting Belly', *The Yale Gertrude Stein*, ed. Richard Kostelanetz (New Haven: Yale University Press, 1980), 48.
32. For further analysis of this passage of 'Lifting Belly' and of Stein's writing as a lesbian, see Catharine Stimpson, 'The Somagrams of Gertrude Stein', *Poetics Today*, 6 (1985), 67–80.
33. See Richard R. Bozorth, *Auden's Games of Knowledge: Poetry and the Meanings of Homosexuality* (New York: Columbia University Press, 2001); Edward Mendelson, *Early Auden* (New York: Viking Press, 1981) and *Later Auden*; and Gregory Woods, *Articulate Flesh: Male Homo-eroticism in Modern Poetry* (New Haven, CT: Yale University Press, 1987).
34. W. H. Auden, 'Lay your sleeping head, my love', *The English Auden*, 207.
35. See especially Adrienne Rich, 'Vesuvius at Home: The Power of Emily Dickinson' and 'Women and Honor: Some Notes on Lying', *Adrienne Rich's Poetry and Prose*.
36. Rich, Poem XVII, 'Twenty-One Love Poems', *Adrienne Rich's Poetry and Prose*, 84.
37. *Ibid.*, 83.
38. Mark Doty, *Sweet Machine* (New York: Harper, 1998), 111.

13

The queer writer in New York

'Are we talking about literally New York or some kind of imagined scene?'
Eileen Myles asks Dennis Cooper, even though she knows that the two cannot
be separated, for what makes New York so powerful a place for gay and
lesbian writers is that the 'literal' city can sustain and inspire so many
imagined ones.[1] People find in New York what they desire to imagine even
as they imagine what they desire. This multiplicity and diversity of New
Yorks is the starting point for both Edmund White's guide to gay life in the
city in *States of Desire* (1980) and Samuel R. Delany's spirited defence in
Times Square Red, Times Square Blue (1999).

But to understand some of the power of New York as a place of and for the
imagination, one must look at its physical design. By New York, people mean
Manhattan and not the outer boroughs which along with Manhattan make
up the actual jurisdiction. Unlike London, Paris, Rome or Moscow, which are
all transected by rivers, Manhattan is an island surrounded by them.
According to *Geology of the City of New York* (1909), Manhattan is
a thirteen-mile-long outcrop of gneisses, granites, limestone and schist only
superficially covered by drifts of river muds and sands.[2] In the thirties Carl
Van Vechten wrote that in New York no one can escape the sounds of
blasting, 'which reminds one that Manhattan, like the Church of Rome, is
built on solid rock'.[3] Walt Whitman describes his *Mannahatta* as a '*rocky
founded island – shores where ever gaily dash the coming, going, hurrying sea
waves*'.[4] He may have been among the last, for John Gillis claims that New
Yorkers gave up thinking about Manhattan as an island at least by the time
the Brooklyn Bridge opened in 1883. And yet Alfred Corn seems quite aware
that Manhattan 'has the shape of / A boat with the Battery / For prow'.[5] And
Allen Ginsberg apostrophizes 'This port / Of seasonal departures, this starry
island'.[6] Moreover, Manhattanites retain the characteristics of island people:
provinciality, self-involvement and intensity. Nevertheless, the mindset of
Manhattanites differs in at least one important respect from that of other
islanders: whereas most islanders feel the need for the mainland, New

Yorkers are contemptuous of the mainland's need for them. Suburbanites who flock to Manhattan for excitement, culture and sexual possibilities are sneeringly referred to as 'the bridge-and-tunnel crowd'. Some New Yorkers would like to raise the bridges around their moated castle.

If most New Yorkers have forgotten that they live on an island, queer Manhattanites, in contrast, are keenly aware of the rivers that surround them. The Harlem River, the shortest, is also the saddest. In his bluesy 'Reverie on the Harlem River', Langston Hughes discovers that sitting beside its waters makes you 'wonder what you got left'.[7] Adrienne Rich compares it to a 'toxic swamp'.[8] On the other hand, Paul Goodman claims that 'The Lordly Hudson' 'has no peer in Europe or the East'.[9] Yet it, too, speaks of loneliness and self-destruction. Eileen Myles's ex-lover Chris runs out of Puffy's, a lesbian bar near the Hudson, and lifting 'her arms in a pure Isadora Duncan type pose' attempts suicide by throwing herself into it.[10] The East River, separating Manhattan from Brooklyn and Queens, has inspired writers since Whitman, who 'many and many a time cross'd the river of old' and

> Saw the white sails of schooners and sloops, saw the ships at anchor
> The sailors at work in the rigging or out astride the spars
>
> . . .
>
> The large and small steamers in motion, the pilots in their pilot-houses.[11]

Hart Crane hears 'by the River that is East' 'the echoes assembling, one after one, / Searching, thumbing the midnight on the piers. / Lights, coasting, left the oily tympanum of waters.'[12] In 1883, Emma Lazarus – a wealthy New York Jew, who could not in her lifetime print her openly lesbian poem 'Assurance' – symbolically finds in the Statue of Liberty a 'Mother of Exiles', who welcomes 'The wretched refuse' to New York's 'teeming shore'.[13] Whether her sexuality led her to such sympathies, we cannot say, but the tradition of openness to the strange, foreign or merely different has made New York a place where lesbian and gay writers have felt more accepted than in most places. The physical reality of New York is a starting point and a source of inspiration for queer writers. But it hardly determines how queer artists will see the city. For in truth, what remains natural in the New York landscape – the river, the palisades of the Jersey coast – is dwarfed by what has been built on it. Even Central Park, New York's great homage to nature, is an engineered fantasy.

One place, however, where nature and man have merged is on the waterfront. Even after the maritime business left the city, the liminal and transitional space of the piers and docks filled the queer *imaginarium*, that depository of images, myths and styles. Indeed, it seems that the very vacuum left by the shipping industry has been reoccupied by the erotic – as the stevedores were sucked off the docks by late capitalism, the queens and clones moved in. In his novel *Hold Tight*, about spies and waterfront whore-houses in the 1940s, Christopher Bram describes the area around West Street and Gansevoort in noir-ish terms: 'The street opened on a square, a cobble-stone bay where five or six streets met at odd angles. Two flatbed trucks were parked in the middle. There were houses ... three of them wedged together in the narrow corner.'[14] On a more romantic, if not decadent note, Edmund White detects 'the trapped smell of sweat on bodies' just beneath the odour of brine in the decaying piers along West Street and makes them into a cathedral with 'communicants telling beads or buttons pierced through denim, the greater number shuffling, ignoring everything in their search for a god among us'.[15] Richard Howard recalls in 'A Sybil of 1979' looking down 'at the big meat-trucks parked on West Street, empty now / but not as they would be after dark, [with] men / furtively climbing in and out' and being asked by Muriel Rukeyser, 'Do you ever go to the trucks?'[16] Emanuel Xavier nostalgically describes the West Street docks in the 1980s as 'the days when the piers belonged to the children of the [voguing] houses. Those ... days before the West Side Highway piers had become a roller rink for the steroid-enhanced, salon-tanned muscle boys.'[17] West Street from Soho to the Village has produced a genealogy of gay images starting as a seedy locale of long-shoremen and whorehouses, to a crumbling cathedral of sex, to the hang-out for Puerto Rican and black drag queens and finally emerging as a roller rink for the muscle queens of the AIDS era.

I begin with these literary postcards to suggest the importance of various scenes for the queer New York literary imagination, and by *scene* I do not mean just the cityscape, but also the social environments that historically have made up New York's cultural spaces. I use the term *scene* to describe these clusters because unlike *circle* it does not imply a clear boundary. One scene can dissolve into another scene; one can perform simultaneously in several different scenes in either a starring role or a supporting position, or by waiting in the wings for a walk-on. If there are no fixed dramatic personae (although they can have charismatic leaders), there are also no required oaths of alle-giance. Nevertheless scenes tend to have metonymic locations – Greenwich Village, Harlem, the Lower East Side. But even when writers and artists gravitate to certain quarters of the city, outliers, extras, fellow travellers blur the boundaries and make it difficult to map them neatly.

Consider Jerry Cooke's now iconic 1948 *Life* photo taken at the Gotham Bookmart to celebrate Edith and Osbert Sitwell's arrival in New York (Fig. 1). Such a high-brow queer event provides a snapshot of New York literary life. Of those amassed for the occasion, even those who were not homosexual were, as in the case of Marianne Moore and Dame Edith, decidedly queer. By my count almost half of the group was lesbian, gay or

Fig. 1. New York authors by Jerry Cooke for *Life Magazine*, 1948.
Reproduced by permission from Getty Images.

bisexual. In the same tiny room are gathered Elizabeth Bishop and Marianne Moore, Gore Vidal and Tennessee Williams. Charles Henri Ford sits crossed-legged on the floor; Stephen Spender stands with one knee bent and, finally, towering over everyone, W. H. Auden leans on a step-ladder. It is not surprising that Marya Zaturenska and Horace Gregory – the only married pair in the photograph – huddle shyly in a corner or that Randall Jarrell, whose own sexuality is a matter of question, looks away from the camera as if he wished he were somewhere else.

That such disparate groups came together suggests the ways that queer scenes can overlap with one another and with straight scenes as well as the extent to which New York is a crossroad between Europe and the rest of the United States. Auden, who had become an American citizen two years before the photograph, had his own American friends – Carson McCullers, Jane and Paul Bowles – with whom he had formed a communal house in the early forties. Auden had little contact with Gore Vidal or Tennessee Williams, but had known Charles Henri Ford in Europe. With Moore he had a special friendship dating back to 1939 when he first visited her.[18]

Because so many gay and lesbian writers live in New York, and because lesbian and gay writers outside of New York pass through the city, queer authors find themselves thrown into contact with those with whom they would otherwise have no connection. The possibility of contact and networking is, I shall suggest, more common in New York than in London or Paris because of the greater egalitarianism of New York.

Networks and *contacts* are two social processes that make scenes possible according to Samuel R. Delany in his study of the Times Square district. According to Delany:

> Networking tends to be professional and motive-driven. Contact tends to be more broadly social and appears random. Networking crosses class lines only in the most vigilant manner. Contact regularly crosses class lines ... Networking is heavily dependent on institutions to promote the necessary propinquity ... Contact is associated with public spaces and the architecture and commerce that depends on and promotes it.[19]

In New York, people bump into one another and start talking. Larry Kramer helped Andrew Holleran get *Dancer from the Dance* (1978) published after meeting him at a gym. Richard Howard helped Edmund White get *Forgetting Elena* (1973) published after encountering him at the baths.[20] Yet Holleran and White met by no accident – it was a case of social networking that occurred when Robert Ferro and his lover Michael Grumley put together the gay writers group, The Violet Quill.[21] Gay and lesbian cultures probably foster opportunities for contact and networking because they are a 'fundamentally urban phenomenon'[22] and queer life encourages the intersection of desire and ambition, the two engines, according to Delany, that produce contacts and networks.[23] Yet one needs to be careful to avoid supporting fears of 'a homosexual international conspiracy in the arts', or what has been called the *homintern*.[24] A network is not a cabal.

Interwar years

When queer literary scenes started in New York is unclear, but in the interwar years homosexuality and literary culture came together in both Harlem and Greenwich Village. Wallace Thurman commented in 1932 that 'Harlem is a state of mind, peopled with improbable monsters.'[25] Yet Harlem until the Depression was more integrated than it became and still retained small garden allotments, which Claude McKay celebrates in his novel *Home to Harlem* (1928).[26] It is this tension between Harlem's homey domesticity and its 'promiscuous thickness' and 'hot desires' that queer writers found particularly difficult to navigate. In *Passing* (1929), Nella Larson shows how a woman passing as white can shatter the stable domestic world of a Harlem apartment, but the novella, it has been argued, is 'about sexual attraction and identification' as well as about passing as straight.[27] Although not lovers, Wallace Thurman and Richard Bruce Nugent shared an apartment together (Langston Hughes rented another apartment in the same building for a while). It was from this flat that they issued in 1926 the groundbreaking journal *Fire!!*, which lasted only one number. *Fire!!* situated the 'New Negro' writers and artists, many of whom were queer, in conflict with the bourgeois sensibilities of the Harlem establishment and the well-meaning but timid tastes of white do-gooders. As Thurman put it, the New Negro writers refused to be 'patted on the head by philanthropists and social workers'.[28] Later Thurman and Nugent were given the chance to develop a home for African-American artists, 267 West 136th Street, dubbed 'Niggerati Manor', where low rents and the stimulation of other artists would produce, it was hoped, a steady stream of work that would realize the talent of its residents, but their nightly parties and disruptive behaviour put an end to the experiment, a failure mourned in both Thurman's *Infants of the Spring* (1932) and Nugent's posthumously published *Gentleman Jigger* (2008).

Although Harlem might be 'hunting for joy' by 'fooping or jig-jagging the night away',[29] it also had its share of homophobia. *Home to Harlem* is haunted by Bessie Smith's 'Foolish Man Blues', in which the bisexual Smith asks: 'there's two things in Harlem I don't understan' / It is a bulldyking woman and a faggotty man ... what are you?'[30] Ma Rainey, who sometimes wore men's clothes, asserts both that she 'don't like no man' and that she has a right to privacy. Because 'ain't nobody caught me / They sure got to prove it on me'.[31] The most notorious lesbian blues singer of Harlem, Gladys Bentley, sang obscene parodies of well-known songs, dressed in men's clothing and pounded the piano as if it were dough, but under the pressure of McCarthyism and religion, she married and renounced her ways.[32]

Many black writers and artists, and especially queer black writers, attended the white salons of the heterosexual Muriel Draper and Mabel Dodge Luhan through the networking of Carl Van Vechten, the homosexual (but married) critic, photographer and novelist. The world of these salons reflects Van Vechten's sense that 'New York ... is in a constant state of mutation ... New York is fluid: it flows.'[33] Flow it did. With art and ideas, tears and blood, and especially bootlegged liquor. In Van Vechten's *Parties* (1930), David and Rilda Westlake are indiscriminate sexual magnets. David's best friend Hamish desires them both. Roy Fern is so besotted by David that he kills a man to please him. In the social and erotic currents people were bound to collide. At Mabel Dodge Luhan's, one could meet 'Socialists, Trade Unionists, Anarchists, Suffragists, Poets, Relations, Lawyers and Murderers',[34] and not a few were queer since the guest list might include the poet and novelist Djuna Barnes; the painter and poet Marsden Hartley; Langston Hughes; Jean Toomer, the author of *Cane*; and the novelist and social critic Charlotte Perkins Gilman. Draper's parties attracted the poet Hart Crane; the composer and critic Virgil Thomson; the writer, editor and cultural entrepreneur Lincoln Kirstein; as well as the novelist Glenway Wescott and his publisher lover Monroe Wheeler, who together forged a *ménage à trois* with the photographer George Platt Lynes. Later, there was the salon of the lovers Margaret Anderson and Jane Heap, who together produced *The Little Review*, one of the most important avant-garde journals in America. New York represented the place in which artists, writers and thinkers could get some of the intellectual and artistic stimulation in America that they could get in Europe.

But the notoriety of these queer writers did not mean acceptance. In Ernest Boyd's nasty satirical essay, 'Aesthete Model 1924', queers were pictured as sirens luring red-blooded American writers to their downfall. The danger begins in college, when the prototypical undergraduate naïvely makes friends with those who had the 'avowed intention of not being he-men' and who 'welcomed a new recruit'. Luckily the straight writer can be cured, the first signs of recovery being 'dreams haunted by fears of Sodom and Gomorrah'. Released from the grip of those who 'join in a tribute to Proust', he finally regains 'pep in the swing of his fist' and obtains 'a regular and well-paid job'.[35] Boyd's criticism met its mark, and the heterosexual Malcolm Cowley, for one, 'began to feel harried and combative [by being] forced to defend his masculinity against whispers'.[36] Queer men and women writers within the literary world were accepted, but only so far, and ultimately with uneasiness.

The stock market crash of 1929 ended such silliness. The poet and biographer Muriel Rukeyser found that 'New York is quiet / as a doped man walking to the electric chair'.[37] In Charles Henri Ford and Parker Tyler's *The Young and the Evil* (1933), considered by some to be the first truly gay novel because of its unapologetic homosexual characters and its use of gay slang, the city is full of men who are 'debonair, destitute, devouring'.[38] Greenwich Village is laced with tearooms, dancing parlours, 'gangsters, dark girls and children who played street games'.[39] When two characters are beaten up by sailors and arrested for solicitation, they are released by a sympathetic magistrate who 'leaned over and said sweetly but be more careful next time!'.[40] Ford is a figure who bridges generations. In the thirties, he typed Djuna Barnes's manuscript for *Nightwood* (1936), the seminal novel of lesbian Paris, and in the sixties he shepherded Andy Warhol through the New York high artistic world. His co-author Parker Tyler made a name as a serious film critic; his *Screening the Sexes: Homosexuality in the Movies* (1972) broke new ground in cultural criticism.

Post-war years

The rise of Hitler brought many Americans who had been living in Europe and many European émigrés to New York. Edwin Denby was among them. A dancer in Europe, he fled back to the United States in 1933, after being warned to get out of Germany. For a while he shared a loft with Paul Bowles, who was then a composer and not yet a novelist married to the lesbian writer Jane Bowles. At the time, Bowles was writing the music for his and Charles Henri Ford's opera *Denmark Vesey* (1938). On his return to the States, Denby started writing regular dance criticism known for its insight, elegance, intellect and independence.

After the Second World War, Denby articulated a new attitude towards New York. He asked New Yorkers to see the city as a sort of ballet. In a lecture he was too shy to give, he tells his audience of dance students, 'There is no point in living here, if you don't see the city you are living in', and lectures them, 'If you were observant, you would have long ago enjoyed the many kinds of walking you can see in this city, boys and girls, Negro and white, Puerto Rican and Western American and Eastern, foreigners, professors and dancers, mechanics and businessmen, ladies entering a theatre with half a drink too much, and shoppers at Macy's.'[41]

Denby, handsome, distinguished and shy, is an important figure, who is often forgotten in surveys of gay literature because he was extremely reticent about his private life and his ostensible subject, dance, is so marginalized. This neglect is unfortunate, for dance – like music and art, which have been widely studied – had an important impact on queer New York writing. Edmund White wrote that the theatre in which the New York City Ballet performed 'had been the drawing room of America, and that ... Americans saw in the elaborate *enchaînements* on stage a radiant vision of society'.[42] William Meredith watching from 'the paunchy dark' sees in the 'bold genitals' of the gay male dancers 'a longer affliction of splendor: / That it cannot reproduce its kind.'[43] If Lincoln Kirstein laid the practical ground for the New York City Ballet, Denby laid the critical ground.

In addition, Denby is important because he and Fairfield Porter were father figures for what has been dubbed The New York School of Poetry, whose leading members were Frank O'Hara, John Ashbery, James Schuyler and Kenneth Koch, all but the last gay. O'Hara and Ashbery became two of the most important figures in American poetry. They were lured to New York by the artistic and cultural possibilities the city provided. More than other writers, they befriended painters, and Ashbery and Schuyler ended up as art critics and O'Hara as a museum curator. O'Hara was especially charismatic. Warm, open and restless, he was a magnet for other writers and painters. The energy of the initial group of New York poets attracted a 'second generation' which included Joe Brainard, who was also an artist, and Jim Carroll, who was also a musician. They were followed by a third generation (but the generations get blurred), which includes Eileen Myles, Tim Dlugos and David Trinidad. These writers brought a directness, gentleness and humour to American poetry, mixing the mundane, the arcane, high and low culture into a wild dance. Gay life in New York invited this sudden alternation between the lofty and the lumpen. O'Hara gleefully moves from Balanchine to cheeseburgers, and Ashbery from Vasari to Van Camp's Pork and Beans. By the sixties, this style had become a signature of gay life, according to Daniel Harris, and magazines meant for a gay audience, like *After Dark*, would juxtapose 'pinups of leering body builders' with lengthy reviews of Marlowe's *Edward II*.[44]

The very title of Frank O'Hara's poem, 'A Step Away from Them', indicates its relationship to dance. O'Hara partners us through his lunch hour: 'First, down the sidewalk / where laborers feed their dirty / glistening torsos sandwiches / and Coca-Cola', then to Times Square where 'A / Negro stands in a doorway with a / toothpick.' He passes a blonde chorus girl, gets something to eat, and watches as 'A lady in / foxes … puts her poodle / in a can.' And just as he had counted down the incidents of his walk, he tallies up the deceased: 'First / Bunny died, then John Latouche, / Then Jackson Pollock.'[45] Yet he moves on. The poem ends with 'A glass of papaya juice / and back to work. My heart is in my / pocket, it is Poems by Pierre Reverdy.'[46] In New York, the movements of construction workers and chorus girls compete for attention with Jackson Pollock and Pierre Reverdy.

New York's vibrancy stood in contrast to many European cities, which after 1945 lay in ruins. Indeed, by virtue of the United Nations, New York had become the capital of the world. Even its slums radiated excitement and beauty. One measure of this new way of seeing New York is the operatic *West Side Story* (1957), which was created by an exclusively gay (and Jewish) battery of artists – the music by Leonard Bernstein, the lyrics by Stephen Sondheim, the book by Arthur Laurents and the staging and choreography by Jerome Robbins. New York, for them, is the new Verona.

Of course, this was the white perception of the city; James Baldwin saw things quite differently from his Harlem perspective. Harlem had erupted into violence during the Second World War, and afterwards conditions got worse. Rents were higher than in the rest of the city; food was more expensive, and jobs scarcer.[47] For many queer artistic Harlemites, the only place to survive was Europe. By the 1970s Harlem is even worse. Audre Lorde walks 'down the withering limbs / of New York' and determines:

> There is nothing worth salvage left in this city
> but faint reedy voices like echoes
> of once beautiful children.[48]

By the late sixties, however, the vibrancy of the city was ending even for white gay artists and even as gay liberation and lesbian feminism created a greater sense of community and new publishing opportunities. Poverty, corruption and neglect had allowed the city to decay. Muriel Rukeyser notes how the American Academy of Arts and Letters, located north of Harlem, has been covered with graffiti, so that

> painted upon the stones, Chino, Bobby, Joey,
>   Fatmoma, Willy, Holy of God
> and also Margaret is a shit and also fuck and shit;
> far up, invisible at the side of the building
> WITHOUT VISION THE PEO
> and on the other side, the church side . . .
> IVE BY BREAD ALONE[49]

The hallowed, high-sounding words are invisible and broken, but the scrawled names and obscenities are in plain sight. Similarly, Marilyn Hacker watches as

> Mrs. Velez of the Tenants' Association
> zig-zags her top-heavy shopping cart through
> the usual palette of dogshit, brick-red
> to black on grimy leftover snow.[50]

'You've got to be tough to live here', Edward Field, one of O'Hara's lovers, reminds himself as he drops another cockroach into an ashtray to the horror of his out-of-town guests.[51] But the toughness that the queer New Yorker develops often leads to the comic. May Swenson imagined 'two white whales . . . installed at / the Waldorf' escaping via the heliport atop the Pan Am building.[52] The Beat movement, although associated with San Francisco, had its origins in New York when Allen Ginsberg, a Columbia University student, first made contact with William S. Burroughs and Herbert Huncke and the bisexual Neil Cassidy. Ginsberg understood that New York was both a joyous place where Blake spoke to him uptown and a dangerous one where downtown addicts were ready to 'knife a poet'.[53] When he is mugged in middle age, he portrays himself not as a hardened city-dweller but as a slightly comic patsy reciting 'Om Ah Hūm' while an 18-year-old boy, looking for money, fingers his back pocket and discovers that Ginsberg's wallet is empty of all but credit cards (Mobil, Amex) and identification (instructor at Naropa, Chief Boo-Hoo Neo American Church New Jersey & Lower East Side).[54]

Ginsberg's language is energized by the cross-class contacts New York offers. He experimented with Hunke's hustler slang; he calls Times Square 'the teahead's sensate garden',[55] a reference both to marijuana and to the bathrooms (or tearooms) used in Times Square subway stations, which since the 1930s were referred to as the 'Sunken Gardens'.[56] Like the novelist Bruce Benderson, Ginsberg needs to forge a 'vital link with the culture of poverty', which is nowhere more apparent than in Times Square.[57] John Rechy has the narrator of *City of Night* (1963), a groundbreaking novel, begin his life of hustling in Times Square:

> From the thundering underground – the maze of the New York subways – the world pours into Times Square. Like lost souls emerging from the purgatory of the trains (dark rattling tunnels, smelly pornographic toilets, newsstands futilely splashing the subterranean gray depths with unreal color), the newyork [*sic*] faces push into the air: spilling into 42nd Street and Broadway – a scattered defeated army.[58]

During the 1990s, Mayor Rudolph Giuliani was obsessed with cleaning up Times Square to make it safer, not for queers and queer artists, but for tourists and suburbanites who had more money to spend. Cleaning up New York meant shaping it to the bland commercial preferences of out-of-towners rather than to the indigenous desires of the rich and poor men and women who found uncommon ground in X-rated movie theatres, strip joints and hustler bars.

Times Square was not the only neighbourhood cleaned up. The Lower East Side in the 1990s went through major renovations, driving out many of the artists and local residents who could no longer afford to live there. But in the 1960s it was still a place of cheap rents, where young artists and writers gravitated. Formerly the home of immigrants – mostly Jews and Eastern Europeans – who packed the tenements and still clung on in smaller numbers, the neighbourhood became the backdrop of the East Coast counterculture – its streets lined with headshops and bodegas among the kosher delis. By the eighties, headshops were replaced by 'shooting galleries', places where people could inject drugs. Sarah Schulman, the novelist and playwright, whose works are set in New York, writes about a 'particular brand of dingy' not to be confused with poverty. 'There was a special kind of neglect that felt like sabotage ... No mothers yelled to kids from tenement windows. No music floated down from the lips of thin musicians in crowded apartments ... Too many junkies had taken over too much territory.'[59]

Despite the crime, gay and lesbian writers and artists held on to the neighbourhood because of its cheap rents and ongoing artistic community. Eileen Myles, who for several years ran the Poetry Project at St Mark's Church, one of the most important incubators of poetry in the country, gives homage to this artistic genealogy in her book *Chelsea Girls* (1994), written about the late 1970s. The title is drawn from Andy Warhol's 1966 film, which capitalized on the iconic Chelsea Hotel, which has been described as a 'myth loaded with old denizens', a place where Herbert Huncke, William S. Burroughs, Gore Vidal and Tennessee Williams once stayed, and hence the perfect setting for illicit sex.[60] But the title also celebrates James Schuyler, who, after many hospitalizations for mental illness, came to reside there. Myles is Schuyler's assistant. The book concludes with Myles's taking a woman she has met to the Chelsea. Between bouts of love-making, Myles attends to Schuyler; in doing so she connects herself to the generations of queer artists who came before her, a connection extended symbolically by the books scattered on Schuyler's floor: Firbank, Virginia Woolf's diaries, John Ashbery's *As We Know*.[61] Myles tells Schuyler about the woman she has waiting in a nearby room, and he delights to hear her stories.

This continuity of artistic life inspired Dennis Cooper when he lived in New York in the mid eighties. 'I'd go to a party', he recalls, 'and there would be slightly older writers like Joe Brainard and Kenward Elmslie and Ron Padgett, and then the established greats like Ashbery and Schuyler and Edwin Denby ... an incredibly multigenerational group of artists'. However, Cooper has come to feel that 'it was the end of that world, the last golden hours of the New York School'. For Cooper and Myles, the New York School comes to an end because the scene became 'dominated by heterosexuals'.[62] For Daniel Kane, one of the salient features of the New York School was its 'resistance to machismo', which is why lesbian writers like Myles, Schulman and Joan Larkin were so attracted to it.[63]

For lesbians, the aesthetic of the New York School had another drawing card related to its resistance to machismo: it gave a writer 'permission to be local, as if one were famous'.[64] O'Hara made references to his friends who were then unknowns with the same exuberance as he refers to such cultural icons as Lana Turner or Billie Holiday. For artists who felt themselves disenfranchised, as so many lesbian writers did, this permission to see their local lives as not only worthy of notice but surrounded by the aura of fame was liberating.

AIDS and New York

Many factors brought the New York School to its end, but none as definitive as the AIDS epidemic. AIDS vastly shifted the way gay writers saw their city. For years many lesbian and gay writers had accepted the city's benign indifference as an opportunity to forge their own communities. Bohemianism, after all, has a strong anarchistic strain. But the AIDS epidemic required the city to act, and it remained unmoved. 'Homosexuals are not men who sleep with other men', Roy Cohn declares in a crucial scene in Tony Kushner's *Angels in America* (1993). 'Homosexuals are men who in fifteen years of trying cannot get a pissant antidiscrimination bill through City Council. Homosexuals are men who know nobody and who nobody knows.'[65] AIDS revealed, as Larry Kramer argued, that the gay community was powerless to move not only the Health Department but also the other city institutions such as *The New York Times* and Mayor Ed Koch, who was rumoured to be gay. Kramer wrote in one of his invectives, 'Until the day I die, I will never forgive this newspaper and this mayor for treating this epidemic . . . in such an irresponsible fashion.'[66] But indifference and homophobia did not alone account for the lack of response. For Sarah Schulman, a member of ACT UP and the Lesbian Avengers, there was a more malevolent force at work. In her *People in Trouble* (1990), much of which is stolen in the musical *Rent!* (1996), the activist character James tells demonstrators that the developer Ronald Horne has 'bought buildings with fifty percent gay tenants in the hope that we will drop dead and leave him with empty apartments'.[67] Builders did not want just to clean *up* New York, according to Schulman, they wanted to clean *out* New York to make room for the wealthy and healthy.

She was not alone. AIDS brought out the Kafkaesque in New York. The writer, performer and visual artist David Wojnarowicz, one of the most extraordinary figures to emerge in this period, reports that when a Senate panel discovered that in the next 18 months 33,000 homeless people with AIDS would be living on the streets, New York officials assured the investigators that 'these people were dying so fast from lack of health care that . . . there would be no visible increase' in the corpses lying on the sidewalk.[68] Meanwhile as he sits in the hospital with a friend dying of AIDS, Wojnarowicz watches preparations for the first Gulf War in which kids 'yakking about how they were going to march straight to Baghdad' fill out their wills and Dick Cheney raises questions of who deserves to be 'diagnosed with dementia' by exhibiting 'that weird lust in his eyes and bits of brain matter in the cracks of his teeth'.[69] AIDS turned New York into an unreal estate market in which the death rate of gay men had to be maintained in order to control the number of homeless people living on the streets.

AIDS's relation to housing finds it way into David B. Feinberg's works. One of the most acidly funny writers of the time – and AIDS writing was often filled with gallows humour – he turns his withering gaze at everything and everyone he sees either directly in essays or through his autobiographical persona B. J. Rosenthal in his novels *Eighty-Sixed* (1989) and *Spontaneous Combustion* (1991). All of Feinberg's work is shadowed by AIDS and his increased disabilities. Gay people are no less a target of attack than straight ones. In *Queer and Loathing* (1994), his final book, he recounts the story of trying to find a new apartment. He makes an appointment with Gil, 'everybody's favorite Chelsea real-estate agent' and Gil shows Feinberg several apartments; the first, Gil points out, would be 'perfect for sex parties ... The second has a sauna'.[70] The third is fitted with railings to which sex partners can be handcuffed. Despite the epidemic, the selling features of the apartments all have to do with dangerous sex. When he leaves Gil, Feinberg runs into Bruce, whose dying lover may have been the last person with whom he had unprotected sex. In short, the community he goes to for help are the same people who created the culture that has infected him. Like Kushner, Feinberg captures the conflicts of distrust and need that shaped New York.

Yet AIDS writing is not universally dark or embittered with gallows humour. In her novel *Push*, the African-American writer Sapphire (born Ramona Lufton in 1950) creates a narrator, Claireece Precious Jones, who has almost everything going against her: she has two children before she is sixteen, both of whom are the product of rape by her father. The eldest is born with Down's syndrome. Precious is poor, black and virtually illiterate, surrounded by drugs, crime and hopelessness. She is also HIV-positive. But somehow the machinery of the city catches up with her. She is placed in a shelter and in an alternative school, Each One Teach One, where she encounters Miz Rain, who changes her life. In some ways, *Push* follows a fairly standard trajectory of redemption, yet in this context redemption is the last thing one would expect.

The events of 9/11 have only confirmed the sense that the city's hubristic monuments to power and money are also its symbols of destruction. The poet Edward Field, who watched the World Trade Towers collapse from his apartment window, ironically returns to Whitman in order to 'digest' these events. For just as Whitman can be found 'under your boot-soles', so, too, the disaster is present in 'the grit under [his] shoe soles', a grit of the victims' 'pulverized bones'.[71] However, despite terrorists and developers, queer writers continue to find something endearing about the island. The ex-hustler, ex-drug dealer, Puerto Rican/Ecuadorian writer Emanuel Xavier includes in his anthology of 'queer spoken word poetry' the work of Cheryl Boyce-Taylor, a Trinidadian student of Audre Lorde. 'I want to scream / this is a crazy filthy city / with shit and stink', but she also loves

> this crazy city
> and poets and trinis
> and pan insulin boys
> world music rum bread pudding
> rollover minutes fresh lilacs

lavender oils American girls
hot tubs foot rubs and
my lover's rubber duckie
and rainy morning stained with the sticky taste
of your sinful mouth.[72]

NOTES

1. Dennis Cooper and Eileen Myles, 'Afterword. The Scene: A Conversation between Dennis Cooper and Eileen Myles', in Brandon Stosuy, ed., *Up Is Up But So Is Down: New York's Downtown Literary Scene, 1974–1992* (New York: New York University Press, 2006), 463.

2. L. Gratacap, *Geology of the City of New York*, 3rd edn (New York: Holt, 1909), 8–9.

3. Carl Van Vechten, *Parties* (New York: Knopf, 1930), 141.

4. Walt Whitman, *The Complete Poetry and Collected Prose* (New York: Library of America, 1982), 309. Whitman's italics.

5. John Gillis, *Islands of the Mind: How the Human Imagination Created the Atlantic World* (New York: Palgrave, 2004), 125; Alfred Corn, *A Call in the Midst of the Crowd* (New York: Viking, 1978), 43.

6. Allen Ginsberg, 'Ode to Decadence', *The Book of Martyrdom and Artifice: First Journals and Poems 1937–1952*, ed. Juanita Lieberman-Plimpton and Bill Morgan (New York: Da Capo, 2006), 419.

7. Langston Hughes, *Selected Poems* (New York: Vintage, 1974), 42.

8. Adrienne Rich, *Your Native Land, Your Life* (New York: Norton, 1986), 36.

9. Paul Goodman, *Collected Poems*, ed. Taylor Stoehr (New York: Random House, 1973), 365.

10. Eileen Myles, *Chelsea Girls* (Santa Rosa, CA: Black Sparrow Press, 1994), 252.

11. Walt Whitman, *The Complete Poetry and Collected Prose* (New York: Library of America, 1982), 309.

12. Hart Crane, *The Poems of Hart Crane*, ed. Marc Simon (New York: Liveright, 1986), 101.

13. Emma Lazarus, *Selected Poems*, ed. John Hollander, American Poets Project (New York: Library of America, 2005), 58.

14. Christopher Bram, *Hold Tight* (New York: Signet, 1988), 12.

15. Edmund White, *Nocturnes for the King of Naples* (New York: St Martin's Press, 1978), 4–5.

16. Richard Howard, *Inner Voices: Selected Poems 1963–2003* (New York: Farrar, Straus and Giroux, 2003), 377.

17. Emanuel Xavier, *Christ-Like* (New York: Painted Leaf, 1999), 214.

18. Charles Molesworth, *Marianne Moore: A Literary Life* (New York: Atheneum, 1990), 302.

19. Samuel R. Delany, *Times Square Red, Times Square Blue* (New York and London: New York University Press, 1999), 129.

20. David Bergman, *The Violet Hour: The Violet Quill and the Making of Gay Culture* (New York: Columbia University Press, 2004), 3.

21. *Ibid.*, 34.
22. Delany, *Times Square*, 126.
23. *Ibid.*, 129, 168.
24. Michael S. Sherry, *Gay Artists in Modern American Culture: An Imagined Conspiracy* (Chapel Hill: University of North Carolina Press, 2007), 1.
25. Wallace Thurman, *Infants of the Spring* (New York: Modern Library, 1992), 137.
26. Claude McKay, *Home to Harlem* (Boston, MA: Northeastern University Press, 1987), 280.
27. Siobhan B. Somerville, *Queering the Color Line* (Durham, NC: Duke University Press, 2000), 145.
28. Thurman, *Infants*, 123.
29. McKay, *Home to Harlem*, 30.
30. *Ibid.*, 36–7.
31. Gertrude Rainey, 'Prove it on Me Blues', in Angela Y. Davis, ed., *Blues Legacies and Black Feminism: Gertrude 'Ma' Rainey, Bessie Smith and Billie Holiday* (New York: Pantheon, 1998), 238.
32. Carmen Mitchell, 'Creation of Fantasies / Construction of Identities: The Oppositional Lives of Gladys Bentley', in Delroy Constantine-Simms, ed., *The Greatest Taboo: Homosexuality in Black Communities* (Los Angeles: Alyson, 2001), 221.
33. Carl Van Vechten, *Parties* (New York: Knopf, 1930), 138.
34. Mabel Dodge, quoted in Andrea Barnet, *All Night Party: The Women of Bohemian Greenwich Village and Harlem 1913–1930* (Chapel Hill, NC: Algonquin Books of Chapel Hill, 2004), 143.
35. Ernest Boyd, 'Aesthete Model 1924', in Lawrence E. Spivak and Charles Angoff, eds., *The American Mercury Reader* (Philadelphia, PA: Blakiston, 1944), 298–303.
36. Malcolm Cowley, *Exile's Return: A Literary Odyssey of the 1920s* (New York: Viking, 1951), 190.
37. Muriel Rukeyser, *The Collected Poems of Muriel Rukeyser*, ed. Janet E. Kaufman and Anne R. Herzog (Pittsburgh, PA: Pittsburgh University Press, 2005), 45.
38. Charles Henri Ford and Parker Tyler, *The Young and the Evil* (New York: Gay Presses of New York, 1988), 196.
39. *Ibid.*, 29.
40. *Ibid.*, 191.
41. Edwin Denby, *Dancers, Buildings and People in the Streets* (New York: Horizon Press, 1965), 199–200.
42. Edmund White, *Skinned Alive* (New York: Knopf, 1995), 210.
43. William Meredith, 'The Ballet', *Partial Accounts: New and Selected Poems* (New York: Knopf, 1987), 30.
44. Daniel Harris, *The Rise and Fall of Gay Culture* (New York: Hyperion, 1997), 68.
45. V. R. 'Bunny' Lang was an obscure poet and friend of O'Hara's from college; John La Touche was a celebrated lyricist who wrote the libretto for *The Ballad of Baby Doe* (1956); Jackson Pollock was a famous abstract painter.
46. Frank O'Hara, *Selected Poems*, ed. Donald Allen (New York: Knopf, 1974), 110–11.
47. James Baldwin, 'The Harlem Ghetto', *Notes of a Native Son*, 2nd edn (Boston, MA: Beacon Press, 1984), 57.

48. Audre Lorde, *Undersong: Chosen Poems Old and New*, revised edn (New York: Norton, 1992), 137.

49. Rukeyser, *Collected Poems*, 446–7.

50. Marilyn Hacker, *First Cities: Collected Early Poems 1960–1979* (New York: Norton, 2003), 263.

51. Edward Field, 'Roaches', *Counting Myself Lucky: Selected Poems, 1963–1992* (Santa Rosa, CA: Black Sparrow Press, 1992), 265.

52. May Swenson, 'Wednesday at the Waldorf', *Nature: Poems Old and New* (Boston, MA: Houghton Mifflin, 2000), 157.

53. Ginsberg, *The Book of Martyrdom*, 423.

54. Allen Ginsberg, *Collected Poems: 1947–1980* (New York: Harper and Row, 1984), 626.

55. Ginsberg, *The Book of Martyrdom*, 424.

56. George Chauncey, *Gay New York: Gender, Urban Culture and the Making of the Gay Male World 1890–1940* (New York: Basic Books, 1994), 197.

57. Bruce Benderson, *Toward the New Degeneracy: An Essay* (New York, Paris and Turin: Edgewise, 1997), 31.

58. John Rechy, *City of Night* (New York: Grove, 1963), 34.

59. Sarah Schulman, *After Delores* (New York: Dutton, 1988), 33.

60. Eileen Myles, *Chelsea Girls* (Santa Rosa, CA: Black Sparrow Press, 1994), 272.

61. *Ibid.*, 273.

62. Cooper and Myles, *Up Is Up*, 466.

63. Daniel Kane, *All Poets Welcome: The Lower East Side Poetry Scene in the 1960s* (Berkeley: University of California Press, 2002), 24.

64. Cooper and Myles, *Up Is Up*, 466.

65. Tony Kushner, *Angels in America: A Gay Fantasia on National Themes* (New York: Theatre Communications Group, 1995), 51.

66. Larry Kramer, '2,339 and Counting', *Reports from the Holocaust: The Making of an AIDS Activist* (New York: St Martin's Press, 1980), 70.

67. Sarah Schulman, *People in Trouble* (New York: Dutton, 1990), 118.

68. David Wojnarowicz, *Memories that Smell like Gasoline* (San Francisco: Artspace Books, 1992), 51.

69. *Ibid.*, 43–4.

70. David B. Feinberg, *Queer and Loathing* (New York: Viking, 1994), 151.

71. Edward Field, *After the Fall* (Pittsburgh, PA: University of Pittsburgh Press, 2007), 49.

72. Cheryl Boyce-Taylor, 'Crazy: Cheryl's Rant', in Emanuel Xavier, ed., *Bullets & Butterflies* (San Francisco, CA: Suspect Thoughts, 2005), 126–7.

General

Abelove, Henry, Michèle Aina Barale and David M. Halperin, eds. *The Lesbian and Gay Studies Reader*. New York: Routledge, 1993.

Haggerty, George E. and Molly McGarry. *A Companion to Lesbian, Gay, Bisexual, Transgender and Queer Studies*. Oxford: Blackwell, 2007.

Summers, Claude J., ed. *The Gay and Lesbian Literary Heritage: A Reader's Companion to the Writers and their Works, from Antiquity to the Present*. New York: Routledge, 2002.

Literary

Austen, Roger. *Playing the Game: The Homosexual Novel in America*. Indianapolis: Bobbs-Merrill, 1977.

Bergman, David. *Gaiety Transfigured: Gay Self-Representation in American Literature*. Madison: University of Wisconsin Press, 1991.

Bristow, Joseph. *Effeminate England: Homoerotic Writing After 1885*. New York: Columbia University Press, 1995.

Bristow, Joseph, ed. *Sexual Sameness: Textual Differences in Lesbian and Gay Writing*. London: Routledge, 1992.

Brookes, Les. *Gay Male Fiction since Stonewall: Ideology, Conflict and Aesthetics*. New York: Routledge, 2009.

Butters, Ronald R., John M. Clum and Michael Moon, eds. *Displacing Homophobia: Gay Male Perspectives in Literature and Culture*. Durham, NC: Duke University Press, 1989.

Carlston, Erin. *Thinking Fascism: Sapphic Modernism and Fascist Modernity*. Stanford, CA: Stanford University Press, 1998.

Castle, Terry. *The Apparitional Lesbian: Female Homosexuality and Modern Culture*. New York: Columbia University Press, 1993.

Castle, Terry, ed. *The Literature of Lesbianism: A Historical Anthology from Ariosto to Stonewall*. New York: Columbia University Press, 2003.

Crompton, Louis. *Byron and Greek Love: Homophobia in Nineteenth-Century England*. Berkeley: University of California Press, 1985.

d'Arch-Smith, Timothy. *Love in Earnest: Some Notes on the Lives and Writings of English Uranian Poets from 1889 to 1930*. London: Routledge and Kegan Paul, 1970.

Foster, Jeannette. *Sex Variant Women in Literature: A Historical and Quantitative Survey.* 1956. Tallahassee, FL: Naiad, 1985.

Goldberg, Jonathan. *Sodometries: Renaissance Texts, Modern Sexualities.* Stanford, CA: Stanford University Press, 1992.

Goldberg, Jonathan, ed. *Queering the Renaissance.* Durham, NC: Duke University Press, 1994.

Hennegan, Alison, ed. *The Lesbian Pillow Book.* London: Fourth Estate, 2000.

Jagose, Annamarie. *Inconsequence: Lesbian Representation and the Logic of Sexual Sequence.* Ithaca, NY: Cornell University Press, 1992.

Jay, Karla and Joanne Glasgow, eds. *Lesbian Texts and Contexts: Radical Revisions.* New York: New York University Press, 1990. Reprinted London: Onlywomen Press, 1992.

Kellog, Stuart, ed. *Literary Visions of Homosexuality.* New York: Haworth Press, 1983.

Love, Heather. *Feeling Backward: Loss and the Politics of Queer History.* Cambridge, MA: Harvard University Press, 2007.

Martin, Robert K. *The Homosexual Tradition in American Poetry.* Austin: University of Texas Press, 1979.

Moore, Lisa Lynne. *Dangerous Intimacies: Toward a Sapphic History of the British Novel.* Durham, NC: Duke University Press, 1997.

Prins, Yopie. *Victorian Sappho.* Princeton, NJ: Princeton University Press, 1999.

Raitt, Suzanne. *Vita and Virginia: The Work and Friendship of V. Sackville-West and Virginia Woolf.* Oxford: Clarendon Press, 1993.

Raitt, Suzanne, ed. *Volcanoes and Pearl Divers: Essays in Lesbian Feminist Studies.* London: Onlywomen Press, 1994.

Reade, Brian, ed. *Sexual Heretics: Male Homosexuality in English Literature from 1850 to 1900: An Anthology.* London: Routledge and Kegan Paul, 1970.

Sedgwick, Eve Kosofsky. *Between Men: English Literature and Male Homosocial Desire.* New York: Columbia University Press, 1985.
  Epistemology of the Closet. Berkeley: University of California Press, 1990.
  Tendencies. London: Routledge, 1994.

Sedgwick, Eve Kosofsky, ed. *Novel Gazing: Queer Readings in Fiction.* Durham, NC: Duke University Press, 1997.

Sinfield, Alan. *Cultural Politics, Queer Reading.* London: Routledge, 1994.
  Out on Stage: Lesbian and Gay Theatre in the Twentieth Century. New Haven, CT: Yale University Press, 1999.

Smith, Bruce R. *Homosexual Desire in Shakespeare's England: A Cultural Poetics.* Chicago: University of Chicago Press, 1991.

Smith, Patricia Juliana. *Lesbian Panic: Homoeroticism in Modern British Women's Fiction.* New York: Columbia University Press, 1997.

Traub, Valerie. *The Renaissance of Lesbianism in Early Modern England.* Cambridge: Cambridge University Press, 2002.

Vanita, Ruth. *Sappho and the Virgin Mary: Same-Sex Love and the English Literary Imagination.* New York: Columbia University Press, 1996.

Woods, Gregory. *Articulate Flesh: Male Homo-eroticism in Modern Poetry.* New Haven, CT: Yale University Press, 1987.
  A History of Gay Literature: The Male Tradition. New Haven, CT: Yale University Press, 1998.

History

Boswell, John. *Christianity, Social Tolerance, and Homosexuality: Gay People in Western Europe from the Beginning of the Christian Era to the Fourteenth Century*. Chicago: University of Chicago Press, 1980.

Same-Sex Unions in Premodern Europe. New York: Villard Books, 1994.

Bray, Alan. *Homosexuality in Renaissance England*. 1982; updated edn, New York: Columbia University Press, 1995.

Chauncey, George, Jr. *Gay New York: Gender, Urban Culture, and the Making of the Gay Male World, 1890–1940*. New York: Basic Books, 1994.

Cook, Matt. *London and the Culture of Homosexuality, 1885–1914*. Cambridge: Cambridge University Press, 2003.

Cook, Matt, H. G. Cocks, Robert Mills and Randolph Trumbach, eds. *A Gay History of Britain: Love and Sex Between Men Since the Middle Ages*. Oxford: Greenwood World Publishing, 2007.

Crompton, Louis. *Homosexuality and Civilization*. Cambridge, MA: Harvard University Press, 2003.

D'Emilio, John. *Sexual Politics, Sexual Communities: The Making of a Homosexual Minority in the United States, 1940–1970*. Chicago: University of Chicago Press, 1983.

Making Trouble: Essays on Gay History, Politics, and the University. New York: Routledge, 1992.

D'Emilio, John and Estelle Freedman. *Intimate Matters: A History of Sexuality in America*. New York: Harper & Row, 1988.

Doan, Laura. *Fashioning Sapphism: The Origins of a Modern English Lesbian Culture*. New York: Columbia University Press, 2001.

Donoghue, Emma. *Passions Between Women: British Lesbian Culture 1668–1801*. London: Scarlet, 1993.

Dover, Kenneth James. *Greek Homosexuality*. Cambridge, MA: Harvard University Press, 1978.

Duberman, Martin Bauml. *About Time: Exploring the Gay Past*. New York: Meridian, 1991.

Duberman, Martin Bauml, Martha Vicinus and George Chauncey, Jr, eds. *Hidden from History: Reclaiming the Gay and Lesbian Past*. London: Penguin, 1991.

Faderman, Lillian. *Surpassing the Love of Men: Romantic Friendship and Love Between Women from the Renaissance to the Present*. London: Women's Press, 1985.

Odd Girls and Twilight Lovers: A History of Lesbian Life in Twentieth-Century America. New York: Columbia University Press, 1991.

Foucault, Michel. *The History of Sexuality: An Introduction*. Trans. Robert Hurley. London: Allen Lane, 1979.

The History of Sexuality, vol. II: *The Use of Pleasure*. Trans. Robert Hurley. Harmondsworth: Penguin, 1987.

The History of Sexuality, vol. III: *The Care of the Self*. Trans. Robert Hurley. Harmondsworth: Penguin, 1988.

Fuss, Diana. *Essentially Speaking: Feminism, Nature and Difference*. New York: Routledge, 1989.

Gerard, Kent and Gert Hekma, eds. *The Pursuit of Sodomy: Male Homosexuality in Renaissance and Enlightenment Europe.* New York: Harrington Park Press, 1989.

Halperin, David M. *One Hundred Years of Homosexuality, and Other Essays on Greek Love.* New York: Routledge, 1990.

How to Do the History of Homosexuality. Chicago: University of Chicago Press, 2002.

Houlbrook, Matt. *Queer London: Perils and Pleasures in the Sexual Metropolis, 1918–1957.* Chicago: University of Chicago Press, 2005.

Katz, Jonathan Ned. *Gay American History: Lesbians and Gay Men in the U.S.A.: A Documentary.* New York: Crowell, 1976.

Gay/Lesbian Almanac: A New Documentary. New York: Carroll and Graf, 1994.

Licata, Salvatore J. and Robert P. Petersen, eds. *The Gay Past: A Collection of Historical Essays.* New York: Harrington Press, 1985.

Norton, Rictor. *Molly Clap's Molly House: Gay Subculture in England, 1700–1830.* London: Gay Men's Press, 1992.

Rocke, Michael. *Forbidden Friendships: Homosexuality and Male Culture in Renaissance Florence.* New York: Oxford University Press, 1996.

Rousseau, G. S. *Perilous Enlightenment: Pre- and Post-modern Discourses, Sexual, Historical.* Manchester: Manchester University Press, 1991.

Saslow, James M. *Ganymede in the Renaissance: Homosexuality in Art and Society.* New Haven: Yale University Press, 1986.

Sinfield, Alan. *The Wilde Century: Effeminacy, Oscar Wilde, and the Queer Moment.* London: Cassell, 1994.

Smith-Rosenberg, Carroll. *Disorderly Conduct: Visions of Gender in Victorian America.* New York: Oxford University Press, 1985.

Trumbach, Randolph. *Sex and the Gender Revolution: Heterosexuality and the Third Gender in Enlightenment London.* Chicago: University of Chicago Press, 1998.

Turner, Mark. *Backward Glances: Cruising the Queer Streets of New York and London.* London: Reaktion Books, 2003.

Weeks, Jeffrey. *Sexuality and its Discontents: Meanings, Myths, and Modern Sexualities.* London: Routledge and Kegan Paul, 1985.

Sex, Politics, and Society: The Regulation of Sexuality since 1800. London: Longman, 1989.

Coming Out: Homosexual Politics in Britain from the Nineteenth Century to the Present. London: Quartet, 1990.

Weeks, Jeffrey and Kevin Porter, eds. *Between the Acts: Lives of Homosexual Men, 1885–1967.* London: Routledge, 1991.

Theory and politics

Bersani, Leo. *Homos.* Cambridge, MA: Harvard University Press, 1995.

Bristow, Joseph. *Sexuality.* London: Routledge, 1997.

Bristow, Joseph and Angelia R. Wilson, eds. *Activating Theory: Lesbian, Gay, Bisexual Politics.* London: Lawrence & Wishart, 1993.

Butler, Judith. *Gender Trouble: Feminism and the Subversion of Identity.* New York: Routledge, 1990.

Bodies that Matter: On the Discursive Limits of 'Sex'. New York: Routledge, 1993.

Dean, Tim and Christopher Lane, eds. *Homosexuality and Psychoanalysis*. Chicago: University of Chicago Press, 2001.

De Lauretis, Teresa. *The Practice of Love: Lesbian Sexuality and Perverse Desire*. Bloomington: Indiana University Press, 1994.

Dollimore, Jonathan. *Sexual Dissidence: Augustine to Wilde, Freud to Foucault*. Oxford: Clarendon Press, 1991.

Edelman, Lee. *Homographesis: Essays in Gay Literary and Cultural Theory*. New York: Routledge, 1994.

   No Future: Queer Theory and the Death Drive. Durham, NC: Duke University Press, 2004.

Fuss, Diana. *Essentially Speaking: Feminism, Nature and Difference*. New York: Routledge, 1989.

Fuss, Diana, ed. *Inside/Out: Lesbian Theories, Gay Theories*. New York: Routledge, 1991.

Hocquenghem, Guy. *Homosexual desire*. Trans. Daniella Dangoor. 1978. Durham, NC: Duke University Press, 1993.

Roof, Judith. *A Lure of Knowledge: Lesbian Sexuality and Theory*. New York: Columbia University Press, 1991.

Warner, Michael, ed. *Fear of a Queer Planet: Queer Politics and Social Theory*. Minneapolis: University of Minnesota Press, 1993.

Transgender

Halberstam, Judith. *Female Masculinity*. Durham, NC: Duke University Press, 1998.

   In a Queer Time and Place: Transgender Bodies, Subcultural Lives. New York: New York University Press, 2005.

Prosser, Jay. *Second Skins: The Body Narratives of Transsexuality*. New York: Columbia University Press, 1998.

Stryker, Susan. *Transgender History*. Berkeley, CA: Seal Press, 2008.

Stryker, Susan and Stephen Whittle, eds. *The Transgender Studies Reader*. London: Routledge, 2006.

Volcano, Del LaGrace. *The Drag King Book*. London: Serpent's Tail, 1999.

Race and culture

Bose, Brinda and Subhabrata Bhattacharyya, eds. *The Phobic and the Erotic: The Politics of Sexuality in Contemporary India*. Calcutta: Seagull, 2007.

Gopinath, Gayatri. *Impossible Desires: Queer Diasporas and South Asian Public Cultures*. Durham, NC: Duke University Press, 2005.

Hawley, John C., ed. *Post-Colonial Queer: Theoretical Intersections*. Albany: State University of New York Press, 2001.

Parker, Andrew, Mary Russo, Doris Sommer and Patricia Yaeger, eds. *Nationalisms and Sexualities*. New York: Routledge, 1992.

Patton, Cindy and Benigno Sánchez-Eppler, eds. *Queer Diasporas*. Durham, NC: Duke University Press, 2000.

Stockton, Kathryn Bond. *Beautiful Bottom, Beautiful Shame: Where Black Meets Queer*. Durham, NC: Duke University Press, 2006.

Vanita, Ruth, ed. *Queering India: Same-Sex Love and Eroticism in Indian Culture, and Society*. New York: Routledge, 2002.

Vanita, Ruth and Saleem Kidwai, eds. *Same-Sex Love in India: Readings from Literature and History*. New York: St Martin's Press, 2000.

AIDS

Bersani, Leo and Adam Phillips. *Intimacies*. Chicago: University of Chicago Press, 2008.

Carter, Erica and Simon Watney, eds. *Taking Liberties: AIDS and Cultural Politics*. London: Serpent's Tail, 1989.

Crimp, Douglas. *AIDS: Cultural Analysis, Cultural Activism*. Cambridge, MA: MIT Press, 1988.

Dean, Tim. *Unlimited Intimacy: Reflections on the Subculture of Barebacking*. Chicago: Chicago University Press, 2009.

Foertsch, Jacqueline. *Enemies Within: The Cold War and the AIDS Crisis in Literature, Film and Culture*. Champaign: University of Illinois Press, 2001.

Halperin, David M. *What do Gay Men Want?: An Essay on Sex, Risk, and Subjectivity*. Ann Arbor: University of Michigan Press, 2007.

Kruger, Steven. *AIDS Narratives: Gender and Sexuality, Fiction and Science*. New York: Garland, 1996.

Patton, Cindy. *Inventing AIDS*. New York: Routledge, 1990.

Watney, Simon. *Policing Desire: Aids, Pornography, and the Media*. Minneapolis: University of Minnesota Press, 1987.

INDEX

Cambridge Companions to . . .

AUTHORS

Edward Albee edited by Stephen J. Bottoms

Margaret Atwood edited by Coral Ann Howells

W. H. Auden edited by Stan Smith

Jane Austen edited by Edward Copeland and Juliet McMaster (second edition)

Beckett edited by John Pilling

Bede edited by Scott DeGregorio

Aphra Behn edited by Derek Hughes and Janet Todd

Walter Benjamin edited by David S. Ferris

William Blake edited by Morris Eaves

Brecht edited by Peter Thomson and Glendyr Sacks (second edition)

The Brontës edited by Heather Glen

Frances Burney edited by Peter Sabor

Byron edited by Drummond Bone

Albert Camus edited by Edward J. Hughes

Willa Cather edited by Marilee Lindemann

Cervantes edited by Anthony J. Cascardi

Chaucer edited by Piero Boitani and Jill Mann (second edition)

Chekhov edited by Vera Gottlieb and Paul Allain

Kate Chopin edited by Janet Beer

Caryl Churchill edited by Elaine Aston and Elin Diamond

Coleridge edited by Lucy Newlyn

Wilkie Collins edited by Jenny Bourne Taylor

Joseph Conrad edited by J. H. Stape

Dante edited by Rachel Jacoff (second edition)

Daniel Defoe edited by John Richetti

Don DeLillo edited by John N. Duvall

Charles Dickens edited by John O. Jordan

Emily Dickinson edited by Wendy Martin

John Donne edited by Achsah Guibbory

Dostoevskii edited by W. J. Leatherbarrow

Theodore Dreiser edited by Leonard Cassuto and Claire Virginia Eby

John Dryden edited by Steven N. Zwicker

W. E. B. Du Bois edited by Shamoon Zamir

George Eliot edited by George Levine

T. S. Eliot edited by A. David Moody

Ralph Ellison edited by Ross Posnock

Ralph Waldo Emerson edited by Joel Porte and Saundra Morris

William Faulkner edited by Philip M. Weinstein

Henry Fielding edited by Claude Rawson

F. Scott Fitzgerald edited by Ruth Prigozy

Flaubert edited by Timothy Unwin

E. M. Forster edited by David Bradshaw

Benjamin Franklin edited by Carla Mulford

Brian Friel edited by Anthony Roche

Robert Frost edited by Robert Faggen

Gabriel García Márquez edited by Philip Swanson

Elizabeth Gaskell edited by Jill L. Matus

Goethe edited by Lesley Sharpe

Günter Grass edited by Stuart Taberner

Thomas Hardy edited by Dale Kramer

David Hare edited by Richard Boon

Nathaniel Hawthorne edited by Richard Millington

Seamus Heaney edited by Bernard O'Donoghue

Ernest Hemingway edited by Scott Donaldson

Homer edited by Robert Fowler

Horace edited by Stephen Harrison

Ibsen edited by James McFarlane

Henry James edited by Jonathan Freedman

Samuel Johnson edited by Greg Clingham

Ben Jonson edited by Richard Harp and Stanley Stewart

James Joyce edited by Derek Attridge (second edition)

Kafka edited by Julian Preece

Keats edited by Susan J. Wolfson

Lacan edited by Jean-Michel Rabaté

D. H. Lawrence edited by Anne Fernihough

Primo Levi edited by Robert Gordon

Lucretius edited by Stuart Gillespie and Philip Hardie

Machiavelli edited by John M. Najemy

David Mamet edited by Christopher Bigsby

Thomas Mann edited by Ritchie Robertson

Christopher Marlowe edited by Patrick Cheney

Andrew Marvell edited by Derek Hirst and Steven N. Zwicker

Herman Melville edited by Robert S. Levine

Arthur Miller edited by Christopher Bigsby (second edition)

TOPICS